"Everyone knows that Tolstoy's nonviolence inspired Gandhi, Martin Luther King, and millions of others. Far fewer know how directly Tolstoy's vision was rooted in the Sermon on the Mount, though thinkers as diverse as Bonhoeffer, Wittgenstein, and Dorothy Day certainly did. Steve Hickey's recovery of this forgotten Christian tradition is a reminder that when we think of nonviolent movements for justice around the globe, we are in fact reconsidering the truth of the teaching of Jesus."

—BRIAN BROCK
Professor of Moral and Practical Theology, Department of Divinity and Religious Studies, King's College, Aberdeen

"Hickey's book takes Jesus' Sermon on the Mount as seriously as Tolstoy did. By rigorously explaining Tolstoy's interpretation and locating it firmly within the broader Christian tradition despite Tolstoy's idiosyncrasies, it makes a compelling case for fellow Christians to live by the ethics of the Sermon. A must-read for those curious about Tolstoy's religious and political writings, and especially for those interested in Christian ethics."

—ALEXANDRE CHRISTOYANNOPOULOS
Senior Lecturer in Politics and International Relations, Loughborough University

"This comprehensive study irradiates Tolstoy's neglected religious writings with a new clarity, sympathy, and optimism. The great Russian novelist is presented as a major Christian commentator who deserves to be read by all 'pastors and seminarians' and included in the modern religious curriculum. Then comes the real challenge: the Sermon on the Mount should be seen as 'liveable and to be lived.' Steve Hickey will show you how."

—ANTHONY BRIGGS
Translator of *War and Peace* and *Resurrection*

"*Second Tolstoy* is a unique study in the faith and public theology of the nineteenth-century Russian novelist. Tolstoy attempted to live directly by the teachings of Christ's Sermon on the Mount. He had a central influence on Mahatma Gandhi, Martin Luther King Jr., Ludwig Wittgenstein, and Dietrich Bonhoeffer. . . . I remember the young Steve, the bright young seminarian who planted a church in South Dakota and led it to become a church of more than a thousand persons while also serving in the South Dakota State Legislature. Stricken by a cruel and disabling affliction, he buried himself in Tolstoy. Now teaching in an Alaskan College, his impassioned spiritual research has given us not only a unique study in Tolstoy—Steve also enflames our own passion for Christ and his kingdom."

—PAUL EMANUEL LARSEN
President emeritus, The Evangelical Covenant Church

Second Tolstoy

Second Tolstoy

The Sermon on the Mount as Theo-tactics

STEVE HICKEY

PICKWICK *Publications* · Eugene, Oregon

SECOND TOLSTOY
The Sermon on the Mount as Theo-tactics

Copyright © 2021 Steve Hickey. All rights reserved. Except for brief quotations in critical publications or reviews, no part of this book may be reproduced in any manner without prior written permission from the publisher. Write: Permissions, Wipf and Stock Publishers, 199 W. 8th Ave., Suite 3, Eugene, OR 97401.

Pickwick Publications
An Imprint of Wipf and Stock Publishers
199 W. 8th Ave., Suite 3
Eugene, OR 97401

www.wipfandstock.com

PAPERBACK ISBN: 978-1-7252-8535-4
HARDCOVER ISBN: 978-1-7252-8536-1
EBOOK ISBN: 978-1-7252-8537-8

Cataloguing-in-Publication data:

Names: Hickey, Steve, author.

Title: Second Tolstoy : the sermon on the mount as theo-tactics / Steve Hickey.

Description: Eugene, OR : Pickwick Publications, 2021 | Includes bibliographical references and index.

Identifiers: ISBN 978-1-7252-8535-4 (paperback) | ISBN 978-1-7252-8536-1 (hardcover) | ISBN 978-1-7252-8537-8 (ebook)

Subjects: LCSH: Tolstoy, Leo, graf, 1828–1910—Political and social views. | Tolstoy, Leo, graf, 1828–1910—Religion and ethics. | Sermon on the mount.

Classification: PG3415.R4 .H53 2021 (paperback) | PG3415.R4 .H53 (ebook)

11/10/21

Holy Bible, New International Version® Anglicized, NIV® Copyright © 1979, 1984, 2011 by Biblica, Inc.® Used by permission. All rights reserved worldwide.

There is a way which seems right to a man,
but its end is the way of death.

—Proverbs 14:12

For as the heavens are higher than the earth,
so are my ways higher than your ways
and my thoughts than your thoughts.

—Isaiah 55:9

You have heard that it was said . . .
but I tell you . . .

—Matthew 5:28–29

difficult is the way which leads to life,
and there are few who find it.

—Matthew 7:14

but when you are tempted,
He will also provide a way out

– 1 Corinthians 10:13

Contents

Abstract | xiii
Acknowledgments and Dedication | xv
Pertinent Chronology | xvii

0.0 Introduction: Why Give Gandhi All the Glory? | 1
    0.1 A Sympathetic Reading and the Problem of Secular Subjectivity | 2
    0.2 The Under-Appreciated Prophet | 3
    0.3 Heretics and the Other Side of the Gospel | 7
    0.4 A Three-Part Framework for Appreciating Second Tolstoy | 8
    0.5 New and Original Contributions Herein | 9
    0.6 The Ins and Outs of the Religious Tolstoy | 11

PART ONE: THE DOCTRINE OF JESUS | 13

1.0 The Overlapping Life and Literature of Leo Tolstoy | 15
    1.1 Second Tolstoy | 18
    1.2 *A Confession* (1879–81) — [*abbr.* CF] | 21
    1.3 *A Critique of Dogmatic Theology* (1881–82) — [*abbr.* DT] | 29
    1.4 *The Four Gospels Harmonised and Translated: Volumes* 1, 2 (1881–82) — [*abbr.* HM] | 33
    1.5 The Gospel in Brief (1882–83) — [*abbr.* TGB] | 36
    1.6 NIV-UK/TGB Parallel Comparison of Matthew 5–7 | 40

2.0 The Centre of Second Tolstoy; *What I Believe and The Kingdom of God is Within You* | 44
    2.1 *What I Believe* (1884) — [*abbr.* WB] | 45
    2.2 *The Kingdom of God Is within You* (1893) – [*abbr.* KG] | 51
    2.3 Tolstoy's Diatribes as Prophetic Unction, Rhetoric and Echoes from the Mount | 63
    2.4 The September Ninth Train to Tula | 65

- 3.0 Tolstoy's Sermon on the Mount as a New Life Conception | 72
    - 3.1 For Tolstoy, the Sermon on the Mount Is All the Bible You Really Need | 73
        - 3.1.1 Tolstoy atop Mars Hill; Religious Pluralism or Moral Universalism | 74
    - 3.2 A New Life-Conception Is Tolstoy's Term for the Teaching within the Sermon on the Mount | 80
    - 3.3 For Tolstoy, Resist not Evil (Matt 5:39) Is the Key to the Rest of the Sermon on the Mount; In Fact It Is the Essence of Christianity | 83
    - 3.4 Tolstoy Believed the Sermon on the Mount Is Not to Be Interpreted as an Ethic for an Ascetic Withdrawal from the World, nor Is Its Application Limited to Interpersonal Relationships | 85
    - 3.5 Tolstoyan Sermon on the Mount Interpretations Led Him to Radicalized Applications Far Surpassing Common Christian Devotional Practice and Lifestyle | 87
- 4.0 Divine Command Ethics: Universal Principles and Law in Second Tolstoy | 89
    - 4.1 For Tolstoy, the Moral Perfection of Matthew 5:48 Is within Reach | 91
    - 4.2 Tolstoy Differentiated between Moral Guidance by External Precept or Law, and Internal Moral Guidance by Being Shown the Ideal in the Sermon on the Mount, and Having This Ideal Directing and Leading from Within | 93
    - 4.3 For Tolstoy, Distinguishing between an Eternal Law and the Written Law Is the Only Way to Make Sense of Matthew 5:17–20 | 96
    - 4.4 Tolstoy Believed the Eternal Law Was Set Forth Most Clearly in Five New Commandments Given by Jesus in the Sermon on the Mount | 98
        - 4.4.1 The First Commandment: Be Not Angry | 99
        - 4.4.2 The Second Commandment: Do Not Commit Adultery | 100
        - 4.4.3 The Third Commandment: Take No Oaths | 101
        - 4.4.4 The Fourth Commandment: Resist Not Evil | 102
        - 4.4.5 The Fifth Commandment: Do Not Make War | 102
    - 4.5 Obedience over Orthodoxy | 103
        - 4.5.1 Tolstoy's Unorthodox Doctrine of God, and Jesus as God | 108
- 5.0 Letters, Legacy, and the Ghost of Tolstoy | 113
    - 5.1 Searching for Second Tolstoy in 8500 Letters | 114

5.2 Letter #257: To the Emperor Alexander III, March 8–15, 1881 | 115
5.3 Letter to a Hindu and a Letter to Hitler | 119
5.4 The Tolstoy Bonhoeffer Never Knew | 123
5.5 Tolstoy's Discrepancies; Accuse Me and Not the Path I Follow! | 130
5.6 Bauman: Ghost of Tolstoy Haunts a Century of Sermon on the Mount Interpretation | 137

PART TWO: THE DOCTRINE OF THE CHURCH | 143

6.0 **Tolstoy among the Reformers of Constantinian Christendom** | 145
    6.1 Petr Chelčický's Ninety-Five Theses | 147
    6.2 Tolstoy and the Constantinian Heresy | 154
    6.3 Embracing the Religion of the Sword, the Eusebian Myth, and the Unrealized Reformation | 158
    6.4 *Hic Sunt Leones* | 161
    6.5 Chelčický, Tolstoy, and Jean Lasserre—Missing Voices in the Modern Dialogue | 164

7.0 **Matual and Laurila: Plausible but Not Palpable, Loopholes and Tolstoy's Blindspot** | 174
    7.1 David Matual: Tolstoy as Translator | 176
    7.2 Kaarle Laurila: The Finnish Layman Who Offered the Lengthiest Critique to Date | 177
    7.3 An Intermittent Ethic: Laurila on Tolstoyan Reception in Finland | 179
    7.4 Pitting Luther against Tolstoy | 181
    7.5 Laurila's Reading of Tolstoy's Sermon on the Mount Interpretation | 184
    7.6 Tolstoy's Blindspot; the Tension between Neighborly Love and Enemy Love | 189

PART THREE: THE DOCTRINE OF THE WORLD | 193

8.0 **Sexual Self-Disarmament: Tolstoy's Eccentricity on Sex and Marriage** | 195
    8.1 Tolstoy on the Secularist's Couch: Misogyny, Masochism, and the Absent Mother | 197
    8.2 Tolstoy's Second Commandment: Abstinence in Singleness, Minimization in Marriage | 199
    8.3 *The Christian Teaching* on Sensual and Sexual Sins | 201

8.4 *Confession* and Diaries: A Whole Catalog of Active Sexual Life Going Back Twenty Years | 204
8.5 *The Kreutzer Sonata* as a Prophetic Challenge to Immoral Society | 206
8.6 Anke Pie and the Indian Tolstoy: Asceticism and Non-violence | 211

9.0 Matthew 5:38–39 as an Alternative Politic | 215
   9.1 Tolstoy against Social Darwinism | 215
      9.1.1 Rudolf Steiner on Tolstoy and Darwin (1904) | 218
      9.1.2 Hugh McLean on Tolstoy and Darwin (2008) | 219
      9.1.3 The Sermon on the Mount as the Antithesis of Survival of the Fittest | 221
   9.2 Tolstoy against Marxist-Leninism | 222
      9.2.1 Tolstoy on the Superstition of Progress, Human Brotherhood, and Non-violent Means | 223
      9.2.2 Lenin: The Weakness and Subtle Poison of Tolstoy's Sermon on the Mount | 226
      9.2.3 Leon Trotsky's 1908 Tribute to Leo Tolstoy | 232

10.0 **Tolstoy against State Violence: Theo-tactical Altruism (TtA)** | 236
   10.1 The Sermon on the Mount Is Not State-Crafting, Nor Is It Theocracy | 238
      10.1.1 Tolstoy Was a Radicalized, Radical, Theo-tactical Altruist | 240
      10.1.2 The Juxtaposition of Anthro-tactics with Theo-tactics | 241
      10.1.3 Theo-tactics as a Pressurised Faucet or Well-Spring, Not a Deep Bucket | 246
      10.1.4 Tolstoy Did Not Envision a Stateless, Lawless Utopia | 247
   10.2 Walter Wink and the Third Way | 251
      10.2.1 The Theo-tactics of the Turned Cheek, Extra Cloak and Second Mile | 253
      10.2.2 The Cross as Theo-tactical | 254
      10.2.3 Theo-tactics for the Most Intense Times in the Most Brutal of Places | 255
   10.3 John Howard Yoder on Tolstoy as a Pacifist | 256
   10.4 Hopton and Christoyannopoulos on Tolstoy and Anarchism | 257
      10.4.1 Tolstoy an Adherent of the Christianity *of Christ* | 258
      10.4.2 The Twentieth-Century Struggle to Hear Tolstoy's Voice | 259

10.5 A Modern Appropriation: Antifa, the Righteous Wind, and
   Theo-tacs | 263
   10.5.1 The Wind of Righteous Rhetoric | 265

11.0 Conclusion | 267
   11.1 Three Misreadings: What We Get Wrong | 268
      11.1.1 The Marginalization of Tolstoy | 269
      11.1.2 The Secularization of Tolstoy | 269
      11.1.3 The Pluralization of Tolstoy | 270
   11.2 Four Main Findings: What Tolstoy Got Right | 270
      11.2.1 Simple Obedience | 271
      11.2.2 Living Martyrdoms | 273
      11.2.3 Enemy Love | 274
      11.2.4 Theo-tactics | 275

12.0 Appendices | 277
   12.1 NIV-UK/TGB Parallel Comparison of Matthew 5–7 | 279
   12.2 Letter to Tsar Alexander III, 8–15 March 1881 | 289
      12.2.1 Tolstoy's handwriting: Draft of 1881 Letter to Tsar Alexander
         III | 296
   12.3 First English Translation of Tolstoy's Foreword to Chelčický's *Net
      of Faith* | 297
   Preface by Leo Tolstoy, Translated for Steve Hickey by Olga
      Sevastyanova | 297
   12.4 Depictions of Tolstoyan Christianity in Art | 302
      12.4.1 *What Is Truth,* Nikolay Ge | 302
      12.4.2 *Tolstoy in Hell,* Fresco, 1883 | 304
      12.4.3 *Christ Embracing Tolstoy,* by Jan Styka | 305
      12.4.4 Ilya Glazunov's *Eternal Russia* | 306
      12.4.5 *Do Not Repay Evil with Evil*: Petr Chel`čický at Vodňany by
         Alfons Mucha (1918) | 307
   12.5 Matthew 5:11 and the Tolstoy Anathema Iron | 308

13.0 Bibliography | 311
   13.1 Primary Source Material | 312
      13.1.1 Tolstoy Non-fiction Work | 312
      13.1.2 Related Tolstoy Fiction | 317
      13.1.3 Tolstoy Family | 317
   13.2 Secondary Source Material | 317
      13.2.1 Books, Journal Articles, Essays and Papers | 317
      13.2.2 Video and Documentary | 328
      13.2.3 Annotated Bibliographies
         and Online Searchable Archives | 328

Abstract

SINCE JESUS FIRST GAVE his Sermon on the Mount, very few if any have devoted more years to practicing and teaching others to practice its precepts than Leo Tolstoy. Tolstoy's take on the Sermon on the Mount stands apart in the history of Sermon on the Mount interpretation and has had enormous influence on others and other countries. Yet, often Gandhi gets the glory, or others. Tolstoy is remembered as a great writer, but his religious and philosophical works are by and large unknown or disparaged, even in Tolstoyan scholarly circles. It remains that his contribution is substantially under-appreciated and misunderstood. This project seeks to capture the particulars and dynamics of Tolstoy's interpretation of the Sermon on the Mount from a deliberately sympathetic vantage point. Underlying this project is shared belief with Tolstoy that the Sermon on the Mount is liveable and to be lived. This project assumes that from the vantage point of traditional orthodoxy Tolstoy got much wrong but there remains a lack of consideration of and appreciation for what he got right, radical obedience to the teachings of Jesus. After a careful overview of Tolstoy's post-conversion period, and his subsequent writings which constitute a Second Tolstoy corpus of literature, his hermeneutic is explored and his teachings treated generously. Tolstoy's interpretive adversaries and allies are given voice with the intention of better comprehending his interpretations and their perceived implications and failings. A new vocabulary is proposed to more precisely capture Tolstoyan lived theology, namely the political and social expressions of Tolstoyan Christianity, with the intention these theories and practices will gain a wider consideration, understanding and following.

Acknowledgments and Dedication

AT MY AGE, AND considering my health and uncertain future, the aim of my research was never merely to be awarded a Doctorate of Philosophy. Frankly, if this work only achieves that goal and then collects dust on the shelves of some academic library, it will be a disappointment and a prayer gone unanswered. My interest to pursue Tolstoy as an important interpreter of the Sermon on the Mount is motivated by a deep sense that God is again seeking to underscore a radical obedience to the teachings of Jesus in the Body of Christ today. My prayer is the insights herein will make their way into the hands of a new generation of disciples who embrace radical obedience to the Sermon on the Mount, and who seek to live theo-tactically wherever God has placed them.

Working with the religious literature of Tolstoy, but particularly key secondary sources, required quality translations from several languages and appreciation and acknowledgements are due those who translated articles and book sections for me; Thanks to Olga Sevastyanova and Tatiana Shingurova both here in Aberdeen, and to Svetlana Zhuravleva, Svetlana Volovshchikova and Margarita Babakina in Tula, Yasnaya Polyana, and Moscow for Russian translations and research help. Thanks to Rebecca Elder and Christiane Lasserre for translations from French. Thanks to Stuart Hay for translations from German. Also thanks to Tom Lock who shared his Czech to English translation and work on Petr Chelčický which was invaluable for those sections of my project. Also I'm grateful to esteemed colleagues in Tolstoy studies who communicated with me to encourage me at various points along the way; Dr. Anthony Briggs, Professor Emeritus at Birmingham University, Dr. Alexandre Christoyannopoulos of Loughborough University, Dr. Charlotte Alston of Northumbria University, and especially for the help of Dr. Galina Alexeeva at Yasnaya Polyana. Galina sent me home from Yasnaya Polyana with far more than I was able to use here and really inspired me to take my Tolstoy interests even further. I'm grateful to Dr. Radha Balasubramanian for sending her work on Tolstoy and India to me and encouraging my research in these common areas of interest. Special thanks to my Divinity and Ethics department colleagues, Emily Hill who served as an occasional research assistant to me, and Alex Mason, as well as my daughter Kaitlyn Hickey for finding and retrieving various journal articles when needed. It was my good fortune that my research timeframe on this project coincided with Dr. Stanley Hauerwas's time as chair in Theological Ethics here at the University of Aberdeen. At several points, especially the chapter on the Constantinian heresy, his interaction was helpful. I cherish his personal notes to me about my work here; "You have taught me much about Tolstoy I had no idea about . . . very interesting . . . very good . . . well written and well argued—well done." My doctoral supervisor Dr. Brian Brock gets credit for being the one who steered me in the direction of Tolstoy's Sermon on the Mount interpretation. Throughout, this dissertation is better because he pushed me (often via rewrites) to think about Tolstoy at a deeper level than I have thought about anything before. Dr. Michael Laffin also examined my work critically and offered numerous valuable suggestions. And to my beloved Kristen, like everything else these last thirty-plus years, we walked this one out together.

Dedicated to a new generation of Siders, that is mountainsiders– those who gather together desiring to radically adhere to the way of Jesus given on that mountainside. Glory to God as more meet up with Jesus on the mountainside and truly seek to emulate him in the world today.

Pertinent Chronology

30 AD	The Sermon on the Mount given by Jesus on the hillside in Galilee
314	Donation of Constantine and the onset of Constantinian Christianity
1443	Bohemian Reformer Petr Chelčický wrote the ninety-five section *Net of Faith*
1517	Martin Luther posted his ninety-five theses against the Church
1828	Leo Tolstoy born August 28 at Yasnaya Polyana
1833	Tolstoy's brother tells him of the green stick hidden in the ravine with the secret of happiness and peace
1844	Tolstoy at Kazan University
1852–56	Tolstoy in the army, at war, return to Yasnaya Polyana
1857	Trip to Paris and Switzerland; Tolstoy witnesses executions in Paris
1859	Darwin's *Origin of the Species* published
1860	Tolstoy's brother Nicholas died
1860	Travels to Italy, Paris and London
1862	Marries Sophia Andreyevna
1865–69	Writes *War and Peace*
1866	Defends soldier at a court martial
1867	Marx publishes first volume of *Das Kapital*
1875–77	Writes *Anna Karenina*

PERTINENT CHRONOLOGY

Second Tolstoy period

1879–81	Writing *Confession*
1881–82	Writing *A Criticism of Dogmatic Theology* and his *Gospel Harmony*
1881	Wrote his *Letter to the Tsar (Alexander III)*
1882	Buys house in Moscow
1884	Writes *What I Believe*
1885	Becomes a vegetarian
1889	Writes *The Kreutzer Sonata*
1891	Renounces copyrights and divides property among his family
1891–2	Russian Famine, Tolstoy provides relief
1893	Writes *The Kingdom of God is Within You*
1887	Lenin's brother executed by Alexander III radicalizing Lenin against the state
1898	Tolstoy advocates on behalf of the persecuted Doukhobor Christian sect
1899	Writes *Resurrection*, in part to fund the relocation of the Doukobors to Canada
1901	Excommunicated by the Orthodox Church on February 22
1903	Protests against Jew baitings
1905	Failed revolution attempt in Russia
1908	Tolstoy wrote *Letter to a Hindu*
1908	Lenin writes for Tolstoy's 80th birthday claiming Tolstoy is to blame for failed 1905 revolution
1909–10	Tolstoy correspondence with Mahatma Gandhi
1910	Tolstoy flees his wife/Yasnaya Polyana on October, 28, dies November 7 at Astapovo train station
1910	Gandhi establishes the Tolstoy Farm in South Africa
1914–18	World War I
1917	Russian Revolution
1918–20	Red Terror and Russian Civil War, Bolsheviks in power
1919	Tolstoy secretary/friend/biographer Paul Biriukov exiled to Geneva, befriends Henri Lasserre
1920	Bonhoeffer as a youth writes that he enjoys reading Tolstoy

1927	Bonhoeffer graduated Berlin University having studied under Karl Holl
1928	Bonhoeffer at Barcelona gives a rationale for killing in war
1930	Bonhoeffer and Jean Lasserre become friends at Union Seminary in New York
1930	Gandhi's Salt March
1934	Bonhoeffer spoke at Fano, Denmark ecumenical conference against war and killing
1934	Bonhoeffer corresponds with Gandhi for a visit to India, Niebuhr discourages it
1935–37	Bonhoeffer's underground seminary at Finkenwalde
1936	Reichbishop Ludwig Müller published a "Germanised" Sermon on the Mount
1937	Bonhoeffer writes *Discipleship*
1939	Bonhoeffer writes *Life Together*
1939–45	World War II
1940	On Christmas Eve, Gandhi writes Hitler asking him to end the war
1944	Kaarle Laurila writes against Tolstoyan Christianity in Finland
1944	Henri Lasserre writes book on Tolstoyan Communities
1945	Bonhoeffer executed April 8 at Flossenbürg Concentration Camp
1947	India Independence
1948	Gandhi assassination January 30
1962, 65	Bonhoeffer friend Jean Lasserre writes *War & The Gospel* and *Christians and Violence*

~ 0.0 ~

Introduction
Why Give Gandhi All the Glory?

ON THE THRESHOLD OF a century of brutal global wars, nuclear bombs, holocausts, genocides, and bloody revolutions, a middle-aged novelist of world-renown morphed into a troubled prophet spending every ruble of his considerable credibility to champion the way of peace, calling his countrymen away from the distracting dogmas of Christendom back to the simple teaching of Jesus in the Sermon on the Mount. From the vantage point of traditional Christian orthodoxy, this pesky prophet got more wrong than he got right. However, what he got right was a simple Sermon on the Mount obedience which, according to Jesus, continues to be the sole factor determining and distinguishing the greatest from the least in the Kingdom of Heaven (Matt 5:19). In the last three decades of the eight he lived on earth, having achieved the height of literary success writing what is often considered the world's greatest novel, Leo Tolstoy broke stride with both the Doctrine of the Church and the Doctrine of the World (his vernacular) and ventured down Christ's narrow path seeking to practice and teach others to practice the painfully clear and uncompromising tenets of Jesus' Sermon on the Mount, what Tolstoy considered to be the Doctrine of Jesus.

Tolstoy can be considered the most significant interpreter of the Sermon on the Mount since Jesus stood on that mountainside—a bold claim but not hyperbole. What sets Tolstoy apart as a Sermon on the Mount interpreter is at least fourfold:

1. The number of decades he devoted to practicing and teaching the Sermon on the Mount has few parallels in church history.
2. The number of books and pamphlets he devoted solely to Sermon on the Mount obedience places his contribution above and apart.
3. The reach of his Sermon on the Mount interpretation and application profoundly influencing contentions in other continents in the century to follow; India and Israel, France, Germany and Great Britain, Canada and the United States.

However, as significant as each of those factors are, most significant is what remains ahead of us in this project,

4. Tolstoy's interpretation of the Sermon on the Mount as a new way of life (New Life-Conception) given by Jesus who intended his followers to simply obey and not reason against.

0.1 A Sympathetic Reading and the Problem of Secular Subjectivity

By way of preliminary remarks it is important to explain why little credence will be given herein to common criticisms of the religious Tolstoy and the religion of Tolstoy. What follows is a long overdue sympathetic treatment of the religious Tolstoy and particularly his interpretation of the Sermon on the Mount. In his introduction to *Religion from Tolstoy to Camus*, Walter Kaufmann observed: "The world has been exceedingly kind to the author of *War and Peace*, but it has not taken kindly to the later Tolstoy."[1] In his literary comparison and essays in contrast of *Tolstoy and Dostoevsky*, George Steiner similarly finds an intrinsic generosity toward Tolstoy's fictional literature but a marked disdain toward his later religious writings:

> Literary criticism should arise out of a debt of love. In a manner evident and yet mysterious, the poem or the drama or novel seizes our imaginings. We are not the same when we put down the work as when we took it up. . . . I say this because contemporary criticism [of Tolstoy] is of a different cast. . . . [I]t often comes to bury rather than praise.[2]

A. N. Wilson, who wrote a more recent significant Tolstoy biography begins with a personal recollection about sitting in a 1967 R. V. Sampson lecture on

---

1. Kaufmann, *Religion from Tolstoy to Camus*, 7.
2. Steiner, *Tolstoy or Dostoevsky*, 3–4.

Tolstoy when Sampson referenced a Jewish proverb—"If God came to live on earth, people would smash his windows." Wilson writes:

> Professor Sampson went on to say that people had been smashing Tolstoy's windows ever since he had enunciated his great principles of life. I was amazed that anyone could speak of a novelist as if he were divine . . . that excitement, and that amazement continue to this hour. I have never got over Professor Sampson's lecture. He will certainly regard the present book as an exercise in window-smashing.[3]

This book however, is not an exercise in window-smashing. It fills a gap in the literature, ironically, in even asking what Tolstoy got right. One can make significant errors and mistakes along the way and still discern significant truths. For those who prefer Tolstoy's transgressions be central, the bibliography included here is well-stocked with volumes highlighting the religious Tolstoy's trespasses. If indeed one would be ill-advised to get their Christology or eschatology from Tolstoy, there most definitely are other things he can teach us, even in his weak attempts to live them himself. There are a rare few examples of thorough scholarship wading through his negatives to retrieve these positives.

0.2 The Under-Appreciated Prophet

In the pages that follow, Tolstoy will be read as an under-appreciated prophet. His influence has been global, but often Gandhi gets the glory, with no mention of Tolstoy. In their two volume annotated bibliography of English language sources from 1878 to 2003, David Egan and Melinda Egan amassed 3,303 citations related to Tolstoy studies; mainly books, articles, chapters and dissertations—totalling 578 pages of listings. The last fifteen years are not represented. Only 18 percent of the 3,303 secondary literature citations have to do with Tolstoy's (1) politics, (2) philosophy, and (3) religion—basically the entire Second Tolstoy corpus (better defined in the next chapter, Section 1.1). Considering Tolstoy spent the last thirty years of his life devoted to his religious views, it is quite striking that only 6 percent is the amount of secondary source material related to his religious writings, or 211 citations total out of 3,303.

A central contention in this project is that there is great need for more work in this area; that Tolstoy's contributions to Political Theology and Christian Ethics are significant; and that he should be read in every

---

3. Wilson, *Tolstoy*, ix.

theological academy alongside the variety of other thinkers like Bonhoeffer, Yoder, and Hauerwas; that he is the baseline in Sermon on the Mount scholarship for the following century (argued in subsection 5.6); and that he is just upstream of every expression and discussion today about nonviolent resistance. Tolstoy's interpretation of the Sermon on the Mount (that it is to be strictly obeyed, not reasoned against) is unique in its intensity and consistency and he defended it across a large corpus of theological writing over several decades. The influence of his religious writings in non-violent political revolutions in Russia, India, and beyond have earned him a prominent place in the company of the religious thinkers we expose divinity students to today, alongside the likes of Bonhoeffer, Yoder, and Hauerwas. It is regrettable those named three did not engage Tolstoy in any notable way as there is substantial overlap of Tolstoy with each of their theological contributions particularly those relating to the Sermon on the Mount and to war and peace studies. Dr. Alexandre Christoyannopoulos is on a very short list of academics presently engaging Tolstoyan religio-political literature and he too argues for Tolstoy's positive contributions for our modern situation:

> [M]ore specifically on the political implications of Christianity, Tolstoy raised several points that could offer interesting first steps on pathways for further thinking. His approach itself may not always be careful tolerant, or academic, but his message is still pertinent and worth pondering in today's political climate, because he highlights a peaceful yet often forgotten dimension of Jesus' message to humanity.[4]

Tolstoy's critics may be correct in their assessment that he threw the baby out with the bathwater, however, in future analysis of the religious Tolstoy care must be taken that one does not do the same.

The main problem in the reception of Tolstoy's religious writings is the interpreters incomprehension about the shape of his piety. Alexander Root's approach is an example of this in the extreme. In the 1970s the Russian KGB kicked philologist and polemicist Alexander Root out of Russia. More recently Root wrote a blistering, and remarkably sarcastic and sour, book-length rant against Tolstoy and Tolstoyan Christianity. Root contends even Tolstoy's long white beard and simple robe were part of the intentionally calculated deception of a false prophet who viewed himself as God; his "disheveled visage [was] deliberately modelled on the crude public perception of God's appearance."[5] Root insists that, as in modern marketing, Tolstoy was carefully "repositioning and repackaging. (Let us not forget that Tolstoy was

---

4. Christoyannopoulos, "Turning the Other Cheek to Terrorism," 28.
5. Root, *God and Man according to Tolstoy*, 6.

primarily a communicator, not a contemplator.) He had to make the world accept him not just as a writer but as a God-like figure, a Christ surrogate."[6]

Tolstoy was not Jesus. In fact, he would have vehemently rebuked any who even confused him with a Christian cleric, much less with any sort of Christ. However, to this day he presents a challenge to many in all the various streams of Christendom who frankly, look and act nothing like Christ. For these reasons, he is a prophet worthy of a fair hearing. If one is looking for a prophetic voice or a philosopher who is completely consistent with watertight propositions, keep looking. There is much in Tolstoy to criticise. Yet it will be shown here how some of the criticism is a biased misreading of Tolstoy by those who begin their analysis of Tolstoy with either an animosity toward the Christian faith, or conversely, with an animosity toward any who speak against a traditionally orthodox interpretation of it. When A. N. Wilson, that aforementioned award-winning Tolstoy biographer, refers to the Sermon on the Mount as a "counsel of craziness" it seems apparent the way of Jesus is as much the rub as anything of Tolstoy himself:

> It is possible to read the rest of Tolstoy's life as a heroic attempt to live as Jesus Christ told his followers that they should live. That, up to a point, is what it was. But it is also possible to read the next thirty years as an extraordinary demonstration of the fact that the Sermon on the Mount is an unliveable ethic, a counsel of craziness which, if followed to its relentless conclusion as Tolstoy tried to follow it, will lead to the reverse of peace and harmony and spiritual calm which are normally thought of as concomitants of the religious quest. Tolstoy's religion is ultimately the most searching criticism of Christianity which there is. He shows that it does not work.[7]

Though Wilson's biography is quite good on many counts, Colm McKeogh of the University of Waikato in New Zealand summed up the entire biography saying "A. N. Wilson presents Tolstoy as a headstrong fool and sees little of worth outside his literature."[8] Certainly, from the vantage point of the unbelieving world the way of Christ is the way of fools. Tolstoy was certainly a radicalized follower of the ways of Christ, a holy fool who took the teaching of Jesus more seriously than most anyone else in his day, and our day.

Tolstoyan criticism throughout the past century has suffered on occasion from the subjectivity of an unbelieving disposition. Discernment is needed first to ascertain if the critique is first and foremost a critique of

---

6. Root, *God and Man according to Tolstoy*, 66.
7. Wilson, *Tolstoy*, 300–1.
8. McKeogh, *Tolstoy's Pacifism*, 197.

Jesus, a critique of the reasonableness of living the Sermon on the Mount, or merely a critique of Tolstoy. Any hoped-for objective analysis becomes subjectively tainted by preconceived negations of the Sermon on the Mount lifestyle Tolstoy was weakly trying to emulate. Outside Russian Orthodoxy in the nineteenth century,[9] some of his earliest twentieth-century criticism, and the most unflattering ones were from violent Marxist revolutionaries like Lyubov Axelrod and Georgi Plekhanov.[10] Of course they have nothing good to say about the non-violence and pacifism of Tolstoyan religio-politics. Perhaps deep down and unbeknownst to even themselves he reminds them of the Jesus they reject. An analysis of Tolstoyan Christianity tends to result in some form analysis of one's own self along the way.

The Church of the twentieth century effectively put Tolstoy out and ignored his existence and memory. Even so, there is no reformer or theologian in Christian history who comes without quirks, controversies and questions. What if Christians were to cast crazy Ezekiel aside on account of his bizarre antics? Ezekiel's radical obedience to the Lord meant he went about naked and barefoot for three years. Then he laid down on each side for a few years not to mention his otherworldly visions and diet. Hosea married a prostitute. People of faith believe God can indeed raise sons of Abraham from the roughest of stones and use even an ass to speak a needed truth. In his book *The Religion and Ethics of Tolstoy* written only a few weeks after Tolstoy's death, Alexander H. Craufurd eulogized him with this disclaimer: "The spiritual vision of the greatest prophets is often confused, perplexing, and to some extent inconsistent or at least incoherent."[11] Tolstoy was guilty on all accounts. However, theologians into the present day engage notable others who also dealt devastating blows to the status quo of Christendom. The ideas of Nietzsche, Hegel, and Kant, are continually raised from the dead, in fact, they are required reading. Yet there is and has been a curious but unfortunate veil over Tolstoyan Christianity.

Nietzsche, Hegel, and Kant remain such colossal figures in theological conversation that no doubt it will seem too far a stretch to list Tolstoy in that league. However, Tolstoy had a global following as an author among all classes of people; he was considered as influential among the population of his day as the Tsar; he wrote dozens of volumes and articles on various aspects of Sermon on the Mount obedience and its implications; and Tolstoyan communities emerged by the thousands across Russia and into Europe, Canada, and the United States. What more does one have to do to

---

9. Bulgakov, S.N. editor., *On the Religion of Lev Tolstoy*, Moscow: Put', 1912.
10. *Karl Marx and Lev Tolstoy* in Plekhanov, *Selected Philosophical Works*, vol. 5.
11. Craufurd, *Religion and Ethics of Tolstoy*, 154.

be located on the radar as a serious religious thinker and reformer? There has been a peculiar veil concealing him, perhaps even a demonic veil suppressing his call to Sermon on the Mount obedience (only his flaws and faults are recalled) while the ideas of those who have declared God dead enjoy some measure of diabolical amplification. There being some truth in all of the above reasons Tolstoy has been neglected in theological circles in the last century, the disregarding of the Sermon on the Mount itself is the real underlying factor and the disinterest in Tolstoyan Christianity is merely another chapter in that much longer story. In other words, it is the radical Sermon on the Mount message people struggle to swallow, and every messenger is easily stripped and driven away.

0.3 Heretics and the Other Side of the Gospel

Tolstoy is the focus of the last chapter of Walter Nigg's lengthy book on heretics and Nigg's positive hermeneutic toward heretics is shared in this project at least as it related to Tolstoy. Nigg argued heretics play a vital role in our faith and play an important role and function for the Church, even a supporting role not just an opposing role: "[spurring] the church to the self-criticism which alone could act as a rejuvenating force."[12] Nigg articulated how desperately Christianity needs this today, and in times past: "[heretics] afford us new insight into the Gospels. . . . [They] represent a different conception of Christianity. . . . [They] advocate a view of Christianity different from that of the victorious churches."[13] Nigg's defence of heretics captures the sense of this project, that Tolstoy was far from a total loss, but rather an important ambassador to a Church that herself had ventured far out into dangerous heretical waters. Nigg precisely articulates the reading of Tolstoy in the forthcoming pages: "We might put it that he attempts to bring to the fore the other side of the Gospel. . . . The heretics, then, represent a repressed interpretation of Christianity."[14]

12. Nigg, *The Heretics*, 9.
13. Nigg, *The Heretics*, 11.
14. Nigg, *The Heretics*, 11–15. "We might put it that he attempts to bring to the fore the other side of the Gospel. . . . The heretics, then, represent a repressed interpretation of Christianity. . . . Out of the history of the heretics there emerges a buried truth which unexpectedly begins to glow with new radiance. . . . The heretic's special contribution to church history is to be found in their incessant endeavours to advance the other, the overlooked and misunderstood conception of Christianity. . . . The heretics resemble the saints. . . . The heretic's life almost always becomes a tragedy . . . viewed as disobedience to the church, the heretic was punished by being expelled from its communion. . . . The bloodied pages of the story of heresy tell a tale of martyrs within Christendom.

No argument is made here defending every heretic, or to gloss over the damage they can do, especially in how people can be eternally led astray. Even so, this work proceeds in some measure of agreement with Nigg, at least as his sentiments quoted above can be said of Leo Tolstoy. As Nigg wrote: "Tolstoy was indeed the great discoverer of the Sermon on the Mount in our day and age. Once again it was a heretic who after many centuries sought to hammer that sermon home to the conscience of Christendom."[15] No defence is given in the pages that follow for what Tolstoy got wrong. Rather, a careful ear is attuned to what he got right. It is this prophetic edge of Tolstoy that this project seeks to amplify for a new generation's consideration as they seek to follow Christ into Christlikeness.

0.4 A Three-Part Framework for Appreciating Second Tolstoy

Tolstoy's religious thought, his reading and application of the Sermon on the Mount, can be most succinctly captured using his three-part framework: (1) Doctrine of Jesus, (2) Doctrine of the Church, and (3) Doctrine of the World. It is this three-part framework which will serve as the larger structure of the chapters in this project: (1) the Doctrine of Jesus set against (2) the Doctrine of the Church and (3) the Doctrine of the World. The first five chapters will give careful articulation to Tolstoy's Doctrine of Jesus.

The first chapter introduces the overlapping life and literature of Leo Tolstoy with primary attention placed on the first four of the six volumes which constitute the main religious works of Tolstoy which will be referred to as Second Tolstoy. The second chapter is a survey of the remaining two of the six main works of Second Tolstoy. The third and fourth chapters survey Tolstoy's unique interpretation of the Sermon on the Mount by identifying the major hermeneutical moves he made with and within the Sermon itself. These first four chapters are intentionally descriptive with very little analysis. The aim is to present Tolstoy's reading of the Sermon on the Mount. The fifth chapter considers the epistolary work of Tolstoy and then his legacy in a century of Sermon on the Mount scholarship.

The middle section contains two chapters dealing with the Doctrine of the Church. The sixth chapter seeks to capture the Constantinian shift which Tolstoy deemed the departure point for subsequent centuries of

---

With their heart-rending readiness to suffer, the heretics represent a continuation of the Passion of Christ, which will go on until the end of the world. . . . The story of the persecuted heretics leads directly to the heart of Christianity."

15. Nigg, *The Heretics*, 389.

ecclesial apostasy and a rejection of Sermon on the Mount ethics. The seventh chapter is the first and long overdue analysis of the lengthiest critique to date of Tolstoyan Christianity by a Finnish layman who sought to use Luther as the best retort to Tolstoy.

The final section contains three chapters pertaining to the Doctrine of the World. Chapter eight covers Tolstoy's sexual self-disarmament and his views on marriage. Chapter nine sets forth Tolstoy's reading of Matthew 5:38-39 as an alternative politic presenting a serious challenge to the prevailing ideas of his time, specifically Social Darwinism and Marxist-Leninism. The final chapter introduces needed vernacular changes breaking from the traditional use of Christian anarchy and pacifism to describe Tolstoy as related to state violence and war. Themes of obedience, living martyrdom, blind love and theo-tactics emerge in the conclusion amidst other significant findings throughout this research and analysis.

This project is my second work on Tolstoy's interpretation of the Sermon on the Mount. The earlier project was a Master's thesis entitled—*Tolstoy's Novel Idea: Obey the Sermon on the Mount*. In that work, an inordinate amount of time was spent sparring with secondary sources against Tolstoy. For this reason, generally this thesis does not engage these secondary sources all over again, except as needed and more briefly. Deliberately, this project limits who else is drawn in resulting, hopefully, in an intentional amplification of what Tolstoy had to say. The intention in this second project, now a PhD dissertation, was that Tolstoy would be heard properly and appreciated, leaving to a lesser place what others have said about and against him. This is not to say secondary sources are neglected, it is to say they are not given a prominent place or extended treatment as some might expect (again, because they were given greater and proper due in the earlier project). The aim of this work is to focus on Tolstoy and what Tolstoy said and what he meant, and less on what others thought about it.

0.5 New and Original Contributions Herein

A notable success of this thesis is in the numerous original contributions to Tolstoyan studies found within these pages. These original and new contributions include:

1. The project itself is a first, the first book-length treatment of the Sermon on the Mount in Second Tolstoy.

2. Herein is the first parallel, technical comparison of Matthew 5–7 in Tolstoy's *Gospel in Brief* with a contemporary English translation (NIV-UK).

3. There is the inclusion and analysis of newly found and newly translated material on Tolstoy and Chelčický, on Tolstoy and Lassarre, on Tolstoy and Laurila, and new historical connections made between Tolstoy and Bonhoeffer.

4. Tolstoyan passages that stand apart and stand out for their notable prophetic unction and fervor are treated as a new and important genre for further study: the genre of Tolstoy's diatribes.

5. Particularly important is the basis given for an original and radical re-reading of what has heretofore been considered Tolstoy's failed marriage and lovelessness. What has long been considered negatively is shown to be a positive in that Tolstoy's adherence to Christ cost him family harmony.

6. A plausible alternative history is proposed in light of Tolstoy's letter to the Tsar and the radicalization of Vladimir Lenin.

7. The most significant original contribution of this thesis is in the new verbiage and vernacular given in these pages to better describe Tolstoyan Christianity to a new generation, that verbiage being theo-tactics.

8. Lastly there is a delightful new find, included in the appendices (subsection 13.5) which I am calling the *Tolstoy Anathema Iron*, making its first appearance in Tolstoyan studies.

0.6 The Ins and Outs of the Religious Tolstoy

The chapters that follow will not pursue the philosophical influences on Tolstoy. The interest herein is hermeneutical and ethical; how did Tolstoy interpret and apply the Sermon on the Mount? There is no question he was a product of the Enlightenment, though probably it is more precise to view him as an early Post-Enlightenment thinker. There is no question significant early philosophical influences exist, especially that of Rousseau and Schopenhauer. Those questions will be largely left alone. The validity and legitimacy of Tolstoy's Christian conversion, a key tenet throughout my reading of Tolstoy, severs, or at least diminishes his earlier ideological ties and dependancies with Enlightenment thinkers. However, to at least acknowledge those influences, and to visually present those influences on Tolstoy, and the influences of Tolstoy on others, the graphic is provided. Downstream of Tolstoy there were a number of notable people in different parts of the world who took up the main aspects of his Sermon on the Mount interpretations and engaged them in their own lives and settings; of course Gandhi to Martin Luther King Jr., but also Ludwig Wittgenstein and William Jennings Bryan, Clarence Darrow, Ernest Howard Crosby, and Dorothy Day. Tolstoy influenced the Kibbutz movement in Israel, and Andre Crocme and the Lasserre's in France who influenced Dietrich Bonhoeffer. More to come in subsection 5.4 on considering Bonhoeffer as an important downstream development in what can be seen as Tolstoyan Christianity.

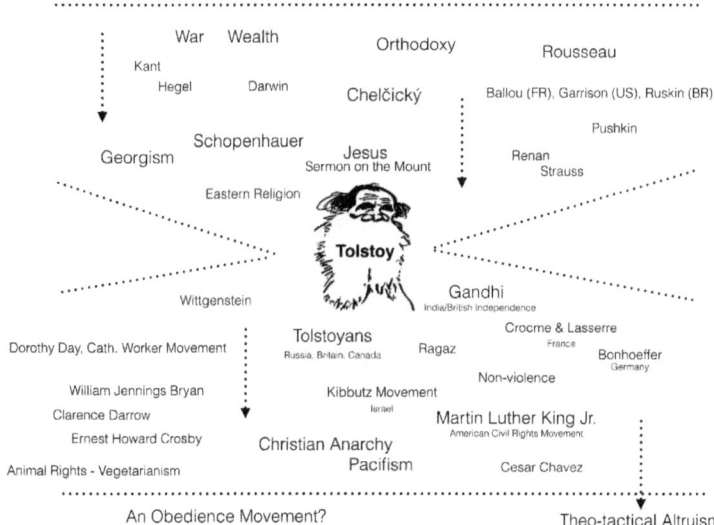

PART ONE

The Doctrine of Jesus

~ 1.0 ~

The Overlapping Life and Literature of Leo Tolstoy

> At that time [age 26] I began to write through vanity, avarice, and pride. In my writings I did the same as in life.
>
> —Tolstoy, *A Confession*

THE LITERATURE OF LEO Tolstoy can only be properly studied alongside a study of the life of Leo Tolstoy as his literature and his life are entirely and inextricably intertwined. The corpus of his earlier fictional literature, what could be dubbed First Tolstoy, was written within a popular genre of his day, Nineteenth Century Russian Realism, as it is known today. These fictional works were realistic, situated in the social and political setting of the author's own day. First Tolstoy includes his semi-autobiographical trilogy *Childhood, Boyhood,* and *Youth* (1852, 1854, 1856), *Sevastopol Sketches* (1855), *Family Happiness* (1859), *The Cossacks* (1863), his main novels *War & Peace* (1869), *Anna Karenina* (1877) and his other novels and novellas from the 1850s, 1860s and early 1870s. The middle of the nineteenth century was a time of great political and social angst in Russia and realism literature became a popular venue for criticism, analysis, social challenge and reform. Tolstoy's characters were both fictional and historical—approximately 160 of the 567 characters in *War & Peace* were real historical figures.[1] However, and of

---

1. Pevear, "Introduction," viii–ix.

greater import, even some of his main fictional characters bear a striking resemblance to his own self and life in earlier time and place.

It is widely understood Pierre Bezukhov in *War & Peace* was a reflection of Tolstoy himself; his fringe status among the Upper Class, his social awkwardness, excessive partying and sexual exploits, financial foolishness, impulsive emotions, periods of irrationality and his search for morality and meaning in life. Tolstoy's own story was seamlessly weaved into his storyline.

> The Rostovs and Bolkonskys are thinly-disguised versions of Tolstoy's own family members, who came from an ancient Russian noble line. For example, the character of Nikolay Rostov borrows a lot from Tolstoy's father, Nikolay, who was also a hero of the Patriotic War of 1812 and a lieutenant colonel in the Pavlograd regiment, which is mentioned in the novel by name. Marya Bolkonskaya bears a great resemblance to Tolstoy's mother, Marya Tolstaya, née Volkonskaya. The description of their wedding ceremony is similar to that of Tolstoy's parents, and the same is true of the characters' estate, Lysye Gory, which resembles Tolstoy's own home, Yasnaya Polyana.[2]

The first line in *Anna Karenina*: "Happy families are all alike; every unhappy family is unhappy in its own way" has given astute readers some measure of justified suspicion that Tolstoy's own unhappiness was partially woven into subsequent pages. His mother died when he was two years old and it is not difficult to notice his own reflection in the young Seryozha. As a prolific diarist over the course of many decades, Tolstoy unwittingly gave modern unsympathetic psychoanalytical literary critics much to work with, especially as this missing mother figure weighed on him emotionally and psychologically throughout his life.[3] Orphaned at age ten after an accident claimed the life of his father, Tolstoy's preoccupation with life and mortality in his real life were only lightly veiled before being written into his novels. He later said: "I wrote everything into *Anna Karenina*, and nothing was left over" alluding to how much of himself was written into the characters and storyline.[4] It is apparent *Anna Karenina* (1877) was a pivotal book for

---

2. Viesel, "War and Peace."

3. Rancour-Laferriere, *Tolstoy's Quest for God*, 180. "If Tolstoy's vehement rejection of the Russian Orthodox 'Mother Church' of his ancestors and of his childhood was a repudiation of his mother, then the grandiose pantheism of his later years aims at reconciliation with his mother. She with her precious breast abandoned him early on, but sheath her ubiquitous body is not with him forever. Tolstoy's quest for God thus begins and ends with his quest for his mother." See also Subsection 8.1.

4. Popoff, "Why People Write about Tolstoy?" On her blog, noted Tolstoy scholar Alexandra Popoff mentions the quotation in this way: "McGasko quotes Tolstoy as

Tolstoy and marked his departure from writing fiction to writing about his faith. In addition to the genre of Russian Realism and the strong similarities between his own life and that of his fictional characters, Tolstoy found space in his main novels for lengthy sections—interjected throughout the storylines—of his philosophical thought and commentary on the social order, social justice, government, theology and history. So extended are these essays in *War & Peace*, to better market the book to popular readers early translator Huntington Smith separated it into two volumes placing the storyline in one volume and Tolstoy's extended essays on history in the other creating a 222 page volume Smith titled: *The Physiology of War; Napoleon and the Russian Campaign*. Whether in two volumes or one, much in First Tolstoy is Tolstoy himself and in no way could be construed as entire fictions alien to his person and setting made up to entertain the reader.

The literature and life of Leo Tolstoy are intertwined in even more intimate ways than his genre of realism. Making him a moving target for his critics, Tolstoy's literature follows the course of his spiritual journey, in particular his conversion to a radicalized form of Christianity with his discovery of Sermon on the Mount obedience as the path to life and happiness. Tolstoy's pre-conversion literature will be considered First Tolstoy in the pages that follow and his post-conversion literature Second Tolstoy. Tolstoy was born September 9, 1828; he lived eighty-two years dying November 20, 1910. His pre-conversion period, birth to approximately age fifty,[5] resulted in a tangible darkness permeating his writings; a sordid interest and even fixation on the pain of life and love, war, meaninglessness, despair, suicide and death. His post-conversion period literature reveals evidence of a light having dawned within him which burned consistently for the remaining thirty-two years of his life. Of his overlapping life and literature Tolstoy wrote: "You think that I am one thing and my writing is another. But my writing is the whole of me."[6]

In 1891 at the age of sixty-three Tolstoy made a list of one hundred "Works Which Made An Impression" dividing them up into five ages of man and ranking them according to their degree of influence on him; *enormous, v. great,* or merely, *great.*[7] The second listed age bracket *Age 14 to 20*

---

supposedly saying, "I wrote everything into *Anna Karenina*, and nothing was left over." I don't know where he got this quote."

5. It is Tolstoy himself who points to his conversion at the approximate age of fifty. Certainly his conversion did not happen overnight. Innesa Medzhibovskaya's thorough book on Tolstoy's conversion follows the course of his spiritual pilgrimage over a period of nearly forty years. See Medzhibovskaya, *Tolstoy and the Religious Culture*.

6. Christian, *Tolstoy's Letters: Volume II*, 399.

7. Mikhail Mikhailovich Lederle, a St. Petersburg publisher, bookseller, author and

begins with "Matthew's Gospel: Sermon on the Mount – Enormous." Importantly, the Sermon on the Mount more than anything else held sway with him throughout his entire life, especially commanding his allegiance across the last three decades of his life. His novels and religious writings aside, Tolstoy ultimately sought to locate his life within the lines of Jesus' Sermon on the Mount, Matthew 5–7 and play a part in God's story.

1.1 Second Tolstoy[8]

No doubt, even the title of the work, *Second Tolstoy*, will cause some measure of consternation in Tolstoyan scholarly circles as the consensus of late

---

member of the Petersburg Committee on Literacy wrote 2000 "professors, scholars, artists, and men of letters, public figures, and other luminaries" asking for a list of the one hundred books that most influenced them. Tolstoy made and attached his list to an October 25, 1891 letter to Lederle written from Yasnaya Polyana. Christian, *Tolstoy's Letters: Volume II*, 373–74.

8. The full listing of non-fiction works within the Second Tolstoy period is as follows: *A Confession* (1879)—Volume 1 of an untitled four-part work; *A Criticism of Dogmatic Theology* (1880)—Volume 2 of an untitled four-part work; *The Gospel in Brief*, or *A Short Exposition of the Gospel* (1881); *The Four Gospel Unified and Translated* (1881)—Volume 3 of an untitled four-part work; *Church and State* (1882); *What I Believe* (also called *My Religion*) (1884)—Volume 4 of an untitled four-part work; *What Is to Be Done?* (also translated as *What Then Must We Do?*) (1886); *On Life* (1887); *The Love of God and of One's Neighbour* (1889); Supplementary essay for Timofei Bondarev's *The Triumph of the Farmer or Industry and Parasitism* (1888); *Why Do Men Intoxicate Themselves?* (1890); *The First Step: On Vegetarianism* (1892); *The Kingdom of God Is within You* (1893); *Non-Activity* (1893); *The Meaning of Refusal of Military Service* (1893); *Reason and Religion* (1894); *Religion and Morality* (1894); *Christianity and Patriotism* (1894); *Non-Resistance*: letter to Ernest H. Crosby (1896); *How to Read the Gospels* (1896); *The Deception of the Church* (1896); *Letter to the Liberals* (1898); *Christian Teaching* (1898); *On Suicide* (1900); *The Slavery of Our Times* (1900); *Thou Shalt Not Kill* (1900); *Reply to the Holy Synod* (1901); *The Only Way* (1901); *On Religious Toleration* (1901); *What Is Religion and What Is Its Essence?* (1902); *To the Orthodox Clergy* (1903); *Thoughts of Wise Men* (compilation; 1904); *The Only Need* (1905); *The Grate Sin* (1905); *A Cycle of Reading* (1906); *Do Not Kill* (1906); *Love Each Other* (1906); *An Appeal to Youth* (1907); *The Law of Love and the Law of Violence* (1908); *The Only Command* (1909); *A Calendar of Wisdom* (1909).

Tolstoy's fiction writing during this post-conversion Second Tolstoy period strongly reflects his religious convictions: *The Death of Ivan Ilyich* (1886); *The Kreutzer Sonata* (1889), *Resurrection* (1899); *The Forged Coupon* (1911); *Hadji Murat* (1912). This listing only includes his novels and novellas during this period and not his numerous short stories and plays.

Second Tolstoy also must include his diary entries, and even more-so a large grouping of his letters, specifically the letters of "Tolstoy the Thinker" according to the tripartite grouping of Tolstoy's immense collection of extant letters by R. F. Christian into the three groupings; Tolstoy the writer, the thinker, and the man. The last thirty-two

is that there really is only one Tolstoy, that his later philosophical concerns can be discerned even in his earliest life and writings.⁹ This project makes no argument against those established facts, it *is* the case that from childhood—*the green stick!*—Tolstoy was concerned to find what was true and discover what gave meaning and happiness to life. However, it is also clear that there is a distinct Second Tolstoy corpus. The fact that Russian literature scholars in universities all over the world spend little or no time on his later writings is evidence enough there is a clear break between the literature of First and Second Tolstoy. Even more, Tolstoy himself regarded his earlier works of far lower importance than his latter works. Perhaps most telling is that his wife absolutely regarded the early Tolstoy as different from the later Tolstoy. Certainly the Russian censors saw the earlier writings of Tolstoy as benign and the latter writings as subversive. There can be little argument these differences are real and go far beyond the differences in genre between First and Second Tolstoy. Therefore, it is appropriate and overdue that a new area of appreciation in Tolstoy scholarship become Second Tolstoy.

The scope of the analysis in the following pages is narrowed to the first fourteen years of Tolstoy's post-conversion literature period, 1879–93, dates which were selected corresponding with the writing and publication

---

volumes of the enormous ninety-volume Soviet addition of *Count Tolstoy's Collected Works* ('Jubilee Edition'; Moscow, 1928–58) contain his approximately 8,500 letters. "The germ of almost everything that has come to fruition in his thinking and writing after 1880 can be found in one or other of his letters of the previous thirty years: his pacifism, his rejection of capital punishment, his hostility towards state institutions and bureaucratic practices, his unconventional views on primary and secondary education, his distrust of university professors, doctors and journalists, his hatred of big cities and an urban society based on buying and selling of property, his painful awareness of the contrast between his own material well-being and the poverty surrounding him and his concern to justify his art in terms of its usefulness to the community as a whole. There are many such pointers in Tolstoy's earliest letters to the direction in which his thoughts were leading him, but none are so obvious, perhaps, as those which indicate his attitude towards death and the meaninglessness of life. . . . What is revealed in these letters is Tolstoy's absolute conviction of the paramount importance of religion, his impatience with Orthodox ritual and dogma, and his belief that the essence of Christian feeling is love and unselfishness and that these qualities were not only the most desirable virtues in themselves, but were conspicuously lacking in those adherents of official Orthodox Christianity with whom he was most familiar." Christian, *Tolstoy's Letters: Volume I*, viii–ix.

9. Wilson, *Tolstoy*, 301. "It is very hard not to think of his life as falling into two distinct halves, divided by the publication of Anna Karenina. It is right to point out as nearly all writers on Tolstoy do, that there is a continuity between his former and his later self. . . . All his life he had sought, for at least some of the time, a spiritual solution to the eternal questions. Yes, yes, but this is to miss the obvious point that after Anna Karenina there are no great novels."

dates of the most significant six of his main non-fiction (religious) books comprising the first half of the Second Tolstoy period of his life:

Second Tolstoy – Main Post-Conversion Non-Fiction Religious Works (1879–93)

1. *A Confession* (1879–81) – [*abbr.* CF]
2. *Critique of Dogmatic Theology* (1881–82) – [*abbr.* DT]
3. *The Four Gospels Harmonised and Translated: Vols. 1, 2* (1881–82) – [*abbr.* HM]
4. *The Gospel in Brief* (1882–83) – [*abbr.* GB
5. *What I Believe* (1884) – [*abbr.* WB]
6. *The Kingdom of God Is within You* (1893) – [*abbr.* KG]

After relatively brief introductory treatments of the first four books, the analysis in the three subsequent chapters will be on Tolstoy's interpretation of the Sermon on the Mount in the latter two selected books. The first four books amount to a research sequence and personal discovery process of essential preparatory study serving to solidify Tolstoy's convictions and ready him to write his fifth and most defining and compendious religious book, *What I Believe*. The implications of his Sermon on the Mount interpretations became the primary devotion of the last three decades of Tolstoy's life. As will be evident, these first four books of this post-conversion period tell the story of his (a) spiritual pilgrimage through darkness to light, (b) his coming to discover what he believed to be the errors of Orthodox doctrine, and (c) the dawning of light primarily from his comprehensive exegetical work on the Gospels which informed and became the foundation for his unique interpretation of the Sermon on the Mount and again, particularly the two main books on Sermon on the Mount obedience, *What I Believe* (1884), *The Kingdom of God Is within You* (1893). Hereafter the following abbreviations will be used on most occasions to refer to these aforementioned significant six post-conversion books; CF, DT, HM, GB, WB, and KG.

Initially it would seem it was not Tolstoy's original intent to publish these first books in his shift to religious writing as these projects served a more personal purpose of discovery and confirmation of his suspicions and growing convictions. It is common in popular reprints of Tolstoy works to find a life chronology of Tolstoy printed in the back with the years 1879–83 marked "makes intensive theological study."[10] Though at this point in his celebrity life as an author he no doubt had a sense that every word he wrote on any matter would one day be collected and disseminated to the interested public, Tolstoy was not primarily writing in this period for publication but more for personal discovery. Even so, at some point in the course of his work on these manuscripts Tolstoy began to envision a four-part work beginning with (1) *A Confession* as Volume I, then (2) *A Critique of Dogmatic Theology* becoming Volume II, then (3) *The Four Gospels Harmonised & Translated* as Volume III, and it is assumed that (4) *What I Believe* became his envisioned Volume IV. These four were never published accordingly, as any sort of four-part set that belonged together or as a progression or series despite his intention these books be appreciated in sequence.[11] The first, second and fourth books in this envisioned four-part set were published separately and each very popular on their own right. However, even now this third book, Tolstoy's Gospel harmony, stirs little interest and is only available within the many volumes of his *Complete Works* and never as a stand alone publication like the other three parts of the envisioned set of four. In 1891, ten years after he completed his Gospel harmony his friends encouraged him to officially publish it and he agreed with the following disclaimer: "The work is far from being finished, and there are many defects in it. I no longer feel the strength to correct and finish it, because that concentrated, ecstatic tension of my soul, which I constantly experienced during the whole time of this long work, can no longer be renewed" (HM, Vol. I, 3). Again the integration of his life and spiritual journey with his literature is evident. His agreement to publish was with the hope it might communicate "even a small part of that enlightenment which I experienced when I wrote it, and of that firm conviction of the truth of the path which has been revealed to me, and on which I travel with every greater joy, the longer I live" (HM, Vol. I, 3).

1.2 *A Confession* (1879–81) — [abbr. CF]

The first work in Second Tolstoy is *A Confession,* though contrary to the four-part schema envisioned above, there are hints, at least initially, Tolstoy simply intended his CF to serve as the introduction to his subsequent *Critique of Dogmatic Theology*. Both appear in one volume, Volume 13 of Leo Weiner's *Collected Works* in a shared table of contents with CF listed as: *My Confession: Introduction to the Critique of Dogmatic Theology and Investigation of the Christian Teaching* (DT, 8). Topically and materially there is

---

10. Tolstoy, *Great Short Works,* 680.
11. Tolstoy, *Gospel in Brief,* 7.

obvious overlap between these two works and they should be appreciated together even though *Confession* immediately took on a life of its own with any sense that it was a prelude to something larger being entirely lost. The trajectory throughout CF points directly to the beginning of DT.

Conversion narratives and Confessions became a genre of their own across the history of Christian thinkers and literature and Tolstoy's *Confession* is often appraised in comparison to Augustine's *Confession* and the similar but secular *Confession* of Jean-Jacques Rousseau.[12] Much more than the former, the latter was carefully read and reread by Tolstoy. In 1928 Milan Markovitch carefully filled over four hundred pages assessing Tolstoy's dependance on, or departure from, his early intellectual interests in Rousseau.[13] Tolstoy's comments about Rousseau's great impression on him are commonly remembered: "I idolised Rousseau to such an extent that I wanted to wear his portrait on my breast beside the saints picture."[14]

> Tolstoy worshiped Rousseau, largely because he recognised in him one whose spirit was akin to his, and because Rousseau expressed plainly what was as yet confused in his own brain; the feeling that something was wrong, that the contrasts in society were too great, that the culture which he saw and in which he lived was only a varnished barbarism: these things he had felt for a long time, and Rousseau's call for a return to unspoiled nature harmonised with his feelings and found a ready response.[15]

It is true in his twenties and thirties Tolstoy was heavily influenced by Rousseau. However, Tolstoy's *Confession* and Augustine's, are both notably different from Rousseau's in that Rousseau took his *Confession* in a secularized direction, not ending in a conversion to God or Christianity. If there is something significant to say about the three together it is that from Augustine, Rousseau took the genre in a direction away from God and Tolstoy reversed it back again: "a turn from the secular, literary mode back to the religious mode."[16]

The most obvious difference between these three well-known Confessions is in the length; in similar font and formatting Tolstoy's CF is only 61 pages in length; while Augustine's is 352 pages and Rousseau's is 649 pages in length. This brevity is fitting with the probability Tolstoy's CF was

---

12. Bullitt, "Rousseau and Tolstoy." And Coetzee, "Confession and Double Thoughts."

13. Markovitch, *Jean-Jacques Rousseau et Tolstoï*.

14. Steiner, *Tolstoy the Man*, 47.

15. Steiner, *Tolstoy the Man*, 48.

16. Paperno, "Who, What Am I?", 64.

meant to serve as an auto-biographical foreword of a spiritual pilgrimage or testimonial sort to set up the context, rationale and motivations behind his subsequent *Critique of Dogmatic Theology* and further work on his exhaustive Gospel harmony. For any who would make too much of Tolstoy's *Confession* in relation to Augustine's and Rousseau's it is noteworthy that Tolstoy had no title for this work when he submitted it to typesetters in 1882, he simply called it *"Introduction to an Unpublished Work."* The work was censored and illegal copies of proofs began to circulate: "Before long, family members, friends, editors, and reviewers alike started to call the work 'Confession.'"[17] Regardless of whether or not Tolstoy was consciously producing a traditional religious literary Confession, it is a concise example of the basic framework of a conversion narrative classic to a religious literary Confession.

Tolstoy's *Confession* is sixteen short segments, or chapters. Beginning with his baptism and education in the Orthodox Christian faith where he never really believed in earnest, Tolstoy quickly moved to give the account of his early defection from the faith. At age eleven a boy told him there was no God and that everything they were being taught were fabrications. That, and reading Voltaire set him on the course of questioning. At age fifteen he began reading philosophy and at age sixteen he stopped praying, attending church and preparing himself for communion. The next ten years he recalled with "dread, loathing and anguish of heart. . . . I killed people in war and challenged to duels to kill; I lost money at cards, wasting the labour of the peasants; I punished them, fornicated, and cheated. Lying, stealing, acts of lust of every description, drunkenness, violence, murder – There was not a crime which I did not commit, and for all that I was praised, and my contemporaries have regarded me as a comparatively moral man" (DT, 8–9). Then he began to write as he lived repeatedly mentioning in his *Confession* that he wrote and taught "myself not knowing what" (DT, 10–12). He saw himself as a priest of culture. "Thus I lived, abandoning myself to that insanity for six years longer until my marriage" (DT, 13). There were two deaths that revolted him and crushed his beliefs in the "superstition of progress"; witnessing an execution in Paris, and the death of his brother. He began to see the lie that "everything develops, and I, too, am developing" (DT, 14). Tolstoy "grew sick, mentally rather than physically, and went to live with the Bashkirs of the steppe, – to breath air, drink kumys, and live an animal life" (DT, 15). Another fifteen years passed and there is no mention in his *Confession* of the successful writing he was doing during this period. Instead he wrote what was going on inside: "I felt that what I was standing on had

---

17. Paperno, *"Who, What Am I?"*, 60.

given way, that I had no foundation to stand on, that that which I lived by no longer existed, and that I had nothing to live by" (DT, 18).

"My life came to a standstill.... I could breathe, eat, drink, and sleep ... but there was no life.... The truth was that life was meaningless" (DT, 19). Tolstoy felt his "life [was] a stupid, mean trick played on [him] by somebody" even though this was a period of his life when "[he] was on every side surrounded by what is considered to be complete happiness. [He] had a good, loving, and beloved wife, good children, and a large estate, which grew and increased without any labour on [his] part. [He] was respected by [his] neighbours and friends, more than ever before, was praised by strangers, and, without any self-deception, could consider [his] name famous" (DT, 20). Even so, during this period he had to hide the rope in his bedroom and not carry a gun lest he succumb to the strong internal impulses to use them on himself. He could not "ascribe any sensible meaning to a single act, or to my whole life" (DT, 21).

Tolstoy recalled at this point an old story about a traveller jumping into a waterless well to save himself from being overtaken by a beast. At the bottom of the well there was a dragon ready to eat him. He could not climb out because of the beast above, nor go lower because of the beast below, so he clutched a twig and hung there as weakness increased within him. At this point he noticed two mice, a black one and a white one, both nibbling at the trunk of the limb that held him up. He noticed also honey dripping off the leaves and he licked a couple drops for relief. Tolstoy said those two drops of honey which distracted him briefly from the cruel reality of his existence and hopeless predicament were the love of family and of authorship, or art. However, he came to believe that even art was "an adornment of life, a decoy of life" (DT, 22). In the pages that follow Tolstoy recounted how he began a search in all the branches of knowledge in case "perhaps, I overlooked something, or did not understand something right" (DT, 25). He search was for the answer to one question: "My question, the one which led me, at fifty years, up to suicide, was the simplest kind of question, and one which is lying in the soul of every man, from the silliest child to the wisest old man, – 'What will come of what I am doing to-day and shall do to-morrow? What will come of my whole life?'" (DT, 26). Neither the experimental sciences nor speculative sciences had answers to these questions. His own life proved the error of those who were speculating "everything develops ... and moves in the direction of complexity and progress." His story was that he stopped developing and his muscles were growing weaker and his teeth were falling out. It was self-evident to Tolstoy that "there could be no law of endless development ... [or that] in endless space and time everything was developing, perfecting itself" (DT, 27–28). Nothing in science answered these repeated questions which "present themselves to every man, 'What am I?' or, 'Why do I live?' or 'What shall I do?" (DT, 29). He found the answers of speculative science deeply dissatisfying.

> [A]bout the origin of species and of man . . . the answer in this sphere of knowledge to my question what the meaning of my life was, was always; "You are what you call your life; you are a temporal, accidental conglomeration of particles. The interrelation, the change of these particles, produces in you that which you call life. This congeries will last for some time; then the interaction of these particles, produces in you that which you call life and all your questions will come to an end. You are an accidentally cohering globule of something. The globule is fermenting. This fermenting the globule calls its life. The globule falls to pieces, and all the fermentation and all questions will come to an end. . . . I want to know the meaning of my life, but the fact that it is a particle of the infinite not only gives it no meaning, but even destroys every possible meaning. (DT, 33)

From the emptiness of evolution theory, Tolstoy turned to philosophy for answers; to Socrates, Schopenhauer, Solomon and Buddha.

Despite spending a number of years of his life reading and resonating with Schopenhauer, in the end he departed ways after finding nothing positive to answer the deep questions about the meaning and value of human life and existence. Tolstoy found Solomon's assessment no different than his own at that point, all under the sun is vanity and meaningless. Also in Buddhism, "'it is impossible to live with the consciousness of inevitable suffering, debility, old age, and death, – it is necessary to free oneself from life, and from every possibility of life' . . . Thus, my wandering among the sciences not only did not take me out of my despair, but even increased it" (DT, 39).

From the sciences and disciplines of knowledge, Tolstoy turned his attention to observing people and noted:

> [T]here were four ways out from the terrible condition in which we all are. . . . The first way out is through ignorance. . . . The second way out is though Epicureanism [knowing life is hopeless we should simply enjoy such good as there is]. . . . The third way out is through . . . a noose about the neck, the water, a knife to pierce the heart with, railway trains. . . . I saw that that was the worthiest way out. . . . The fourth way out is through weakness . . . to live in the condition of Solomon, of Schopenhauer, – to know that life was a stupid joke played on me, and yet to live, wash and dress myself, dine, speak, and even to write books.

That was repulsive and painful for me, but I still persisted." (DT, 41–44).

The shift in CF for Tolstoy begins in section eight of the sixteen sections, as he realized reason was not the only thing at work in life. He wrote about a force that made him observe more beyond reason, a force that compelled him to look at the lives of the peasant class and envy them for seeming to possess what he did not. His discovery was that "rational knowledge did not give any meaning to life" and in fact it "excluded life" (DT, 49). He came to see that an irrational knowledge of faith held answers to his questions. However, "from faith it followed that in order to understand life, [he] must renounce reason" (DT, 50).

Tolstoy's search for life's meaning then took him back to the "believing men of [his] own circle, to learned men, to Orthodox theologians, to old monks, to theologians of the new shade, and even to so-called new Christians, who professed salvation through faith in redemption. [He] clung to these believers and questioned them about their beliefs, and tried to find out in what they saw the meaning of life" (DT, 57). To his dismay, Tolstoy did not find clarity in their explanations, but only more "obfuscation of the meaning of life . . . [and worse they] lived just as bad, if not worse, than the unbelievers" (DT, 58). Tolstoy turned next to "cultivate the acquaintance of the believers among the poor, the simple and unlettered folk, of pilgrims, monks, dissenters, peasants . . . [and] saw that the whole life of these people was passed in hard work, and that they were satisfied in life . . . in contradistinction to the fact that the more intelligent we are, the less do we understand the meaning of life. . . . [He] began to love these people [the poor]. . . . Thus [he] lived for about two years, and within [him] took place a transformation, which had long been working in [him], and the germ of which had always been in [him]" (DT, 59–61).

Tolstoy used an analogy of a boat to describe his life at this point. It was as if he was put in a boat and "pushed off from some unknown shore [and] had pointed out to me the direction toward another shore, had a pair of oars given into my inexperienced hands, and was left alone" (DT, 70). With the current against him and his incompetence with oars he drifted away from the goal, and came across many others in his situation: "lonely oarsmen, who continued to row; there were large boats, immense ships, full of people; some struggled against the current, others submitted to it" (DT, 70). Downstream he went, next he heard the rapids and saw boats wrecked there. Then he regained his senses: "That shore was God, the direction was tradition, the oars were the freedom given me to row toward the shore, – to unite myself with God. Thus the force of life was renewed in me, and I began to live once more" (DT, 71).

Tolstoy then renounced the life of those in his class of men who he had come to view as parasites, and more fully immersed himself in the lives of the peasant class. He returned to church services, the fasts, the relics and the images, even communion: "I wanted with all the forces of my soul to be able to become one with the masses, by executing the ritualistic side of their faith; but I was unable to do so. I felt that I should be lying to myself and making light of what for me was holy, if I did it" (DT, 74). He again sought out the theologians who told him: "the fundamental dogma of faith is the infallible church. From the recognition of this dogma follows, as its necessary consequence, the truth of everything professed by the church. The church as a collection of believers united in love and, therefore, in possession of the true knowledge. . . . Truth will be revealed to love, and so, if you do not submit to the ritual of the church, you impair love; and if you impair love, you are deprived of the possibility of discovering the truth" (DT, 74–75). Tolstoy, still seeking to be open and honest, followed the "rites of the church, [and] humbled reason and submitted [him]self to that tradition . . . [and] unconsciously concealed from [him]self the contradictions and obscurities of the doctrine" (DT, 75, 77). He committed himself again to the Sabbath, Holy Days, and the Eucharist "and swallowed this blood and body without any blasphemous feeling, with the desire to believe, but the blow had been given me" (DT, 79). He could not continue for long and frequently envied the illiteracy and ignorance of the peasants (DT, 81). For three years he fully applied himself to the path of Orthodoxy and ultimately widened his search to "the other churches, to Catholicism and to the so-called dissenters . . . believers of different creeds. . . . [He] wanted to be a brother to these people (DT, 81–82). However, they each believed they were in sole possession of the truth and that the others were heretics: "This hostility increases in proportion as the knowledge of doctrine increases. And I, who had assumed the truth to be in the union of love, was involuntarily startled to find that that religious teaching destroyed precisely that which it ought to build up" (DT, 82). Tolstoy went again to see "archimandrites, bishops, hermits, ascetics, and asked them, and not one of them made even an attempt at explaining that offensive state of affairs (DT, 83). Then Tolstoy

> turned [his] attention to what was being done in the name of religion, and I was frightened and almost entirely renounced Orthodoxy. . . . [The] relation of the church to vital questions was its relation to war and capital punishment. Just then Russia had a war on its hands and Russians began to kill their brothers in

> the name of Christian love ... [and] they prayed in churches for the success of our arms, and the teachers of religion acknowledged this murder as a business which resulted from faith. ... I saw the orders of the church, her teachers, monks, and hermits, approve the murder of erring, helpless youths. I turned my attention to what was done by men who professed Christianity, and I was horrified. (DT, 85)

Tolstoy's conclusion to the main body of his *Confession* was that "the lie was mixed in with the truth ... That in the teaching there is truth, there can be no doubt for me; but it is equally certain to me that it also contains the lie, and I must find the truth and the lie and separate one from another" (DT, 87). In that final sentence is found the driving motivation fuelling each of his subsequent projects in logical sequence: *Critique of Dogmatic Theology*, the *Four Gospel Harmony and Translation*, the *Gospel in Brief* and *What I Believe*. With the life and literature of Tolstoy overlapping and being so intertwined, it was important to give the above page by page synopsis of his first fifty years as his life story is essential to fully appreciating his subsequent religious works and to make sense of his unique interpretations of the Gospel and particularly the Sermon on the Mount.

Tolstoy had finished his CF in 1879 as is evident by the dating on the final page of the manuscript proper. However, there is an brief addendum dated three years later, 1882, where he told of a recent prophetic dream or vision he had that "expressed to me in concise form what I had lived through and described" in CF (DT, 88–90). In his dream Tolstoy was lying on a bed though not comfortably with regard to his legs. He noticed there were plaited rope strips attached to the sides of the bed and in trying to push against one to allow his legs to be outstretched the strips broke and others under his thighs also gave way. Eventually, the lower half of his body was slipping down and he realized he was over a great height. It was too terrible to look down into the abyss so he looked up to the infinity above: "The infinity below repels and frightens me; the infinity above me attracts and confirms me." A voice in the dream told him "Observe! It is it!" He noticed that he was being firmly held by one strip at the middle of his body attached to a pillar and there was no longer a question of him falling. Again the voice spoke: "Remember? Do not forget." The meaning of the dream for Tolstoy was that it was a picture of his life and how what previously had supported him, even if uncomfortably, gave way when he pushed against it, and how ultimately he found his security in one strip attached to a pillar. That strip attached to the pillar he came to discover in the Doctrine of Jesus found in the Gospels and the Sermon on the Mount. The strips that gave way were the Doctrines of Orthodoxy. In this way Tolstoy ended his *Confession* where his *Critique of Dogmatic Theology* then began.

1.3 *A Critique of Dogmatic Theology* (1881-82) — [abbr. DT]

The second work of these six main post-conversion works (regarded here as Second Tolstoy) is *A Critique of Dogmatic Theology*. There is a logical inquiry sequence and research progression in these six books; first his *Confession* setting the stage for the systematic critique of Orthodox dogma which was necessary, mostly for his own benefit and personal reassurance, to justify his break from traditional dogma. Initially, Tolstoy was a hesitant heretic. Decades of layering disappointment with the Orthodox Church and an ever-widening disbelief in Orthodox doctrines and devotional practices resulted in Tolstoy determining the Church over the centuries had come to a point of grave error. Even so, sentimentality and regard for the faith he was reared in, and some niggling fear of the Lord, inclined him to first make double sure he was not the one who was wrong. He was open to, and perhaps even hopeful to prove himself wrong and the Church right: "I did not then assume that the doctrine was false, - I was afraid of supposing that, - for one untruth in that doctrine destroyed the whole doctrine, and then I should lose the main support which I had found in the church as the carrier of truth, as the source of knowledge of the meaning of life which I was trying to find in faith" (DT, 92). This was a period of ardent inner contention for Tolstoy: "For a long time I wavered in doubt, did not permit myself to deny what I did not understand, and with all the forces of mind and soul tried to understand that teaching in the same way as those understood it who said they believed in it, and demanded that others, too, should believe in it" (DT, 95). Tolstoy's review of Orthodox theology was thorough: "I used up a great deal of paper, analysing word after word, at first the Symbol of Faith, then Filarét's Catechism, then the Epistle of the Eastern Patriarchs, then Makari's Introduction to Theology, and then his Dogmatic Theology. . . . [I] finally reached a point when I knew the Theology like a good seminarist, and I am able, following the trend of thoughts which have guided the authors, to explain the foundation of everything. . . . When I attained to that, I was shocked" (DT, 94-95). He explained, had it not been the case that he was honestly seeking the meaning of life and faith, "I, after reading these books, not only would have turned an atheist, but should have become a most malignant enemy of every faith, because I found in these doctrines not only nonsense, but the conscious lie of men" (DT, 95).

In English, including a brief introduction and conclusion, DT is 358 pages in length and is divided into two main sections comprised of the following seventeen subsections.

The Complete Works of Count Tolstoy – Volume XIII

Critique of Dogmatic Theology – Part One

I. Introduction; the aim, the subject, the origin of Orthodox Christian dogmas, division of the dogmas, the character of the plan and method, a sketch of the history of the science of dogmatic theology (98–103)

II. Of God in himself, and of his general revelation to the world and to man (104–14)

III. Of God, one in substance (115–29)

IV. Of the Essence of God (130–60)

V. Of God Trine in Persons (161–88)

VI. The personal attribute of God, the Holy Ghost (189–206)

VII. The image and likeness of God in man (207–16)

VIII. The descent of the sin of the first parent to the whole human race: prefatory remarks (217–26)

IX. Of God as the Provider (227–38)

Critique of Dogmatic Theology – Part Two

X. Of God the Saviour and his special relation to the human race (239–47)

XI. About our Lord Jesus Christ, and about the mystery of the incarnation (248–77)

XII. About the acts of salvation performed by our Lord Jesus Christ, or about the mystery of the redemption (278–303)

XIII. About God as a sanctifier (304–39)

XIV. Of divine grace as a force with which the Lord sanctifies us (340–58)

XV. By the words sanctification of man are meant the sacraments (359–71)

XVI. Of the sacraments of the church, as means through which divine grace is communicated to us (372–406)

XVII. Of God as the Judge and Retributer (407–30)

XVIII. Conclusion (431–51)

Each subsection contains Tolstoy's analysis and refutation to subsections within Macarius Bulgakov's standard *Orthodox Dogmatic Theology* which totalled six volumes and was published in St. Petersburg in the years 1847–53. Macarius Bulgakov (1816–82) later became Macarius I (spelled Makari in DT), the twelfth Metropolitan of Moscow serving in that position during this very period of Tolstoy's life (Macarius I; 1879–82). In his unrestrained mordant appraisal of the theology of the church, Tolstoy had dared to systematically dismantle the bulwark and fortifications of one of the most prominent, regarded, powerful and influential Orthodox fathers of his time and place. Cited earlier was a passage illustrating Tolstoy did possess some fear of the Lord, yet there is no indiction he feared the lex talionis of either church or state. Not surprisingly, DT did not get past the Orthodox/Russian censors.[18]

There are other places to properly and formally develop Tolstoyan theological distinctives and draw attention to points of divergence in doctrine between Tolstoy and the renowned theologians of the Russian Orthodox Church. Considering the intentional brevity of these post-conversion book overviews, it must suffice here to succinctly draw the following conclusions to generally encapsulate Tolstoy's main findings, in what could even be so negatively construed as his autopsy of dogmatic theology, as he found no life left there.

(1) Tolstoy rejected the lack of freedom for different interpretations on doctrinal matters: "[I]t is not permitted to understand them in any other way. He who understands them differently: anathema" (DT, 431).

(2) Tolstoy rejected the notion that only the church may sanctify, a point the church justified through belief in apostolic succession which Tolstoy also rejected. In the preface to his subsequent harmony of the Gospels he reviewed his earlier time of analysis of Orthodox doctrine:

> I was brought to the conviction that there was no church at all. All the differently believing Christians call themselves true Christians and deny each other.... Indeed, there are a thousand traditions, and each denies and curses all the others, and regards its own as the true one: Catholics, Lutherans, Protestants, Calvinists, Shakers, Mormons, Greek Orthodox, Old Believers, the Popish and Popeless sects, Milkers, Mennonites, Baptists, Mutilators, Dukhobers, etc., etc., all of them equally assert about their own faith that it is the only true one.... There are a thousand faiths, and each calmly considers itself to be holy ... and all the others as heresies. It will soon be eighteen hundred years that this self-deception has been going on. (HM, 6–8)

---

18. Tolstoy, *Gospel in Brief*, 7.

For Tolstoy the answer was "simple and obvious. The cause of the division of the Christians is precisely this teaching about the church" (HM, 9). He believed that the way to unite Christians was not in any proscribed set of doctrines, but in how one ought to live. Something he saw "in all those different sects of Christians [was] complete agreement in the conception of what is good, what evil, and of how one ought to live" (HM, 10). His conclusion was the "truth of faith is not to be found in the definite interpretations of Christ's revelation, those interpretations which have divided the Christians into a thousand sects, but is to be found in the very first revelation of Christ himself. And so I turned to a study of the Gospels" (HM, 10).

(3) Tolstoy came to believe the sacraments, the means of sanctification dispensed only by the church, were the seven manipulations of the church. The church insists in "these manipulations lies that means for salvation which God has invented" (DT, 435). Tolstoy's personal spiritual journey led him to discover a very different path to life, the original path that Christ asked his disciples to follow him down, that path of life Jesus revealed from the Mount. Tolstoy further rejected the deception of the sacraments being effectual "independently of the spiritual condition of the priest and of him who receives the sacrament" (DT, 435).

(4) Tolstoy found nothing in Orthodox dogma that gave meaning to human life and to his life in particular: "According to this teaching the meaning of my life is an absolute absurdity, much worse than what presented itself to me by the light of my reason" (DT, 437). It was ludicrous to Tolstoy that if his "relatives absent-mindedly [forget] to pray for me, I shall just as must go to hell and remain there" (DT, 437). This was a central question that drove his spiritual search: "I was frightened by the meaninglessness of my own life and by the insolubility of the question: What are my strivings, my life, for, since all that will end?" (DT, 437).

(5) Tolstoy concluded the moral applications of Orthodox dogma were nil, and did not answer the question how should we live except that we "must have popes around us, or live near a monastery, and leave as much money as possible [to the] memorial masses" of the church (DT, 437–38).

(6) Tolstoy took church dogma to task for the impression that God's will is arbitrary and for there being nothing good or hopeful for those who do not accidentally come in contact with the sanctifying action of the church, only that they should be eternally tormented by devils (DT, 436).

(7) Tolstoy ended his critique of dogmatic theology with the inflammatory assertion that the blasphemy of the Holy Ghost from which there is no forgiveness is nothing other than "the terrible teaching of the church, the foundation of which is the teaching about the church" (DT, 436).

1.4 *The Four Gospels Harmonised and Translated: Volumes 1, 2* (1881-82) — [*abbr.* HM]

Overlapping the same frame of time he worked on *Critique of Dogmatic Theology* (1881-82), Tolstoy engaged in a massive and painstakingly comprehensive project to harmonize and translate the four Gospels. His first sentences in the fifth book of Second Tolstoy, *What I Believe*, are statements explaining his objectives and reasoning in these two earlier works:

> I shall explain elsewhere, in two voluminous treatises, why I did not understand the doctrine of Jesus, and how at length it became clear to me. These works are a criticism of dogmatic theology and a new translation of the four Gospels, followed by a concordance. In these writings I seek methodically to disentangle everything that tends to conceal the truth from men; I translate the four Gospels anew, verse by verse, and I bring them together in a new concordance. The work has lasted for six years. Each year, each month, I discover new meaning which corroborate the fundamental idea; I correct the errors which have crept in, and I put the last touches to what I have already written. My life, whose final term is not far distant, will doubtless end before I have finished my work; but I am convinced that the work will be of great service; so I shall do all I can to bring it to completion. (written 1883, WB, 12)

Tolstoy distinguished this as the "outward work upon theology and the Gospel" and he did not return to it or ever complete his HR but spent his remaining twenty-seven years devoted to the "inner work of an entirely different nature" not with anything "systematic or methodological" (WB, 12). This inner work of an entirely different nature he believed to be "love, humility, self-denial, and the duty to return good for evil" all of which he considered the substance of Christianity, the doctrine of Jesus (WB, 12-13).

Tolstoy's HM was well over eight hundred pages in length and it was comprehensive in that it was as much a careful translation, interpretation and commentary on the texts as it was an attempt to harmonise four Gospel stories into one, chronologically or historically. Having mastered Greek a decade earlier, Tolstoy's work was done entirely in the Greek manuscripts, lexicons and dictionaries (HM, Vol. I, 17). At his disposal Tolstoy had several other Gospel harmonies which appear to have been either standards and/or merely available in his time: "Arnolde de Vence, Farrar, Reuss, (and) Grechulévich" each of which he viewed as attempts to harmonize the Gospels on a purely historical basis (HM, Vol. I, 18). Much of Tolstoy's HM was set against that of Édouard Reuss[19] and Archimandrite Vasilij Grechulévich as is evident throughout by the long sections included from both, especially long sections in French from Reuss. He took both as "the basis of my work, collating . . . and departing from both whenever the sense demanded it" (HM, Vol. I, 18). Tolstoy's HM differed from these others in that, in his words: "I leave the historical meaning entirely alone, and harmonise only in the sense of the teaching." Tolstoy believed the teaching of Christ was buried beneath all the legends about Christ also recorded in the Gospels—mainly referring to the miracles but also the Resurrection. It was his contention that there are two parts to the Gospels: "two sharply distinguished parts of the expositions: one the exposition of the teaching; the other, an attempt at proving the truth of the teaching, or, more correctly, the importance of the teaching, such as are the miracles, prophecies, and predictions." Tolstoy came to see that the "proofs, which, no doubt, were proofs, now form the chief stumbling-block in the acceptance of the teaching" (citations above all from HM, Vol. II, 357).

His grievance with the legends, as he called them, was in how they eventually and entirely eclipsed the teaching of Jesus, or a best obscured it: "There comes a time, when all the false legends take the place of the teaching, all are gathered into one, are formulated, and are expressed as dogma, that is, as decrees" (HM, Vol. II, 359). He believed these Gospel legends were largely to blame for superstition and mysticism eventually becoming the centre of Orthodox dogma and devotion instead of the plain teaching of Christ and the way of life. Referencing an old Russian proverb, Tolstoy believed common people are left with only two alternatives, to "get furious at the lice and chuck the fur coat into the stove, that is to reject the whole as absurd, as ninety-nine of every hundred men actually do, or to subvert reason, as the church commands us to do, and accept everything stupid and unimportant with what is wise and important" (HM, Vol. II, 359).

More than he believed the legends were false or fictitious, he believed they were of lesser importance, unnecessary additions by Gospel authors of a subsequent period which became complete distractions and diversions from the path of life clearly set forth in the teachings of Christ. He wrote the "miracle was not a proof of the truth, but of the importance of the matter. The miracle attracted attention, – the miracle was an advertisement" (HM, Vol. II, 360). The truth was in the teaching, not the advertisement. Tolstoy reasoned "the belief in them (miracles) aided in the propagation of the faith, – they have been useful; but the teaching has been disseminated

---

19. Reuss, *Geschichte der Heiligen Schriften*. Or Reuss, *History of the Sacred Scriptures*.

and confirmed, and the belief in miracles has become useless and harmful" (HM, Vol. II, 361). Shocking as it may seem to read Tolstoy had such low regard for the miracles and earthly mercies of Christ, it is important to remember and appreciate his context where Orthodox superstition had entirely displaced the path to life and had become a wide road leading the masses down a path that led to destruction, in his view. It is in that sense that he deemed the miracle legends useless and even harmful: "I need no proofs that it (truth) exists: it does exist. So let us leave out what was necessary at some past period, in order to make the forest grow, – to form the teaching of Christ" (HM, Vol. II, 361). Further, Tolstoy was no Thomas needing additional supernatural verification. Tolstoy believed divinity was more than evident in the way of life prescribed by Christ.

Tolstoy's harmony of the four Gospels spans 845 pages in two volumes of the *Complete Works of Count Tolstoy* edited and translated in 1904 by Leo Weiner (XIV, XV). It is organised as follows:

The Complete Works of Count Tolstoy – Volume XIV

The Four Gospels Harmonised and Translated – Volume One

   Preface / Introduction
   I. The Incarnation of the Comprehension. The Birth and Childhood of Jesus Christ (50–106)
   II. General Remark. The New Worship in the Spirit by Works. The Rejection of the Jewish God (107–56)
   III. The Kingdom of God. Christ's Testimony Concerning John (157–206)
   IV. The Law (The Sermon on the Mount). The Rich and the Poor (207–307)
   V. The Fulfilment of the Law Gives the True Life. The New Teaching about God. (308–69)
   VI. The Food of Life. Man Lives Not by Bread Alone. On Carnal and Spiritual Kinship (370–451)

The Complete Works of Count Tolstoy – Volume XV

The Four Gospels Harmonised and Translated – Volume Two

   VII. Proof of the Truth of the Teaching. Demanding Proofs of Christ (3–77)
   VIII. There is No Other Life. Of the Rewards in the Kingdom of God (78–136)
   IX. The Offences (137–227)
   X. The Struggle Against the Offences (228–84)

XI. The Farewell Discourse (285–325)
XII. The Victory of the Spirit (326–51)
Conclusion to the Investigation of the Gospel
Short Exposition of the Gospel
Contents of Gospel in Brief
Conclusion

Related specifically to forthcoming chapters in this project, note that ninety-five pages of the first volume of HM comprise Tolstoy's treatment of: *The Law "The Sermon on the Mount"* (HM, Vol. I, 207–302). The perceptive might notice in Tolstoy's title of this work the emphasis on the "Four Gospels Harmonised" which gives indication he treated equally the Gospel of John and the three Synoptics. His interest being the meaning of the teaching of Christ and not historical, philosophical or theological criticism, Tolstoy had to no reason to join the mainstream flow of New Testament scholarship in his day which treated John's Gospel separately: "and so, if all four are the exposition of one and the same revelation of truth, then one must confirm and elucidate the rest. And so I considered them by uniting them, without omitting the Gospel of John" (HM, Vol. I, 18).

1.5 *The Gospel in Brief* (1882–83) — [*abbr.* TGB]

Using classic Enlightenment trope, Tolstoy's metaphor for the intention behind his extensive Gospel harmony project was to peel back the layers of obscurity over a wonderful painting to uncover again (after 1800 years) the teaching of Christ which Tolstoy most succinctly sought to reveal in his subsequent abridgement (written for publication), his *Gospel in Brief* (HM, Vol. II, 362). This TGB was the sought-after outcome of his Gospel harmony. This abridgement mainly contained what Tolstoy believed to be the doctrine of Jesus, his teachings. Tolstoy's HM was the place he dealt with every single text in the four Gospels. Tolstoy's Gospel was not built on the hermeneutics of *Jefferson's Bible*, essentially taking a scissors to it and eliminating the undesirable parts.[20] Tolstoy's Gospel harmony (HM) included even the parts he considered unnecessary to prove Jesus' divinity such as the prophecies, the miracles and the resurrection:

> In the full exposition, the third part [HM] everything in the Gospels is set down without any omissions. But in the present rendering [TGB] the following are omitted; the conception and birth of John the Baptist, his imprisonment and death, the birth

20. Levitysky, "Tolstoy Gospel in the Light of the Jefferson Bible."

of Jesus, his genealogy, his mother's flight with him to Egypt; his miracles at Cana and Capernaum; the casting out of the devils; the walking on the sea; the blasting of the fig-tree; the healing of the sick; the raising of the dead; the resurrection of Christ himself, and the references to prophecies fulfilled by his life. Those passages are omitted in the present short exposition because, containing nothing of the teaching but only describing events that took place before, during, or after the period in which Jesus taught, they complicate the exposition. Those verses, however they may be understood, do not contain either contradiction or confirmation of the teaching. Their sole significance for Christianity was to prove the divinity of Jesus to those who did not believe in it.[21]

Tolstoy intended his TGB to contain only the plain, unobscured revelation of the way to life set forth by Christ. It is properly understood when it is viewed not for what he eliminated, but for what he was hoping to highlight. His intent was to make the divinity more evident, more perceptible, not to remove what is traditionally known as the supernatural aspects to either confirm the divinity of Christ, or portray his humanity and compassion. In Tolstoy's view, so evident was the divinity of the way of Christ even the miracles were deemed a diversion from that path of life.

Tolstoy saw in the Lord's Prayer the perfect outline for his TGB and though it is difficult to see this as clearly as he did, he sought to make the twelve chapter divisions in the Gospel brief fit the stanzas of the prayer: "When I had finished my work I found to my surprise and joy that the Lord's Prayer is nothing but a very concise expression of the whole teaching of Jesus in the very order in which I had arranged the chapters, and that each phrase of the prayer corresponds to the meaning and sequence of the chapters" (TGB, 9). The overlay and outline is as follows; the passages reordered into each section were noted by Tolstoy and are listed for reference in the footnotes below:

Chapter 1 The Son of God – Our Father[22] (22)

Chapter 2 Which Art in Heaven[23] (27)

21. Tolstoy, *Gospel in Brief*, 9–10.

22. Matt 1:18–19; Luke 2:40–52; 3:23. Matt 3:1; Mark 1:4; Matt 3:4; Mark 1:4; Luke 3:4–6, 10–14; Matt 3:5–8, 10–13, 4:1–3. Luke 4:3; Matt 4:3; Luke 4:4; Matt 4:4; Luke 4:9–11; Matt 4:7–8; Luke 4:5–6, 9, 7–8; Matt 4:10; Luke 4:13; John 1:36–47, 49, 51; Luke 4:16–21.

23. Matt 12:1; Mark 2:23; Luke 6:1; Matt 12:2, 7; Luke 13:10–14; 14:3, 6, 5. Matt 12:11–12, 9–13; 15:1 Mark 7:1; Matt 15:2; Mark 7:3–5, Matt 15:3; Mark 7:10–13; Matt 15:7–9; Mark 7:8, 14–15; Luke 11:41; Mark 7:16–21, 23; John 2:13–20; Matt 12:6–7;

Chapter 3   Hallowed Be Thy Name[24] (34)

Chapter 4   The Kingdom of God – Thy Kingdom Come[25] (40)

Chapter 5   The True Life – Thy Will Be Done[26] (48)

Chapter 6   A False Life – As in Heaven So on Earth[27] (58)

Chapter 7   I and the Father Are One – Give Us Our Daily Bread[28] (67)

Chapter 8   Life is Not Temporal – Each Day[29] (76)

Chapter 9   Temptations – Forgive Us Our Debts as We Forgive Our Debtors[30] (83)

Chapter 10 The Struggle Against Temptation – Lead Us Not Into Temptation[31] (92)

John 2:23–25; 4:4–6, 8, 7, 9–10, 13, 14, 19–21, 23–26; 3:22–27, 31–36; Luke 11:37–39, 41; 7:37–48; 18:10–14; 5:33–38.

24. Matt 11:2–7, 16, 18–19, 16, 17, 19, 8–9, 11; Luke 16:16; 17:20, 23–24, 21; John 3:1–6, 8, 7, 9–13, 15–21; Matt 13:3–5, 7–8; Mark 4:26–29, 33, 24–25, 27, 29–30, 47–48, 10–11, 15, 18, 19–23, 12; Luke 8:18; Matt 13:31.

25. Matt 9:35–36; 5:1–2; Luke 6:20–25, 20; Matt 5:13–24; 19:7, 9, 33–34, 37–41; Luke 6:30, 37; Matt 7:1, 3; Luke 6:39–40; Matt 7:6; 5:39, 43–44, 46; 7:12; 6:1–12; Mark 11:25–26; Matt 6:16–34; Luke 11:9; Matt 7:9–11, 13–14; Luke 12:32; Matt 7:15–17; Luke 6:45; Matt 7:21–27; Luke 4:32; Matt 4:14, 16; 12:19–21.

26. Matt 11:25, 28–30; John 4:31–38; 5:1–2, 4, 2–3, 5–11, 15–17, 19–31, 36–40, 43–44; Luke 19:11–22; Matt 25:26–27; Luke 19:23–24; Matt 25:28; Luke 19:25–26; Matt 25:30; John 6:1–3, 5, 7; Matt 14:17; John 6:9–11, 26–33, 35–57, 60–63; Luke 10:1–3; Matt 10:16; Luke 10:4. Mark 6:10–11; Matt 10:22–23, 19, 23, 26–34; Luke 12:49, 51–53; 14:26; Matt 12:15, 24, 26–29, 31–32, 30, 33.

27. Luke 8:19; Matt 12:46; Luke 8:20–21; 11:27–28; 9:57–58; Mark 4:35, 37–38, 40; Luke 9:59–62; 10:38–42; 9:23–25; 12:15–21; 13:2–8; 12:54–56; 14:25–33; 15–16, 18–23; 16:1–6, 8, 9–11, 13–17, 19–31; Mark 10:17–27; Luke 19:1–10; Mark 12:41–44; Matt 26:6–13; 21:28–29.

28. John 7:1–3, 5, 3, 4, 6–9, 11–12, 14–19, 21–29, 33–34, 38–40, 42–52; 8:12–14, 18–19, 21, 24–26, 28–29, 31–32, 34–44, 46, 48–59; 9:1–3, 5–9, 11, 13–21, 24–31, 33–34; 11:2; 10:1–3, 1, 5, 7–14, 17–18, 15, 17, 16, 24–38, 20–21, 39–42; Matt 16:13–18.

29. Matt 10:38–39; 19:27; Mark 10:29–31; Matt 20:1–3, 8–16; Mark 10:35, 37–40; Matt 20:23; Mark 10:41–42; Matt 20:25–27; Mark 10:45; Matt 18:11–12; Luke 15:8, 10; 14:8–11; 15:11–13, 15–18, 20–32; Mark 12:1–8; Matt 21:40–43; Luke 17:5–10; 12:35–39; Matt 24:45–46, 48–51; Mark 13:33; Luke 21:34; Matt 25:1–7, 10; Luke 13:24–25; Matt 16:27; 25:32, 34.

30. Matt 19:13–14; Luke 18:17; Matt 18:3, 5; Luke 9:48; Matt 18:10, 14, 6–8; Luke 17:3; Matt 18:15–16; Luke 17:4; Matt 18:17, 23–35, 25; 18:18–20; Mark 10:2; Matt 19:3–6, 8–12; 17:24–25, 27; 22:16–21; 23:15–22; Luke 9:52–56; 12:13–14; John 8:3–11; Luke 10:25, 27, 29–35; Matt 16:21; Mark 8:32–34; Matt 22:23–25, 28; Luke 20:34–36; Matt 22:31–32, 34–37, 39–40, 42–43; Luke 12:1; Mark 8:15; Matt 16:11–12; Luke 20:46; Matt 23:2–8, 13, 15–16, 23, 28, 27, 30–31. Mark 3:28–29; Matt 23:37–38, 24:1–4, 12, 14.

31. Luke 11:53–54; John 11:47–48; Luke 19:47–48; John 11:49–50, 52–57, 7–10;

Chapter 11 The Farewell Discourse – But Deliver Us From Evil[32] (99)

Chapter 12 The Victory of the Spirit Over Flesh – For Thine is the Kingdom, The Power, and the Glory[33] (105–11)

These twelve chapters of Tolstoy's *Gospel in Brief* (TGB) are only brief if compared to the eighty-nine chapters of the four Gospels, together which, in 1611 KJV English, total 82,590 words. In Aylmer Maude's English translation, the twelve chapters of GB amount to 47,779 words, a little more than half a long as Matthew, Mark, Luke and John combined. However, GB is more than double the length of the twenty-eight chapters of Matthew's Gospel (23,343 words in length). The author of *War & Peace* is not known for brevity and so the sense in which this is indeed a brief must be qualified. Tolstoy's aim was more to be straightforward and clear with the teaching of Jesus than to be concise. As can be seen in my detailed parallel comparison (subsection 13.1), Tolstoy's Sermon on the Mount was 16.5 percent longer than Matthew's Sermon on the Mount. Importantly, there is no inclusion of any extra-Biblical stories or statements of Christ in the twelve chapters of TGB, for example, the likes of which are included in apocryphal *The Gospel of Thomas*. The additions are comprised mainly of Tolstoyan commentary and summarizations of canonical Gospel material and meaning.

Tolstoy's Sermon on the Mount is found in chapter four of GB which is a chapter titled: *Thy Kingdom Come*. In the Appendices, subsection 12.1, a careful parallel comparison of Tolstoy's *Gospel in Brief* (BG) with the NIV-UK of Matthew 5–7 can be found with notations that call attention to (a) NIV-UK text(s) omitted in TGB and (b) TGB text additions not found in the NIV-UK. The discoveries and decisions Tolstoy made in his Gospel harmony study shaped his *Gospel in Brief* paraphrase translation and in many cases (to be discussed in the following chapter) informed his unique Sermon on the Mount interpretations spelled out best in his subsequent and fifth post-conversion work, *What I Believe*. The unique Tolstoyan Sermon of

---

12:2–5, 8, 7, 12–14; Matt 21:10–11; Mark 11:15; John 12:19; Mark 11:18; John 12:20–28, 31–32, 34–36, 44–45, 47–50, 42–43; Matt 26:3–5, 14–16, 17–20; John 13:11; Matt 26:21; Mark 14:18; Matt 26:23, 26–28. Luke 22:18; John 13:4–7, 10, 12, 14, 17–18, 21–27, 30–35; Matt 26:30–31, 33–35; Luke 22:35–36, 38; Matt 26:36; John 18:1. Matt 26:37–45.

32. John 13:36–38; 14:1–28, 15:1–2, 4–27, 16:1–13, 15–31, 17:1, 3, 6, 4, 7–11, 15, 17, 18, 21, 23, 25–26.

33. Matt 26:56; John 18:12–14; Mark 14:53; Matt 26:58, 69–75; Mark 14:53; John 18:19–23; Matt 26:59–61; Mark 14:59; Matt 26:62–68, 27:2; John 18:28–32; Luke 23:2; John 18:33–38; Luke 23:5. Mark 15:3–5. Luke 23:6–15; Matt 27:23, 21–23; John 19:4, 6–15, 12, 15, 13; Matt 27:24–25; Luke 23:23; John 19:13; Matt 27:26, 28–29; John 19:16; Matt 27:31; John 19:18; Luke 23:34–35; Mark 15:29–32; Luke 23:39–43; Matt 27:46–48, 50; John 19:28–30; Luke 23:46.

the Mount interpretations which later greatly influenced Mahatma Gandhi, Martin Luther King Jr. and others on several continents have their origins right here in the findings and fruit of Tolstoy's exegesis.

1.6 NIV-UK/TGB Parallel Comparison of Matthew 5–7

Included in subsection 12.1 are ten technical plates containing my line by line analysis of the Sermon on the Mount chapters of Tolstoy's *Gospel in Brief* (TGB) with Matthew 5–7 of the *Holy Bible, New International Version, Anglicised, NIV*, known more commonly as the NIV-UK. Twenty-two notes are bracketed within this parallel analysis and several of those numbered notations will be referenced here in this preceding section containing my findings and observations. Superficially as was previously stated, the TGB is perceptively but not significantly longer than what is found in the NIV-UK of Matthew 5–7. Precisely, it is 16.5 percent longer (3,012 English words in the former, 2,586 English words in the latter) and this additional length is almost entirely attributable to Tolstoy's commentary and summation of certain pericopes in the first third of the Sermon on the Mount. There is no extra-canonical material added and only four relatively minor instances where he inserted material from other parts of the Bible; (a) to craft his narrative introduction, Tolstoy drew briefly from Matthew 9:35 (Jesus went from town to town having compassion on the crowds as they were like sheep without a shepherd); (b) for his Beatitudes, Tolstoy borrowed from the Lukan woes from the Sermon on the Plain; (c) as Note 8 indicates, an inference can be made from 1 Samuel 15:22 (God does not require sacrifice) and (d) Tolstoy draws again on Luke's Sermon on the Plain much more from Isaiah 9 in his expanded conclusion to the parable of the wise and foolish builders (Notes 21–22). There are no rants or diatribes the likes of which are the focus here in subsection 2.3; there is no biting rhetoric; and, he did not appeal to reason. The discernible differences between the TGB and the NIV-UK can be summarized as (1) some reordering, (2) some reiteration and review and 3) some rephrasing and interpretive rendering.

Two observations can be made about the opening section of the TGB. First, again, Tolstoy reordered narrative traditionally located in Matthew 9:35 to his Sermon on the Mount introduction. Second, he interpreted blessedness as happiness to be found only in obedience to the will of God. Four times in the first three verses he referred to God's will: "the happiness of doing the Father's will." Clearly he believed the Sermon on the Mount to contain the will of God for how we should live. Having re-positioned Matthew 9 (where Jesus was saddened by the sight of crowds as sheep without a shepherd), Tolstoy began his Sermon on the Mount with Jesus feeling "sorry for the people because they perish without knowing what true life consists of." Twice more he reiterated the happiness that comes from following the will of God, the source of this true life which results in happiness. Tolstoy believed the Sermon on the Mount contained the expressed will of God for all people and the only path that led to happiness and meaning in life. In his greatly abbreviated rendering of the Beatitudes, again, he drew mainly from the Lukan woes. Tolstoy's emphasis was God's concern for those in physical poverty as against those who have material wealth (Notes 3-4). Tolstoy's own conversion and testimony shine through in repeated references to the poor and homeless being the true teachers of happiness for in his search for happiness and the meaning of life he learned more of the way of life from the peasant class than from any philosopher or theologian (*A Confession*, Chapters 10, 15).

Interpretive rendering and reiteration stand out most noticeably in the following pericope on the fulfilment of the law. Tolstoy made clear distinction between the Eternal Law and the Written Law. This vital distinction in Tolstoyan Sermon on the Mount interpretation was briefly mentioned in subsection 1.4 and will receive more thorough analysis in three forthcoming subsections 2.1, 4.3 and 4.4. Tolstoy had exegetical and textual justifications to conclude Jesus was abolishing the Written Law which Christians commonly confused, he believed, with the Eternal Law. His most significant re-ordering example is found here as he borrowed the pericope on not judging from Matthew 7:1-6 and relocated it in its entirety after 5:42. Believing the section on *no oath taking* applied primarily to court tribunals, he deemed this passage on *no judging* to be better located earlier. It is in this section on law where Tolstoy added length to his version of the Sermon by calling attention to what he deemed were the five new commandments and giving brief exposition on them and a final summation. Several interesting omissions occur in these sections. First, Tolstoy omitted eternal consequences for breaking the commandments. For example, "will be in danger of the fires of hell" and, "in danger of your whole body being thrown into hell" are excluded. These omissions are indicative of his disinterest in matters eschatological. However, he also omitted any natural consequences: "or your adversary may hand you over to the judge ... the officer ... prison ... not get out until you have paid the last penny." For Tolstoy, it was consequence enough that those who disobey the commandments forfeit the happiness and meaning of life.

Finally, Tolstoy left out Jesus' admonition to "be perfect as your heavenly Father is perfect." More will be said on Tolstoy's conception of perfection in subsection 4.1 as moral perfection was central to Tolstoy's life long spiritual journey and to his conception of Christian living. In short, perfection for Tolstoy was simple, he believed perfection simply meant goodness. In his *Harmony of the Four Gospels*, this verse was not omitted but instead rendered "Be therefore good to all men, as your father in heaven in good to all" (HM, 263, 271). Only a slight trace of this Jesus command "be perfect" or "therefore be good" can be discerned in the TGB at this point of omission where he begins "Do good to men of your own nation," and at the beginning of the next section on almsgiving, "So if you do good to others . . ." Again, on the matter of consequences, he did make reference to "your reward is from your father in heaven" which, in context, again seems to deny eternal rewards and place any benefits of obedience in the here and now. There are a three places where it is clear Tolstoy was rewriting the Sermon on the Mount for the context of his place and time. Instead of the righteousness of the Pharisees and teachers of the law, Tolstoy gave the rendering, "the virtue of the Orthodox legalists." Also, where Jesus spoke on these religious men who love to pray standing in the synagogues, Tolstoy used the word churches instead. Thirdly, in the conclusion the traditional passage about the amazement of the crowds that he taught with authority unlike the teachers of the law is recast, "the teaching of Jesus was quite different from that of the Orthodox professors of the law." As much as Tolstoy worked to capture the original meaning of the Sermon on the Mount it was equally important to him that the Sermon on the Mount speak this original meaning to those he was contending with in his own time and place.

Tolstoy's interest in the Sermon on the Mount was mainly concentrated in the first third of the three chapters, Matthew 5–7. The latter two thirds of the Sermon on the Mount receive very little doctoring except one omission and two additions. The omission is the *do unto others* Golden Rule of Matthew 7:1. Only a possible hint of it in vague form remains in his summarization of the earlier law section: "Treat foreigners as I have told you to treat each other" (Note 20). The two additions are underscored in Note 21 and Note 22. In the section on true and false teachers, Tolstoy inserted material from Luke's Sermon on the Plain (6:44–45):

> A good man out of his good heart brings forth all that is good. But an evil man out of his evil heart brings forth all that is evil. For from the overflow of the heart the lips speak. And therefore if teachers tell you to do to others what would be bad for yourselves, if they teach violence, executions, and wars–then you may know that they are false teachers.

In the conclusion Tolstoy again referenced "the Orthodox teachers of the law" and added notably to the traditional ending of the Parable of the Wise and Foolish Builders:

> And the people were all astonished at this teaching, for the teaching of Jesus was quite different from that of the Orthodox professors of the law. They taught a law that had to be obeyed, but Jesus taught that all men are free. And in Jesus Christ were fulfilled the prophecies of Isaiah: that a people living in darkness, in the shadow of death, saw the light of life. That he who brought this light of truth did no violence or harm to men, but was meek and gentle. To bring truth into the world he neither disputes nor shouts, nor is his voice raised, and he will not break a straw or put out the smallest light, and all the hope of men is in his teaching.

For this expanded conclusion Tolstoy added references to how, in Jesus Christ, the prophecies of Isaiah 9 were fulfilled. Functionally he used Isaiah 9 in a similar way to how Luke in chapter four used Isaiah 62 to communicate the same about Christ.

~ 2.0 ~

The Centre of Second Tolstoy; *What I Believe* and *The Kingdom of God is Within You*

. . . presenting Christ's teaching as something new after 1800 years of Christianity.

—Tolstoy in Miscellaneous letters and essays, 23:335.

THE TWO CHAPTERS SUBSEQUENT to this one will draw out the distinctive and paramount aspects of Tolstoy's interpretation of the Sermon on the Mount which are found in concentrated form in his two main books on Sermon on the Mount obedience, *What I Believe* (1884) and the *Kingdom of God Is within You* (1893). The brief introductions to these two post-conversion works now ahead in this second chapter are intentionally abbreviated in certain sections so as to avoid unnecessary reiteration between this second and the coming third and fourth chapters. Nevertheless, the brevity of these two introductions must not be interpreted as an indication they are of lesser significance to Tolstoyan Christianity. In fact, these two works are the most significant and deserve the additional treatment they receive in the following two chapters.

2.1 *What I Believe*[1] (1884) — [*abbr.* WB]

Writing this fifth and most important post-conversion book in such a relatively concise and uncluttered fashion was possible because Tolstoy first wrote four books chronicling the path he traversed in his spiritual search up to this point. *What I Believe* was written to be clear and straightforward as Tolstoy thought the teachings of Jesus most certainly were. It is written conversationally in the same testimonial prose as his *Confession* and the reader is casually treated to the story of his coming upon the truth of the Doctrine of Jesus. In WB, Tolstoy wrote honestly about the impossibilities and problems he found in traditional interpretations of the text, calling out as he saw them 1800 years of eisegetical obfuscations layered over and hiding the true meaning. He wrote plainly of the exegetical fruit of his six years of personal study which resolved for him the classic tensions which, he believed, commentators since the fourth and fifth centuries relaxed even by changing the text itself to avoid the implications of what it really and plainly said. It was Tolstoy's contention that Jesus meant his sermon to be understood on that mountainside by unlearned ordinary people and WB was similarly written to be read by the masses whose attention Tolstoy had won. Throughout his exposition of the Sermon on the Mount in WB, Tolstoy walked the reader through his steps at resolving problems in the text and finding clarity of originally intended meaning. First he consulted the text, the words and grammar. Then he consulted the commentaries and traditions of the Church demonstrating how the difficult meaning of the text was, at times, softened or changed by subsequent interpreters who had reason to make the text more palpable to a generation in Christendom who had abandoned the demanding doctrines of Jesus of the Mount. Though there are strands within the book containing indictments against the church, WB was not written to theologians and ecclesiastics to be nailed to church doors hoping for reforms. Tolstoy's heart was with the people and his gift was communication. WB was his response to the masses who wondered what changed their beloved novelist such that he would walk away from his craft, the height of his success, and stoop to renouncing his literary masterpieces. These first five post-conversion books are reminiscent of the man who sold everything to buy the field where he found the treasure.

The twelve chapters of WB bear no titles and the temptation to label them according to the major ideas within is best resisted so as to not draw

---

1. In most publications and reprints today this volume is titled *My Religion—What I Believe*. Tolstoy's original title was simply *What I Believe* and for that reason I will refer to it as such in the pages that follow. See Maude, *Life of Tolstoy, Vol. II*, 25. Maude insists the correct title is *What I Believe* and later additions of *My Religion* are incorrect.

away from one matter and overemphasis another. That said, the first chapter introduces what Tolstoy considered to be the substance of Christianity, something he now claims to have known since the days of his childhood: "the doctrine of Jesus which inculcates love, humility, self-denial, and the duty of returning good for evil" (WB, 12). He announced he "could not become a disciple of the Church" because of "the indifference of the Church to what seemed to me essential in the teachings of Jesus" (WB, 13, 14). The key to Christianity he found in Matthew 5:39—"resist not evil." In that, Tolstoy "understood that Jesus meant neither more nor less than what he had said" (WB, 16). This was the very path Jesus took himself and the very path he called his followers to take. It captured Christlikeness and therefore what would constitute a Christian.

In the second chapter, Tolstoy addressed the usual concern that such a difficult command was impossible to obey; to which he replied that Jesus "saw no such impossibility.... Nowhere did he say that obedience would be difficult; on the contrary, he said ... 'My yoke is easy and my burden is light' ... If my master says to me, 'Go; cut some wood,' and I reply, 'It is beyond my strength,' I say one of two things: either I do not believe what my master says, or I do not wish to obey his commands" (WB, 19–20). Tolstoy began chapter three with a statement building toward the main stream of his hermeneutic and application of the Sermon on the Mount: "We are wrong when we say that the Christian doctrine is concerned only with the salvation of the individual, and has nothing to do with questions of State" (WB, 24). The clear choice Christ placed before his followers on that mountainside Tolstoy brought into focus, the choice between divine/eternal and human law. Tolstoy gave internal proofs within the text that Jesus forbade the participation of his followers in human law courts and tribunals; speak no evil means do not accuse and judge not means do not condemn, both inherent to societal institutions based on retributive justice. In part, Tolstoy's argument was that "Christianity before Constantine regarded tribunals only as an evil" (WB, 30). In chapter four, a case was made that human laws of resistance to evil only augment it. Paraphrasing, Tolstoy rephrased the words of Jesus: "You believe that your laws reform criminals; as a matter of fact, they only make more criminals. There is only one way to suppress evil, and that is to return good for evil, without respect for persons. For thousands of years you have tried the other method; now try mine, try the reverse" (WB, 34). A repeated lament for Tolstoy was: "The doctrine of Jesus is understood in a hundred different ways; but never, unhappily, in the simple and direct way which harmonizes with the inevitable meaning of Jesus words. Our entire social fabric is founded upon principles that Jesus reproved" (WB, 35). With brief reference to Strauss and Renan who considered Jesus teaching "charming nonsense" and "nothing but chimerical ideas" Tolstoy gave no ground:

> Jesus understood his doctrine, not as a vague and distant ideal impossible of attainment, not as a collection of fantastic and poetical reveries with which to charm the simple inhabitants on the shores of Galilee; to him his doctrine was a doctrine of action, of acts which should become the salvation of mankind. (WB, 37)

Tolstoy argued the way of violence was contrary to the inclination of human nature: "No one will deny that not only to kill or torture a man, but to torture a dog, to kill a fowl or a calf, to inflict suffering is repugnant to human nature ... and yet our existence is so organised that every personal enjoyment is purchased at the price of human suffering contrary to human nature" (WB, 38). Humanity is able to distance herself from an awareness of her culpability in such violence by diverting the direct responsibility for it to "administrative machinery" (WB, 38). In the Sermon on the Mount Tolstoy understood Jesus to issue a directive to his disciples to not participate in this machinery of the State.

Chapters five and six are expositions of Tolstoy's paramount and unique interpretations of the Sermon on the Mount; namely (a) the differentiation between the Written Law of Moses and the Eternal Law of God, and (b) the five new commandments taken from Matthew chapter five. Succinctly put: "Jesus abolished the Mosaic law, and gave his own law in its place" (WB, 52). So important are these expositions to Tolstoyan Christianity it is at this point they will only be mentioned as chapter four is focused on these specifically. In short, Tolstoy determined the five new commandments of Jesus to be: (1) Be not angry; (2) Do not commit adultery; (3) Take no oaths; (4) Resist not evil; (5) Do not make war (WB, 165). Tolstoy's religion starts to emerge in articulations as this: "The establishment of the kingdom of God depended upon our personal efforts in the practice of Jesus doctrine as propounded in the five commandments, which instituted the kingdom of God on earth" (WB, 78). Returning to WB chapter seven to the persistent complaint that these teachings of Jesus are unattainable, Tolstoy deemed it a false conviction found "in pseudo-Christian religion which men had been teaching for fifteen hundred years" (WB, 86). Beginning here to use phrases that later permeated much of his remaining two decades of religious writing, Tolstoy referred to this "false conception of life" which has

> (through the dogma of the Fall) debarred man from the most important and legitimate field for the exercise of his powers, and has deprived him entirely of the idea that he can of himself do

> anything to make his life happier or better. Science and philosophy, proudly believing themselves hostile to pseudo-Christianity, only carry out its decrees. . . . Ethics and moral instruction have disappeared from our pseudo-Christian society without leaving a trace! (WB, 88)

In addition to the dogmatists of his day, Tolstoy skewered the science and philosophical minds of his time for espousing the false conception of life. This being an important area of confrontation for Tolstoy against the intellectual current and academic consensus of his day, a later chapter in this project (subsection 9.1) provides a more comprehensive assessment of Tolstoy's belief that the Sermon on the Mount is the antithesis of an evolutionary ethic and the antidote to the lethal implications of the emergence Social Darwinism.

Chapter eight of WB is troubling for any who ascribe to the traditional tenets of orthodox Christianity; repentance, resurrection and eternal life. "Jesus taught us, not of a life beyond the grave, but of that universal life which comprises within itself the life of humanity, past, present, and to come. . . . According to the doctrine of Jesus, the personal life is saved from death by the accomplishment of the will of God as propounded in the commandments of Jesus" (WB, 106). Using a story about being lost with companions in a snowstorm Tolstoy compared seeing a light with seeing a path. The light is like a mirage, even imaginary, but the path under their feet is real: "Ah, but if we continue to travel toward the imaginary light, we shall perish; if we follow the road, we shall surely arrive at the haven of safety" (WB, 109–10). Dogmas about life-ever-after appeared as a mirage to Tolstoy and his preference was to place the next step of his trust on the narrow path Jesus spoke of on the mountainside, believing it was the road that led to life which few would find. Tossing out the bathwater of sacred doctrines leaves Tolstoy open to the charge that he tossed out the baby as well, preferring a path of works to the finished work of Christ. Perhaps to alleviate the concerns, Tolstoy ended chapter eight as follows:

> Understanding this, I understood and believed that Jesus is not only the Messiah, that is, the Anointed One, the Christ, but that he is in truth the Saviour of the World. I know that he is the only way, that there is no other way for me or for those who are tormented with me in this life. I know, that for me as for all, there is no other safety than the fulfilment of the commandments of Jesus, who gave to all humanity the greatest conceivable sum of benefits. (WB, 111)

Whether or not this a sufficient confession for Christian salvation remains contentious.

If one were to place a title on chapter nine of WB, a suggestion might be "Faith is in the Acts it Inspires." Using the New Testament epistle which another reformer considered straw, Tolstoy drew heavily on James to implore followers of Christ to obey and act according to the commandments of Jesus. At this point he started to write about the renunciation of one's personal life and the virtue of living for others. In chapter ten he taught the happiness of work, and martyrdom, and the calling to live in community with other believers. The community he encouraged was not the removed existence of old monasticism, a form of self-denial he considered slow suicide (WB, 123). He believed it was impossible to live the Sermon on the Mount in such isolation; that Christ

> has given us the example of his life. All his life that is known to us was passed in the company of publicans, of the downfallen, and of Pharisees. The principal commandments of Jesus are that his followers shall love others and spread his doctrine. Both exact constant communion with the world. And yet, the deduction is [erroneously] made that the doctrine of Jesus permits retirement from the world. That is, to imitate Jesus we may do exactly contrary to what he taught and did himself. (WB, 124)

Again putting forth concepts that he used again and again in his books and booklets in the next couple decades, Tolstoy brought a sharp contrast between the disciples of Jesus and the disciples of the world, between the doctrine of Jesus and the doctrine of the world. In a perceptive way Tolstoy made a case for the doctrine of the world to have claimed many more lives than any amount of martyrs following the doctrine of Jesus:

> Go through our great cities and observe the emaciated, sickly and distorted specimens of humanity to be found therein; recall your own existence and that of all the people whose lives you are familiar; recall the instances of violent deaths and suicides of which you have heard, and then ask yourself for what cause all this suffering and death, this despair that leads to suicide, has been endured. You will find, perhaps to your surprise, that nine-tenths of all human suffering endured by men is useless, and ought not to exist, that, in fact, the majority of men are martyrs to the doctrine of the world... For each Christian martyr there have been a thousand martyrs to the doctrine of the world, and the sufferings of each one of them have been a hundred times more cruel than those endured by others. (WB, 127, 133)

In a remarkable way, the suffering and privations of refusing military service seem far less than the sufferings of those who die on the battlefield or survive to live out their lives mentally and physically maimed. Tolstoy outlined five conditions of earthly happiness supported by the Gospels: (1) expose to nature, the outdoors and sunshine, (2) work, (3) family, (4) "sympathetic and unrestricted intercourse with all classes of men" and (5) bodily health (WB, 129–31). He concluded chapter nine with: "Which, then, is more reasonable; which offers the more joy and the greater security, a life according to the doctrine of the world, or a life according to the doctrine of Jesus?" (WB, 143).

In chapter ten there is a further comparison between the doctrine of Jesus and the doctrine of the Church which conceals and even attempts to cancel the doctrine of Jesus. Summarizing some of his findings in his *Critique of Dogmatic Religion* Tolstoy asserted the doctrine of the Church "seemed to me so entirely pagan, so wholly out of accord with Christianity" (WB, 146). In Church catechisms and publications Tolstoy observed each "commandment is followed by a reservation which completely destroys its force" (WB, 147). In this chapter are concentrations of an important aspect of Tolstoyan Sermon on the Mount interpretation, that being the case he made for the corruption of the Christianity fully underway by the time of Constantine's reign. A later chapter in this project, chapter six, will return to this Constantinian shift which Tolstoy deemed the departure point for subsequent centuries of ecclesial apostasy and a rejection of Sermon on the Mount ethics. Tolstoy argued for a return to the doctrine of Jesus and held to interest or hope for a reformation in the doctrine of the Church: "but now the time is come when the Church has lost its usefulness, and the world, having no other means for sustaining its true existence, can only feel it's helplessness and go for aid directly to the doctrine of Jesus" (WB, 163).

In the final chapter of *What I Believe*, the twelfth, Tolstoy developed five temptations that destroy happiness each of which corresponds to one of the five commandments of Jesus: (1) enmity toward men, (2) debauchery, (3) swearing to the oath, (4) resort to violence, and (5) the "distinction that we make between compatriots and foreigners" (WB, 169–74). The last of these five is of vital importance for the major moves he made in his Sermon on the Mount interpretation—that it doesn't just apply to the individual but also to the State; for the follower of Jesus in the world, to recognise their fellowship with the rest of the world and to treat everyone including enemies with love and as equals (WB, 175). Tolstoy wrote of that "gross imposture called patriotism" which also will become a consideration in the forthcoming pages which concentrate on Tolstoyan conceptions of socialism, anarchy, the renunciation of war and the Sermon on the Mount as a political program, and love as a foreign policy. Tolstoy ended *What I Believe* with: "Now, as eighteen hundred years ago, this Church is made up not of those who say 'Lord, Lord,' and bring forth iniquity, but of those who hear the words of truth and reveal them in their lives" (WB, 179).

2.2 *The Kingdom of God Is within You* (1893) – [*abbr.* KG]

So scant has been the interest in and awareness of Tolstoyan religious literature over the past century and a quarter, apart from Tolstoy's *Kingdom of God Is within You,* even academics in related fields today would be hard pressed to name another volume in what is construed here as Second Tolstoy. Curiously, KG has become the most reprinted and best known (relatively speaking) of any of Tolstoy's six most significant post-conversion religious writings. This is unfortunate because it is clearly not his main exposition of his religion, Sermon on the Mount obedience. Rather, that main volume is *What I Believe*. In similar fashion to Luke/Acts—"in my former book, Theophilus, I wrote about . . ."[2] Tolstoy began *Kingdom of God* with a sentence about how nine years earlier: "In 1884, I wrote a book entitled *What I Believe,* wherein I formulated my creed" (KG, 8). To read *Kingdom of God* as a stand alone volume is certainly beneficial, as is reading the Book of Acts by itself. However, as the Gospel of Luke captures the impetus driving the actions, obedience and applications which flow from it into the Book of Acts, so *What I Believe* dynamically relates to its sequel the *Kingdom of God Is within You*. This section, 2.2, contains a digest of the main of the KG twelve chapter book. The next section, 2.3, locates and investigates within the main of the book a number of prophetic impulses, referred to here as Tolstoy's diatribes. The final section 2.4 of this chapter expounds on the ninety page train ride story Tolstoy told as a conclusion to KG. Tolstoy first published KG in Germany in 1894 after it was banned in Russia. The title, *Kingdom of God Is within You,* Tolstoy drew from Luke 17:20–21 "[Jesus] answered, 'The Kingdom of God is not coming with things that can be observed; nor will they say, 'Look, here it is!' or 'There is is!' For, in fact, the kingdom of God is within you.'"

In the *Preface* of KG a succinct statement is provided which captures Tolstoy's beliefs to date and the purpose of this book: "In this book I have endeavoured to show that our modern Christianity has been tried and found wanting, that the armed camp of Europe is not Christian, but Pagan, as its latter-day religion, of which the present state of affairs is the outcome" (KG, 7). In the *Introduction* to follow he provided an expanded

2. Acts 1:1.

title giving further insight into his views on the paganism that had become Orthodoxy: "The Kingdom of God Is within You: Or, Christianity not as a Mystical Doctrine, But as a New Life Conception" (KG, 8). He discussed his earlier book, *What I Believe*, which despite being censored "excited curiosity" and subsequently put him into contact with others in various parts of the world who sympathized with his ideas and interpretations. These interactions made him aware of others who had come to similar conclusions in the past and gave him more clarity to develop the ideas within his earlier book, *What I Believe*. The title to his first chapter is an acknowledgement that he had come to discover others before him believed along similar lines: "Doctrine of Non-Resistance to Evil from the Origin of Christianity, Has Been, and Still Is, Professed by the Minority of Men" (KG, 10). The chapter begins with the Quakers, Fox, Paine and Dymond as examples of "men who have long since recognised the impossibility of harmonising Christianity and war" (KG, 11).

The son of American abolitionist William Lloyd Garrison contacted Tolstoy to make him aware of a comparable work by his father a half century earlier, a book called *Non-Resistance*.[3] Tolstoy included a seven page section reprinting from Garrison's book a declaration from an 1838 Peace Convention held in Boston.[4] Tolstoy lamented at this point and in a number of subsequent parts of KG his dismay that such articulate expressions of the doctrine of Christian non-resistance did not make "a deeper impression on men . . . [or] become a subject for universal consideration. . . . On the contrary, not only is it unknown in Europe, but even among . . . Americans . . . there are but few who are familiar with this" (KG, 17). It is a repeated

---

3. In January 1904, Tolstoy received a copy of a biography on Garrison from Vladimir Tchertkoff (Tchertkoff and Holah *A Short Biography of William Lloyd Garrison*) and sent back, in letter form, a tribute which was published in future additions. The tribute, titled *What I Owe to Garrison*, was also included in later additions of Garrison's book *Non-Resistance*, 46–55. The tribute begins as such: "Reading it, I lived again through the spring of my awakening to true life. While reading Garrison's speeches and articles I vividly recalled to mind the spiritual joy which I experienced twenty years ago, when I found out that the law of non-resistance to which I had been inevitably taught by the recognition of the Christian teaching is its full meaning, and which revealed to me the great joyous idea to be realised in Christian life – was even as far back as the forties not only recognised as proclaimed by Garrison (about Ballou I learned later), but also placed by him at the foundation of his practical activity in the emancipation of the slaves. My joy at that time mingled with bewilderment as to how it was that this great Gospel truth, fifty years ago explained by Garrison, could have been so hush up that I had now to express it as something new."

4. William Lloyd Garrison organized a peace convention held in Boston in September of 1838. At this convention Garrison formed the *New England Non-Resistance Society* with forty members present, including Adin Ballou, signing the Society's *Declaration of Sentiments* from which Tolstoy drew these extended citations.

marvel to Tolstoy in KG there is such a veil over these Gospel truths. It becomes apparent in these and other examples given by Tolstoy that the veil has been more effective than any open resistance to these ideas as there is little resistance needed for ideas that are widely unknown and ignored.

Moving next to another American ambassador of Christian non-resistance, Adin Ballou, minister and social reformer, Tolstoy included lengthy citations.[5] Here there is the first mention of a major Tolstoyan Sermon on the Mount interpretation, that there are both micro and macro applications of these teachings of Jesus (see also subsection 3.4). Tolstoy quoting Ballou, "Man stealing is a great crime in one man, or a very few men only. But a whole nation can commit it, and the acts becomes not only innocent, but highly honourable" (KG, 19). Other champions of Christian non-resistance are named in chapter one, but most notably Tolstoy's discovery of the Czech Petr Chelčický and his book *The Net of Faith* which became important to Tolstoyan Sermon on the Mount interpretation.[6] Contending for reform a hundred years before Luther was Bohemian reformer Petr Chelčický in the Kingdom of Bohemia (modern day Czech-Republic). Chelčický's book helped Tolstoy make his case against what scholars today know as the Constantinian heresy, the fourth century integration of imperial government and violence into Christendom, all of which is the subject of chapter six of this project.

In chapter two of KG, Tolstoy addressed the two classes of criticism, religious and secular, from both foreign and domestic readers of his earlier book, *What I Believe*, to the case he made for Christian non-resistance. Their dissent he "summed up under five headings" (KG, 37–41).

> (1) "From men of high position, either in Church or State, who feel quite sure that no one will venture to combat their assertions ... these men, intoxicated for the most part by their authority, have forgotten that there is a Christianity in whose name they hold their places" (KG, 37).
> (2) Though Christ did "teach us to turn the other cheek ... the world abounds with evildoers and if these wretches are not subdued by force, the righteous will perish and the world will be destroyed" (KG, 38).

---

5. The discovery of Adin Ballou (1803–90) and his fifty years of preaching non-resistance (and his 1840 founding of the short-lived *Hopedale Community* in Massachusetts) was a welcomed support for Tolstoy bolstering his own solidifying convictions. Subsequent correspondence with Ballou included receipt of his works; pamphlets, writings and perhaps an earlier form of a book published posthumously in 1910; *Christian Non-Resistance*.

6. Chelčický, *Net of Faith*.

He found this second argument coming from as early a churchman as St. John Chrysostom.

> (3) Affirming that "the commandment of non-resistance is every Christian's duty, when the injury is a personal one, it ceases to be obligatory when harm is done to one's neighbour" (KG, 38).
> (4) "asserting that this commandment is not denied but acknowledged like all the others; it is only the special significance to it by sectarians that is denied" (KG, 40).

The fifth Tolstoy asserted to be most popular of them all

> 5) "in quietly evading reply, pretending that the question was solved ages ago, in a cogent and satisfactory manner, and that it would be a waste of words to reopen the subject." (KG, 41)

In summary, Tolstoy wrote:

> Such were the views of the clergy, of the professors of Christianity, in regard to my book [*What I Believe*], nor could anything different have been expected; they are in the bonds to their inconsistent position, believers in the divinity of the Teacher and yet discrediting His plainest words. (KG, 45)

About his Russian secular critics he wrote they were

> apparently ignorant of all that had been said and done in regard to non-resistance to evil, seemed to think that I had invented the principle myself, and attacked it as if it were my idea, first distorting and then refuting it with great ardour, bringing forth timeworn arguments that had been analysed and refuted over and over again. (KG, 46)

Commenting on the political environment of his time, Tolstoy noted "the principle of non-resistance to evil by violence was attacked from two opposite camps: the Conservatives... and the Revolutionists" (KG, 47).

The title "The Misconception of Christianity by Non-Believers" was Tolstoy's choice for his third chapter though the designation "Non-Believers" refers here to the church, its priests and its membership for they, in Tolstoy's view, were obviously not believers in the non-violent way of Christ (KG, 50). The notion and language of conceptions emerges more consistently from this point on in the book as Tolstoy addresses misconceptions here, and starts to contrast false conceptions of Christianity with the true conception. The "tradition of this false conception has been handed down for ages" Tolstoy maintained, as the plain meaning of Christ began to be concealed by "strange" "perversions," including an emphasis on the mystical and the miraculous (KG, 51):

> The more mystical grew the apprehension of Christ's teaching, the more miraculous element entered into it; and the more miraculous it became, the further it was from its original meaning; and the more complicated, mystical, and remote from its original meaning it came to be, the more necessary it was to declare its infallibility, and the less intelligible it became. (KG, 55)

Tolstoy's observation was "the more widely spread Christianity became, and the larger the number of uninstructed men it received, the less it [a true conception of Christianity, the doctrine of Jesus] was understood" (KG, 57). His claim was the church had failed to produce disciples of Jesus calling people instead to the Credo which he noted contained nothing of the Sermon on the Mount. In focusing on the Credo instead of the doctrine of Jesus, the Church quickly became divided on dogma. Tolstoy posited sections of the Catholic catechism against the Orthodox catechism and against the Lutheran catechism (KG, 58–60). Each sect claiming to be in possession of the truth, dissenters are regarded as heretics and persecuted, even executed. Tolstoy defined heresy to be "every opinion which does not accord with the code of dogmas that we have professed at any given time" (KG, 62). Using church history to support his claim Tolstoy wrote that each "advance that has been made towards the comprehension and the practice of the doctrine [of Jesus] has been accomplished by heretics: Tertullian, Origin, Augustine, and Luther, Hus, Savonarola, Chelčický, and others were all heretics" (KG, 65). His most biting assessment of the misconception of the Christianity he reserved for his own Orthodox tradition as he walked the reader from birth to death and thereafter the superstitions that church held dear; infants immersed three times, swallowing bread and wine, praying to saints, crossing oneself, Confession, Marriage, feast day abstentions, money and lighting wax tapers, saying repeated prayers to secure heaven for the departed. Tolstoy found it to be everything but what was in the Bible, and told a story about a visitor in a monastery shop who could buy any and every superstitious trinket of saints and icons but no Russian Bible (KG, 73). His accusation included the Church using "hyponotism [as] one of its chief agents. Every art, from architecture to poetry, is enlisted in order to move and intoxicate the human soul" (KG, 77).

After he laid bare the misconceptions of the Church as he saw them, Tolstoy devoted chapter four to the misconceptions of Christianity by Scientists. Importantly here, Tolstoy names three distinct life conceptions: (1) the individual or animal life conception, (2) the social or pagan life conception, and (3) the divine life conception (KG, 82). He described history as "but the transcript of the gradual transition from the animal-life conception to the individual to the social, and from the social to the divine" (KG, 83). Near to the end of the age of enlightenment and at the beginning of the rise of evolutionary theory and Social Darwinism, Tolstoy chided the arrogance of scientific thought and method—"in believing that they possess such infallible methods of studying their subject"—and he insisted progress in humanity was to be found only in the doctrine of Jesus and not in these "lower life conceptions" (KG, 87, 89). He underscored the five new commandments of Jesus to be the real "stepping-stones on the way to perfection" (KG, 93). Running against the current of survival of the fittest theories and ideologies, Tolstoy underscored the doctrine of Jesus teaching that love must go beyond ones-self, even beyond the love of one's own race and nation. Tolstoy believed the Sermon on the Mount to contain the antithesis of Social Darwinism and its indifference, hostility and violence toward the other:

> Humanity? Where is its limit? Where does it end and where does it begin? Does it include the savage, the idiot, the inebriate, the insane? If one were to draw a line of demarcation so as to exclude the lower representatives of the human race, where ought it to be drawn? Ought it to include the Negro, as they do in the United States, or the Hindus, as some Englishmen do, or the Jews, as does another nation? (KG, 95)

Sounding like a forerunner in the civil rights movements yet to come, Tolstoy wrote of the "necessity for widening the sphere of love" and how "Christian love only comes from a Christian life-conception" (KG, 96–97). In a decided rejection of the myth of evolutionary progress and the lethal error of the hypothesis that the human story started somewhere in a chemical cesspool slowly over time improving everyone, Tolstoy wrote: "The Christian doctrine restores to man his original consciousness of self, not the animal self, but the godlike self, the spark of divinity... in human form" (KG, 97).

Identifying the principle reason for the misconception regarding the doctrine of Jesus even in the Church, Tolstoy observed how men look upon the doctrine of Jesus as optional: "as one that may be accepted or rejected, without any special change in one's life" (KG, 99). Chapter five in KG addressed the contradictions between how Christians live and what they believe. The following section of this analysis, subsection 2.3, seeks to draw out the momentum swell that becomes discernible at this point in KG with regard to the passion and prophetic unction in Tolstoy's writing. He writes as if writing to all of civilised humanity, "the time has come, and it is already at hand" for humanity to embrace the higher life of Christ: "equality, brotherly love, community of good, non-resistance of evil by violence . . . at this very moment we are experiencing one of these transitions. Humanity has outgrown its social, its civic age, and has entered a new epoch . . . [yet] man's whole life is a continual contradiction of what he knows to be his duty" (KG, 102-3). Tolstoy took aim at the division of our fellow beings into "two classes, the one in poverty and distress, which labours and is oppressed, the other idle, tyrannical, luxurious" (KG, 105). The Sermon on the Mount was to Tolstoy a call to a radical reversal of the social order. Dealing blows to careers of oppression, unjust laws, civil power, economic injustice and the sins of hypocrisy of the upper class Tolstoy dialed up his rhetorical gifts to plead the case that "we are all brothers" (KG, 107). His plea was not as much to the individual Christian, but to "We, Christian nations. . ."; yet again he called out the discrepancy between being Christian-in-name-only: "We live in a time replete with contradictions, writes Count Komoravsky, the Professor of International Law in his learned treatise; 'Nevertheless, the governments increase the military force year after year. . . How are the word and deed at variance!" (KG, 110-11). Instead of the spirit of Jesus possessing men, "this spirit of rivalry favours the chances of war" (KG, 111). As he did in chapter one using extensive supporting quotations from others, Tolstoy included a series of extended quotes again from Komarovsky, Enrico Ferri, Charles Booth, Frédéric Passy and this from Sir Wilfrid Lawson: "In Europe great Christian nations keep among them 28,000,000 of armed men to settle quarrels by killing one another instead of by arguing. This is what the Christian nations of the world are doing at this very moment. . . [either] Christianity is a failure, or . . . those who profess to expound Christianity have failed in expounding it properly" (KG, 113-14). Enlisting the similar views of others instead of saying these types of things again and again himself, Tolstoy appears to be effectually putting credible witnesses on the stand in his case against the so deemed Christian State. After drawing attention to the suicide rate of soldiers, Tolstoy ended this chapter—"in short, every man to be at once a Christian and a gladiator" (KG, 118).

Chapter six of KG continues Tolstoy's Sermon on the Mount-based case against the Christian at war, universal armament, and military conscription. Why leading men, the enlightened men, advanced thinkers of his time were so apt on plunging society "into a condition worse than pagan – into a state of primeval barbarism" is his concern here and Tolstoy identified three prevailing vantage points as possible answers to the question" (KG, 121). "First, that the state of affairs came about accidentally and the attitude of those in [this] first category [expect] deliverance from war by means of diplomatic and international mediation" (KG, 122). Tolstoy included several pages of highlights from the London Peace Conference as an example of this approach followed by various rebuttals demonstrating the inadequacies; including that it is too utopian and it is a suicidal policy (KG, 131, 132). Tolstoy concluded "Christianity is subversive of every government" and "they have established a Christianity which serves to prop up government rather than destroy it" (KG, 133). Second, he identified the vantage point that "the fate of humanity [is] to be forever striving after love and peace, [though] it is nevertheless abnormal and inconsistent (KG, 134). Tolstoy found this view about the "sensitive men of genius, who see and realise all the horror, folly and cruelty of war, but by some strange turn of mind never look about them for any means of escape" (KG, 134). He cited famous French writer Maupassant, Victor Hugo, and an extensive bit of sarcasm from Von Moltke on "assembling in herds by the hundred thousands, marching . . . sleeping in the mud, living like a wild beast in a perennial state of stupidity; plundering cities, burning villages, ruining whole nations . . . to be saved from falling" (KG, 135-36). Thirdly, Tolstoy saw a group of men who "have lost all conscience, and are consequently dead to common sense and human feeling . . . [quoting extensively] Moltke . . . Doucet . . . Jules Clarette . . . Emile Zola . . . Vogue . . . and of Darwin" (KG, 141-45). These men without conscience "believe in the law of evolution and look upon war as not only unavoidable but even useful, and therefore desirable – such men are fairly shocking, horrible in their moral aberration" (KG, 145).

The significance of military conscription is the subject of chapter seven of KG. Tolstoy challenged the conception of authority: "as the word is commonly understood, is a means of coercion, by which a man is forced to act in opposition to his wishes" (KG, 148). He rejected physical violence as "the basis of authority" (KG, 149). Recounting two thousand years of history, Tolstoy illustrated how governments "increase [their] armies in order to support their authority . . . Thus each government finds itself obliged to outdo its neighbour in the increase of its army . . . [and] The despotism of governments increases exactly in proportion to the increase of their strength" (KG, 153, 155, 156). Writing of the "fatal significance of the general conscription" Tolstoy maintained "every citizen who becomes a soldier likewise becomes a supporter of the State system. . . . He who performs his military duty becomes a participant in all these acts . . . , and which are inmost cases directly opposed to his conscience" (KG, 158). Conscription, he believed, was the last step in the process of government coercion. With prophetic fervency Tolstoy exclaimed: "The time has come when the ever-growing abuses of governments and their mutual contexts have required from all their subjects not only material but moral sacrifices, till each man pauses and asks himself, Can I make these sacrifices? And for whose sake am I to make them? . . . And of what use is it?" (KG, 159). Tolstoy's claim was "there is no longer any reasonable ground for such sacrifices" (KG, 161). The chapter ends with a brief comparison of the disadvantages of submission versus non-submission to government. The disadvantages of non-submission would possibly be a trial, imprisonment, exile, or perhaps execution. The disadvantages of submission however, are always being "arrayed in the garments of a clown" obeying the word of superior officers being put through rigorous training to go to a place to execute the orders given and being "forced to slay fellow men of other countries who never did me any harm . . . [and] being sent to a place where I may be mutilated or killed" (KG, 162). At least in the former Tolstoy wrote, "he will enjoy the assurance that he is doing God's business" (KG, 163).

Referring to the conclusion of the Sermon on the Mount, the story of the wise and foolish builders, Tolstoy began chapter eight of KG declaring the prophecy to have come true: "And thus, after eighteen centuries, the prophecy has been fulfilled. As the result of the abandonment of Christ's teaching, having disregarded the principle of non-resistance to evil, men have unwittingly fallen into the condition of imminent peril foretold by Christ to those who refused to follow his precepts" (KG, 166–67). Two paths were placed before humanity on that Mount and people chose the one over the other. Again giving a short recollection of Christian history, the teachings of Jesus accepted initially by a few but ultimately being rejected by many, Tolstoy described the cycle of violence the world finds itself in: "Nowadays every government, the despotic as well as the most liberal, has become what Herzen has so cleverly termed a Genghis Khan with a telegraphic equipment, that is with an organisation of violence" (KG, 171). That cycle of violence he saw to be made up of four expedients: (1) intimidation, (2) bribery, (3) hypnotism, and (4) conscription. In the hypnotic condition they "cease to be men and become imbecile and docile machines in the hands of the hypnotiser."

> Intimidation, bribery, and hypnotism force men to become soldiers; soldiers give power and make it possible to execute and to rob mankind (with the aid of bribed officials), as well as to hypnotise and to recruit men who are in their turn to become soldiers. The circle is complete, and there is no possibility of escape from it. (KG, 174)

Especially interesting considering the weakened status of the family in the modern era, Tolstoy noted the one "domain of human activity, and only one, has hitherto escaped the encroachments of the governments – the domain of the family, the economical domain of private life and domestic labour.

But now even this domain, in consequence of the struggle of socialists and communists, is gradually passing into the hands of governments" (KG, 175). Hoping out loud, Tolstoy wondered if the passing of eighteen centuries of compromised Christianity and subsequent human misery have been in vain or if "these eighteen centuries have made men realise all the miseries of the pagan state" (KG, 176). The chapter ends with descriptions of "the glaring contradiction[s] between this state of affairs and those Christian feelings and ideals with which all modern men are penetrated (KG, 181).

Deliverance from the miseries of pagan life comes only from the acceptance and practice of the Christian life-conception Tolstoy found in the Sermon on the Mount. Chapter nine of KG gives assurance it is still not too late: "A man has but to assimilate this life-conception and he will be set free as a matter of course from the fetters that now restrain him, and feel as free as a bird who spreads his wings and flies over the wall that has kept him a prisoner" (KG, 188). This freedom, Tolstoy maintained, includes being set free from the State:

> For a Christian to promise to subject himself to any government whatsoever – a subjection which may be considered the foundation of state life – is a direct negation of Christianity [as the individual] promises beforehand to obey implicitly every law that men may enact, by that promise utters an emphatic denial of Christianity, whose very essence is obedience in all contingencies to the law which he feels to be within him – the law of love (KG, 189).

To Tolstoy, in the Sermon on the Mount Jesus was crystal clear; no man can serve two masters. Using an illustration of bees acting in a swarm to describe the present condition of humanity, Tolstoy observed all it takes is for one bee to be willing to change its position and be willing to start and the swarm would follow suit: "If the man who has assimilated the Christian life-conception waits for others before he proceeds to live in accordance with it, mankind will never change its attitude. And as all that is needed to change a solid mass of bees into a flying swarm is for one bee to spread its wings and fly away, when the second, the third, the tenth, and the hundredths will follow suit" (KG, 191). When men come along and make laws, demand taxes, establish courts and coerce people to fight in wars, Tolstoy wrote "one would think that in these days there could be but one reply from any man in his senses" so ask, "Why should I?" (KG, 194–95). Tolstoy contended the Sermon on the Mount was a grave threat to the established order:

> These are the bees who are the first to separate themselves from the swarm, and still hovering near, they wait for the whole

swarm to rise and follow them. The governments are aware of this, and look upon such occurrences with more apprehension than upon all the socialists, anarchists, and communists, with their conspiracies and their dynamic bombs. (KG, 198)

Tolstoy wrote as if to enlist young men in a greater cause, one that he believed to be far more dangerous to governments than socialists, communists and anarchist pose—all because they refuse to be coerced and enlisted with all the others (KG, 203): "All the institutions of the State are opposed to the conscience of a Christian: the oath of allegiance, taxation, courts of law, and armies; while the whole authority of government is dependant upon them" (KG, 204). Tolstoy believed the Sermon on the Mount mounted a revolution of another sort: "Revolutionary foes struggle against the government, but Christianity enters not into this contest; internally, it destroys the principles on which government is based" (KG, 205). Drawing from an analogy of a conqueror who seeks to destroy a town by fire, Tolstoy described the outbreak of several of these small fires and ended the chapter with: "'I come to send fire on the earth,' said Christ. And this is the fire that begins to burn" (KG, 207). Incendiary language for sure, but such was the blazing nature of the revolution Tolstoy believed the Sermon on the Mount sought to kindle.

Noting how "no one need tell the young birds when it is time to burst from the shell" Tolstoy sought to discern if "the time has come for men to cast aside the customs of the State and establish a new order" (KG, 211). For him the issues were clear: "the love of power is incompatible with goodness . . . to possess power and to do violence are synonymous terms . . . it is absurd to speak of Christians as sovereigns or rulers" (KG, 213, 214, 215). In chapter ten of KG more of the futility of the way of violence is described: "violence never really overcomes evil" (KG, 217). Tolstoy recalled there have been examples of leaders, Charles V, Ivan the Terrible, and Alexander I, who "having realised the evils of power and its futility, renounced it, because they recognised it as a calamity, having lost all pleasure in the deeds of violence which they formerly enjoyed." Tolstoy's aim in these pages was to inspire others to "go over to the new truth" (KG, 222). Making it seem easy, Tolstoy explained: "If public opinion would but frown upon violence, it would destroy all its power . . . that power which is the convergence of the invisible, intangible, spiritual forces of all humanity is public opinion" (KG, 226). Trying to convert by violence has never worked and Tolstoy asserted "In order to convert uncivilised nations, who do us no harm, whom we have no motive for oppressing, we ought, above all, to leave them in peace, and act upon them only by our showing them an example of the Christian virtues of patience, meekness, temperance, purity and brotherly love" (KG,

227). His lament was "we, in fact, rob them; we sell them wine, tobacco, and opium, and thereby demoralise them; we establish our own customs among them, we teach them violence and all its lessons; we teach them the animal law of strife, that lowest depth of human degradation, and do all that we can to conceal the Christian virtues we possess" (KG, 227).

The final chapter of KG, eleven, is followed by a ninety page conclusion which is of such significance it will be treated by itself in the subsequent section numbered 2.4. Chapter eleven posits the Sermon on the Mount as the means of societal transformation and not just for any sort of much needed church renewal. Tolstoy takes the reader through series of applications of the New Life-Conception beginning with the hard truth that there are many places a true Christian cannot work; as a spy, detective, usurer, tavern-keeper, police officer, courtiers, judges, as ecclesiastical or military masters, and bankers (KG, 232–33). He challenged high-minded youth to vocations as doctors, engineers, artists, writers and farmers rather than as priests or soldiers. He raised concern about who gets celebrated in society with monuments, generals or inventors. He presented a direct challenge to his wealthy readers, those in the army, those who were judges and lawyers, gaolers and turnkeys, executioners, even land owners and manufacturers. His call was to found "schools, hospitals, and savings banks, institute pensions, and build houses for the workmen" (KG, 235). Tolstoy saw the leaven of the Kingdom quietly working behind the good changes that were underway in society: "it will continue to influence men more and more, until it brings about a change in their mode of life and reconciles it with that Christian consciousness already possessed by the most advanced" (KG, 236). Here in the final formal chapter of the book, Tolstoy writes as if he is presenting the dream, the possibility that God's Kingdom can come on earth. However, Tolstoy could not conceive of such a reform coming from within the church: "The same priests, bishops, churches, and synods, but it becomes more and more evident to all that these men themselves have long since ceased to believe what they preach, and are therefore unable to persuade any one of the necessity of believing what they no longer believe themselves" (KG, 237). The chapter ends with what can be construed as a glimpse into Tolstoy's eschatology:

> Hence the prophecy: that a time will come when all men will hearken unto the word of God, will forget the art of war, will melt their swords into ploughshares and their lances into reaping hooks; which, being translated means when all the prisons, the fortresses, the barracks, the palaces, and the churches will remain empty, the gallows and the cannon will be useless. This

is no longer a mere Utopia, but a new and definite system of life towards which mankind is progressing with ever increasing rapidity. But when will it come? Eighteen hundred years ago Christ, in answer to this question, replied that the end of the present world – that is, of the pagan system – would come when the miseries of man had increased to their utmost limit; and when, at the same time, the good news of the Kingdom of Heaven – that is, of the possibility of a new system, one not founded upon violence – should be proclaimed throughout the earth. (KG, 241)

In company with the prophets, Tolstoy set forth these promises and hopeful possibilities.

2.3 Tolstoy's Diatribes as Prophetic Unction, Rhetoric and Echoes from the Mount

Luther had his 95 *Theses* for the Roman Church and three centuries later Tolstoy pounded his prophetic protest of the Orthodox Church into at least eight diatribes in his *The Kingdom of God Is within You*. A diatribe is an assertive and poignant verbal sally against someone or something, and these eight were unctions entirely of that sort. The careful reader of this, his second book on obedience to the Sermon on the Mount may notice a number of shifts in cadence and in Tolstoy's occasional use of repetition of rhetoric. These diatribe sections could be likened to the Pentecostal preacher when he 'falls under the anointing,' or to Martin Luther King Jr.'s unforgettable "I have a dream" speech. Tolstoy's eight diatribes pack an equally prophetic punch and yet it appears no one in the last one hundred and twenty-five years has called any attention to them. For this reason I highlight them here, and those who notice new things get to name them which is what I have done here in dubbing them Tolstoy's Diatribes. My hope is that others will note this curious and distinct Tolstoyan prophetic rhetoric as a new categorical genre. Like contractions getting closer together and more intense toward the end, these diatribes are initially eighty pages apart, then forty, then twenty-five, then ten, then one; and, they seem to crescendo in intensity and urgency. Tolstoy's eight main prophetic diatribes are listed below without any summation of content, except Diatribe #7 is included below as a sampling.

Diatribe #1:	*"We Are Brothers"*	page 107
Diatribe #2:	*"Why Should I?"*	page 195
Diatribe #3:	*"What Use To Us"*	page 238
Diatribe #4:	*"What Does It Mean?"*	page 256
Diatribe #5:	*"One Wonders Why"*	page 275
Diatribe #6:	*"It is Possible!"*	page 302
Diatribe #7:	*"Return Sons of Men!"*	page 311
Diatribe #8:	*"No matter"*	page 312

People have used many labels to describe Tolstoy; diarist, artist, novelist, soldier, pacifist, aristocrat, ascetic, activist, heretic, social reformer, subversive, moralist, madman, anarchist, apostle. Whether one agrees with his message or not, a diatribe as follows puts Tolstoy in the classification of prophet. Space constraints will only tolerate the citation of one of the eight mentioned above:

> Return to yourselves, sons of men, and have faith in the Gospel, and in its doctrine of eternal happiness! If you heed not this warning, you shall all perish like the men slain by Pilate, like those upon whom the Tower of Siloam fell; like millions of other men, who slew and were slain, who executed and suffered execution, who tortured and were tortured; as perished the man who so foolishly filled his granaries, counting on a long life, on the very night his soul was required of him. Return, sons of men, and believe the words which Christ uttered 1800 years ago, words which He repeats today with greater force, warning us that the evil day He foretold is at hand, and that our life has reached its last descent of folly and wickedness. (KG, 311)

As these prophetic diatribes ebb and flow amidst the rest of the paragraphs in the book it is not always easy to discern where precisely one starts and ends. In fact, the last two seem to overlap. Others can join in the study of these diatribes and help determine whether or not they were truth spoken in love; whether or not they represent the core of Tolstoy's prophetic challenge; and whether or not they bear repeating in subsequent ages as course corrections. Bible and theological schools tasked with raising up reformers would do well to familiarise students with Tolstoy the reformer and Tolstoy the prophet. Perhaps the urgency of obedience to Christ is something that could be passed on as a holy contagion to those who are drawn close to it in a study of Tolstoy the obedient.

2.4 The September Ninth Train to Tula

Unlike some academics and intellectuals of his era, Leo Tolstoy can never be accused of espousing incomprehensibles; or, of writing a sentence, either philosophical or theological, that needs to be read closely and carefully two or three times to glean any sense of the involved and strained bloviation therein. It was a repeated point in the development of Tolstoy's greater thesis how Jesus intended to be understood by the simple, unsophisticated, and uneducated on that mountainside. Similarly, there is evidence of Tolstoy being more interested in being understood by the everyman than only by the elite. His ability, nay his gifting to vividly tell a story and convey in a compelling manner had achieved him world-renown across the general populace. In 1901 his friend and biographer Aylmer Maude wrote:

> Frankness and clearness have a great charm for Tolstoy. The mistakes and errors of a man who is clear are more likely to be of use than half truths of those who are content to be indefinite. On any matter, to express yourself so that you cannot be understood is bad. [Noting that Tolstoy was hard to please with poetry, Maude wrote:] Why, [Tolstoy] asks, need men hamper the clear expression of their thoughts by selecting a style which obliges them to choose, not the words which best describe their meaning but those that best enable them to get the lines to scan. If we can say what we have to say in three words, why use five?[7]

Maude once asked Tolstoy how he accounted for "the supreme rank among authors" accorded to Shakespeare. Tolstoy's reply was that he "explained it to himself by the fact that the 'cultured crowd' [has] no clear idea of the purpose and aim of life, and can most readily and heartily admire an author who is like themselves in this respect – i.e. one with no central standpoint from which to measure his relation to all else."[8]

These comments in this slight excursus to the introduction of this final section of KG are intended to underscore, perhaps that in part, plain speech

---

7. Maude, "Talks with Tolstoy," in *Tolstoy and His Problems*, 192–93.

8. Maude, "Talks with Tolstoy," in *Tolstoy and His Problems*, 194. In the second of Aylmer Maude's two-volume biography of Tolstoy, still the standard, he mentioned the downside of Tolstoyan plain speak: "Though he was sincere and wise, he, like other mortals, made mistakes—and did so just because he, too, oversimplified, and wished to solve the complex problems of property, sex, and Government, by the all too simple method of rejecting those things entirely.... One must sympathise with Tolstoy's desire to centralise, unify and simplify, life's teaching; that is what all who take life seriously should aim at, but the dilemma is, that as soon as opinions are reduced to concise formula—whether it be 'the blood of Jesus', the 'infallible Church', the non-use of physical force' or, what not—we find that such formulas fail" (Maude, *Life of Tolstoy, Vol. II*, 414).

attracted Tolstoy to the Sermon on the Mount, but even more to underscore the general readability and practicality of these religious works of Tolstoy by the general population. Tolstoyan Christianity, if it was anything, it was practically applied, applicable and pragmatic. This trademark Tolstoyan praxis can be easily seen in his extended conclusion to the *Kingdom of God Is within You*. Across seventy-two pages, Tolstoy took his readers on a trip to some common scenes and situations in late nineteenth century Russian society—on a September 9 train ride to Tula—describing what he was seeing and thinking from the perspective of the New Life-Conception of the Sermon on the Mount.

The first scene was at a station where his train met up with the train that carried the Governor and troops armed and ready to "go torturing and murdering the famine-stricken peasants" (KG, 247). The flogging of peasants who were merely pushing back against the injustices of their landowners was commonplace and considered necessary for order in society. Tolstoy described the brutality of those scenes which sometimes ended with musket fire into the crowds leaving dead and wounded fathers, women and children. Tolstoy likened the battalion of soldiers on board the train to "the modern Genghis Khan predicted by Herzen" and the Governor "intoxicated with power . . . utterly intoxicated by the sight of blood" (KG, 250–51). Tolstoy's story drew in those who no doubt considered themselves outside the circle of culpability for such wicked deeds: "Not only did the magistrates, the officers, and the soldiers sanction this act by their presence, but they took part in it, preventing the crowd from interfering with the order of its execution" (KG, 252). But even more,

> the entire organisation of our life rests not on any principle of justice, as men occupy and enjoy advantageous positions under the existing system like to imagine, but on the rudest and most barefaced violence, on the murder and torture of human beings. Those who possess large estates and large capital, or who receive high salaries collected from the needy working classes, from the people who often lack the necessaries of life; merchants, clerks, doctors, lawyers, artists, scientists, writers . . . cooks and valets . . . fondly believe that the privileges they enjoy are not the outcome of violence (KG, 252).

Tolstoy made the case that all of society was based on violence and coercion. Echoing some of Hegel's master-slave dialectic Tolstoy claimed: "for every man who lives at ease there are ten overworked, hungry, and often cruelly suffering families of working men, all the privileges of the rich, all their luxury, all their superfluities are acquired and maintained only by tortures, imprisonments, and executions" (KG, 255). For Tolstoy, there was no distance between the harsh reality of every day life in society and the claims the doctrine of Jesus placed on the disciple of Jesus. He found the Sermon on the Mount relevant to all that was going on in the society around him.

One of the strengths within Tolstoyan literature is in the way he was able to get into the psychology of his fictional characters and this is also the case as he described those around him on that September 9 train to Tula. Particularly the soldiers, hanging around

> smoking, laughing, and jesting, some cracking seeds and spitting out the shells . . . chatting [and] good natured. . . . These men, who were on their way to murder starving fathers and grandfathers, seemed as unconcerned as though they were off on the pleasantest, or at least the most everyday business in the world. . . . All these men on their way to commit murder, or to torture the starved and defenceless peasants by whose toil there were supported. (KG, 256)

Tolstoy remarked that he knew the men, not as individuals, but he knew they would each say their deeds arose from a conviction that the State system had to be maintained. Tolstoy presumed to know those men "have rarely, if ever bestowed a single thought upon political science" and even more egregious, "every one of them professes Christianity" and, they are men who have mothers and wives and children and, who for the most part are "kindly, gentle [and] tenderhearted . . . abhor[ing] any kind of cruelty, to say nothing of killing" (KG, 257). Repeatedly Tolstoy asked, what does it mean?: "[T]hey are within a half-hour's ride of the spot where they will inevitably find themselves compelled to do such deeds" (KG, 258). He chided the spectators who stood by and did nothing, who "remained perfectly calm . . . [with] no sign of remorse" (KG, 258). The irony of it all, the hypocrisy of it all, was a marvel to Tolstoy: "Not one of those officials would steal a purse . . . Not one of those officers would cheat at cards. . . . Not one of those soldiers would dare reject the sacrament, or even taste meat on Good Friday" (KG, 259). Yet, they were willing to do the unthinkable believing it to be "the sacred duty of every man to maintain" the present social order (KG, 261). Tolstoy pressed in further to discover what their convictions could possibly be founded upon. For those in the upper echelons of society there was the belief that the present system was beneficial to their interests. For those in the lower echelons of society, Tolstoy found they derived no advantages. He postulated what might be if the regular people in society refused to play the submissive role in such a system which only perpetuates it: "All these deeds of injustice and cruelty have become an integral part of the existing system of life, only because there are men ready to execute them. If there were no such men, the multitude of human beings who are now the victims of violence would be spared" (KG, 263–64). Repeatedly Tolstoy asserted . . . "if there were no men to obey the will of others. . . . It is to this crowd of submissive slaves, ready to obey all orders, that we owe the deeds of a whole series of tyrants" (KG, 264).

Citing the Russian military code, Tolstoy explained how the will of a person is turned over to another, namely the State or superior officer. He called it a delusion that men "may violate every law, human and divine, as long as he does not violate his oath of allegiance to him who, at a given time, happens to be in power . . . [and it is a delusion to think] men are set free from their obligations to God and to their own consciences, and bound to obey the will of a casual superior" (KG, 267). Moving next to the "insane business" of military conscription, Tolstoy was vivid in detail how men leave "their wives and mothers, giving up everything that is sacred to them, only to become senseless tools of murder . . . [noting how it] is too painful if one's senses are not stupefied with wine" (KG, 268). He described the enlistment day which traditionally ended with carousing and brawling throughout the night in a tavern such that they were still under the influence when made to assemble the next morning. Next, Tolstoy recounted how that priest arrives in the morning to swear them all in. The Father

> opens the Bible wherein an oath is forbidden, lifts the cross, that cross on which Christ was crucified for refusing to do what this person, his supposed servant, commands men to do, all these defenceless and deluded young men repeat after him the lie so familiar to his lips. . . "I promise and swear to the Lord Almighty, upon His Holy Bible," etc. to defend (that is murder all those whom I shall be ordered to murder) and to do whatever those men, strangers to me, who regard me only as a necessary tool to be used in perpetrating the outrages by which they oppress my brethren and preserve their own positions, command men to do. All the recruits stupidly repeat the words." (KG, 270)

Tolstoy continued with his descriptions noting the wives and mothers cry and wail bitterly knowing they will be abandoned for years, and how the fathers say little, or perhaps sigh or click their tongues to indicate their sorrow and dismay. Again and again Tolstoy mentioned the role of vodka to stupefy and insulate them from what was really transpiring.

In what can be construed as a discipleship of a different sort, after a year of military exercises, drills, lies, blows and vodka, "the good, kindly, and intelligent fellows will have become as brutal as their teachers" (KG,

272). The end result of this other sort of discipleship was the creation of an instrument of violence and to Tolstoy's astonishment, it is all with ecclesiastical blessing. Tolstoy challenged any sort of "moral doctrine [that] permits murder for any object whatsoever . . . [as] Every code of morals must be founded first of all upon the acknowledgement that human life is to be held sacred. . . . Life is a substance which can neither be weighed, measured, nor compared; hence the taking of one life for another makes no sense" (KG, 273). Tolstoy believed the "most violent and rapacious band of robbers is less to be feared than such an organisation" (KG, 273).

He continually posed the question, why? Why does this go on? The answer has much to do with the matter of moral responsibility: "When such deeds are committed, there are so many instigators, participants, and abettors that no single individual feels himself morally responsible" (KG, 277). In a rich exposition on moral responsibility Tolstoy described how it can be that no one feels the responsibility on their own shoulders: "Some demand the crime, some propose it, some determine it, some confirm it, and some order it, and some execute it. . . . [W]e find a number of intermediaries . . . and they too wash their hands of all responsibility" (KG, 277, 278). Tolstoy denied there could be any transference of responsibility from one person or thing to another. Blaming also the imaginary superiority certain classes and races of people have come to believe they have over other classes and races of people—the popular Darwinistic ideology in his time—Tolstoy reminded the reader of the responsibility humans have, one to the other.

Using the concepts of intoxication and hypnosis, Tolstoy continued on describing the psychology that enabled the violence on which the present social order was founded. There was an intoxication of authority "to which men succumb, under conditions like parades, pageants, religious ceremonies and coronations" which fed this "delusion in regard to human inequality" (KG, 280). And from these ranks came the hypnotisers, Tolstoy's term for those who so masterfully stupefied entire sectors of society, "all the great mass of workers, who are completely absorbed by their labour, all those of weak mind, all the enfeebled, the many who have come under the subjection of nicotine, alcohol, opium, or what not – all these are not in a position to think for themselves, and consequently they submit to those who stand on a higher intellectual level" (KG, 283). Tolstoy held out hope that those who slumber as such would awaken, and the "stifled voice of conscience" would be revived . . . [and that men would] come to their senses" (KG, 285, 286). "If only a few of these men come to their senses and refuse to do the deed, and fearlessly express their opinion of the wickedness of such deeds" Tolstoy believed society could change (KG, 288). Everything depended on "the degree of consciousness that men possess of Christian truth" (KG, 288).

Tolstoy wrote of "the new metaphysic of hypocrisy" whereby a man may "pass for a virtuous man and still pursue his evil career" (KG, 293). One can be engaged in most any wicked pursuit as long as "he gives but the least part of his money to the church or to the poor, then he is deemed an exemplary Christian indeed" (KG, 293). In several pages on this hypocrisy Tolstoy made applications to those in a variety of vocations and lifestyles. And, he again challenged scientific theory which, while insisting on the fraternity of all men on the one hand, gave justification on the other for the extermination "of whole races of so-called savages, etc." (KG, 295).

In wrapping up his extended arguments and expositions in KG, Tolstoy contended that no one can now feign ignorance and no one can say now that they did not know.

> We know perfectly well that as we finish our dinner, see the new play . . . enjoy a merrymaking at Christmas, take a walk, go to a ball, a race, or a hunt, we owe it to the policeman's revolver or the ball in the soldier's musket, which will pierce the hungry belly of the disinherited man who, with watering mouth, peeps around the corners at our pleasures, and who might interrupt them if the policeman or the soldiers in the barracks were not ready to appear at our first call. (KG, 300)

Tolstoy's final appeal was (a) to truth, and (b) to the free agency of man. He distinguished between three kinds of truth: (1) truth that has long been recognized; (2) truth which men perceive as but dimly and far; and (3) truth which God is presently revealing in an unmistakable way (KG, 305). Tolstoy's exposition he believed to be an exposition on that third category of truth and that this truth was forcing itself on the present age of men. He believed in the free agency of man to respond to God's truth: "in his power to become, through recognising and professing the truth that has been revealed to him, a free and willing labourer at the eternal and infinite work performed by God and his universe" (KG, 306). With prophetic unction in back to back diatribes intended to garner a response to these truths, Tolstoy provoked the imagination: "What will become of mankind if each one fulfils that which God demands through the conscience that is in him? (KG, 310). He concluded: "The only significance of life consists in helping to establish the Kingdom of God" (KG, 318).

The main work of this chapter has been to recapture and re-present the development and basis for Tolstoyan Sermon on the Mount interpretation in the two main works of the Second Tolstoy corpus: *What I Believe* and *The Kingdom of God Is within You*. Also, the identification of a new genre has been claimed and called Tolstoy's prophetic diatribes. The chapter concludes with a closer appreciation of the extended narrative Tolstoy included at the end of KG which has been called here: *The September Ninth Train to Tula*. In each of these sections Tolstoy has been shown to be a unique, creative, timely and passionate interpreter of the Sermon on the Mount. His insights and exegetical work into Matthew 5 are unique in the history of the interpretation of these famous texts for their non-negotiable literal applications and moral demand on the hearer, their intensity and consistency. And, they are creative in the hard work and new thinking he did to answer questions that in his view no one else was adequately answering (i.e., on the exceptions to divorce). They are also innovative in their application, applying the commandments of Jesus to very timely and touchy aspects of Russian life during his time. Finally, it has been shown these two books at the centre of Second Tolstoy are impassioned and prophetic. A tangible urgency and force has been demonstrated particularly in the latter half of *The Kingdom of God Is within You* in his intense and always intensifying prophetic diatribes. Chapters three and four each build on the foundation of this chapter by identifying and analyzing important distinctives that mark and drive Tolstoyan Sermon on the Mount interpretation.

~ 3.0 ~

Tolstoy's Sermon on the Mount as a New Life Conception

> *...presenting Christ's teaching as something new after 1800 years of Christianity.*
> —Tolstoy in Miscellaneous Letters and Essays, 23:335.

THE PURPOSE AND IMPORTANCE of this chapter and the next is to set forth a synthesis of the main and virtually unique distinctives of Tolstoyan Sermon on the Mount interpretation building off the mostly descriptive work accomplished in the previous chapters. It was Tolstoy's intention to remove all the layers of obscurity which, over eighteen centuries, had clouded the simple meaning Jesus intended to convey. These layers were eisegetical to Tolstoy in that they were applications and rationalizations based on misconstructions and misinterpretations of the actual text. The thrust of this chapter and the following is to set forth the central and virtually unique distinctives of Tolstoyan Sermon on the Mount interpretation which are most worthy of consideration. They emerge primarily from within the two central works of Second Tolstoy, *What I Believe* (1884), and the second book written nine years later, *The Kingdom of God Is within You* (1893).

3.1 For Tolstoy, the Sermon on the Mount Is All the Bible You Really Need

For Tolstoy, the Sermon on the Mount (which expressed the Doctrine of Jesus, which he later referred to as the New Life-Conception) was the most important and most inspired part of the Christian Bible:

> To me [the Sermon on the Mount] has always been the substance of Christianity.... [Hoping to find what his heart recognized as truth in the religion taught by the Orthodox Church], I soon saw that I should not find in its creed the confirmation of the essence of Christianity; what was to be essential seemed to be in the dogma of the Church merely an accessory. What was to be the most important teaching of Jesus was not so regarded by the Church.... Of all the other portions of the Gospels, the Sermon on the Mount always had for me an exceptional importance. I now read it more frequently than ever. Nowhere does Jesus speak with greater solemnity, nowhere does he propound moral rules more definitely and practically, nor do these rules in any other form awaken more readily an echo in the human heart; nowhere else does he address himself to a larger multitude of the common people. If there are any clear and precise Christian principles, one ought to find them there. (WB, 13–14)

For Tolstoy, the rest of the Gospels, including the miracles (GB, 9–10) and even the Resurrection of Christ himself were deemed unnecessary to establish the divinity of the Doctrine of Jesus contained in the Sermon on the Mount (WB, 99f.). As curious (or misguided) as his disinterest in the miracles of Jesus may be, he viewed them as a potential distraction to the believer (KG, 55). Vital to properly understanding Tolstoy's disdain for miracles and the mystical, consideration must be given to the fact that the Russian Orthodox Church was his context, an Orthodoxy that revered the miraculous relics and icons encouraging adherents to adore, kiss and kneel before these artefacts. In that context Tolstoy came to believe all that to be mystical, superstitious chicanery and a grand diversion away from simple obedience to the plain teaching of the miracle worker himself. There is much to say about Tolstoy's *Gospel in Brief* and the misinformation that surrounds it. Though it has been compared to *The Jefferson Bible* (see subsection 1.5) for all that it omits, Tolstoy's *Gospel in Brief* was intended only to capture mainly the teaching ministry of Jesus.[1] The teaching ministry of Jesus was, for Tolstoy, the substance of the Gospel. His *Gospel in Brief* is brief, but his much longer

---

1. Levitysky, "Tolstoy Gospel," 347–55.

Harmony of the Gospel is over 800 pages and includes all the events, miracles and stories he is accused of omitting.[2] Though the Bible for Tolstoy would have meant the Eastern Orthodox canon of seventy-six books, it was not the case that he deemed each book equally inspired or equally important. In a quote some attribute to him sentiments that are very much Tolstoyan are conveyed: "To believe that everything in a book considered holy is true is idolatry of books."[3] For Tolstoy, the divinity of the One who gave the Sermon on the Mount is sufficiently evident in the content of the message itself and even miracles are not needed to convince people otherwise. Though he drew from other parts of the canonical Bible, both Old and New Testaments, the Sermon on the Mount was scripture enough for Tolstoy to follow Christ as Lord.

3.1.1 Tolstoy atop Mars Hill; Religious Pluralism or Moral Universalism

Tolstoy's well-known interest in, and even high regard for some aspects of Eastern religious teaching, philosophy and wisdom traditions and the sacred texts of other religious and secular philosophers has left him open to the charge of religious pluralism. Shortly it will be shown how the Sermon on the Mount and the Gospels were for Tolstoy the texts by which these other texts were tested for truth. Even so, undeniably there was for Tolstoy a wider canon as a source of Truth and he did not hesitate to draw spiritual wisdom grabbing general revelation he believed was articulated in the traditions and texts of other religious thinkers and philosophers, of every age. A very concentrated and now convenient source to analyze this wider canon of inspiration and divine guidance is in his *Calendar of Wisdom* (1904), sometimes called his *Circle of Reading*.

Over the course of a couple decades in his later life (earliest mention of his interest in such a project was in 1884, notation below) Tolstoy developed a collection of sacred sayings and texts, grouping many of them by themes, adding a few sentences of his own and placing 3–5 pithy wisdom statements per day—his *Circle of Reading* became a collection for 365 days of the year exposing the reader to what Tolstoy deemed the best in sacred wisdom and truth from a wide circle of contributors, classic and modern. At first glance the format appears to be that of a Christian daily devotional book with a

---

2. Matual, *Tolstoy's Translation of the Gospels*, 31–35.

3. Not presently able to confirm the authenticity of this statement attributed to Tolstoy. Gleaned from here: https://twitter.com/tolstoysays/status/637076732923674624 and it circulates elsewhere on the internet as a Tolstoy quotation.

reading for each day of the year. However, a closer look reveals it is more of a spiritual or general spirituality book than any sort of Christian one, at least it would appear so to one not used to seeing the sacred writings of other religions being used to, by and large, reinforce what certainly is true according to the Christian Scriptures. In the main, the non-Christian citations are congruent with Scriptural truth.

Tolstoy was near the top of a very short list of the most widely read people in the world at that time. His 22,000 volume personal library with books in forty languages at Yasnaya Polyana easily demonstrates that claim (Dr. Galina Alexeeva at Yasnaya Polyana has undertaken an enormous "Tolstoy and World Literature" project and so far has carefully catalogued 5000+ of his books, including his personal notations, into a multi-volume, annotated bibliography). Tolstoy's *Circle of Reading* places him most comfortably atop Mars Hill engaging respectfully with the prophets, philosophers and poets of the day—pulling truth, virtue and wisdom out of their own best thinkers and revealing how what they knew in part came most clearly in the Gospels and the Doctrines of Jesus. Publication of *Circle of Reading* in Russia ceased from 1912 all the way until 1995 when democratic reforms took place there. The first English translation appeared in 1997 by Peter Sekirin who wrote: "This was Tolstoy's last major work. . . . It was his own favourite everyday reading, a book he would turn to regularly for the rest of his life."[4] The March 15, 1884, entry in Tolstoy's diary says: "I have to create a circle of reading for myself: Epictetus, Marcus Aurelius, Lao-Tzu, Buddha, Pascal, The New Testament. This is also necessary for all people."[5] Sekirin made a case in his introduction to the *Circle of Reading* for how significant a book this was for Tolstoy referencing a 1885 letter to his colleague Vladimir Chertkov:

> I know that it gives one great inner force, calmness, and happiness to communicate with the great thinkers as Socrates, Epictetus, Arnold, Parker. . . . They tell us about what is most important for humanity, about the meaning of life and about virtue. . . . I would like to create a book . . . in which I could tell a person about his life, and about the Good Way of Life.[6]

It was late in 1902 when he first started writing the *Circle of Reading*.

All total, not including himself, Tolstoy drew from 143 religious figures, sacred texts, thinkers and philosophers. Tolstoy's wider canon of truth even included some of his contemporaries which he justified as such:

4. Tolstoy, *Calendar of Readings*, 6.
5. Tolstoy, *Calendar of Readings*, 6–7.
6. Tolstoy, *Calendar of Readings*, 6–7.

There is much good to be learned from the Koran, from the Buddhists, from Confucius, from the Old Testament, from the Indian Upanishads, and from the New Testament. But the closer religious thinker or philosopher is to us in time, the more he can help us draw from these teachings in the light of our present day lives.[7]

In alphabetical order this listing here is meant to demonstrate the breadth of the sources used most; Geneva philosopher Henri Frédéric Amiel (22 sayings included), second century Roman emperor and philosopher Marcus Aurelius (26), Chinese Proverbs (30), first century Roman philosopher and orator Marcus Tullius Cicero (20), Chinese philosopher Confucius (17), Eastern Wisdom (12), American poet Ralph Waldo Emerson (21), Greek philosopher Epictetus (15), Indian Proverb (19), German Philosopher Immanuel Kant (25), nineteenth century Italian leader in the struggle for Independence Giuseppe Mazzini (19), French mathematician and theologian Blaise Pascal (25), French philosopher Jean Jacques Rousseau (13), English author and critic John Ruskin (26), first century Roman Stoic philosopher Seneca (17), German philosopher Arthur Schopenhauer (15), nineteenth century American poet Henry David Thoreau (14), and the Talmud (38). To a lesser degree many others were included, including; St. Augustine (1), Black Hawk (1), Buddha (1), St. Chrysostom (5), Egyptian Wisdom (1), Erasmus (1), American economist Henry George (6), Russian Novelist Nikolai Gogol (3), Thomas Jefferson (2), Thomas à Kempis (1), Martin Luther (1), Mohammed (4), Greek historian Plutarch (3), sixteenth century Dutch philosopher Benedictus Spinoza (4), seventeenth century French author Francois Voltaire (2) and Zoroaster, the founder of Zoroastrian religion (2). The most quoted source, other than himself, was the Christian Bible (69) and clearly in Tolstoy's own statements there is significant Christian content. Each of the 365 days readings, again, typically comprised of 4–5 short statements, begin with the first and last statement being from Tolstoy himself. Some days he only sited one or two other thinkers besides himself. Twenty-five of the 365 days he drew inspiration from no where or no one else except his own thoughts. The *Circle of Reading*, though widely sourced with many other thinkers through history is very much as compilation of Tolstoy's own wisdom as an aged, spiritual sage, and his own advice and insights for spiritual direction. Other thinkers are included where they support his own views.

It is also important and insightful to notice what Tolstoy did not include. Of the 69 references to canonical texts, 56 were text gleaned from

---

7. Tolstoy, *Calendar of Readings*, 303.

the four Gospels especially from the Sermon on the Mount. Notably, as mentioned above, there are 38 Talmudic texts but only four of the 69 canonical texts are from the Old Testament (one law text on land ownership; two psalms on muzzling the tongue and from the lips of children; and one prophetic text from Isaiah on hands stained with blood). Considering Tolstoy's general ill-regard for Paul and the rest of the New Testament it is no surprise to find only four texts in the entire work from Paul (against passing judgment on another, on the importance of every member of Christ's body, on not working yet eating, and the importance of testing everything).[8] If there is a glaring omission in Tolstoy's *Calendar of Wisdom* it is in the fact that he did not include even one Proverb or anything from the Biblical wisdom literature. The elevation of Gospel and Sermon on the Mount texts in the *Circle of Reading* is notable, and demonstrates his belief that in Jesus there was special revelation. Tolstoy believed the other traditions shared with Christianity general virtues for all humankind.

Tolstoy had come to believe truth and falsehood were both mixed, in good measure, into every faith and tradition; and certainly he believed this included the Christian faith and teaching by the time of Constantine and long thereafter. In embracing a particular religion's expression of truth he was not endorsing everything else the religion espoused. For example, he drew from Hindu wisdom traditions where they aligned with his adherence to the doctrines of Jesus but he definitively renounced eastern superstitions, including reincarnation, a rub that Gandhi asked him to retract. Tolstoy replied that he would not, and that he wished Gandhi would leave what he wrote alone. However, for the sake of the wider publication of the rest Tolstoy gave Gandhi license to amend as he desired for a wider Indian audience. Though modern Bahá'í adherents claim Tolstoy as an early endorser of their faith, it can only be said his praise was limited to that within Bahá'ísm which was congruent with his Sermon on the Mount convictions. In quotations that are dubiously attributed to him through Martha Root, an American Bahá'ín who claimed to have gleaned the citations from her conversations

---

8. Tolstoy's study had led him to the conclusion that the shift away from the teachings of Jesus started very early in the church, even with the Apostle Paul: "Therefore, the arbitrary separation of the metaphysical and ethical aspects of Christianity entirely disfigures the doctrine [of Jesus], and deprives it over every sort of meaning. The separation began with the preaching of Paul, who knew but imperfectly the ethical doctrine set forth in the Gospel of Matthew, and who preached a meta-physico-cabalistic theory entirely foreign to the doctrine of Jesus; and this theory was perfected under Constantine, when the existing pagan social organisation was proclaimed Christian simply by covering it with the mantle of Christianity." Tolstoy, *Kingdom of God Is within You*, 150–51.

with Tolstoy's former secretary, Valentin Bulgakov in 1927, Root presented Tolstoy as a hearty endorser of Baháísm:

> [Tolstoy speaking as recalled by Bulgakov and recorded by Root:] We spend our lives trying to unlock the mystery of the universe but there is a prisoner, Bahá'u'lláh, in Akka, Palestine, who had the key.[9]
>
> I sympathise with all my heart with Bábism, *insofar as* it preaches brotherhood and equality between all men, and the sacrifice of material life in the service of God.[10]
>
> Bábism, which has evolved into Baháísm, (Bahá'u'lláh), and which has its roots in Islam, is one of the highest and purest of religious teachings.[11]
>
> There exists the Bábi sect whose religious teachings are of a very high order. The successor to the Báb's cause, Bahá'u'lláh, was exiled by the Turkish authorities to Akka where his son now lives. The members of this sect recognise no external form of religion, and the basis of religion is, according to them, the goodness of life, that is to say, love for one's neighbour and non participation in the evil projects carried out by governments.[12]
>
> Very profound. I know of no other [religion] so profound.[13]

Much within that citation sounds like Tolstoy and is generally consistent with statements that are directly attributable to him. However, these statements, twice-filtered through others (two decades after the supposed fact), are still a misrepresentation if they are considered a Tolstoyan endorsement of all that is Baháísm.[14] Even granting some legitimacy to the accuracy of the quotations, a careful reading will not glance passed the words "*insofar as*" which limit Tolstoy's tolerance of Baháísm to the points of agreement it shares with his convictions rooted in his interpretations of the doctrines of Jesus. In his article *Tolstoy's Views on the Bahá'í and Mormon Faiths*, Serge van Neck noted:

---

9. Neck, "Tolstoy's Views on the Bahá'í and Mormon Faiths."
10. Stendardo, *Leo Tolstoy and the Bahá'í Faith*, 32–33. Italics added.
11. Stendardo, *Leo Tolstoy and the Bahá'í Faith*, 40.
12. Stendardo, *Leo Tolstoy and the Bahá'í Faith*, 43.
13. Stendardo, *Leo Tolstoy and the Bahá'í Faith*, 56.
14. Root, *Count Leo Tolstoy and the Baha'i Movement*.

Yet notwithstanding his obvious admiration and respect for the Baháʼí Faith, some of the teachings turned him off. Primary among these is the idea of the Manifestations of God as being fundamentally different from ordinary human beings, including their essential infallibility. For this reason his initial response to reading the Kitáb-i-Íqán (The Book of Certitude) was strongly negative, although that did not seem to diminish his appreciation for the Faith overall.[15]

Tolstoy believed: "We should teach our children those principles that are common to all religions– Buddhist, Muslim, Christian, Jewish, and so on, that is, for the moral science of love and the unification of all people."[16] Here too, a correct reading would be to say—insofar as these other faiths are congruent with the doctrines of Jesus they are to be well regarded; regardless of the source, there are universal truths to affirm.

Tolstoy was not a religious pluralist believing all paths divine, or even lead to the divine. For Tolstoy, the major religious traditions and founders had each come upon a measure of truth in their earliest quests for it. That universally regarded truth and absolutisms were discernible in the wider canon of religious and philosophical texts and traditions convinced Tolstoy of the reality and importance of a moral universalism, and was evidence to him that the same revelatory source was behind the common truths of love and universal brotherhood. He believed the doctrines of Jesus were not just for Christians, but that they were the divine way of life for all of the world, and this he found evident in the fact that many of these truths were not unique to Christianity. His method was similar to the method adopted for this dissertation; Tolstoy was not worried about what was wrong in the Koran, for example, or any other non-Christian or secular source. He was interested to commend what they got right and use it as a collaborative witness to the way espoused by Christ. Tolstoy certainly treated his own religious tradition, Christianity, more harshly than the traditions of others. It is not likely he was oblivious to how evil masquerades as an angel of light as he spent most of his energies in the latter period of his life fighting this very thing within Christendom. With such a log in the eye of the doctrines and traditions of Christendom, rather than point out a speck in another traditions he generally treated them with respect and had regard for what he believed they got right.

---

15. Neck, "Tolstoy's Views on the Baháʼí and Mormon Faiths," 4.
16. Tolstoy, *Calendar of Readings*, 288.

3.2 A New Life-Conception Is Tolstoy's Term for the Teaching within the Sermon on the Mount

In the nine intervening years between the publishing of Tolstoy's first and second books on Sermon on the Mount obedience there were minor progressions or developments of his thought on matters related to the central themes of these works. One notable development in those intervening years is in how he had become aware of the various forerunners in earlier centuries who shared his reading of the teaching of Jesus and similar interpretations, particularly on non-resistance and war, and the Constantinian shift which justified the antithesis of Sermon on the Mount living. Whereas in the earlier book he wrote with no mention of others who had or were also discovering Jesus' teaching anew for the first time in 1800 years, in the second book he began with an entire chapter devoted to the support of his positions by earlier people and groups. The chapter title explains: "Doctrine of Non-Resistance to Evil From the Origin of Christianity, Has Been and Still Is, Professed by the Minority of Men." As novel as his Sermon on the Mount interpretations and applications may have seemed to him in 1884, he was not feeling so alone by 1893. Citing the support of others adds credibility to one's conclusions which perhaps lends to a wider reading, increased acceptability and receptivity, something any author would want especially one whose books and pamphlets were being censured as were Tolstoy's.

A second discernible progression of thought between his 1884 and 1893 publications on the same subject matter has to do with definitional clarity. Consistently in his first work he referred to the Doctrine *of Jesus*. Nine years later he exclusively referred to this as the Doctrine *of Christ*. There is no place where he explained this subtle shift in the direction toward divinity in reference to the teaching of Jesus of Nazareth leaving the reader to draw their own conclusions. Tolstoy did reject Albert Schweitzer's predecessors, the Strausses and Renans, and their search for the historical Jesus and became increasingly convinced that the teaching of Jesus was divine, the only Way, the Truth and the Life (WB, 36). Even so, at best Tolstoy's was a low Christology as he rejected the Trinity accepting the divinity of Christ's teaching but not the divinity of Jesus. William Nickell summaries this well:

> Tolstoy's Christ underscores a key element in Tolstoy's debate with the Church; for all his belief in God Tolstoy nonetheless joined in the modern deconstruction of Christian metaphysics. When he argued that "The Kingdom of God Is Within You" he described a Protestant sense of personal ethical responsibility but also a different relationship to God. He had resolved an existential crisis by finding faith in a mortal Christ who had offered

redemption to humanity not by dying on the cross but by living a moral life.[17]

Whereas the Church was adhering to the divinity of the teacher, Tolstoy's concern was in the divinity of the teaching.[18]

The most important definitional development between the 1884 and 1893 books is that by 1893 Tolstoy was speaking of the teaching of Jesus as a "New Life-Conception." This phrase does not appear in the 1884 work but rose to subtitle status, or even alternative title status, for the 1893 work: "*The Kingdom of God Is within You: Or, Christianity not as a Mystical Doctrine, But as a New Life-Conception.*" In the preface of this book he stated his primary aim to communicate "three principle ideas – the first, that Christianity is not only the worship of God and a doctrine of salvation, but is above all things a new conception of life which is changing the whole fabric of society" (KG, 7). In chapter two he stated "to set forth that conception of Christ and his doctrine has been the object of my book" (KG, 46). Tolstoy's word *conception*, the Russian концепция or kontseptsiya, means idea, concept or conception. As he used the word in context, repeatedly, the meaning of a frame of mind, or framework of belief, or worldview, each help to more fully capture his probable meaning. If Tolstoy were writing to the twenty-first century reader it could be he would make his case arguing the Sermon on the Mount is an alternative lifestyle choice, a higher and better way of living, a divine pattern for life for relating to God and others. Even though no one in the past one hundred years has re-translated these two books for the reader today, it is doubtful a better or more contemporary word than *conception* would convey the correct meaning to the modern reader.

Tolstoy wrote of this New Life-Conception, this higher way of life, in the context of naming other lower, life-conceptions—particularly the animal life-conception and slightly higher social life-conception. The third and highest conception he considered to be this New Life-Conception of the Sermon on the Mount: "Thus far there have been three of these, life-conceptions; two of them belong to a bygone era, while the third is of our

17. Nickell, *The Death of Tolstoy*, 58.

18. Earlier in subsection 2.1 Tolstoy was quoted: "Understanding this, I understood and believed that Jesus is not only the Messiah, that is, the Anointed One, the Christ, but that he is in truth the Saviour of the World. I know that he is the only way, that there is no other way for me or for those who are tormented with me in this life. I know, that for me as for all, there is no other safety than the fulfilment of the commandments of Jesus, who gave to all humanity the greatest conceivable sum of benefits" (WB, 111). My subsequent comment was "whether or not this a sufficient confession for Christian salvation remains contentious." To repeat the intention of this project, the interest is in what Tolstoy got right about Sermon on the Mount obedience and not so much on what he got wrong from the vantage point of traditional orthodoxy.

own and is called Christianity.... These three life-conceptions are – firstly, the individual or animal; secondly, the social or pagan; and thirdly, the universal or divine.... History is but the transcript of the gradual transition from the animal life-conception of the individual to the social, and from the social to the divine" (KG, 82–83). In his philosophy of history this animal life-conception referred to the earliest times of "primeval savagery, to the lowest dregs not only of pagan life, but of animal life, which we outlived 5000 years ago" (KG, 120). The subsequent shift to a social life-conception is not given any specific dating by Tolstoy except that as history progressed humanity moved away from "his life's object [being to] gratify his desires ... to gratify[ing] the will of communities and individuals" (KG, 82). The Classical Period of 500–300 BC, considered the golden age of philosophy in Greece, might be the most likely place Tolstoy would mark this second shift in life-conceptions. Tolstoy dated the Sermon on the Mount eighteen centuries ago as the beginning of the shift from the social to the New Life-Conception. "[T]he doctrine of Christ is not a doctrine of rules for man to obey, but unfolds a new life-conception, meant as a guide for men who are now entering a new period, one entirely different from the past" (KG, 100).

In developing the notion of this New Life-Conception, Tolstoy further parsed out and identified two fallacious conceptions of life and Christianity; the churchman's conception and the scientific conception, respectively. The former could be considered the deceptive counterfeit within Christendom of the real, and the latter could be understood as the short-sightedness of science as a conception unable to conceive anything beyond the temporal and material. In Christ-like manner, Tolstoy reserved his harshest criticisms for the religious leaders: "The activity of the Russian Church, despite the veneer of modernity ... consists not only in encouraging the people in a course and grotesque idolatry, but in the strengthening and promulgating superstition and religious ignorance, and in endeavouring to destroy the vital conception of Christianity that exists in the people side by side with this idolatry" (KG, 73). From that statement he proceeded to tell a story of visiting a monastery and watching an old peasant be able to purchase every sort of religious trinket, icon, relic and holy day description but not being able to buy a Russian Bible. He wrote that all the while the true conception of a Christian exists and is clear, it continues to seem vague to those who should be the very stewards of it: "its sense has become more and more vague, reaching at last such a degree of obscurity that men fail to understand the simplest commands expressed in the Bible, even when couched in the plainest possible language" (KG, 51). That plainest possible language was the doctrine of Jesus in the Sermon on the Mount, this New Life-Conception, and yet the churchman's conception was the only acceptable view.

Similarly, Tolstoy found the scientific conception to be just as fallacious and the Sermon on the Mount to represent the antithesis of the superior race and dysgenic race theories gaining wider and wider popularity during his time.[19] For Tolstoy, the Sermon on the Mount was incompatible with the notion of survival of the fittest as it commanded a concern for all of humanity. Darwinian militarism stood directly opposed to the teaching of the one who told us to love enemies. Perhaps it could be said that Tolstoy viewed Darwinism as the antithesis to the Sermon on the Mount and its greatest conceptual enemy (more on this theme in subsection 9.1). Tolstoy would no doubt have concurred with the comments of a later devotee of Tolstoyan religious writings—William Jennings Bryan, the American politician and lawyer of the famed Scopes Trial on evolution theory. Bryan contended Darwinism aided in "lay[ing] the foundation for the bloodiest war in history."[20] For Tolstoy, these other life-conceptions were not simply benign errors in understanding. They were the very wide and popular life-paths that led exactly where the Sermon on the Mount said they would lead, to destruction individually and collectively (Matt 7:13–14). At the onset of a new century of horrific global wars, holocausts and genocides, Tolstoy's prophetic warnings and invitations to embrace this New Life-Conception were by and large unheeded.

3.3 For Tolstoy, Resist not Evil (Matt 5:39) Is the Key to the Rest of the Sermon on the Mount; In Fact It Is the Essence of Christianity

Commonplace in Sermon on the Mount studies is to regard the Beatitudes as a grand preamble to a Constitution of the Kingdom of God, or to regard the Sermon on the Mount as the essence of Jesus' teaching and the Beatitudes as the essence of the essence. In Tolstoy's engagements with the Sermon on the Mount, the Beatitudes take a back seat while the texts that underscore enemy love are brought to the forefront: "This was the passage that gave me the key to the whole: 'Ye have heard that it hath been said, an eye for an eye, and a tooth for a tooth: but I say unto you, that ye resist not evil' (Matt. 5:38–39). . . . These words, 'Resist not evil' when I understood their significance, were the key that opened up all of the rest. Then I was astonished that I had failed to comprehend words so clear and precise" (WB, 16–17). "When I apprehended clearly the words 'Resist not evil' my conception of

---

19. Vucinich, *Darwin in Russian Thought*.
20. Bryan, *In His Image*, 124–25.

the doctrine of Jesus was entirely changed; and I was astounded, not that I have failed to understand it before, but that I had misunderstood it so strangely. . . . When we say, 'Turn the other cheek' 'Love your enemies,' we express the very essence of Christianity" (KG, 19).

In the preface to *The Kingdom of God Is within You* Tolstoy began: "In this book I have endeavoured to show that our modern Christianity has been tried and found wanting, that the armed camp of Europe is not Christian, but Pagan, as is latter-day religion, of which the present state of affairs is the outcome" (KG, 7). Tolstoy viewed the "principle deviation" from the doctrine of Christ to be "the evasion of the commandment that forbids man to resist evil by violence, as a striking example of the perversion of the doctrine of Christ by ecclesiastical interpretation" (KG, 7). Convinced he had uncovered the essence of true Christianity and Christlikeness in resist not evil, Tolstoy measured everything against that standard; the New Testament letters, the early church fathers, the commentaries of the faith, the creeds of the Church, the claims of Church after Constantine that Christians could be soldiers, and the armed nations that consider themselves Christian. All of the above he tried and found wanting. He was not even willing to consider any of it pseudo-Christianity, if it tolerated retaliation and violence he considered it entirely pagan. Immediately after Jesus said love enemies he said in Matthew 5:46–47: "If you love only those who love you, what reward will you get? . . . Do not even pagans do that?" For the Christian, the calling is greater than loving and protecting your own family and country. There is nothing unique, spiritual or Christlike about that at all. Tolstoy's uncovering of this essence of Christianity launched him into a very unsettled season in his long conversion as it was his hope to find the Doctrine of the Church he was reared in to be true to the faith. However he found in the doctrines of the Church, particularly after Constantine (see chapter 6 on Tolstoy and the Constantinian Heresy), the very opposite of the value system of Christ and he rejected nearly every aspect of both eastern and western orthodox dogma and devotion. Much like the one who found the pearl of great price, to obtain the field containing that treasure, Tolstoy dispensed of nearly everything else, including the written law of the Old Testament. Granted, for Tolstoy, his devotion to the treasure was more about the divine pathway than the person of Christ himself. For Tolstoy, the essence of Christianity was not so much the person and work of Christ except to the degree it can be said that Christ loved and died for his enemies, and this is also the very essence of those who seek to be like him, and are called by his name.

3.4 Tolstoy Believed the Sermon on the Mount Is Not to Be Interpreted as an Ethic for an Ascetic Withdrawal from the World, nor Is Its Application Limited to Interpersonal Relationships

The two main interpretive questions when approaching the Sermon on the Mount are: (1) Is it liveable? and (2) To whom is it for? The first question is about attainability. Certainly Tolstoy believed Jesus gave attainable expectations for his followers on the mountainside that day. Tolstoy can be listed among the few interpreters of the Sermon on the Mount who believed Jesus meant for his followers exactly what he said to those who would be called his followers. For Tolstoy it was folly to convince oneself that Jesus said all he said though neglected to mention his teaching would not work in the complexity of their real world. The second question concerns the intended audience. Was the Sermon on the Mount a micro-ethic only for the small interactions believers have with each other, or did he intend for both micro and macro applications, adherence and obedience to his teaching? Was its application to be limited only to interpersonal relationships or even more limited to the extra-spiritual lifestyles of those of some monastic order, or does the Sermon on the Mount also have bearing on the international policies of a Prime Minister, President or Monarch who bends his/her knee before the Lordship of Christ?

Though attracted to the monastic order having visited monasteries several times in his life, and at key points in his life, Tolstoy found the Sermon on the Mount impossible to live in such seclusion. He believed this Doctrine of Christ should be proclaimed from the rooftop until "this doctrine penetrates every phase of human life, domestic, economical, civil, politic, and international" (KG, 51). He rejected the notion that there were only two ways; either (a) "to participate in the organised evil about us, or [(b)] to forsake the world and take refuge in a convent or monetary . . . [which is] to renounce life for what is the equivalent to slow suicide." He continued: "The erroneous belief that it is better for a man to retire from the world than to expose himself to temptations . . . is entirely foreign . . . to the spirit of Christianity . . . [so we] ought not to fly from men, but live in communion with them" (WB, 123). "The principle commandments of Jesus are that his followers shall love others and spread this doctrine. Both exact constant communion with the world. And yet the deduction is made that the doctrine of Jesus permits retirement from the world. That is, to imitate Jesus we may do exactly contrary to what he taught and did himself" (WB, 124). "Jesus did not teach salvation by faith in asceticism or voluntary torture.... Jesus told men that in practising his doctrine among unbelievers they would be, not more unhappy, but, on the contrary, much more happy, than those who did not practice it" (WB, 125).

At the onset of the long and yet ongoing era of Constantinian Christianity (again, see chapter 6 regarding this Constantinian shift), it became the primary rationale for rejecting the demands of the Sermon on the Mount to conclude they apply only to individuals and have no bearing on Christians in positions of government or authority; nor that it is applicable to Christian soldiers who are merely in the service of government. Effectually any real application of the Sermon on the Mount, particularly loving enemies, is reasoned away and, Tolstoy believed, Christians fall to the spirit of vengeance becoming as bloodthirsty in war as pagans. Yet, regarding pagans, in Matthew 6:3, Jesus said "do not be like them." Appearing in the very centre of the Sermon on the Mount, that verse captures the central matter of the Sermon, that Christians have been given a very different value system which should govern their interactions with others in the world around them. They are now those who turn the other cheek. To the degree that Christians retaliate and disobey the command to turn the other cheek, they forfeit Christlikeness. It was this very obvious but unfortunate self-contradiction (that Christians look nothing like the Sermon on the Mount) that so deeply concerned Tolstoy.

For Tolstoy the matter was settled with clarity via a couple of simple word studies from one text: "You have heard that it was said, 'Love your neighbour and hate your enemy.' But I tell you: Love your enemies." Tolstoy explained: "[N]eighbour in the Hebrew language meant, invariably and exclusively, 'a Hebrew'" (WB, 72). He noted it is the same word and meaning as in Luke 10:29 where the "neighbour" is a Samaritan– someone a Hebrew would have clearly not regarded as a neighbour. Finding the same meaning in Acts 7:27, his conclusion is "'neighbour' in Gospel language, means a compatriot, a person belonging to the same nationality. Therefore the antithesis used by Jesus in the citation, 'love thy neighbour, hate thine enemy,' must be in the distinction between the words 'compatriot' and 'foreigner.'" Tolstoy contended his supposition was further confirmed when seeking the Jewish understanding of enemy. "The word enemy is nearly always employed in the Gospels in the sense, not of a personal enemy, but, in general, of a 'hostile people'" (WB, 72).

Based on the words Jesus used, Tolstoy's conclusion was that it is not possible that Jesus intended his teaching to be applicable only on the interpersonal level. Tolstoy spoke of the widening sphere of love and believed a nation could be loved:

> After having transferred the consciousness and love for the individual to the family, and from the family to the race, the nation, and the state, it would be perfectly logical for me, in order to escape the strife and disasters that result from the division of mankind into nations and states, to transfer their love to humanity at large.... Where does it end and where does it begin? Does it exclude the savage, the idiot, the inebriate, the insane? If one were to draw a line of demarcation so as to exclude the lower representatives of the human race, where ought it to be drawn? Ought it to exclude the Negro, as they do in the United States, or the Hindus, as some Englishmen do, or the Jews, as does another nation. (KG, 95)

Jesus never differentiated between loving a neighbour and loving a neighbouring nation.

3.5 Tolstoyan Sermon on the Mount Interpretations Led Him to Radicalized Applications Far Surpassing Common Christian Devotional Practice and Lifestyle

The Sermon on the Mount demands a different lifestyle. One can not embrace it and remain as they were. It was intended to change people and make them like Christ. Adherents to this inaugural address of the Kingdom of God should look different and live different having encountered Christ on the Mount. In his epistle James distinguished between hearers and doers and this is what sets Tolstoy in a league of his own as a Sermon on the Mount interpreter. He allowed the Sermon on the Mount to change his life; how he spent money, how he spent his time, what he ate, how he treated people and animals, how he related to enemies and government, the aristocracy and the poor, clerics and the Church. The Sermon on the Mount changed his ambitions, how he worked, how he played. It changed who he was and who he wanted to be. It changed the entire course of his life; it took over his life and possessed him, and he used the language of possession to describe the location and depth of grip the Sermon on the Mount had on him. What is unique about his Sermon on the Mount interpretations can be seen in his radicalized applications; prohibiting and/or discouraging sex and even marriage, living in cities, eating meat, owning private property, military conscription and oath swearing for country, judging in the court system; and advocating anti-clericalism, anti-death penalty, non-retaliation, non-violence, anti-war and an early form of Christian political anarchy.

Each of Tolstoy's seemingly radical applications came from his exegesis of the text of Matthew 5–7. For each it would take a paragraph even to briefly sketch his justifications. A more thorough analysis of several of these main radicalizations is forthcoming in subsequent chapters of this book. One example will suffice for the purposes of this chapter and suffice in concluding this section. Careful word studies from the text of the Sermon on the Mount provided for Tolstoy the clarity to make applications that challenged long-accepted and seemingly justifiable practices in civilised society, like participation in tribunals and courts of justice. In Matthew 7:1 Jesus famously said "Do not judge, or you too will be judged" just prior to his admonition that his followers inspect the fruit of others and make a judgment as to whether it be good or bad. "Judge not" has long been a difficult text for Christians who know intuitively God would not be asking them to turn off their conscience capacity to discern right from wrong, or good from evil. Among the generally Biblically-illiterate population of secular society this text is well-known and Jesus' words here are often used against followers of Christ who appear so judgmental. Tolstoy entirely avoided this common misinterpretation by focusing on the meaning of the Greek word κρίνω, to judge or condemn. Tolstoy asserted that later commentators of the Church and translators, including Luther, were in error to change the meaning to, "to speak evil of." "I found that the word κρίνω had several different meanings, among the most used being to 'condemn in a court of justice,' and even 'to condemn to death,' but in no instance did it signify 'to speak evil'" (WB, 32). "I saw that Christianity before Constantine regarded tribunals only as evil which was to be endured with patience; but it never could have occurred to any early Christian that he could take part in the administration of the courts of justice. It is plain, therefore that Jesus words . . . were understood by his first disciples, as they ought to be understood now, in their direct and literal meaning; judge not in courts of justice; take no part in them" (WB, 30).

~ 4.0 ~

Divine Command Ethics
Universal Principles and Law in Second Tolstoy

> The doctrine of Christ is not a doctrine of rules for man to obey, but unfolds a new-life conception, meant as a guide for men who are now entering a new period, one entirely different from the past.
>
> —*The Kingdom of God Is within You*, 100

THE TWO RECURRENT INTERPRETATIVE questions in Sermon on the Mount studies are (1) Who is it for, and (2) Is it liveable? Regarding the first question, Tolstoy believed Jesus was speaking in the Sermon on the Mount far beyond the ears of the disciples and the crowds on this hillside that day to a very wide and ultimately international audience, to all of humanity about the revealed will of God for the way of life, and even to leaders of nation-states and not just narrowly to individual followers (previous chapter, subsection 3.4). Regarding the second question, Tolstoy was in meagre company believing the Sermon on the Mount was liveable. If it was not liveable, why else would Jesus have plainly told us to live this way? After an exhaustive analysis of nearly two dozen major Sermon on the Mount interpreters starting with Tolstoy on into the modern period, Clarence Bauman noted:

> With astounding ingenuity Christendom developed an amazing variety of reasons why one could not or should not obey the commandments of Jesus [in the Sermon on the Mount]. .

> .. Though an analysis of these various views reveals profound elements of truth in each, most of them nevertheless appear to imply (1) that either Jesus did not mean what he said or did not say what he meant or (2) that what he said applies either to a different time than now or in a different way than then. . . . The Sermon on the Mount has always been an embarrassment to the Church.[1]

Bauman found Tolstoy to be an exception and the structure of his book, by starting with Tolstoy, sets forth Tolstoy as the baseline for modern Sermon on the Mount interpretation as Tolstoy believed it was liveable while others after him generally devised rationalizations to deem it not (see subsection 5.6).[2] Tolstoy most certainly believed the Sermon on the Mount was liveable, even as weak followers of Christ, moral perfection is possible (subsection 4.1) and in part due to the dynamics of this new inner moral guidance (subsection 4.2).

This chapter is a continuation of the previous chapter in presenting a synthesis of the main and virtually unique distinctives of Tolstoy's Sermon on the Mount interpretation which emerge from the two primary works of

---

1. Bauman, *Sermon on the Mount*, 418.

2. Bauman penned a brilliant and helpful listing of his findings: "The Sermon on the Mount is the most important and most controversial biblical text. With incredible ingenuity and astounding diversity, scholars have debated its exegetical meanings, its theological presuppositions, and its ethical implications. In the hope of explaining to whom, when, and how it applies, the Sermon on the Mount has been either dramatised as *imitatio Christi* (St. Francis) or traumatised as Oriental impossibility (Naumann); either clericalised as counsels of perfection (Aquinas) or secularised as metaphysical mind science (Fox); either absolutised as impractical ideal (Kittel) or relativized as eschatological stimulus (Dibelius); either characterised as Jewish wisdom (Windisch) or de-judaised as Aryan humanisation (Müller); either universalised as timeless truth (Harnack) or historicised as a temporal event (Bornhäuser); either categorised as otherworldly (Weiss) or modernised as *Gesinnungsethik* [ethic of ethics] (Hermann); either dogmatised as divine grace (Barth) or rationalised as moral imperative (Kant); either actualised as the Christian way (Miller) or criticised as impossible law (Stange); either symbolised as Oriental hyperbole (Barton); or moralised as philosophy of life (Jones); either psychologised as mental health (Ligon) or romanticised as idyllic fantasy (Renan); either allegorised as Christology (Thurneysen) or sacramentalised as cultic liturgy (Städeli); either politicized as Christian Socialism (Ragaz) or individualised as impossible ideal (Niebuhr); either radicalised as *Nachfolge Christi* (Denck) or naturalised as ethic of creation (Wünsch); either literalised as *nova lex Christi* [new law of Christ] (Tolstoy) or demythologised as self-understanding (Bultmann); either dispensationalised as futuristic (Chafer) or spiritualised as illumination (Prabhavananda); either pragmatised as *satyagraha* (Gandhi) or compromised as ethical paradox (Bonhoeffer); either etherealised as mountain pathways (Waylan) or internalised as pietistic experience (Heim); either eschatologised as Interim Ethic (Schweitzer) or idealised as design for living (Hunter)" (Bauman, *Sermon on the Mount*, 3–4).

Tolstoy on the Sermon on the Mount (WB and KG). In five subsections, matters of Tolstoy's views on moral perfection, moral guidance, Eternal and Written Law and the five new commandments of Jesus are expounded. The chapter concludes with a discussion of moral authority and Tolstoyan obedience to the words of Jesus (the revelation of God on the mountainside) versus an adherence to Christian orthodoxy.

4.1 For Tolstoy, the Moral Perfection of Matthew 5:48 Is within Reach

The notion of moral perfection bears strongly on Tolstoyan Sermon on the Mount interpretation, especially as the Sermon on the Mount itself clearly calls for it: "Be perfect, therefore, as your heavenly Father is perfect" (Matt 5:48). There can hardly be a better starting place to make sense of Tolstoy's understanding of moral perfection than at the decisions he made in translating Matthew 5:48's, *be perfect*. In his *Harmony of the Four Gospels* he rendered verse 48, "Be therefore good to all men, as your father in heaven is good to all."[3] For Tolstoy, moral perfection and goodness were twins of sort but it is too much to say he conceived of them as identical twins, as synonyms. His notation on this translation decision was: "Here the perfection obviously means good which is not limited to certain people. And so I translate it by good" (HR, 263, 271). In interpreting Tolstoy, preference should be made to a simpler reading. As Tolstoy friend and biographer commented: "[Tolstoy] aimed at a direct simplicity of statement such as many writers carefully avoid."[4] To him perfection was simple, when Jesus said be perfect he simply meant be good and Tolstoy believed the Sermon on the Mount set the course of the good and perfect life. To be perfect he believed is to obey the precepts of the Sermon on the Mount: "if one takes the incentives to perfection offered by the teaching of Christ as laws which each man must obey" (KG, 88–89). Perhaps it can be said the twins of good and perfection are only realized in Sermon on the Mount obedience and that for Tolstoy, obedience to the good is moral perfection.

The main nuances of Tolstoy's understanding of moral perfection are most clear in two sections of chapters three and four of his *Kingdom of God*

---

3. Though Tolstoy did include this adapted rendering of Matthew 5:48 in his *Harmony of the Four Gospels*, he entirely left the verse out of his subsequent *Gospel in Brief* version of the Sermon on the Mount (as stated here in subsection 1.6: "Only a slight trace of this . . . can be discerned in the TGB at this point of omission where he begins 'Do good to men of your own nation . . .' and at the beginning of the next section on almsgiving, 'So if you do good to others. . .'").

4. Maude, *Life of Tolstoy, Vol. II*, 99.

Is within You (KG, 52–54, 88–93). Tolstoy understood the Sermon on the Mount to be a guide for interior moral perfection which Jesus repeatedly, in Matthew 5, set against the outward and external perfections of the Written Law.[5] Tolstoy believed "the attainment of this interior perfection was possible for men," and as a consequence of this attainable interior perfection, "the outward perfection foretold by the prophets: the coming of the Kingdom of God, when all enmity shall cease" can be realized (KG, 52). Interior perfection, Tolstoy wrote, "[takes] Christ for our model, and to advance in the direction of interior perfection by the road which has been pointed out for us, as well as in that of exterior perfection, which is the establishment of the Kingdom of God" (KG, 53). Clearly Christ came not only to make humanity more like himself (Christ-like, good and perfect, à la Godly or God-like) but to bring the good and perfect of his Kingdom beyond the individual to the broader society, social life and civilization. Tolstoy would reject any notion of an instantaneous sanctification, or entire sanctification in a Wesleyan-Holiness sense, and taught moral perfection as a process, including there being degrees of perfection (KG, 53). He viewed the opposite of "advanc[ing] toward perfection" and "movement toward perfection" as "the stagnation of the righteous Pharisee," it being much better to even slightly advance toward perfection like Zacchaeus the Publican, the adulteress, or the thief on the cross (KG, 53); the "fulfilment of the doctrine [quoting Matt 5:48—be perfect] lies in a continual progress towards the attainment of a higher truth, and in the growing realisation of that truth within one's self, by means of an ever-increasing love; as well as in a more and more keen realisation of the Kingdom of God in the world around us" (KG, 54).

Regarding the degrees of perfection, Tolstoy differentiated between the "infinite perfection of the Heavenly Father, to which it is natural for every man to aspire, whatever may be his shortcoming" and simply "perfection" which, for clarity sake can be construed as simple perfection (KG, 89). Absolute or infinite divine perfection is the ideal according to Tolstoy, whereas simple perfection is for the believer to take a step in the direction of that ideal. Tolstoy determined the five new commandments according to his interpretation of Matthew 5 were five "mile stones on the infinite road

---

5. There are brief additional places within *Second Tolstoy* where moral perfection is treated. Related to Tolstoy's view of internal or external/outward perfection, Tolstoy wrote two decades later in his 1902 *What Is Religion* treatise: "The law of human life is of such a nature that the improvement of life, of the individual as well as of society, is possible only by inward moral perfecting. Whereas all the efforts of men to improve their life by external influence and coercion serve as the most effective propaganda and example of evil, and therefore fail not only to improve life but on the contrary increase the evil." See Tolstoy, *What Is Religion? And Other Writings*, 49.

to perfection, toward which humanity is struggling, they mark the degrees of perfection which it is possible for [humanity] to attain" (KG, 92). Tolstoy believed these new commandments were liveable, and simple perfection to be attainable: "we must labour now to acquire by degrees habits of self-restraint, until such habits become second nature. . . . [These new commandments] are but stepping-stones on the way to perfection, and must necessarily be followed by higher and still higher ones, as men pursue the course towards perfection" (KG, 93). The ideal "is to bear no malice, excite no ill will, and to love all men. . . . [T]he ideal is perfect chastity in thought [and] purity in married life. . . . [T]he ideal is to take no thought for the morrow, to live in the present . . . taking [no] oath or making promises for the future. . . . [T]he ideal is to use no violence whatsoever . . . return good for evil, endure injuries with patience, and give up the cloak to him who has taken the coat" (KG, 92–93). These, for Tolstoy were stepping stones on Christ's path toward moral perfection. Tolstoy wrote: "God's perfection is the asymptote[6] of human life, towards which it is forever inspiring and drawing nearer, although it can only reach its goal in the infinite" (KG, 90). In geometrical terms Tolstoy was seeking to illustrate God's perfection is continually before the Christian and simple perfection is attainable as the believer (in obedience to the Sermon on the Mount) takes a step toward God's infinite perfection, the consequence of such a step which will be the attainment of good for the individual and another step toward the goodness of God's Kingdom coming to the world.

4.2 Tolstoy Differentiated between Moral Guidance by External Precept or Law, and Internal Moral Guidance by Being Shown the Ideal in the Sermon on the Mount, and Having This Ideal Directing and Leading from Within

Tolstoy believed the Sermon on the Mount articulated the ideal which, when internalized, became the divine voice for moral guidance: "The doctrine of Christ differs from former doctrines in that it influences men not by outward observations, but by the interior consciousness that divine perfection may be attained" (KG, 90). "A Christian, therefore, who submits to the inner, the divine law, is . . . unable to execute the biddings of the outward law when they are at variance with his consciousness of God's law of love" (KG, 189). In Tolstoy's 1889 *Postface to The Kreutzer Sonata* he explained

---

6. In geometry an asymptote is a straight line that continually approaches a given curve but does not meet it at any finite distance.

clearly his view of two different types of moral guidance, internalized and externalized moral guidance:

> Just as there are two ways of indicating to the traveller the path he should follow, so there are two methods of moral guidance for the person who is seeking the truth. One of these consists in pointing out to the person the landmarks he must encounter, and in him setting his course by these landmarks. The other method consists simply in giving the person a reading on the compass he carries with him; he keeps reading as he travels, and by means of it he is able to perceive his slightest deviation from the correct path.[7]

Tolstoy differentiated between moral guidance by external precept or law, and internal moral guidance by being shown the ideal, and having this ideal within, and having the Spirit of Jesus within empowering this journey toward the ideal.

> A person who follows the external law is like someone standing in the light of a lantern that is suspended from a post. He stands in the light shed by this lantern, its light is sufficient for him, and he has no need to go further. A person who follows the teaching of Christ is like someone carrying a lantern before him on the end of a pole of indeterminate length; its light is always in front of him, it constantly prompts him to follow it and at each moment reveals to him a new expanse of terrain that draws him towards it.... It is not a difference in moral demands, but in the way human beings are guided.[8]

The differentiation between external and internal moral guidance is a recurring and dominant theme in the Sermon on the Mount: "you have heard it was said, "Do not commit adultery, but I tell you even a lustful look is a violation." This major interpretive key to the entirety of the Sermon on the Mount is to perceive the monumental change Jesus brought to the dynamic of internal versus external righteousness.

The Sermon begins with eight Beatitudes where the main focus of the first seven is on qualities and characteristics of a righteousness (a Christ-likeness) that, when internalized, will result in the follower of Christ being persecuted for righteousness sake, the eighth Beatitude. The disciple is then encouraged to affect the world around them sometimes only influencing in invisible ways (salt being invisible when it is working) and other times in

---

7. Tolstoy, *Kreutzer Sonata*, 304.
8. Tolstoy, *Kreutzer Sonata*, 305.

visible ways (light as visible influence). Jesus challenged an ascetic lifestyle lived sequestered and hidden under a bushel (Matt 5:16) to a far greater visibility: "In the same way, let your light shine before men that they may see your good deeds and praise your father in heaven." Shortly later however, in Matthew 6:1, he seemingly said the exact opposite: "Be careful not to let your 'acts of righteousness' before men, to be seen by them. If you do you will have no reward from your father in heaven." In the life of the disciple there are these two antithetical temptations; the temptation toward timidity and the temptation toward vainglory. Tolstoy took issue with the monks, the "misguided Jonahs" who, "wishing to remain upright and virtuous, retire from the perverse companionship of men" (WB, 123) as much as he took issue with the parade of clerics in full costume marching through the streets of Moscow: "the ugly idol called the Iverskaya, sacrilegiously carried around Moscow by intoxicated men.... [I]t is only an external worship in the form of idolatry that is propagated" (KG, 70). This tension in the Sermon on the Mount between hiding and showing can be understood best by Jesus speaking words of truth to those who have either succumb to the one temptation or the other. To the ascetic tempted with timidity to hide, Jesus called them forth to show as a light for the world to see. To the ostentatious tempted with religious vainglory Jesus in effect said; but then hide when you are tempted to show. Jesus continued on in chapter six with teachings on hidden giving, not letting your left hand know what your right hand is doing, hidden prayer having a secret life with God, and hidden devotion such as fasting.

In the Sermon on the Mount Jesus called his disciples to a "righteousness [that] surpasses that of the Pharisees and the teachers of the law" (Matt 5:20). The Pharisees and teachers of the law had 248 commandments and 365 prohibitions on their law books, totalling 613. Tolstoy did not interpret these words of Jesus to mean he expected his followers to have and obey at least 614. In fact, Tolstoy interpreted Jesus to reduce all this down even from Ten Commandments to five new commandments he found in chapter five of the Sermon on the Mount. The difference in part, as will be discussed shortly, is the difference between what Tolstoy viewed as the Written Law as opposed to the Eternal Law. For our purposes at this point, the difference in part was a difference between internalized moral guidance and external moral guidance. Tolstoy viewed the Sermon on the Mount as a disruptive force with explosive power to change society and bring the Kingdom of God on earth. He understood this great external change to begin small and within: "The disruptive movement must come from within when the molecule releases its hold on molecule and the whole mass falls into disintegration... This work has been going on for eighteen hundred years. It began when the commandments of Jesus were first given to humanity, and it will not cease till, as Jesus said, '*all things be accomplished*' (Matt. v. 18)" (WB, 179):

> In order to fulfil the doctrine it needs but to take Christ for our model, and to advance in the direction of interior perfection by the road which has been pointed out to us, as well as that of exterior perfection, which is the establishment of the Kingdom of God. (KG, 53)

> The Christian doctrine is not a law which, being introduced by violence, can forthwith change in the life of mankind. Christianity is a life-conception more lofty and excellent than the ancient; and such a new conception of life cannot be enforced; it must be adopted voluntarily, and by two processes, the spiritual or interior process, and the experimental or external process. (KG, 165)

This internal or spiritual reception of the Kingdom of God, for Tolstoy, amounted to the colossal shift Jesus announced that day on that mountainside. He wrote of "the necessity of adopting the Christian ideal, which is subversive of the very structure of our social existence" (KG, 120).

4.3 For Tolstoy, Distinguishing between an Eternal Law and the Written Law Is the Only Way to Make Sense of Matthew 5:17-20

Plainly understood, the statements of Jesus repeated six times in Matthew 5— "you have heard that it was said . . . but I say to you"—mean he was replacing an old law with a new one. This is a very unique position for Tolstoy to have taken on three of the most seminal verses to be found within the Sermon on the Mount, or entire New Testament for that matter, Matthew 5:17-20. But as he explained, though this interpretation runs contrary to centuries of theological and Biblical scholarship, he believed this is a conclusion that comes from a plain reading of the text itself and is supported by the original language and word meanings. From chapter five of *What I Believe*:

> When I came to the words, 'Ye, have heard that it hath been said, An eye for an eye, and a tooth for a tooth: But I say unto you, That ye resist not evil,' the words, 'An eye for an eye, and a tooth for a tooth,' expressed the law given by Moses; the words, 'But I say unto you, That ye resist no evil,' expressed a new law, which was a negation of the first. If I had seen Jesus words, simply, in

their true sense, and not as a part of the theological theory that I had imbibed at my mother's breast, I should have understood immediately that Jesus abrogated the old law, and substituted it for a new law. But I had been taught that Jesus did not abrogate the Law of Moses, that, on the contrary, he confirmed it to the slightest iota, and that he made it complete." (WB, 42)

Repeatedly in chapter five of the Sermon on the Mount Jesus remarked "you have heard that it was said . . . but I say to you," and Tolstoy pointed out "the two laws are directly opposed to one another; that they can never be harmonised; that, instead of supplementing one by the other, we must inevitably choose between the two" (WB, 43). Tolstoy's choice was for the new law of Jesus even if that meant breaking with Church tradition and teaching, the Church fathers, and even the Law of Moses: "We must accept one commandment or the other; and Chrysostom, like all the rest of the Church, accepted the commandment of Moses and denied that of the Christ, whose doctrine he nevertheless claims to believe. Jesus abolished the Mosaic law, and gave his own law in its place" (WB, 52).

Those arguments alone are insufficient to make such a case and to take such a radical position. What then can be made of Christ's words in that seminal text: "For truly I tell you, until heaven and earth disappear, not the smallest letter, not the least stroke of a pen, will by any means disappear from the Law until everything is accomplished" (Matt 5:18)? As he did in other parts of the Sermon on the Mount when Tolstoy found the accepted reading unacceptable to what appeared self-evident, he looked for answers and resolution in word studies and the problems caused by textual variants and later commentators. Tolstoy concluded verse eighteen was not talking about the Law of Moses but rather the Eternal Law. For him, the problem began when early translators made the arbitrary assumption that the *law* this passage refers to is the Written Law. Tolstoy contended if Jesus meant the Written Law he would have used the phrase the "law *and* the prophets. However, Jesus used the expression the "law *or* the prophets" instead. Tolstoy's interpretation also depended on his reading of Luke 16:15-17 where Jesus said "the law and the prophets were until John: since that time the kingdom of God is preached, and every man presseth into it. And it is easier for heaven and earth to pass, than one tittle of the law to fail." Regarding that parallel text Tolstoy wrote: "In the first passage cited he said, 'the law and the prophets,' that is, the written law; in the second he said, 'the law' simply, therefore law eternal" (WB, 45). Citing briefly the history of the variants of the text he commended some for preciseness thereby avoiding a false interpretation but said others, "notably that of Tischendorf, and in the canonical versions, we find the word 'prophets' used, not with the conjunction '*and*,' but with the conjunction '*or*'" (WB, 45). Tolstoy laid the blame on early commentators for changing–*and* into *or*– and obscuring the meaning of the text for centuries thereafter.

In his word study on *law* (both the Greek νόμος and the Hebrew *torah*), Tolstoy concluded there are two primary meanings: "law in the abstract sense, independent of formula; the other, the written statutes" (WB, 46). Tolstoy explained that in Paul and in the books of the prophets like Isaiah the distinction was made by the use of the article, or the absence of an article—Law or the Law: "And so Jesus sometimes speaks of law as the divine law (of Isaiah and the other prophets), in which case he confirms it; and sometimes in the sense of the written law of the Pentateuch, in which case he rejects it. To distinguish the difference he always, in speaking of the written law, adds, 'and the prophets,' or prefixes the word 'your' with 'your law'" as in John 19:7, "It is also written in your law . . ." (WB, 46). Tolstoy lamented how "every prophet, every founder of a religion, inevitably meets, in revealing the divine law to men, with institutions which are regarded as upheld by laws of God. He cannot, therefore, avoid a double use of the word 'law'" (WB, 48). The error of the Church, particularly Ireneaus (according to Tolstoy) is that it asserted "everything old is sacred . . . [but] Jesus could not affirm the whole law; neither could he deny the entire teachings of the law and the prophets, the law which says, 'love thy neighbour as thyself'" (WB, 49). For Tolstoy, there were aspects of the Eternal Law within the Written Law and Jesus upheld these aspects while casting the temporal commandments of the previous aeon aside. To include them, or try to include them alongside the new commandment of Jesus (given in Matthew five) would be to offer "a vague interpretation which introduced needless contradictions, which reduces the doctrine of Jesus to nothingness, and which re-established the doctrine of Moses in all its savage cruelty" (WB, 49). "Jesus selected from what men considered as the law of God the portions which were really divine; he took what served his purpose, rejected the rest, and upon this foundation established the eternal law" (WB, 53).

4.4 Tolstoy Believed the Eternal Law Was Set Forth Most Clearly in Five New Commandments Given by Jesus in the Sermon on the Mount

Any brief reply to an inquiry for an informed sentence or two about Tolstoy's interpretation of the Sermon on the Mount must include mention that Tolstoy identified five new commandments in Matthew 5:21–48. For as much as Tolstoy is considered a Sermon on the Mount interpreter mentioning the Sermon scores of times in various writings over decades, he placed little emphasis on the Beatitudes, or chapters six and seven of Matthew's Gospel. There are places he addressed these other major sections of the Sermon on the Mount but clearly he considered chapter five most important. This section in Matthew 5 on the new commandments of the Eternal Law immediately follow the section discussed above about the replacement of the Written Law with the Law Eternal (Matt 5:17–20). For Tolstoy, it could only be the case having just spoken of the two types of law that now, section by section, Jesus then continued on referencing the old law and replacing it entirely with the new. Typically commentators identify six legislative sections in Matthew 5:21–48, however Tolstoy numbered five because he combined Jesus' teaching on adultery and divorce in 5:27–32 (for the obvious reason that topically the new command pertains singularly to marriage; vis-à-vis relationships with the opposite sex). These five commandments find their way in short form into the later religious writings of Tolstoy, into the rule of subsequent Tolstoyan communities, and again, amount to the substance of what he believed Jesus offered his followers on the mountainside that day. In short form Tolstoy listed these commandments: (1) Be not angry; (2) Do not commit adultery; (3) Take no oaths; (4) Resist not evil; (5) Do not make war (WB, 165). The following is a brief treatment of his reading of these texts in Matthew five and their corresponding commandment.

4.4.1 The First Commandment: Be Not Angry

The old law, according to Matthew 5:21 was "Thou shall not kill." The new law Jesus gave in its stead is "whoever is angry with his brother without a cause will be in danger of the judgment." For Tolstoy, the phrase "without a cause" destroyed the "only clear and direct meaning of the verse" as "I never yet encountered an angry person who did not believe his wrath to be justifiable" (WB, 56–57). Tolstoy's concerns were abated via his word studies in the text and sorting through the textual variants that still bare the fingerprints of copyists. Tolstoy discovered in the oldest manuscripts the word εἰκῆ (without cause) did not appear: "This word, so destructive to the meaning of the doctrine of Jesus, is then an interpolation which had not crept into the best copies of the Gospel as late as the fifth century. Some copyist added the word; others approved it and undertook its explanation. Jesus did not utter, could not have uttered, this terrible word" (WB, 58). Tolstoy paraphrased this first commandment of Jesus: "Live in peace with all men. Do not regard anger as justifiable under any circumstances. Never look upon a human being as worthless or a fool. Not only refrain from anger yourself, but do not regard the anger of others toward you as vain. If anyone is angry with you, even without reason, be reconciled to him, that all hostile feelings may be effaced" (WB, 59).

4.4.2 The Second Commandment: Do Not Commit Adultery

The second commandment emerged for Tolstoy in combining the next sections on adultery and divorce (Matt 5:27–32). As "extinguish[ing] the germ of anger" in the first commandment has global consequence when widely obeyed—people no longer kill each other—a similar global effect is intended, Tolstoy believed, by the second commandment where followers of Christ are admonished to "guard against every idea that excites to sensual desire, and, once united to a woman, never to abandon her on any pretext, for women thus abandoned are sought by other men, and so debauchery is introduced into the world. The wisdom of this commandment impressed me so profoundly. It would suppress all the evils in the world that result from sexual relations" (WB, 59–60). Clearly Tolstoy did not limit the application of the Sermon on the Mount to a small group of followers closed off from the world living away somewhere in their own little utopia. These commandments of Jesus comprised Eternal Laws that lead to life in its fullness on earth. For Tolstoy, the Sermon on the Mount could not be lived in seclusion as obedience to it required living in a contentious world. However, again, Tolstoy took issue with an issue in the text: the divorce exception: "saving for the cause of fornication, which permitted a man to repudiate his wife in the case of infidelity" (WB, 60).

Tolstoy's exegesis of this passage, Matthew 5:27–3, widened to include the other New Testament texts on divorce and marriage: Matthew 19:4–9, Mark 10:5–12, Luke 16:18, and 1 Corinthians 7:1–11. His conclusion was:

> According to Mark, and Luke, and Paul, divorce is forbidden. It is forbidden by the assertion repeated in two of the Gospels that husband and wife are one flesh whom God hath joined together. It is forbidden by the doctrine of Jesus, who exhorts us to pardon everyone, without excepting the adulterous woman. It is forbidden by the general sense of the whole passage, which explains that divorce is provocative of debauchery, and for this reason that divorce with an adulterous woman is prohibited. (WB, 61)

What then is to be made of these exceptions for divorce? Tolstoy's spelled out his struggle to understand: "It seemed to me, that there must be a defect in the translation, and an erroneous exegesis; but where was the source of the error? I could not find it; and yet the error itself was very plain" (WB, 61). Tolstoy concluded the words "fault of adultery" referred to "libertinism, debauchery, or some similar phrase, expressing not an act but a quality" (WB, 63). His word study of πορνείας (v. 32) took him to the corresponding Hebrew *zanah*, the Latin *fornication*, the German *hurerei*, and finally to the French *libertinage* which can never signify the act of adultery, only the state of depravity. Unique in this interpretation, Tolstoy argued πορνείας cannot apply to the wife and "could signify nothing else than the fault of libertinism on the part of the husband and he paraphrased his interpretation as such; Guard against libertinism. Let every man justified in entering into the sexual relation have one wife, and every wife one husband, and under no pretext whatever let this union be violated by either" (WB, 65).

4.4.3 The Third Commandment: Take No Oaths

Unlike his struggle through the obscurity of the exception clause to divorce in the second commandment, Tolstoy's trouble with interpreting the third commandment of Jesus in Matthew 5:33-37 was that it appeared too clear, too simple and too practical (WB, 65). Could Jesus have really meant to never take an oath of any sort? The commentators he consulted were quick to make the case that this certainly could not be an obligatory commandment in all situations as Jesus and Paul effectively swore to oaths invoking God.[9] Even so, for Tolstoy the language of the text was too clear: "How could it be said that Jesus did not perceive this evil when he forbade it in clear, direct, and circumstantial terms? . . . If obedience to the doctrine of Jesus consists in perpetual observance to the will of God, how can man swear to observe the will of another man or other men? The will of God cannot coincide with the will of man" (WB, 67). Tolstoy's application of these text were basis enough for him to condemn military conscription and the taking of oaths which authorities in every country require of their citizens. "The soldier, that special instrument of violence, goes before Russia by the nickname of *prissaiaga* (sworn in). . . . The oath is so indispensable to the horrors of war and armed coercion. . . . [Jesus] came to suppress evil, and, if he did not condemn the oath, he left a terrible evil untouched" (WB, 66). Again there is potential in these new commandments to change the entire world if only they would be obeyed. Tolstoy presented the Sermon on the Mount as a direct challenge to our entire social order, and as a path entirely different than the one all of humanity is on: "We have organised a social order

9. Matt 26:63; Gal 1:20.

which we cherish and look upon as sacred. Jesus, whom we recognise as God, comes and tells us that our social organisation is wrong. We recognise him as God, but we are not willing to renounce our social institutions" (WB, 67). Regarding the oath of a soldier Tolstoy wrote: "They make men swear by the Gospel, that is to say, they do just the contrary of what the Gospel commands. . . . [A]ll oaths are imposed for an evil purpose" (WB, 68).

4.4.4 The Fourth Commandment: Resist Not Evil

As mentioned in the previous chapter (subsection 3.3), the fourth commandment, resist not evil, from Matthew 5:38–42 was for Tolstoy the key to the entire Sermon on the Mount. His paraphrase of it will suffice here to summarize his thoughts: "Jesus said, 'You wish to suppress evil by evil; this is not reasonable. To abolish evil, avoid the commission of evil. . . . Never resist evil by force, never return violence for violence: if anyone beats you, bear it; if anyone would deprive you of anything, yield to his wishes; if anyone would force you to labor, labor; if anyone would take away your property, abandon it at his demand" (WB, 70). Tolstoy was fully aware of the "Christian scholars and freethinkers" who "do not hesitate to correct" the meaning of these words of Jesus: "The sentiments here expressed, they tell us, are very noble, but are completely inapplicable to life; for if we practiced to the letter the commandment, 'Resist not evil' our entire social fabric would be destroyed. . . . If, however, we take the words of Jesus as we would take the words of anyone who speaks to us, and admit that he says exactly what he does say, all these profound circumlocutions vanish away. Jesus says, 'Your social system is absurd and wrong. I propose to you another'" (WB, 69).

4.4.5 The Fifth Commandment: Do Not Make War

Loving enemies and not just your neighbours, the subject of the fifth commandment in Matthew 5:43–48, again presented Tolstoy with textual problems to solve. In each of four previous old commandments Jesus replaced with the new, he cited a specific text from the written law of Moses. Here, in saying, "You have heard that it was said, 'You shall love your neighbour and hate your enemy,'" there is uncertainty about the source of his reference to old law as nowhere is hating enemies to be found in Mosaic law. Tolstoy's word studies revealed to him that rather than citing a specific reference, Jesus was using the words "hate your enemy" to summarize a number of Old Testament scripture passages where Moses directed the people of God to act with hostility toward "hostile peoples." He wrote: "The various passages scattered through the different books of the Old Testament, prescribing the oppression, slaughter, and extermination of other peoples, Jesus summed up in one word, 'hate,' make war upon the enemy. He said, in substance: "You have heard that you must love those of your own race, and hate foreigners; but I say to you, love everyone without distinction of nationality" (WB, 73). For Tolstoy these vital distinctions bring needed clarity to the matter of who this commandment is for, individuals or nation-states as well.

Throughout his treatment of the Sermon on the Mount Tolstoy made use of his own paraphrases to put the intended meaning of Jesus on a level that all can understand. He also used a rhetorical device best described as a diatribe, perhaps unknowingly, when his passion for the truth of the text is most evident. He concluded his treatment of these new commandments with a diatribe that can be called *The Imagined Society* and reading this diatribe and others in his second book remind the contemporary reader of Martin Luther King's *I Have A Dream* speech and other visionary oracles of prophetic types. Tolstoy wants us to imagine

> a Christian society living according to these commandments and educating the younger generation to follow their precepts. . . . [I]magine a state of society where, instead of permitting and approving libertinism in young men before marriage, instead of regarding the separation of husband and wife as natural and desirable . . . instead of regarding it as natural that our entire existence should be controlled by coercion; that every one of our amusements should be provided and maintained by force . . . instead of the national hatred with which we are inspired under the name of 'patriotism'. . . . [I]f in the place of the glory associated with that form of murder which we call war, if, in place of this, we were taught, on the contrary, horror and contempt for all the means military, diplomatic, and political which serve to divide men . . . the observance of his five commandments will bring peace upon the earth. They all have but one object, the establishment of peace among men." (WB, 78–80)

4.5 Obedience over Orthodoxy

Is orthodoxy everything? Is obedience enough? Which is more important, obedience to Christ or adherence to orthodox dogma?[10] These are impor-

---

10. Intentionally in this sentence, *orthodox* is not capitalised. Here the intention is to reference the dogma of the wider spectrum of orthodoxy within the major branches of Christendom, not merely the orthodoxy of the Russian Orthodox Church which was clearly Tolstoy's primary nemesis.

tant questions in grappling with Tolstoyan Christianity. Within the Sermon on the Mount there is indication that Tolstoy could be conceived as standing shoulder to shoulder with those whom God considers the greatest in the Kingdom of Heaven: "but whoever practices and teaches these commands will be called great in the kingdom of heaven."[11] This reference to "these commands" is not a reference to anything the "teachers of the law" were teaching or practising. In the next verse, Jesus said "these commands" are of a righteousness that "surpasses that of the Pharisees and teachers of the law." For the rest of the fifth chapter of Matthew "these commands" are given simply and with clarity. There should be no confusion regarding the importance of these commands, practising and teaching them, for greatness in the Kingdom of Heaven. Tolstoy took Jesus at his word and not because he was motivated to be called great. His life and lifestyle radically changed, so did his message. Tolstoy spent more than thirty years of his life publicly teaching and contending for obedience to the Sermon on the Mount. In light of this text from the Sermon on the Mount, the question of what constitutes greatness in the Kingdom of Heaven should give pause to any who might think orthodoxy to formulas of dogma decided centuries later by the Church rank higher than obedience. The Tolstoyan contention is that Jesus did not spell out on that mountain what to believe but rather how to behave.

Much work is yet to be done on Tolstoy's Christology, his Ecclesiology and Eschatology, his Doctrine of God and Man, Sin and Soteriology. With the exception of Tolstoy's doctrine of God which is the focus shortly in subsection 4.5.1, Tolstoy's doctrinal positions are articulated and examined in this book only to the extent they relate to Sermon on the Mount obedience; such as whether or not obedience amounts to works righteousness or whether or not obedience is salvific. It cannot be said of Tolstoy he may have been a great author but he was only a wannabe theologian and philosopher. Though not formally trained in these disciplines[12], neither were others in church history who unlike Tolstoy we unhesitatingly welcome to contribute

---

11. Matt 5:19–20.

12. Reared in an aristocratic Russian family, tutors taught Tolstoy German and French and it was evident early he had a great capacity for languages and a way with words. At age sixteen he entered Kazon University and studied oriental languages the first year and law the second year. He challenged the university system and syllabus and did not finish his course. He was regarded as "both unable and unwilling to learn" by some on the faculty though one professor said of him: "I gave him an exam today and noticed that he had no desire to study at all. He has such expressive facial features and such intelligent eyes, that I am convinced that with good will and independence he can develop into a remarkable person." Wilson, *Tolstoy*, 42.

to the conversation. They even said of Jesus himself: "How did this man get such learning without having been taught?"[13]

Orthodoxy is determined by authority; be it the authority of Jesus, the authority of Scripture, the authority of church councils, creeds and traditions, the authority of church hierarchy (papal or otherwise) and even the authority of a state. Obedience is a response to recognized authority be it to the authority of a parent, or to the authority of a commanding officer or state, or to these various religious authorities. Obedience is a manifestation of a submission to a sovereignty. Believing the Kingdom of God has come and was coming—*thy Kingdom come, thy will be done*—submission to the will of the coming King becomes a positive affirmation and statement of His Lordship. Under these definitions, Tolstoy emerges as one who does believe, even notably more than his accusers whose lives and religious expression hardly resemble anything in the Sermon on the Mount. In the words of Dietrich Bonhoeffer: "*Only believers obey, and only the obedient believe.*"[14]

Voluntary obedience is of a different sort than coerced obedience, the main distinguishers between the two being agreement and adoration, or love. Obedience is how Christians love God back. Disobedience is to resist *thy Kingdom come* and reject the will of the King. Disobedience is a statement that His judgments are wrong, and the ways of man are right. It is spiritual defiance and rebellion. What separates the sheep and the goats is what they did and did not *do*, not what they did and did not *believe*. The Reformation focus on grace does not cancel obedience. Grace does not give license to disobey or continue in disobedience. Grace includes sufficient empowerment to obey. Obedience is the narrow path that few are on, but it leads to life. Obedience was life not law. Tolstoy believed obedience was the narrow path Jesus walked himself and called others behind him to walk.

Central to the Orthodox/Catholic divisions, and to the Protestant/Catholic divisions and even to the divisions within Protestantism (mainline and evangelical/charismatic) are these issues of authority. Some who are faithful each Sabbath never read Scripture themselves revealing Tradition and Church interpretation are a higher authority than the Scriptures. The notion of a holding to a canon within a canon is practically true of every flavour of Christian though only a rare few go to the length Tolstoy did in trimming the Bible down to what he deemed a few of the most important chapters. The average Christian would be horrified at the thought of taking a scissors to the Bible in such a manner as Tolstoy did, or as did Thomas Jefferson, though functionally the average Christian leaves much of their Bible

13. John 7:15.
14. Bonhoeffer, *Discipleship*, 53, 64.

unread (see subsection 1.5). Before casting stones at Tolstoy for silencing every other revelatory voice and authoritative vantage point, there is room for some concession where one is guilty of the same. For Tolstoy, the teaching of Jesus alone is authoritative, specifically the Sermon on the Mount.

The Sermon on the Mount answered Kant's second question which haunted Tolstoy through several decades of his conversion. Kant's three questions emerged in his *Critique of Pure Reason*:

> The whole interest of my reason, whether speculative or practical, is concentrated in the three following questions:– 1. What can I know? 2. What should I do? 3. What may I hope?[15]

For Kant, the first question was speculative, the second practical, and the third theoretical. For Tolstoy, much relating to orthodoxy was purely speculative and theoretical. For any who place a primacy on orthodoxy, Tolstoy's disregard for central orthodox dogma is at times shocking: "Why do I need to know that he [Jesus] was resurrected? Good for him if he was. For me what is important is knowing what to do, and how I should live."[16] In subjecting orthodoxy to obedience Tolstoy also carved for himself a lonely path in the opposite direction of both theological studies and science. Science was trying to settle the origin of life while Tolstoy cared more about the meaning of life and how we are to live. While Social Darwinists throughout Europe were dividing humanity up by worth and value and cheering on only the fittest for survival, Tolstoy took the side of the poor, the oppressed and taught universal love in obedience to Christ's command.

For Tolstoy, obedience was not unto orthodoxy but unto authority. Behind the teaching of Jesus, for Tolstoy, stood the Logos. In the limited number of Gospel texts Tolstoy believed most important, besides the Sermon on the Mount, he was particularly fond of John 1 and his translation of this first section of John's Gospel is very helpful toward understanding Tolstoy's view of God.

> John 1 . . . 1 The understanding of life has become principle of all things. And the understanding of life has come to replace God. And the understanding of life has become God. 2 It has become the principle of all things instead of God. 3 Everything was born through understanding, and apart from understanding was born nothing of that which is alive and lives. 4 In it life came to be, just as the light of men became life. 5 Just as light shines in the darkness, and the darkness does not overwhelm

---

15. Kant, *Critique of Pure Reason*, 645–46.
16. Bartlett, *Tolstoy*, 287.

it. . . . 18 Nobody has comprehended or will ever comprehend God. The son, having the same nature as the father and being in the father's heart, he has shown the way.[17]

Before immediately dismissing Tolstoy's view of God as nothing beyond an Enlightenment-laden notion deifying Reason, it needs to be noted this is David Matual's English rendering of Tolstoy's Russian translation. As have others, Matual chose the phraseology *understanding of life* in seeking to carefully convey Tolstoy's conception of the Greek *Logos*. Tolstoy's understanding of Logos, and his translation of the word itself is captured in his use of the Russian term; *Razumenie*. In Russian, *Razume* is divine reason and *enie* is consciousness, ability and will.[18] *Razumenie*, God's Word in action, gave us creation—"Everything was born through understanding, and apart from understanding was born nothing of that which is alive and lives." *Razumenie*, God's Word embodied, came into the world in the birth of Jesus—"Nobody has comprehended or will ever comprehend God. The son, having the same nature as the father and being in the father's heart, he has shown the way." Furthermore, for Tolstoy, *Razumenie* comes into the world now through man's action or obedience to *Razumenie*. As Christ came into the world according to the will of God, according to will of God, to co-opt Luther's vernacular, we as little christs continue his life by manifesting God's will on earth through our obedient lives; *thy will be done*. There is a doing not just a believing in Tolstoyan Christianity.

Logos, he believed, is ultimately the authority behind the Doctrine of Jesus (the Sermon on the Mount), and it is this authority that is driving obedience. Jesus embodied Logos on earth, then taught it and modelled it. In a letter to his friend Afanasy Fet, the philosopher, Tolstoy wrote:

> Only *Razumenie* manifested God. . . . I don't know others, I know myself. I know that I live by God, who in my life always stands by me; and I serve God alone. *Razumenie* is God, and about no other God do we have the right to speak."[19] . . . The understanding of life became the beginning of all [John 1:1]. The understanding of life stood by, and for, God. The understanding of life is God.[20]

---

17. Matual, *Tolstoy's Translation of the Gospels*, 68.

18. Medzhibovskaya, *Tolstoy and the Religious Culture*, 201.

19. Medzhibovskaya, *Tolstoy and the Religious Culture*, 203. Quoting from 63:27 in *Tolstoy's Works*.

20. Medzhibovskaya, *Tolstoy and the Religious Culture*, 206.

In her book *Tolstoy and the Religious Culture of His Time*, Inessa Medzhibovskaya asserted that Logos becomes Christ: "Christ achieves his awareness and converts to *razumenie* rather than being born into it. . . . The rendering of *logos*, including the interpretation of the birth of Christ as 'embodied *razumenie*' (24:36–37), Tolstoy considered to be fundamental to his entire project of rewriting the Gospels."[21]

4.5.1 Tolstoy's Unorthodox Doctrine of God, and Jesus as God

It remains a conscious effort to develop and articulate Tolstoy's interpretation of the Sermon on the Mount while leaving to others the work of constructing a proper Tolstoyan theology. Though generally, concerns about his unorthodox views on numerous aspects of Christian doctrine are outside the purview here, it is vital to make space here to address his conception of God, and Jesus as God, especially as the final chapter of this project argues for the notion of Theo-tactics. What then does *Theo* mean to Leo Tolstoy?

David Matual offered two chapters in his book toward this end, a chapter on *God as Logos*, and a chapter on *A Gnostic Christ*. Matual argued that Tolstoy's god, Logos, was nothing beyond "a force, a rational principle."[22] Matual concluded that Tolstoy's rendering of John 1 is laden with "bewildering inconsistency . . . contorted arguments . . . only underscor[ing] the sheer silliness of his final conclusion."[23] In Matual's words, that final conclusion is that Tolstoy

> [w]ith his characteristic ardor . . . attempts to prove that Jesus is not the divine saviour, the Messiah promised to the chosen people, or the herald of a new covenant between God and man . . . he has created a new image of Christ – more gnostic than orthodox, more Tolstoyan than traditional, and more innovative than convincing.[24]

Matual was unimpressed with Tolstoy's positive statements of Christ dismissing them as "banal affirmations." However, Matual conceded that he did see

> the significance [Tolstoy] obviously gave to the words and actions of Christ far exceed[ing] any value he ever attached to the ideas of other men. Indeed Jesus was inestimably important to

---

21. Medzhibovskaya, *Tolstoy and the Religious Culture*, 206.
22. Matual, *Tolstoy's Translation of the Gospels*, 71.
23. Matual, *Tolstoy's Translation of the Gospels*, 71.
24. Matual, *Tolstoy's Translation of the Gospels*, 89.

him. . . . In an undated passage from his notebooks, jotted down sometime in 1880, he remarks that Jesus is God "in a rhetorical sense." In *An Investigation of Dogmatic Theology* he even declares his willingness to accept the basic religious meaning of the traditional belief in Jesus' divinity as long as he remains free to reject the irrelevant historical details. The key phrase in Tolstoy's quarrel with the church over the issue of Christ's identity is "huios tou theo" ("son of God"). . . . [citing Psalm 82 where all men are called the "sons of the Most High"], "the title is not Christ's alone, nor does it exalt him in any way."

Matual overreached in saying Tolstoy's Christ was more gnostic than orthodox. The significant considerations of Tolstoy being situated in the glory days of historical criticism and in the midst of the superstition and mysticism of nineteenth century Russian Orthodoxy are ignored. Without drawing in these considerations which formed the basis for Tolstoy's reconception of the Christian Christ and God, Matual is only able to assess them as having gnostic flavourings:

> Tolstoy's Christ can therefore be seen as the repository of the Gnostic spark, the bearer of the Stoic Spirit, the prophet of Romantic pantheism, or a curious and rather distressing combination of all three.[25]

The seeming confusion in Tolstoy and the inconsistencies in his statements which raise these concerns for Matual are unfortunate as the "divine spark within" is only read through a gnostic lens. A more fruitful avenue to pursue in rightly reading Tolstoy on *God within* would be to pursue Tolstoy's notion of *Imago Dei* and the indwelling Spirit. Certainly Tolstoy's view on God dwelling in us via the Spirit of Jesus is hardly any sort of Romantic pantheism. An important Tolstoy citation rests behind these references to this divine spark within

> religions differ in their external forms but they are all alike in their fundamental principles . . . that there is a God, the origin of all things; that in man dwells a spark from that Divine Origin, which man can increase or decrease in himself by his way of living; that to increase this divine spark man must suppress his passions and increase love in himself; and that the practical means to attain this result is to do to others as you would they should do unto you.[26]

25. Matual, *Tolstoy's Translation of the Gospels*, 114.
26. Tolstoy, "What Is Religion, and Wherein Lies Its Essence?" in *On Life and Essays on Religion*, 12:271–72.

Though his phraseology might be off-putting in traditional circles of Christian orthodoxy, those anxieties can be settled by reading these passages toward Tolstoy's view of *Imago Dei*. Additionally, he was not insinuating that all religions lead to God as he did not believe that to be the case. It was God's revelation in Jesus that Tolstoy believed to be the divine way to life. Though it would be too much to claim Tolstoy held even loosely to trinitarianism, there is merit to the (vague) claim that Tolstoy was a monotheist of the Christian sort.[27]

Reason was rejected by Tolstoy who claimed Faith was necessary. When Tolstoy used words like faith, belief, God and Jesus they can be understood generally in their traditional sense. The contribution of Tolstoy is not in his theological articulations but rather in his success in discerning how God wills us to live. Tolstoy was not taking his cues from the canons, the creeds, the church councils, or the kings of the earth. He distinguished between three doctrines (a) the Doctrine of the World, (b) the Doctrine of the Church and (c) the Doctrine of Jesus, this embodied *Razumenie,* which he spoke of as a *New Life-Conception* articulated by Jesus in the Sermon on the Mount. Tolstoy was not concerned about outcomes or motivated to obey by eschatology. His authority was the Doctrine of Jesus, the *Razumenie/Logos*, which he believed to be the embodiment of an understanding from God, captured and available to us today mainly in this vital teaching of Jesus. There is no argument that Tolstoy did not consider the sixty-six book canon to be authoritative. Tolstoy would likely agree the Acts of the Apostles are not the same as the Acts of the Obedient. In his view, the early church even during the time of Paul and certainly very quickly afterwards focused

---

27. In a 2016 essay, "Leo Tolstoy's Anticlericalism in Its Context and Beyond: A Case against Churches and Clerics, Religious and Secular," Alexandre Christoyannopoulos framed Tolstoy as a Deist as he "reduced religion to morality" and because his "Christianity was anti-metaphysical" (3–6). However, Deism classically construed as belief in a non-intervening God is ill-fitting for Tolstoy who believed in a very active God in the world of his day and in history. He believed God's intervention in the world was through followers of the teaching of Jesus, in-dwelt by the Spirit of Jesus, effectively living out and therefore enacting the will of God on earth. Though not a personal God in any evangelical sense, Tolstoy also did not believe in a detached and removed God, common to deistic conceptions of the Deity. Christoyannopoulos is right in carefully showing how "Clearly, therefore, Tolstoy does embrace the traditional vocabulary of Christianity [faith, belief, revelation], but his understanding of those conventional terms is unconventional" (5). Christoyannopoulos concludes that though Tolstoy borrowed from conventional Christian vocabulary he did so "only within the idiosyncratic grammar of his particular deistic and rational metaphysics . . . [resulting] in a philosophy which is only loosely rooted in traditional Christian understanding, and which exalts a rationalistic understanding of Jesus' ethics" (5). More accurate, in my assessment, is to be content to see Tolstoy, though non-trinitarian, as a monotheist of a Christian sort.

on dogmas rather than doing and were distracted from the obedient life; obedience in particular to the Sermon on the Mount. The question being pressed here is can one adhere to the teaching of Jesus alone and still be considered a Christian? Does obedience trump orthodoxy? From very early on in the Christian movement, some were following Paul, some were following Cephas, some were saying they were following Christ.[28] Tolstoy sought to follow Jesus, as he understood Jesus, not the Jesus of the subsequent early church and certainly not the Jesus of later Constantinian Christianity. He had no regard for apostolic authority, including discernible textual variants in the Gospels he attributed to the apostolic church. So was Tolstoy a Christian, or not? Did he reject too many orthodox dogmas to be considered a fellow believer? The Orthodox Church answered these questions by excommunicating him.

"Get him out! His cross is much too big for our Church."

The contribution of this chapter and the prior chapter has been in presenting a synthesis of the main distinctives of Tolstoy's Sermon on the Mount interpretation. Capturing these distinctives has been a task that is original to this project. To date, there is no other place to look for a succinct listing and commentary on what makes Tolstoy's interpretation of the Sermon on the Mount distinct. It has been argued that Tolstoy should have a more prominent place in theological conversation and education for what he had to say about moral perfection, moral guidance and obedience to moral authority (the revelation of God on the mountainside) against adherence to orthodox dogmas and traditions which generally eclipse entirely

---

28. 1 Cor 1:12; 3:4.

the teaching of Jesus. The next chapter develops further the importance of Tolstoy's legacy in theological and Biblical studies.

~ 5.0 ~

Letters, Legacy, and the Ghost of Tolstoy

ANY INKLING THAT LETTERS are ancillary to a literary corpus should be put to rest by the fact that half the New Testament is comprised of epistles. Correspondence can be a bountiful place to find clarification of ideas and additional and deeper developments of thought. Tolstoy left an enormous collection of letters, over 8500 Tolstoy letters can be found in the ninety volume edition of his collected works. Remarkably, those 8500 letters fill thirty-two of those ninety volumes, Volumes 59–90, and five of those volumes are Tolstoy's letters to one person, Vladimir Chertkov, his close but controversial friend. In the 1970s, R. F. Christian worked through the 8500 letters and selected, edited and translated over six hundred of them, added brief biographical data on the recipients, and contextual notations, and published them in his two volume *Tolstoy's Letters: Volume I* 1828–1879, and *Volume II* 1890–1910.

R. F. Christian felt Tolstoy's letters could easily be grouped into three categories: (1) *Tolstoy the Man* (letters to family and friends); (2) *Tolstoy the Writer* (letters about his writing and novels, and his views on the literature of other writers in Russia, Europe and America); and (3) *Tolstoy the Thinker.* "[There are letters] which concerned Tolstoy the thinker in a broader sense, and expressed his attitude to the times he lived in, contemporary social problems, rural life, industrialisation, education, and more especially in later life, religious and spiritual questions."[1] Tolstoy's letters were to all kinds of people; to his wife and grown children, to his publishers, to other novelists and journalists at home and abroad. There are many letters written to

---

1. Christian, *Tolstoy's Letters: Volume I*, v.

names still remembered today; he wrote to Tsars Alexander II, Alexander III, and Nicholas II and to many in the Russian aristocracy and to foreign diplomats, critics and sympathizers. He corresponded with Ernest Crosby, Henry George, Maxim Gorky, H. G. Wells, Bernard Shaw, and Mohandas Gandhi. He wrote empathetically to the husband of the woman with whom Tolstoy's son committed adultery, and later married. Tolstoy wrote to a lady who asked him if God would forgive her for killing herself. She later said his reply was her salvation. In this third category of *Tolstoy the Thinker*, Tolstoy's letters touched many topics related to Tolstoyan Christianity; prayer, happiness, joy, the soul, consciousness, reason, science, philosophy, the peasant class, Socialism, Communism, Anarchy, revolution, Tolstoyan colonies, capital punishment, sex, marriage, children, violence, war, the 1891–92 Russian famine and his relief efforts, Kant, Nietzsche, Buddhism and other faiths, love, vodka, America, Napoleon, Genghis Khan, fame, Darwin and Malthusian theories, Orthodox superstition, Jews, work, sin, repentance, women's equality, animal cruelty, suicide, death, old age, land ownership, a hypnotised populace and more.

5.1 Searching for Second Tolstoy in 8500 Letters

The analysis that follows is drawn from R. F. Christian's third category of letters, *Tolstoy the Thinker*. More particularly, from the 608 letters R. F. Christian translated, 363 are from the Second Tolstoy period (1879–1910), letters numbered 245–608. From those 363 letters, for the purpose of this study, only two letters have been lifted out and given Second Tolstoy epistolary status because of the content within pertaining to the scope of Tolstoyan Sermon on the Mount interpretation and application (subsections 5.2, 5.3, and 12.2). Of the two main interpretative questions ever-present in Sermon on the Mount hermeneutical dialogue, (1) Is it livable? and (2) Who is it for?, the latter is where Tolstoy made his most significant contribution. His contention was that it did not just apply to a few, but that it presented a course that all of humanity must needs proceed down.

There are numerous examples within his letters in the Second Tolstoy period of the scope of his Sermon on the Mount application. On the one end, in a terse letter to his wife, Tolstoy can be found defending the appropriateness of the Sermon on the Mount for their children. The Countess Tolstoya was insisting it is one thing for a grown man to go the way of a mad man: "it's good for you, but is it good for the children?"[2] Her concern

2. Christian, *Tolstoy's Letters: Volume II*, 396. In Tolstoy's letter #297, to Countess S. A. Tolstoya, December 15–18, 1885.

was that radical obedience to the way of Christ was "even dangerous for the children." Tolstoy was asking for changes such as making their children tend to their own rooms, notice and respect their equality with the peasant class, stop overeating and stop attending the theatre where the really dangerous doctrines of the world were influencing them. For Tolstoy, the Sermon on the Mount was not merely an ethic for a few super Christians. It was God's way of life for all his children, even their own children. He worried about the millstone being placed around their necks for hindering the children from the path of Christ and sending them down the other path, "arranging for them in the form of a refined education with French and English tutors and governesses, music, etc, was the temptation of the love of fame and of exalting oneself above others, a millstone which we were putting round their necks."[3]

5.2 Letter #257: To the Emperor Alexander III, March 8–15, 1881

Tolstoy's letter to Emperor Alexander III demonstrates the scope of Tolstoy's Sermon on the Mount application extended to the furthest point of application; that the Sermon on the Mount is best course for Tsars and nation-states also. In his letter to Alexander III appealing for mercy on behalf of the soon to be executed assassins of the Tsar's father Alexander II, Tolstoy pens with passion and prophetic clarity a letter quite comparable to Martin Luther King Jr.'s famous and widely-circulated *Letter from a Birmingham Jail* (King's 1963 open letter written to fellow clergymen to defend his strategy of nonviolent resistance in the fight against racism). Alternatively it could be seen as Tolstoy's *Philemon* in that as the Apostle Paul penned a mercy plea for Onesimus the runaway slave, Tolstoy penned a mercy plea for the doctrine of Jesus to be applied to matters of civil, criminal and social justice. Tolstoy's letter to the Tsar has had virtually no circulation and consideration by Christians or people in government. This must change so a new generation can consider his prophetic epistle. For this reason it is included in its entirely in the appendix to this dissertation (subsection 12.2). An additional note: It is possible to draw a connection between Tolstoy's letter to the Tsar and the radicalization of Vladimir Lenin (see subsection 9.2.2).

On the first of March 1881 in Petersburg, six members of the revolutionary party, *The People's Will*, assassinated Tsar Alexander II. A little white package wrapped in a handkerchief was tossed on his carriage and exploded. He survived that initial explosion and emerged from the carriage

---

3. Christian, *Tolstoy's Letters: Volume II*, 397.

unharmed, however the team of assassins had a second and third bomb ready and it was the second explosion that took down the Tsar. With his face mutilated, disemboweled and with his legs blown away, members of the Romanov family and a physician rushed to the scene. Lying in the snow, the Tsar bled to death shortly after being given Communion and Last Rites. The reaction to the assassination was violent on both sides. The new Tsar Alexander III, having witnessed his father's gory demise, immediately ordered the suppression of civil liberties in Russia and a mean wave of police brutality ensued. Revolutionaries and anarchists took "their inspiration from the murder of Czar Alexander II in 1881, advocated 'propaganda by deed'—the use of a spectacular act of violence to incite revolution."[4] During the trial and execution preparations to come, as violence was begetting more violence, Tolstoy had another one of his prophetic dreams: "he lay down in his study one day after dinner, fell asleep and dreamed vividly that he was both the executioner and the victim in the punishment of the assassins."[5] Upon waking from this dream Tolstoy wrote his letter to Alexander III asking for mercy for those who killed the Tsar's father. Initially the letter was blocked by Konstantin Petrovich Pobedonostsev, the Orthodox Church official and advisor in the Emperor's court. Through an emissary, Tolstoy redirected the letter around the hostile and bloodthirsty church official to get it into the hands of the Tsar.[6] After reading the letter, the Tsar sent an informal reply to Tolstoy to convey that because the criminal act was not against himself but against his father, he felt it was not in his right to pardon them. Thirty-four days after the assassination, the assassins, one of whom was a General's daughter, were executed. Unlike Tolstoy's *Letter to a Hindoo* which was warmly welcomed in India and, through Gandhi, profoundly influenced an entire nation to heed the non-violent doctrine of Jesus, Tolstoy's letter to the Tsar, to date, has had no discernible effect or further circulation. Had Russia heeded Tolstoy's prophetic word (the doctrine of Jesus) as did India, perhaps they also would have known a peaceful revolution and been spared the horrible bloodbath to come.[7]

4. Palmer, "What Do Anarchists Want from Us?"

5. Christian, *Tolstoy's Letters: Volume II*, 340–41.

6. Christian, *Tolstoy's Letters: Volume II*, 347. "[Pobedonostsev's] personal influence on the last two tsars was enormous. During his Procuratorship the Orthodox Church became more identified with the secular powers than ever before. Persecution of religious sectarians reached its height and censorship was tightened to an unprecedented degree. . . . [Tolstoy] counted in vain on Pobedonostsev's humanitarian and Christian principles to support his proposal to pardon the assassins of Alexander II, for he was one of the most intransigent supporters of capital punishment, and of repression generally, as the solution to the revolutionary problem."

7. Only six years later in March 1887, Vladimir Lenin's older brother Alexander,

Tolstoy began his letter from a posture of humility: "I, an insignificant, unqualified, poor, weak man, am writing a letter to the Russian Emperor."[8] After a couple paragraphs of formalities and acknowledgement of events transpired and the "terrifying nature of the situation," he explained that he would simply write "as man to man" and dispense of the "flourishes of false and servile eloquence which only obscures feeling and thought. . . . My genuine feeling of respect for you, as a man and as a Tsar, will be more evident without these adornments." He continued: "In your soul there must be a feeling of vengeance toward these people as the murderers of your father." Tolstoy couched the situation as presenting a temptation to the Tsar and because before "the obligations of a Tsar there are the obligations of a man." Tolstoy explained "God will not ask you to fulfil the obligations of a Tsar; he will not ask you to fulfil a Tsar's obligations, but he will ask you to fulfil human obligations." Tolstoy then began his Gospel exposition: "Your terrifying situation is terrifying and for that reason alone Christ's teaching is necessary in order to guide us in those fearful moments of temptation which fall to the lot of men." Tolstoy voiced the words of Jesus on the Mount, "Ye have heard that it hath been said, Thou shalt love thy neighbour, and hate thine enemy. But I say to you, Love your enemies . . . do good to them that hate you."

The letter is not brief. Tolstoy articulated his case that "your every step in the direction of forgiveness is a step towards good; or that every step in the direction of punishment is a step toward evil." He expressed his hope "that you, the Tsar, will set the world the greatest example of the fulfilment of Christ's teaching – that you will return good for evil . . . forgive everyone. This and this alone needs to be done; this is the will of God." The rationale from which Tolstoy approached the Sermon on the Mount was that it worked anywhere, in situations big or small: "Truth and goodness are always truth and goodness on earth as well as in heaven." The application of the Sermon on the Mount was effectual on both a micro and a macro-scale. Using the language of remedy, of a new remedy and the old, Tolstoy drew a comparison to ridding a body of an illness:

---

a university student at the time, was arrested for his role in a bombing plot to assassinate Tzar Alexander III. As these years unfolded Lenin's deep bitterness grew as his brothers execution long fuelled the brutality of his revolutionary efforts. He ultimately succeeded where his brother had failed. Had the Tsar taken Tolstoy's prophetic letter six years earlier to heart it is possible history would have taken a very different path for the Romanov family and Russia itself.

8. All the quotations that follow in this section are from Tolstoy's letter to the Tsar, Letter #257, 340–47.

> They treated the sick man with strong remedies and then they stopped giving him strong remedies and allowed his organism to function freely, but neither system has helped: the sick man is getting sicker. There remains yet another remedy – a remedy about which the doctors are completely ignorant, a strange remedy. Why not try it?

Mentioning this remedy has a great advantage over the others in that it has never been used and the others have been used to no avail, he continued: "Why not try in the name of God only to fulfil His law, without thinking about either the state or the good of the masses? There can be no evil in the name of God and the fulfilling of his law." Tolstoy explained to the Tsar the crossroads to which he had come and encouraged him to respond to the hatred that had come against his father by letting the hatred be buried with him. He reasoned the Tsar was presently in a position of innocence having been wronged but that would change if he got blood on his hands in exacting vengeance.

> If you do not forgive, but execute the criminals, you will only have uprooted 3 or 4 individuals from among hundreds and, evil begetting evil, 30 or 40 will grow up in place of these 3 or 4, and you will have lost for ever the moment when you could have fulfilled God's will but you did not do so; you will leave for ever the crossroads where you could have chosen good instead of evil, and will forever be entangled in evil deeds called the interests of the state.

> Forgive, return good for evil, and from among hundreds of evildoers, dozens will come over – not to you and not to them (that is not important) but will come over from the devil to God, and thousands, even millions of hearts will tremble with joy and emotion at the sight of this example of goodness from the throne at such a terrible moment for the son of a murdered father. Sire! If you were to do this, to summon these people, to give them money and to send them away somewhere to America, and were to write a manifesto headed by the words; 'but I say to you, love your enemies', – I don't know about others but I, a poor loyal subject, would be your dog and your slave. I would weep with emotion as I am weeping now, every time I heard your name. But what am I saying – 'I don't know about others?' I know that at these words goodness and love would flow across Russia like a torrent.

Tolstoy's dream inspired him to put before the Tsar a dream, envisioning a Russia God could bless and Tolstoy made the case that the Tsar was right there in that divine moment. He insisted that to "fight against them, one must oppose their ideal with another ideal which will be superior to . . . their ideal." He ended the letter:

> There is only one ideal. . . . Only one word of forgiveness and Christian love, spoken and fulfilled from the height of the throne, and the path of Christian rule which is there for you to tread, can destroy the evil gnawing away at Russia. As wax before fire, every revolutionary struggle will melt away before the Tsar-man who fulfils the law of Christ.

Perhaps one could negatively construe Tolstoy here as playing to the Tsar's flesh, that the way of Christ is the way to greater earthly glory and the adulation of the masses. Clearly Tolstoy was not playing to the Tsar's darker angels clamoring for vengeance. However, in appealing to the good angels of a king's desire to have a flourishing kingdom and subjects, at minimum Tolstoy was acquiescing to the role God had placed the Tsar in and to the understanding that it is God's will that we follow his ways and flourish in the place of our position in life. There is also a hint of Jesus' statement in the Sermon on the Mount that those who practice his commands will be called great in the kingdom of Heaven (Matt 5:19). Tolstoy envisioned for the Tsar how the Kingdom of heaven could be manifest in his kingdom on earth.

5.3 Letter to a Hindu and a Letter to Hitler

The relationship between Leo Tolstoy and Mohandas Gandhi was a hot spark to dry tinder. Though never meeting physically, in important ways they were of one mind and heart spiritually. And though their correspondence was limited to eight letters very late in Tolstoy's life, and limited also to what could be gleaned from a few of Tolstoy's religious books and articles, the interaction and communication was enough to form a bond and transfer that inspired and informed peaceful revolutions in Colonial India, in the American South, ultimately influencing a century of non-violent resistance in numerous places around the planet. At its simplest their relationship was one of mutual admiration and interest. The young Gandhi found in Tolstoy a wise sage who had given decades of thought to the employment of spiritual weapons that win over enemies, and Tolstoy was delighted to see receptivity to his ideas and that they were being tested and tried, picked up and put to work on a national level.

Like Tolstoy, and because of Tolstoy, Gandhi also became captivated by the Sermon on the Mount. Having read Tolstoy's *The Kingdom of God Is within You* while in South Africa in 1894 and being "overwhelmed" by it, Gandhi wrote:

> The Sermon on the Mount went straight to my heart. The verses, 'But I say unto you, that ye resist not evil: but whosoever shall smite thee on thy right cheek, turn to him the other also. And if any man take away thy coat let him have thy cloak too,' delighted me beyond measure.[9]

Mahatma Gandhi became Leo Tolstoy's most famous disciple. Gandhi called him his guru and referred to Tolstoy as the "apostle of non-violence."[10] Separated by nearly six thousand miles and a forty year age difference, a baton was passed as non-violence went from Tolstoy's conception to its most successful application and implementation; 300 million Indian people non-violently resisting oppressive British rule resulting in a free India, enormous geo-political shifts in the region and throughout the Commonwealth, and a modelling and motivation for future peaceful resistance all around the globe. In his comprehensive three-volume treatment of these two 'mahatmas', Martin Green made a careful case that "the modern version of non-violence – and *satyagraha* [firmness in truth], and war-resistance, and one kind of anti-imperialism, even – were in effect invented by Tolstoy and Gandhi."[11] Debate could be had on whether or not Gandhian non-violence was a needed correction to the rigidity of Tolstoyan non-violence, or if it was merely a development and working out of it. An additional option, preferred here, is that Gandhi made compromises where Tolstoy would not. Primarily, Tolstoy interpreted Jesus to mean no violence ever, whatsoever, for any reason. Gandhi was not an absolutist in this regard. Gandhi believed non-violence did have its limits.[12]

---

9. Jones, *Mahatma Gandhi*, 109.

10. Balasubramanian, *Influence of India*, 4. And Gandhi, *My Non-Violence*, 234.

11. Green, *Origins of Nonviolence*, vii. The first and second volumes in Green's trilogy are *The Challenge of the Mahatmas* and *Tolstoy and Gandhi, Men of Peace*.

12. Gandhi spoke against "expedient non-violence" that did not come from within: "I do believe that, where there is only a choice between cowardice and violence, I would advise violence. . . . Time for expedient non-violence passed away a long time ago. Those who cannot be non-violent at heart are under no obligation to be non-violent. . . . Everyone must act on his own responsibility, and interpret the Congress creed [non-violence] to the best of his ability and belief. . . . [M]y non-violence fully accommodated violence offered by those who did not feel non-violence and who had in their keeping the honour of their womenfolk and little children. Non-violence is not a cover for cowardice, but it is the supreme virtue of the brave. Exercise of non-violence

The first document of Tolstoy to appear on Gandhi's radar was Tolstoy's 1908 *Letter to the Hindu*. Rather than position the poor Indian people as weak under the might of Great Britain, Tolstoy asserted the far greater strength of will in 300 million Indians against a hundred thousand Englishmen.[13] This became a central tenet of Gandhi's non-violence:

> But I do not believe India to be helpless. I do not believe myself to be a helpless creature. Only I want to use India's and my strength for a better purpose. Let me not be misunderstood. Strength does not come from physical capacity. It comes from an indomitable will. . . . We in India may in a moment realise that one hundred thousand Englishmen need not frighten three hundred million human beings. A definite forgiveness would, therefore, mean a definite recognition of our strength. . . And so I am not pleading for India to practice non-violence because she is weak. I want her to practice non-violence because of her strength and power.[14]

Like Tolstoy, the greater power came from within, a strength of the will.

Of particular importance, Tolstoy's view of enemies became Gandhi's view as well. There is no better place to see this than in Gandhi's Christmas Eve 1940 letter to Adolf Hitler asking him to end the war. Gandhi began as follows:

> December 24, 1940
>
> DEAR FRIEND,
>
> That I address you as a friend is no formality. I own no foes. My business in life has been for the past 33 years to enlist the

---

requires far greater bravery than that of swordsmanship. . . . Non-violence, therefore, presupposes ability to strike. It is a conscious, deliberate restraint put upon one's desire for vengeance. But vengeance is any day superior to passive, effeminate and helpless submission. Forgiveness is higher still. Vengeance too is weakness. . . . Let there be no cant about non-violence. It is not like a garment to be put on and off at will. Its seat is in the heart, and it must be an inseparable part of our very being" (Gandhi, *My Non-Violence*, 3, 34–35, 37).

13. Tolstoy, "Letter to a Hindu," 427–28. "Do not the figures make clear that it is not the English who have enslaved the Indians, but the Indians who have enslaved themselves? . . . If the people of India are enslaved by violence it is only because they themselves live and have lived by violence, and do not recognise the eternal law of love inherent to humanity. As soon as men live entirely in accord with the law of love natural to their hearts and now revealed to them, which excludes all resistance by violence– as soon as this happens, not only will hundreds be unable to enslave millions, but not even millions will be able to enslave a single individual."

14. Gandhi, *My Non-Violence*, 3–4.

friendship of the whole of humanity by befriending mankind, irrespective of race, colour or creed. . . .

I am, Your sincere friend,

M. K. GANDHI[15]

It remains scandalous to hear or read of Hitler called a "friend" yet Gandhi's rationale was entirely Tolstoyan. Like Tolstoy, Gandhi refused to hate, and love became the tactic to win even the worst human enemy. In writing Hitler, it seems likely Gandhi was taking this right out of Tolstoy's playbook. There is a remarkable resemblance between Tolstoy's 1881 *Letter to the Tsar* (subsection 5.2) and Gandhi's *Letter to Hitler*. Only the imagination can grasp how a very different twentieth century might have unfolded had both Tsar Alexander III and Adolf Hitler heeded the prophetic pleas of the two mahatmas.[16] The contention here is that these two mahatmas were indeed prophetic voices, cut from the same cloth (the Sermon on the Mount) delivering the same message directly to the people with the earthly power to stop widespread killing.

Even so, in a notable departure from Tolstoy's view that the non-violent tactics of the Sermon on the Mount are God's ways for application anywhere, surprisingly, Gandhi had no confidence these non-violent tactics would work against Japan: "Thus we can disown the authority of the British rulers by refusing taxes and in a variety of ways. These would be inapplicable to withstand the Japanese onslaught."[17] Such a view mirrors that of Reinhold Niebuhr in his correspondence with Bonhoeffer about the possibility of Sermon on the Mount tactics working in Nazi Germany. It is widely known that in 1934 Dietrich Bonhoeffer was keen to visit Gandhi in India and the two corresponded to arrange such a visit.[18] Life for Bonhoeffer, unfortunately, took a different turn. Niebuhr explained in his 1968 interview with Larry Rasmussen how he discouraged Bonhoeffer from going because Gandhi was

> an ethical liberal with philosophical footings at great distance from the Weltanschauung of a sophisticated German Lutheran;

---

15. Gandhi, "Letter to Adolf Hitler." In 2011 a film was released in India called *Dear Friend Hitler* loosely based on this correspondence. It was met with negative reviews at the 61st Berlin International Film Festival (TNN, "Gandhi to Hitler").

16. Gandhi's 1881 Letter to Hitler was intercepted by the British and was never delivered to Hitler. Gandhi had written a letter to Hitler the year before that suffered the same fate.

17. Rivett, "Gandhi, Tolstoy, and Coercion," 52, citing a comment made by Gandhi July 5, 1942 in *CWMG*, 76:256.

18. Walsh, *Strange Glory*, 106–9, 441–42nn105–7.

furthermore, Nazi Germany was no place for attempting the practice of nonviolent resistance....

Hitler's creeds and deed bore no resemblance to British ways and means. The Nazis would suffer none of the pains of conscience about using violence which the British did, and organized passive resistance would end in utter failure.[19]

Bonhoeffer did not heed Niebuhr's counsel and proceeded with his plans for a visit to India. Still, that such a meeting never materialized is our loss today; it would no doubt be helpful for peacemakers to know what Bonhoeffer would have gleaned from Gandhian (generally Tolstoyan) non-violence to apply to his resistance against Nazi Germany. Perhaps he would have heard from Gandhi the very things he was hearing from Niebuhr. Regardless this remains a very important part of Tolstoyan Sermon on the Mount interpretation and for his legacy.

5.4 The Tolstoy Bonhoeffer Never Knew

[One should not be] "too ready to ridicule Tolstoy, however right [they are] that Tolstoy should not be confused with the Gospel."[20]

This admonition was given by Dietrich Bonhoeffer's Union Seminary friend Jean Lasserre in his book *War & the Gospel*. In context, this admonition conveys within Lasserre a perceptible sympathy toward the religious Tolstoy particularly and specifically toward Tolstoy's multi-decade commitment to a literal obedience to the Sermon on the Mount and the peace demands therein. Additionally, this conveys Lasserre's admonishment to heed what Tolstoy got right even while disregarding what he got wrong, a contention pervasive throughout this project. Tolstoy rejected the Church entirely, and much that would be considered orthodox, making Tolstoyan Christianity a broad and easy target for ridicule and derision. However, though Tolstoy's critics may be correct in that he metaphorically threw out the baby with the bathwater, Lasserre's admonishment is that we not be quick to do the same to Tolstoy. Lasserre set forth a significant caution that there is something prophetic in Tolstoy's call to Sermon on the Mount obedience for those inclined to hear and heed.

---

19. Rasmussen, *Dietrich Bonhoeffer*, 213.
20. Lasserre, *War & the Gospel*, 18.

This is the Jean Lasserre who profoundly influenced Dietrich Bonhoeffer—the Jean Lasserre whom Eberhard Bethge considered to be the catalyst, or "first impulse" who was used by God to truly convert Dietrich Bonhoeffer to Christ and his teaching in the Sermon on the Mount.[21] This Jean Lasserre, who so profoundly influenced Bonhoeffer to go on to give the world *Discipleship* and *Life Together,* was himself profoundly influenced by Tolstoyan obedience to the Sermon on the Mount.[22] In Geneva around 1919, Jean Lasserre's father, Henri Lasserre, met and became good friends with Tolstoy's biographer and close friend Pavel Biriukov (or Paul Birukoff). Biriukov was a private secretary to Tolstoy and like a son to him, a spiritual son.[23] In her book *Tolstoy and his Disciples,* Charlotte Alston listed Biriukov second on a short list of Tolstoy's most important sympathizers and activists.[24] In Russia, Biriukov started one of the earliest Tolstoyan Sermon on the Mount communities. After Tolstoy's death in 1910, he was exiled to Geneva where Henri Lasserre was living. Biriukov began a Tolstoyan periodical (*Svobodnaya Mysl*) published from Geneva, became a leader among the early Tolstoyan communities in Russia, Europe and beyond. He helped to publish hundreds of thousands of Tolstoyan pamphlets and many of Tolstoy's books. Biriukov wore rubber shoes, a clue that he shared some

---

21. Bethge, *Dietrich Bonhoeffer*, 113. Also DB-ER, 153, and DBW-10, 27.

22. Glen H. Stassen gives credit to Dietrich Bonhoeffer's involvement with the Abyssinian Baptist Church in 1930–31 as the primary inspiration for his notable turn toward the Sermon on the Mount. Perhaps Stassen was playing to his audience as his chapter was included in the book *Bonhoeffer and King* (chapter 15: "Peacemaking"). Stassen wrote: "Many who focus more on white, European influences among his friends that year at Union rightly give credit to the influence of French student Jean Lasserre for paying attention to the Sermon on the Mount and to pacifism. But I urge attention to Bonhoeffer's experience with African American Baptists. . . . [Bonhoeffer's] own letters in that period spend many more words and passion discussing his experience in community with African Americans than his experience with Lasserre." Notably though, all correspondence—except one postcard—between Bonhoeffer and Lasserre was later destroyed and is lost to historians. Regardless, the quotation Stassen cites of Bonhoeffer mentioning his conversion to the Sermon on the Mount was in the context of Lasserre, not the Abyssinian Baptist Church—though certainly Bonhoeffer's turn toward the Sermon on the Mount was a consequence of a confluence of several influences, though primarily Lasserre. (Bethge, *Dietrich Bonhoeffer*, 154–55; January 27, 1936, letter from Finkenwalde to Elizabeth Zinn, 134) There is no mention of Tolstoy in the entire chapter by Stassen or the entire book for that matter—as is the case in most other assessments of Bonhoeffer and King, credit is given to Gandhi for being the source of these Sermon on the Mount non-violent methods. This is a move similar to crediting a student for what his professor taught him.

23. Christiane Lasserre (Jean's daughter) correspondence with Steve Hickey dated September 12, 2016.

24. Alston, *Tolstoy and His Disciples*, 178.

of Tolstoy's more curious Sermon on the Mount applications like not eating meat or wearing leather.[25] However, it was the central admonition to take seriously the Sermon on the Mount which was passed on to Lasserre, both father and son.

Jean Lasserre's father Henri wrote a book in 1945 on Tolstoyan communities[26] based on what Biriukoff had written in a French pamphlet, the *Sayings of Tolstoy (Paroles de Tolstoï)*.[27] In a letter to me, daughter Christiane Lasserre shared how her father and grandfather were close, and that they discussed Tolstoyan obedience to the Sermon on the Mount. She asserts these were also the ideas her father was discussing with Dietrich Bonhoeffer.[28] Jean Lasserre dedicated his book *War and the Gospel* to his Tolstoyan father. It is not the case that the Lasserre's adhered to every Tolstoyan peculiarity. We know Jean Lasserre was not a vegan—in a letter from F. Burton Nelson to his friend Jean Lasserre there are comments reminiscing how delicious the chicken was which Mrs. Lasserre prepared for them on an occasion in 1977 when they were all together at Lasserre's summer chalet in Les Houches.[29] It was Tolstoyan obedience to the Sermon on the Mount that remained for the Lasserre's the central prophetic unction, not any of Tolstoy's more fanciful ideas on diet, land ownership, celibacy, anti-clericalism, or more importantly Tolstoyan dogmatics.

Tolstoy's influence on Bonhoeffer is once removed but from two formative directions; down through the Lasserre's, and down through Gandhi.[30]

25. Alston, *Tolstoy and His Disciples*, 178.
26. Lasserre, *Communities of Tolstoyans*.
27. Birukoff, *Paroles de Tolstoï*.
28. Christiane Lasserre (Jean's daughter) correspondence with Steve Hickey dated September 12, 2016. "I know that my grandfather Henri Lasserre met in Geneva a former secretar von Tolstoï. They became friends. Through that friend the influence of Tolstoï on my grandfather is sure and through Henri on my father. Probably my father spoke with Dietrich Bonhoeffer in New York about Tolstoï during their conversations."
29. Letter dated June 9, 1983, from Dr. F. Burton Nelson to Jean Lasserre. (Covenant Archives and Historical Library, F. Burton Nelson Papers [unprocessed], Box 31, folder "Correspondence with Jean Lasserre").
30. As a child Bonhoeffer eagerly read Tolstoy (*Gespräche mit Tolstoi* by J. Teneromo) and mentioned in a letter to his brother Klaus, dated July 20, 1920, that he didn't understand some of it—particularly the legend of the two old men "who speak about the corruption of truth through participation in social injustice. The young Bonhoeffer may not be aware that Tolstoy refers to himself here" [Note 11]. As a university student Bonhoeffer studied under Karl Holl in Berlin. Holl studied Russian and had a particular interest in Tolstoy, and he was also a leader in peace movements in Germany and peace research. Bonhoeffer, *Dietrich Bonhoeffer Works, Volume 9*, 34; Charfield and Mikhailovna, *Peace/mir*, xxvi. It would be surprising for Bonhoeffer to have studied with Holl and not been exposed to Tolstoyan Christianity. More work needs to be done

Though it is far too much to imply Bonhoeffer was any sort of Tolstoyan, it is not too much to say Tolstoy helped give the world Bonhoeffer, *Life Together* and *Discipleship* and a vision for a new form of monasticism and Sermon on the Mount communities. Only the briefest sketch of this Tolstoyan influence through Lasserre is possible here considering the limited space constraints. Bonhoeffer's new monastic experiment at Finkenwalde (1935–37) was cut short and left largely undeveloped. In similar fashion to how Bonhoeffer's *Ethics* were later recovered, compiled, edited and published by his beloved friend Eberhard Bethge, the challenge and opportunity today is for some new friends of Bonhoeffer to flesh out his unfinished model at Finkenwalde. In our day, a global movement of New Monasticism commonly embraces Bonhoeffer's prophetic statements envisioning a new form of monasticism as their guiding charge. That charge is most clearly articulated in Bonhoeffer's January 14, 1935 letter to his brother Karl-Friedrick:

> I think I'm right in saying that I would only achieve true inner clarity and honesty by really starting to take the Sermon on the Mount seriously. Here alone lies the force that can blow all of this idiocy [alternate translation: hocus-pocus] sky-high--like fireworks, leaving only a few burnt-out shells behind. . . . The renewal of the church will come from a new type of monasticism which only has in common with the old an uncompromising allegiance to the Sermon on the Mount. It is high time people banded together to do this.[31]

What all that might actually look like and mean is a conversation still in its early stages. Bonhoeffer spoke of *"recovering a link with the middle ages."*[32] In Tolstoy there was both a deep attraction to monasticism and a deep dissatisfaction.[33] He and Bonhoeffer would have had much to converse

---

on Holl's teaching in Berlin during this time to determine whether or not it was an additional significant exposure of Bonhoeffer to Tolstoy.

31. Bonhoeffer, *Dietrich Bonhoeffer Works, Volume 13*, 1/193, 285. Also: The next generation of pastors, these days, ought to be trained entirely in church-monastic schools where pure doctrine, the Sermon on the Mount, and worship are taken seriously—none of which are at the university and cannot be under the present circumstances. (DBW 13, 1/147, 217).

32. Bonhoeffer, *Letters and Papers from Prison*, 193. (January 23, 1944, letter from Tegel prison to Renate and Eberhard Bethge).

33. See Medzhibovskaya, "Tolstoy's Hieromonk," 55–63. Also, his short story, *Father Sergius*, written in the last decade of his life "signifies a rejection by Tolstoy of the life of hermit saints and those who perform spectacular acts of self-abasement such as chopping off a finger. According to Tolstoy, a saintly man practises charity and commits no miracles other than the reform of his own sinful life. Father Sergius' flight can also be understood as a projection of Tolstoy's own desire to flee his family as he argued

about, Bonhoeffer speaking of the "need to blow all this hocus-pocus sky high-like fireworks, leaving only a few burnt-out shells behind" (Tolstoy being an expert in this type of pyrotechnics); with Tolstoy chiming in with remarks about how old monasticism "is the equivalent to slow suicide."[34] He and Bonhoeffer both rejected of any sort asceticism that removed the disciple of Christ from the world. Tolstoy believed forsaking the world to

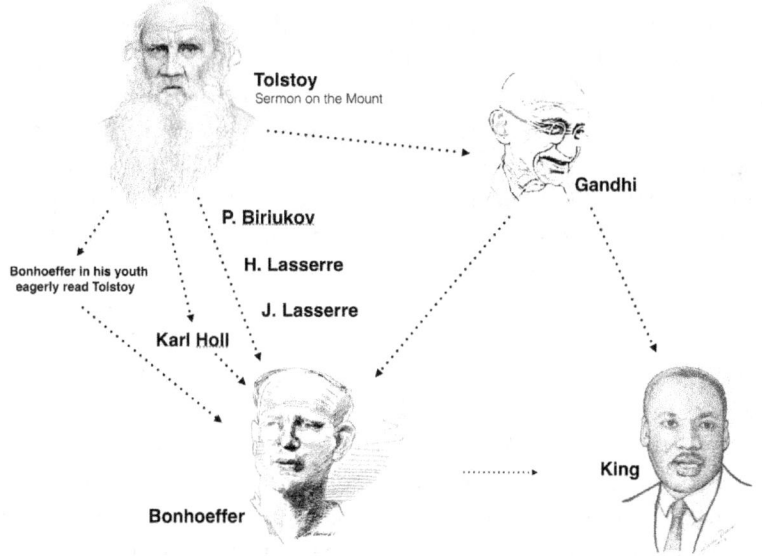

retreat into a convent or monastery made the Doctrine of Jesus impossible to practice, and he likened old monasticism to Jonah as a misguided monk who "wishing to remain upright and virtuous, retire[d] from the perverse companionship of men" and selfishly went out into the desert to make himself a shelter.[35] Bonhoeffer's new monasticism was on the "boundary of the church" but very much still in the world.[36]

---

with his wife about their luxurious way of life" (Tolstoy, "Father Sergius," xxvi–xxvii).

34. Tolstoy, *What I Believe*, 123.

35. Tolstoy, *What I Believe*, 123.

36. Bonhoeffer, *Dietrich Bonhoeffer Works, Volume 5*, 1/32, 46. "The expansion of Christianity and the increasing secularisation of the church caused the awareness of costly grace to be gradually lost.... But the Roman church did keep a remnant of that original awareness. It was decisive that monasticism did not separate from the church and that the church had the good sense to tolerate monasticism. Here, on the boundary of the church, was the place where the awareness that grace is costly and that grace includes discipleship was preserved.... Monastic life thus became a living protest against the secularisation of Christianity, against the cheapening of grace."

Bonhoeffer scholarship in recent decades has only superficially explored Bonhoeffer's interest in Gandhi.[37] Giving Gandhi all the glory for these Sermon on the Mount methods and strategies overlooks or ignores how Gandhi himself pointed back to Tolstoy as his inspiration and influence. Niebuhr cited two reasons to discourage Bonhoeffer's interest in Gandhi yet Bonhoeffer remained unpersuaded.[38] Though wanting to go spend time with Gandhi, Bonhoeffer was keenly interested to see up close what was the world's best example of (Tolstoyan) obedience to the Sermon on the Mount lived in the midst of national conflict and crisis. Work remains to uncover and better understand this linkage between Tolstoy and Bonhoeffer as related to the Sermon on the Mount and this envisioned new form of monasticism toward the renewal of the Church. Granted, for Tolstoy this was hardly about the renewal of the Church – something he viewed as a hopeless enterprise.[39] For Tolstoy, this was about the coming of the Kingdom of God on earth. Even so, Leo Tolstoy may be a good source for better understanding what Bonhoeffer envisioned for the renewal within Christendom; a new type of monasticism that has nothing in common with the old except people banding together in uncompromising allegiance to the Sermon on the Mount.

Questions remain. What might Bonhoeffer have gleaned from spending time with Gandhi visiting his ashram? Are there any insights within Bonhoeffer's concept of *religionless Christianity* which can inform us more precisely on what he was rejecting when he said this new form of monasticism will have nothing in common with the old? Are religionless Christianity and cheap grace developments of similar concerns voiced by Tolstoy? What in religion was this hocus-pocus Bonhoeffer was wanting to blow away to get back to the heart of the Gospel and the teaching of Jesus? It all sounds very Tolstoyan, though Bonhoeffer was likely not consciously drawing directly from Tolstoy, though arguably Tolstoy-through-the-Lasserres was a formative influence for him. Renowned French sociologist and prolific lay theologian Jacques Ellul spoke of Jean Lasserre as "one of France's noblest champions of nonviolence."[40] For decades, since before his friendship with Dietrich Bonhoeffer, Jean Lasserre was an advocate of a Tolstoy-esque Sermon on the Mount obedience. Was Lasserre able to carry forth in France

---

37. Davis, "Bonhoeffer and Gandhi."

38. Rasmussen, *Dietrich Bonhoeffer*, 213. See also Davis, "Bonhoeffer and Gandhi."

39. Rasmussen, *Dietrich Bonhoeffer*, 162: "The Church, by transmitting the truth of the Doctrine of Jesus, has communicated life to the world. Upon this nourishment the world has grown and developed. But the Church has had its day and is now superfluous."

40. Ellul, *Violence*.

through his lifetime of obedient activism what Bonhoeffer envisioned for his own future, and the future of the Church in Germany and beyond?

Reading Tolstoy and reading both Henri and Jean Lasserre on the subject of Sermon on the Mount allegiance and communities all bears a resemblance to reading Bonhoeffer's envisioning of the same.[41] Henri Lasserre's *Tolstoyan Communities* book was not published until 1944, making it unlikely Bonhoeffer even knew of it. Additionally, we know from *Dietrich Bonhoeffer Nachlass* that Bonhoeffer only had one unmarked book of Tolstoy's in his library, Tolstoy's *Gospel in Brief*.[42] Even so, a discernible thread can be substantiated of Tolstoyan influence through Pavel Biriukov, and then through Henri and Jean Lasserre to Dietrich Bonhoeffer leaving a Tolstoyan imprint at Finkenwalde, in *Discipleship* and in Bonhoeffer's embryonic envisionment of this new monasticism emerging globally in our time.

Bonhoeffer was deep into his Sermon on the Mount wrestlings at least from 1930 with Jean Lasserre at Union Seminary through the remaining sixteen years of his life. He wrote *Discipleship*, partially a commentary on the Sermon on the Mount, in 1937. The year before, 1936, Reichbishop Ludwig Müller published a Germanized reading of the Sermon on the Mount twisting Jesus's words to apply only to comrades. Below is a sampling from the Beatitudes, and from the pericopes on murder and enemy love:

> He who always maintains good relations with his comrades will get by in the world. . . . Those of you who keep peace with your comrades are doing God's will. . . . It is in your blood and your fathers taught you it: You should commit no treacherous murder. Such a murderer is guilty and must be sentenced to

---

41. One example will suffice for our purposes here—from Geffrey Kelly's 1972 interview with Jean Lasserre. Lasserre stated, "I would accuse Dietrich of having simplified the matter, of not taking into consideration all the factors. One has to be prudent. I wonder if those who attempted the coup weren't all a bit irresponsible. I believe that the real Hitlerian crime was that Hitler had the Wehrmacht at his disposal. If the Wehrmacht hadn't desired to obey Hitler, Hitler would not have caused all the damage he did. He would not have put Europe to so much bloodshed. Now why did the Wehrmacht obey Hitler? Because practically all the officers of the Wehrmacht, the higher officers and others were Christians, Catholics or Protestants, and they had received a falsified teaching of the Gospel. They had not been taught the Gospel of pacifism. They were taught a nationalistic Gospel which is basically a paganized Christianity. They had been told they always had to obey authority and government. . . . I always say that the real culprits of the Hitlerian drama are the Churches themselves, Protestant and Catholic, which, instead of teaching the young catechism according to the Gospel, taught them Constantinism, which is not the same. . . . Americans are doing the same in Vietnam" (Kelly, *Interview with Jean Lasserre*, 155). This is a statement that has strong echoes of Tolstoy.

42. Meyer, *Dietrich Bonhoeffer Nachlass*, 181.

death. But you must recognise and be clear that the act of murder is the result of an internal development, one which starts with resentment, envy and hate. He who allows such thoughts to surface in him is already guilty. But he who, out of such a mindset, wilfully abuses and persecutes his fellow comrade is truly guilty. However, he who tries to morally annihilate his fellow comrade or threatens him with violence is destroying the national community (*Volksgemeinschaft*), making himself worthy of the harshest punishment before man and God. Do not be unforgiving towards your compatriots with whom you are at enmity. Do not take the argument so far that any understanding and reconciliation becomes impossible. . . . There is an ancient proverb which says, "Love your friend, and hate your enemy." I say to you: If you want to be God's children, you must present yourself differently to your comrades and compatriots.[43]

The books known today to have been in Bonhoeffer's personal library are generally clean copies, however his copy of Reichbishop Müller's Germanised Sermon on the Mount is marked throughout. These are more than interesting but irrelevant details, they demonstrate that Bonhoeffer was writing his commentary on the Sermon on the Mount positioned ideologically in-between the aforementioned Tolstoyan influences on the one side and the Nazi reading of the Sermon on the other side.

5.5 Tolstoy's Discrepancies; Accuse Me and Not the Path I Follow!

Inherent to religious life and practice are inevitable discrepancies between being a doer of the Word or merely being a hearer (Jas 1:22). Only One ever lived a perfect life before God and man and that person was not Leo Tolstoy. Tolstoy, this holy fool who championed universal love to all in the world, critics pounce, was miserable to his own wife, ultimately left her, and was really only in love with himself, or so they say. Tolstoy had strained and severed relationships with some of his children. Alexander Boot broad-brushed as is evident in this example: "people who have too much love for mankind, often have none at all for men. The general subsumes the particular, and the particular disappears–except when it comes to loving themselves. . . . Thus, it was for the sake of abstract love that Tolstoy destroyed love in his own family."[44] Colm McKeogh ended his otherwise very important and insight-

---

43. Müller, *Word of God*.
44. Boot, *God and Man according to Tolstoy*, 35.

ful book on Tolstoy with a final chapter drawing these popular, albeit flawed conclusions, specifically:

> Tolstoy does not love his neighbour as himself. Tolstoy received from God, not love, but law; he gave to his fellow human beings, not love but sacrifice. Having neither personal love nor forgiveness from God, Tolstoy had none to offer his fellow human beings. Tolstoy achieved, not a selfless love, but a loveless self.[45]

One wonders if Boot and McKeogh were referring to the same Tolstoy who signed off his letters to his children—"I kiss you, Your Loving Father"[46]— and to his estranged wife—"I love you, I always will"[47]; the same Tolstoy worked alongside peasants helping them in any way he could; the same Tolstoy who personally wrote the Tsar to get men pardoned; the same Tolstoy who fed thousands every day during the famine; the same Tolstoy who personally paid to relocate persecuted Doukhobor Christians to Canada. This same Tolstoy wrote Gandhi about the infection of love from God hoping it spreads to India.[48] Here, Boot and McKeogh offer readings of Tolstoy that show no appreciation for how Sermon on the Mount obedience can result in dividing families (Luke 12:53) and a white martyrdom.[49]

45. McKeogh, *Tolstoy's Pacifism*, 203.
46. Christian, *Tolstoy's Letters, Volume II*, 663, 669.
47. Christian, *Tolstoy's Letters, Volume II*, 701.
48. Tolstoy, "Letter to a Hindu," 413–15.
49. On the colors of martyrdom: A Celtic monk in the seventh century, in what is called *The Cambrai Homily*, outlined three categories of martyrdom designated by colors; red, green, and white. Red martyrdom refers to when blood is shed; when they lop off your head or throw you to the lions. If Christ is indeed first, personal safety and security are at least a distant second. The problem for those early Celtic saints was that they "had to forgo the bloody 'crown of martyrdom' until the Viking invasions at the end of the 8th century" and therefore they conceived of other forms of martyrdom, living forms because they still knew the call of Christ was to lose your life to find it. After red martyrdom, *The Cambrai Homily* presented green martyrdom to describe those who sell their possessions and give them away to the poor, those who leave behind comforts and pleasures, deny their flesh via monastic ascetics, assuming vows of poverty and chastity, opting for simple living and frugality. White martyrdom is the separation from loved ones. The designation white martyrdom actually goes back four additional centuries being first used by the desert hermit St. Jerome in the third century. White martyrdom is kissing family goodbye before getting on a ship to sail to a faraway place to spend one's life reaching the people God called one to reach. It is also when non-Christian loved ones reject them because of their faith in Christ. My suggestion in regard to these colors of martyrdom is that we conceive of a fourth colors, grey martyrdom. Grey, as I conceive this, can become the color of conviction, the color of foundation stones. The grey martyr pays the high price of standing for and on Christian foundations and core Christian convictions against the crowd, and against the way of the world, even the church world. As every aspiring Reformer of every age discovered,

At stake here is far more than Tolstoy's self-admittedly weak attempts at following the way of Christ.[50] Holding to the lonely view that the Sermon on the Mount was liveable, Tolstoy's failings, exaggerated, have been used to bolster the opposite view, that the Sermon on the Mount presents an impossible ideal. The question is legitimate; do Tolstoy's discrepancies undercut the validity of his postulations on the liveability of the way of Christ, the doctrine of Jesus? Award-winning Tolstoy biographer A. N. Wilson used Tolstoy's failings in just this regard:

> Tolstoy's religion is ultimately the most searching criticism of Christianity which there is. He shows that it does not work.[51]

---

following Jesus and following the Church are not always the same thing. Grey martyrdom as I construe it is when one's credibility, reputation and ecclesiastical standing suffer for Jesus' sake. Jesus himself took a different path than the religious leaders of his day and the cost of his convictions was high. Martin Luther was defrocked. Barth was dismissed from his lectureship at Bonn. Dietrich Bonhoeffer was a grey martyr more than a decade before he was a red one (I assume the legitimacy of his red martyrdom as a Christian martyrdom). My view is that Grey martyrdom is the lot of many reformers who faced rejection from ecclesiastical authority, excommunication, being shunned and regarded as dead. Grey martyrdom is when friendship with Jesus makes one an enemy of their ecclesiastical authority. Tolstoy was a white, green and a grey martyr.

Sources: "The homily expounds on Matthew 16:24 with a selection from the *Homilia in Evangelia* by Pope Gregory I and an explanation of three modes of martyrdom, designated by the colours red, blue (or green, Irish glas), and white. The Cambrai Homily, in reference to the French town *Cambria* where it is kept at the municipal library, is one of the few surviving written sources for Old Irish in the period 700 to 900."

(https://en.wikipedia.org/wiki/Cambrai_Homily cited. . . . Follett, *Céli Dé in Ireland*, 54–56). Also: *The Cambrai Homily* appears in a manuscript of the *Bibliothèque Municipale* (Cambrai, MS. 679, formerly 619, fos. 37rb–38rb).

50. On his weakness and the discrepancy between his actions and his words Tolstoy wrote with a transparency like that of the Apostle Paul in Romans 7: "It makes me feel bad, or rather, awkward, when frequently men well disposed to me take me seriously, seeking and demanding a complete correspondence between my words and my acts. "But how is it that you say one thing, and do another?" I am no saint, and I have never given myself out for a saint; I am a man carried away, and sometimes, or, more correctly, always, say, not fully what I think and feel, not because I do not want to say it, but because I cannot, frequently exaggerate, and simply err. This is so as regards to words. As regards acts, it is even worse. I am an absolutely weak man, with vicious habits, who wishes to serve the God of truth, but who keeps constantly getting off the road. The moment I am looked upon as a man who cannot err, every mistake of mine appears either a lie or a bit of hypocrisy. But if I am understood to be a weak man, the disagreement between my words and my acts will be a sign of weakness, and not of lying and hypocrisy. And then I shall appear as what I really am: bad, but sincerely, with my whole soul, always, and even now, wishing to be absolutely good, that is, a good servant of God." Tolstoy, "Thoughts and Aphorisms," 196–97.

51. Wilson, *Tolstoy*, 300–1. Full quotation subsection 0.2, n7.

On numerous occasions over many years Tolstoy was forthright in responding to such misreadings of the discrepancies of his religious life and practice. In response to questions in a letter from a young journalist Tolstoy replied: "Accuse me – I do this myself – but accuse me and not the path I follow."

> If I know the road home and walk along it drunk, staggering from side to side, does that make the path I follow the wrong one? If it is the wrong one – show me another; if I lose my way and stagger – help me, support me in the real path, as I am ready to support you, and don't make me lose my way, don't rejoice that I have lost my way, don't shout with delight: 'There he is! He says he going home, but he's falling in a swamp.' No, don't rejoice at that, but help me and support me.[52]

After working nine months for the Tolstoy family while they lived briefly in Gaspra, a young man later wrote to Tolstoy that "he had long been sympathetic to his ideas but had been disillusioned by the discrepancy between his way of life and his beliefs after seeing him in close quarters." Tolstoy replied his regret that the young man did not talk to him personally when he had the chance. The main issue was regarding his apparent compromised vegetarianism—"which I have never consciously betrayed in the course of 20 years"—Tolstoy stated, "[I] only learned from your letter that the doctors probably deceived me during my illness by cooking meat broths for me."

> I thank you for the letter and for the denunciations it contains. I continually suffer from the discrepancy between my way of life and the truths which I profess – especially recently as a result of my illness; I try to eliminate this discrepancy and am grateful to those who remind me about it in the way you do in your letter, and force me to try harder to make my life accord with the truths I profess.[53]

Importantly, Tolstoy's frugality and simplicity of lifestyle was stark and apparent to visitors from abroad who called on him. In 1887, American author George Kennan visited Tolstoy at Yasnaya Polyana. Approaching Tolstoy's "plain, white, rectangular, two-story house of brick" he wrote:

> It would be hard to imagine a simpler, barer, less pretentious building. It did not remind of piazza nor towers nor architectural ornaments of any kind. . . . [Inside the] floor was bare;

---

52. Christian, *Tolstoy's Letters, Volume II*, "Letter 271, To M. A. Engelhard From Moscow, December 20(?), 1882 – January 20(?), 1883," 363.

53. Christian, *Tolstoy's Letters, Volume II*, "Letter 490, To G.P. Degterenko, From Yasnaya Polyana, August 20, 1902," 622.

> the furniture was old-fashioned in form, with two or three plain chairs, a deep sofa, or settle, upholstered with worn green morocco, and a small cheap table without a cover. There was a marble bust in a niche behind the settle, and the only pictures which the room contained were a small engraved portrait of Dickens and another of Schopenhauer. It would be impossible to imagine anything plainer or simpler than the room and its contents. More evidences of wealth and luxury might found in many a peasant's cabin in Eastern Siberia.[54]

Despite these occasionally published humble descriptions there persisted the assumption that Tolstoy was living one way while telling others to live another. With so many people assuming he had lots of money he received many requests to give it to this or that person, or cause. He eventually wrote a letter to the editors of the *Russian Gazette* and the *New Times* which was published in September 1907. The gist of the letter was: Please stop asking me for money, I don't have any.

> More than 20 years ago I renounced the ownership of property for certain personal considerations. The real estate that belonged to me I handed over to my heirs as though I has died. I also renounced the right of ownership of my works, and those written after 1881 became public property. The only sums which I still have at my disposal are the monies which I sometimes receive, primarily from abroad, for starving people in particular areas, and the small sums which certain people provide for me to distribute at my own discretion. I distribute them in the immediate neighbourhood for the benefit of widows, orphans, the victims of fires, etc. . . . frivolous newspaper contributions about me have misled and continue to mislead very many people who approach me more and more often and on a bigger and bigger scale for financial help.[55]

Tolstoy mentioned the types of needs people placed before him and how at expressing his regrets he would "get back new letters, angry and reproachful." The letter was published in nearly all the newspapers in Russia and resulted in a bitter backlash against Tolstoy, "where he was pilloried as 'The Great Bankrupt of Russia'" by anonymous letter writers.[56] The letter to the

---

54. Sekirin, *Americans in Conversation with Tolstoy*, 13, 15; also quoted in Kennan, "A Visit to Count Tolstoy," 252–65.

55. Christian, *Tolstoy's Letters, Volume II*, "Letter 550, To the Editors of 'The Russian Gazette' and 'New Times', From Yasnaya Polyana, 17(?) September 1907," 670.

56. Christian, *Tolstoy's Letters, Volume II*, 670.

editor also appeared to have no effect as the solicitations continued at the same rate as before.

Even in the very last months of his life these perceived discrepancies weighed heavily on him. In February of 1910 (Tolstoy died in November), a student at the University of Kiev wrote him and brazenly advised the old sage to "renounce everything – his title, worldly goods and family – and to lead the life of a beggar." Tolstoy's reply demonstrated the seriousness with which he considered this matter of the congruency between one's words and actions. In an atypical longhand personal reply (at this late period he needed secretarial help with correspondence) Tolstoy wrote:

> Your letter deeply moved me. What you advise me to do constitutes my cherished dream, but so far I have been unable to do it. There are many reasons for this . . . but the main one is that I certainly ought not to do it in order to influence other people. This . . . should not govern our activities. What you advise me to do . . . I did more than 25 years ago. But the one fact that I live in my family with my wife and daughter in terrible, shameful conditions of luxury in the midst of surrounding poverty, continually torments me more and more, and there is not a day when I don't think about following your advice.[57]

These latter years of Tolstoy's life were spent between the house in Moscow Tolstoy's wife preferred to live in for the children's sake, and the family estate at Yasnaya Polyana. In the main, Tolstoy found the Moscow lifestyle inwardly gruelling and deeply offensive to his call to simplicity.[58] It was a regular source of consternation in the Tolstoy marriage. On more than one occasion he simply left to escape it and retreat to the estate, or it was arranged that they would live this distance apart and correspond daily. Tolstoy wrote much about marriage to his followers and children and stressed the crucial matter of the husband and wife being of the same mind about what gives meaning to life. It was far better to Tolstoy to not marry than to be caught between ones responsibility to the needs of their spouse against their own obedience to the will of God. No respectable holy man would leave his wife for God and Tolstoy lived within this vivid and painful tension the last three decades of his life. He lived with a sense of being held back by his wife who did not share his convictions and his desperate flight the last week of

---

57. Christian, *Tolstoy's Letters, Volume II*, "Letter 581, To the B. Mandzhos, From Yasnaya Polyana, 17 February 1910," 697.

58. Tolstoy wrote: "The family is the flesh. To reject the family is the second temptation - to kill yourself. The family is a single body. But don't submit to the third temptation - serve not your family but the one God." From PSS, 49:32.

his life can be viewed either as a loveless (which it was not) failed marriage, or as a white martyrdom (see n49), a fulfilled prophecy of Christ that the way of life will divide homes and loved ones.[59] In a long letter to his wife twenty-five years earlier he articulated his dilemma writing:

> There can be no agreement and no loving life between us until you come to what I have come to . . . until you come to me; I didn't say: until I come to you, because that is impossible for me. It is impossible because the things you live by are the very things I have only just escaped from, and from a horrible and monstrous thing which nearly brought me to suicide. I can't go back to the things I lived by, the things in which I found perdition, and which I acknowledged to be the greatest evil and misfortune. But you can try to come to something you haven't yet known . . . when a spiritual revolution was taking place inside me and my inner life changed, you ascribed no significance or importance to it. . . .
>
> You think that I am one thing and my writing is another. But my writing is the whole of me. In life I have not be able to express my views fully; in life I make concessions to the necessity of living together in the family. I live, and in my soul I deny that life.[60]

Four years after his father's death, Tolstoy's son Ilya wrote *Reminiscences of Tolstoy* which underscored a sense of martyrdom in his father's life-choices. Recalling the words of a kinsmen which he felt best conveyed the dynamic in the difficult latter period of his parent's famous marriage: "'What a terrible misunderstanding!' he said. 'Each was a martyr to love for the other; each suffered without ceasing for the other's sake; and then . . . this terrible ending.'"[61] Again, the notion of a white martyrdom (see subsection 5.5, fn 49), the loss of family closeness on account of obedience to Christ, becomes a reasonable consideration in seeking understanding in Tolstoy's seemingly

---

59. Matthew 10:36–37: "A man's foes will be those of his own household. He who loves father or mother more than me is not worthy of me." About this passage, and in relation to Tolstoy, Bunin wrote: "There were many of them, these 'noble youths who abandoned their country for other lands.' For example there were Prince Gantama, Alexis, the man of God, Julian the Hospitaller, and Francis of Assisi. To these must be added the starets Leo from Yasnaya Polyana." Bunin adds the notation that a "staret is an elderly monk or person whose religious life commands respect and authority from mystically-minded disciples." See Bunin, *Liberation of Tolstoy*, 4, 175n8.

60. Christian, *Tolstoy's Letters, Volume II*, "Letter 297, To Countess S. A. Tolstoya, From Moscow, 15–18 December 1885," 393, 399.

61. Tolstoy, *Reminiscences of Tolstoy*, 310.

lovelessness toward his wife, and supposed discrepancy between his message and his marriage.

In other correspondence Tolstoy responded to his noticed discrepancies with comments about the difference between words, deeds and intentions: "The chief difference between words and deeds is that words are always intended for men for their approbation, but deeds can be done only for God . . . deeds you can do quite unknown to men, only for God."[62] On these good intentions which God alone sees, Tolstoy wrote: "I think that we will be judged by our conscience and by God – not for the results of our deeds, which we cannot know, but for our intentions. And I hope that my intentions were not bad."[63] It is unfortunate and hardly fair that one who surpassed so many in society for personal sacrifice and generosity is widely construed as being one who fell short of the cost of discipleship.

5.6 Bauman: Ghost of Tolstoy Haunts a Century of Sermon on the Mount Interpretation

Sermon on the Mount literature since the earliest days of Christianity can be categorized in various ways: (1) homiletical and hermeneutical approaches to the Sermon on the Mount seeking application for Christian living, (2) theological and apologetic approaches devoted to defining and articulating the doctrinal matters raised within the Sermon, i.e. law/Gospel, ethics, eschatology, etc., and (3) historical approaches seeking to capture the long history of interpretation of the Sermon. In this last category there are very few sources of any comprehensive quality but there are a few high calibre expositions, including that of Clarence Bauman.[64] Bauman's treatment, *The Sermon on the Mount: The Modern Quest for Its Meaning*, expressly states the significant role of Leo Tolstoy in the history of Sermon on the Mount interpretation which is of interest now.

The contention here, shared by Bauman, is that Tolstoy (or at least the Ghost of Tolstoy) became the baseline for over a century of subsequent interpretation of the Sermon. That baseline is the absolute or literal position of interpretation that Jesus meant what he said and expected his followers

---

62. Christian, *Tolstoy's Letters, Volume II*, "Letter 499, To Percy Redfern, From Yasnaya Polyana, 23 February 1903," 630–31.

63. Christian, *Tolstoy's Letters, Volume II*, "Letter 479, To John Bellows, From Gaspra, 24 November/7 December 1901," 363.

64. Bauman, *Sermon on the Mount*. Also noteworthy are (1) Kissinger, *Sermon on the Mount*; (2) McArthur, *Understanding the Sermon on the Mount*; (3) Windisch, *Meaning of the Sermon on the Mount*.

to live in this new way. By the ghost of Tolstoy, I intend to convey that Tolstoy, though very often never named, was indeed the absolute position from which all the others creatively departed. Bauman began his extensive survey of the modern era of Sermon interpretation with Tolstoy for this very reason: "Our own analysis begins with Tolstoy because it was through him that the Sermon on the Mount first became a problem to the modern conscience."[65] His conclusion states it even more directly:

> Our history of interpretation began with Tolstoy because it was through him that the hermeneutical possibilities and liabilities of understanding or misunderstanding the Sermon on the Mount were most acutely focused within the developing modern historical consciousness of Western Christian thought. As every great prophet, Tolstoy also proved to be a great divider of men. . . . Virtually every commentator in the modern history of the Sermon's interpretation found reason to contest Tolstoy's view – reason enough to wonder what kernel of eternal truth it contained which could be examined neither by argument nor slander. Tolstoy was convinced Christ meant exactly what he said and intended his words to be taken in childlike truth and not allegorically or casuistically evaded. Jesus did not say his commandments were too hard to keep; he said his yoke is easy. But throughout the centuries the church insisted it is impossible for us to do what Jesus says and that consequently his "Antitheses" are impractical unless accommodated to human weakness.[66]

Bauman presented Tolstoy as the challenge to every subsequent Sermon on the Mount interpreter:

> Tolstoy is not merely a great artist gone astray, whose religious fantasies deserve little claim to serious consideration, especially by theologians. . . . The questions this moral and religious teacher posed to the church during the last thirty-two years of his life demand answers, not just enlightened dismissal or psychological evasion. If Tolstoy has not understood the Sermon on the Mount correctly, it is up to us to say where and how he erred. We may criticise Tolstoy's interpretation, but we cannot afford to ignore it. Even in our critique we ought to remember that polemic against 'fanatics' is to a large extent polemic against the Sermon on the Mount and criticism of Jesus himself.[67]

---

65. Bauman, *Sermon on the Mount*, 7.
66. Bauman, *Sermon on the Mount*, 343–44.
67. Bauman, *Sermon on the Mount*, 34.

Bauman's analysis of the main post-Tolstoy Sermon on the Mount interpreters is that

> One cannot evade the disconcerting impression that they are for the most part motivated by the dubious aim of restricting the scope of its meaning, qualifying the sense of its validity, and limiting the context of its relevance.... With astounding ingenuity Christendom developed an amazing variety of hermeneutical reasons why one could not or should not obey the commandments of Jesus.... The Sermon on the Mount has always been an embarrassment to the Church. Catholicism took the burden of Jesus' demands off the shoulders of its believers by delegating it to professionals.... Meanwhile, Protestant exegesis in prolific variety concluded that the word of Jesus do not really mean what they say.[68]

Tolstoy, or at least the Ghost of Tolstoy, are upstream of most all major modern attempts—successful or otherwise—to apply the Sermon to modern society including Gandhi and E. Stanley Jones in India, Walter Rauschenbusch and the Social Gospel movement in America, Dietrich Bonhoeffer in Nazi Germany, and Martin Luther King Jr. in the American civil rights movement. Bauman's work is important in its exposition of the development from Tolstoy to these other notable Sermon on the Mount interpreters of the last century. Each in some way places a lesser demand on the follower of Christ than Tolstoy believed the Sermon on the Mount literally required of the Christian.

The title of this chapter *Letters, Legacy and the Ghost of Tolstoy*, seeks to bring together the more lasting effects of Tolstoy's ideological reach and influence under one heading. His letters have been shown to be rich depositories of Tolstoyan thought quickly dispersed far and wide. Firstly in subsection 5.2, Tolstoy's heretofore under-appreciated *Letter to the Tsar* is treated here and given near epistolary status among other historic and biblical letters with the hope that it will now gain a wider reading and be heeded in future settings of national conflict. His *Letter to a Hindoo* and subsequent letters to Gandhi are shown in subsection 5.3 to be of catalytic importance to Gandhi's non-violent revolution and the struggle for India's independence. Interaction with Martin Green's trilogy on the two mahatmas contributes to this section of the chapter. New material and findings unique to this dissertation are set forth in subsection 5.4 on the real, albeit indirect, influence of Tolstoy on Bonheoffer traced here through Bonhoeffer friend Jean Lasserre and his Tolstoyan father. An indirect influence of Tolstoyan

---

68. Bauman, *Sermon on the Mount*, 417–18.

Sermon on the Mount interpretation is noted behind the famous work of Bonhoeffer's *Discipleship* and his insistence on simple obedience to the Sermon on the Mount. Tolstoy's legacy has marred by accusations of hypocrisy between his lifestyle and teaching, yet in subsection 5.5 his letters have been shown to absolve him of that charge. And finally, in subsection 5.6, in a brief treatment of Bauman's work, what I'm calling the ghost of Tolstoy is just upstream of many of the Sermon on the Mount interpretations in the past century. In referring to the ghost of Tolstoy, the inference is central to the first stated claims of this project; that often Gandhi gets the glory for what he received from Tolstoy, and how in general, Tolstoy is only infrequently named and remains under-appreciated and overlooked. The hope herein is that these pages will serve to rectify this neglect and restore Tolstoy to a rightful place of prominence in Christian theology and Christian history.

PART TWO

The Doctrine of the Church

~ 6.0 ~

Tolstoy among the Reformers of Constantinian Christendom

ONLY TWICE IN THE span of his long life did Leo Tolstoy leave Russia to travel abroad. The first trip took place in 1857 from February to the end of July and is notable for his witnessing an execution in Paris which profoundly affected him and calcified his abhorrence of and total rejection of state-sanctioned violence and killing.[1] Three years later in July 1860 he traveled abroad again, not returning until the following April. In London he visited schools to better develop his pedagogical theories and later experiments with the education of the youth at Yasnaya Polyana.[2] However, the reformation of education was not the only reformation on his mind.

Tolstoy had been reading the Protestant reformers of the Church and went out of his way to visit Wartburg Castle overlooking the town of Eisenach Germany, where Martin Luther hid after the Diet of Worms. Tolstoy friend and biographer Alymer Maude wrote: "The personality of the great Protestant reformer interested him very much, and after seeing the room in which Luther commenced his translation of the Bible [Tolstoy] wrote in his Diary: 'Luther was great!'"[3] A few days later Tolstoy wrote: "Luther is a

---

1. Maude, *Life of Tolstoy,* Vol. I, 183. "The very next day he saw a man guillotined and made the following entry in his Diary: 'I got up at seven o'clock and went to see an execution. A stout, robust, white neck and breast: He kissed the Gospels and then—death! How senseless!' ... 'I knew it to be unnecessary and bad.'"

2. See Leo Tolstoy's *Tolstoy as Teacher* and *Tolstoy on Education.* Also: Murphy, *Tolstoy on Education.*

3. Maude, *Life of Tolstoy,* Vol. I, 210.

reformer of religion– back to the sources!"[4] In time Tolstoy would also go back-to-the-sources seeking to quarry the teaching of Jesus on that mountainside from underneath eighteen centuries of eisegesis, Church tradition and dogmas. Maude noted that "twenty years later Tolstoy himself when trying to free men's minds from the yoke of an established Church, shaped his chief weapon against the Church by translating not, it is true, like Luther, the whole Bible, but the Gospels."[5]

Importantly the Reformation of Luther was not the earliest or only attempt at reforming Christendom. The reformer who most influenced Tolstoy preceded Luther by nearly a century, Petr Chelčický (pronounced khel-cheet-skee), a Czech from Bohemia. Tolstoy devoted several pages of his *Kingdom of God Is within You* to Chelčický and near the end of his life wrote the foreword to a translation of Chelčický's *Net of Faith*.[6] In what is still the only English biography of Chelčický to be published, Murray L. Wagner wrote: "The scenario that stages church history with clarions and drums as Martin Luther arrives at the Wittenberg door, nails up the *Ninety-five Theses*, and rings up the curtain on an entirely new act of Christian history called 'The Reformation' is a highly mythical interpretation of Protestant beginnings that obscures a long and tortuous history of reformism."[7] Referring to this earlier reformation of Chelčický, Amedeo Molnár proposed that there were two Protestant Reformations the first of which includes all the movements of reform from the twelfth to sixteenth centuries but particularly the Waldenses, Taborites, and the *Unitas Fratum*—an outgrowth of the Czech reforms of Petr Chelčický.[8] Murray writes: "Characteristics common to the 'first reformation' included the recognition of Scripture as sole authority with the actual norm of truth and life narrowed to the synoptic gospels, especially the Sermon on the Mount."[9] The challenge of Chelčický's reform was to return to the doctrines of Christ in the Sermon on the Mount, not the doctrines of Paul as in the later reformation of Luther.

---

4. Christian, *Tolstoy's Diaries, Volume I*, 156–57.

5. Maude, *Life of Tolstoy, Vol. I*, 210.

6. Tolstoy, *Kingdom of God Is within You*, 25–28. And Tolstoy, "Preface," for *Net of Faith*, archived in the Tolstoy personal library and archive at Yasnaya Polyana; translated from Russian in 2017 for Steve Hickey by Olga Sevastyanova. This preface is included in the appendices, subsection 12.3.

7. Wagner, *Petr Chelčický*, 158.

8. Wagner, *Petr Chelčický*, 158.

9. Wagner, *Petr Chelčický*, 158.

6.1 Petr Chelčický's Ninety-Five Theses

In a peculiar stroke of happenstance, Chelčický's major work of protest against the Church, *The Net of Faith* (written 1440–43), has "ninety-five theses" packaged as ninety-five brief chapters, some of which are only a few sentences in length. All of Chelčický's many writings, and he himself, "are literally unknown in what is loosely termed the West."[10] It is apparent from Tolstoy's comments on Chelčický that he was not aware of him when Tolstoy wrote *What I Believe* in 1884. However, nine years later at the writing of *The Kingdom of God Within You*, this work of Chelčický, and Chelčický the reformer himself became important confirmations and clarifications for Tolstoy's own solidifying interpretations of the Sermon on the Mount.[11] Chelčický and his immediate influencers and predecessors (especially the Waldensians), are the earliest articulators and expounders of what is deemed today the Constantinian heresy, Christendom's decisive third-century shift away from the values and teachings of Jesus to an outright embracing and approval of the use of the sword and force.

In this chapter the main intersection points between Chelčický and Tolstoy will be set forth, namely (a) the departure from the doctrines of Christ at the time of Constantine, (b) the centrality of the Sermon on the Mount for Christian living, (c) the conspiracy of silence that continues to muzzle these ideas and these reformers, and (d) real connections between Tolstoy and Bonhoeffer friend Jean Lasserre will be considered as they relate to a little known but important chapter by Lasserre on the Constantinian heresy. Between the Bohemian Petr Chelčický in the fourteenth century and the Frenchman Jean Lasserre in the twentieth century is the Russian Leo Tolstoy in the nineteenth century and each took serious issue with what went on in Rome in the third century. The place to begin is with the most "mature and most representative" of the over fifty extant Chelčický works, his *Net of Faith*.[12]

Net of Faith is designated as such because it is an extended development of Chelčický's unique interpretation of Luke 5:4 where Jesus said to Simon Peter, "Put out into the deep water and let down your nets for a catch." Chelčický's read on this teaching of Jesus is allegorical. The night of "wearisome but fruitless fishing" represents "the spiritual night in which all

---

10. Molnár, *Net of Faith*, iii.

11. Tolstoy, *Kingdom of God Is within You*, 25. "In this work, written four centuries ago, Chelčický, as the Professor [at Prague University] tells me, has expressed exactly the same opinion in regard to true and false Christianity that I did in my work entitled *What I Believe*."

12. Molnár, *Net of Faith*, iii.

human effort is without result. . . . [T]he night is pagan influence and Jewish blindness which passed away when Christ, the Son of God, the True Light, came into the world in order to illumine those who lived in the shadow of death."[13] The net, Chelčický understood to represent the "Holy Scriptures . . . woven and prepared like a physical net, one knot tied to the other, until the whole great net is made; similarly, there are tied one to another the different truths of the Holy Scripture, so that they can enclose a multitude of believers . . . drawn out of the ocean of this world. . . . And this net is capable of pulling out everyone from the sea of deep and gross sins."[14] The net breaks and tears as a multitude of persons are caught, a "great number of repellant things" that are caught in the net, "heretics and offenders, enter the net of faith (Sometimes outwardly being of faith but later – in times of temptation – reverting to abominations and heresies). Such people tear the net."[15]

In his development of this allegorical interpretation, Chelčický paused at this point—now chapter four—to deal with issues that strike at the heart of and bear remarkable similarity to Tolstoy's understandings of these conceptions; the interpretation of the law and the insufficiency of the first law, the Jewish Law. Like Tolstoy, Chelčický believed "many divine words of the first law (footnoted as i.e. the Old Testament) do not bind us."[16] Chelčický shared with Tolstoy similar views on the purpose of the various types of Scripture in the Bible: "Now of course, we have to obey the Scripture. . . but not everything in Scripture is divine. . . . Some portions do not lead us to follow Christ for (they) were written by some only as an (historical) record, and they were never (intended) to have any power."[17] To illustrate his hermeneutic Chelčický stated we are not called today to show ourselves to a priest after we receive prayer for healing even though Jesus cured a man and told him to go find a priest and give a thank offering. Chelčický saw part of that pericope of Scripture containing the act of power and the supporting passages therein only containing a historical record of the deed. This type of consideration of the different types of passages in the Bible and their function bears resemblance to Tolstoy's hermeneutic. For both Chelčický and Tolstoy, the Doctrines of Christ (as they both referred to them) in the Sermon on the Mount, contained the new law of God and changed how Old Testament passages of divine law are to be read and have authority in Christian living today. As reformers of Christendom, Chelčický, Luther

13. Tolstoy, *Kingdom of God Is within You*, 49.
14. Molnár, *Net of Faith*, 52.
15. Molnár, *Net of Faith*, 52–53.
16. Molnár, *Net of Faith*, 55.
17. Molnár, *Net of Faith*, 107.

and Tolstoy each rejected the authority of Church dogma and tradition but Chelčický and Tolstoy differed from Luther with regard to which parts of Scripture possessed supreme authority and power. By bringing the grace doctrines of Pauline Scripture to the forefront and placing a lesser degree of concern on the doctrines of Christ, it is evident the fifteenth century reformers also had their canon within the canon. In Luther's case, regarding the Peasants Revolt, in holding up Romans 13, Chelčický and Tolstoy would construe this as a putting down Matthew 5–7, the section of scripture most dear to them.

Also Chelčický renounced superstitions which are said to be "of faith that are not faith, nor do they resemble it. . . . The straying away from faith has long since become a great movement, and the people are so much steeped in errors that they accept dead, erroneous, and man-made customs introduced as faith. And they are so ignorant that true faith appears to them as a foul heresy."[18] Again, the alignment with Tolstoy is in plain view as Orthodox mysticisms and superstitions were, to Tolstoy, a significant rejection and replacement of what Christ on the mountainside plainly said he expected of his followers.[19] In a series of short chapters beginning with chapter six, Chelčický developed what constitutes the perfect apostolic church which is founded on the law of Christ, "or the religion of Christ tied to his law by many knots of different truths of divine words." Chelčický cited John 17 saying Jesus established the net of faith in his words when he said, "I have given them the words that you gave me, and they have received them." For Chelčický, those words are the teachings of Jesus at the Sermon on the Mount and they constitute the new law of Christ, the new religion of Christ. He underscored the importance of imitating Christ and building only on the foundation of the teaching which Christ laid; citing 1 Corinthians 3:11–12: "For no other foundation can anyone lay than that which is laid, which is Christ. Let each man take care how he builds upon it." Chelčický insisted Christians imitate Christ and follow his laws not obeying the laws of "another authority, pagan and civil, standing in courthouses with lawsuits. . ."[20] There is deep congruity with Tolstoyan Sermon on the Mount interpretation at these points. Chelčický wrote: "The Christians having fallen away from the way of perfection, keep falling deeper and deeper. . . . His law alone can check the fall . . . man can be rescued through his obedience to the laws of Christ."[21]

18. Molnár, *Net of Faith*, 55–56.
19. Tolstoy, *Kingdom of God Is within You*, 49, 68–69.
20. Molnár, *Net of Faith*, 62.
21. Molnár, *Net of Faith*, 99.

Importantly, an additional point central to Tolstoyan Sermon on the Mount interpretation, Chelčický also made noted use of the concept of *an eternal law* beyond the written laws of both sacred and pagan society.[22] Chelčický held up the "sufficiency of Christ's law" and lamented the time of Constantine when "two other laws were added, namely the temporal and the papal law, the Christian society immediately deteriorated in its quality and perished."[23] The other laws, like "poison" mixed in with divine laws, make divine laws "unintelligible, and men finally abandon them."[24] Chelčický was compelled to "expound as much as we can, yet still too weakly, the sufficiency of the law of Christ."[25] His writings are of a kerygmatic genre and clearly he was imploring his readers to return to the true Gospel as he cited supporting passages like Galatians 1:8: "if anyone is preaching to you a gospel contrary to that which you received, let him be accursed," and Jude 3-4: "I appeal to you to contend for the faith that was once for all delivered to the saints. For admission has been secretly gained by some when long ago were designated for this condemnation." Strongly, Chelčický believed he was calling out those who gained secret admission into the net of faith and were not only destroying themselves but many others as well.

As the ninety-five brief chapters of *Net of Faith* proceed, Chelčický devoted space to refuting the claims of various church councils and the engage the arguments of his opponents at those councils.[26] The latter chapters

22. Molnár, *Net of Faith*, 63, 66–67.
23. Molnár, *Net of Faith*, 67.
24. Molnár, *Net of Faith*, 67.
25. Molnár, *Net of Faith*, 68.
26. The outline of *Net of Faith* is as follows: "The Miraculous Fishing chps 1–3"; "Interpretation of the Law chp 4"; "Faith and Superstition chp 5"; "The Perfect Apostolic Church chps 6–12"; "Refutation of the Claims of the Council of Basel and of the Arguments of Juan Palomar chp 13"; "The Church Loses Its Perfection through the Donation of Constantine chp 14"; "The Pope's Guilt in the Transaction Called 'Donatio Constantini' chps 15–18"; "The 'Donation of Constantine' - The Emperor's Guilt In This Transaction chps 19–23"; "The Early & Medieval Church chps 24–25"; "State Authority is Outside Moral Law chp 26"; "The Origin of State Sovereignty chp 27"; "Wyclif's Three Types of Government chp 28"; "The Origin of Church Authority chp 29"; "The Dividing Line Between the Spiritual and the Secular chp 30"; "The Law of Men and the Perfect Law of Christ chps 31–38"; "The Evils of the Church of Rome - Luke 3:14 chp 39"; "Interpretation of Luke 3:14, Refutation of St. Augustine's Argument of Permissible Warfare chps 40–41"; "Interpretation of Romans 13:1–4 chps 42–67"; "Refutation of Aegidius Carlerii Presented at the Council of Basil chps 68–72"; "Refutation of the Arguments of Albertus Magnus of Cologne chps 73–76"; "Resumption of the Arguments of Aegidius Carlerii chps 77–80"; "Military Service and War are Contrary to the Law of Christ chps 81–85"; "Interpretation of Romans 13:5–7 chps 86–91"; "Interpretation of 1 Timothy 2:1–3, There Can Be No Christian Sovereignty chps 92–94"; "Summary chp 95."

include extended expositions of Romans 13:1–7 and 1 Timothy 2:1–3 which very much contain interpretation and conclusions Tolstoy would heartily agree with on government, taxation, death penalty, enemy love, pacifism and war. Chelčický asserted "The whole test of a Christian comes to this: is he willing to love his enemies?"

> For if the Christians believed in this commandment of love, and accepted it among themselves, the sword would immediately fall from their hands, all conflicts and wars would cease among them, no one would threaten them with a sword, but gracefully do good for evil; and should they be hurt and oppressed by others, they would not strike back with their sword but patiently suffer all evil, being more worried about spiritual than physical harm. But the world knew not our Saviour nor did it accept his exalted teaching.[27]

That statement comes from Chelčický's chapter, "*Military Service and War are Contrary to the Law of Christ.*" The phraseological similarities and conceptual overlap with Tolstoy teaching are so exact it would seem Tolstoy found Chelčický and his ideas a decade before we know that he did.

After a ten chapter excursus as detailed above, Chelčický returned to his net of faith allegory. Chelčický began rehearsing the history of the primitive church how formerly the followers of Christ "hid in caves, among rocks and in forests for Christ's name" but how "behold, now the Emperor guides him around Rome, seating him on a white mare – or was it a white horse? No matter! It was always a 'bird of ill omen.'"[28] The reference is to a twelfth century mosaic in the Chapel of St. Sylvester, of the church of Santi Quattro Coronati in Rome where the Emperor Constantine is depicted leading the bridle of Pope Sylvester's horse through Rome after the Donation of Constantine. Chelčický identifies this moment as the tearing of the net:

---

27. Molnár, *Net of Faith*, 134.
28. Molnár, *Net of Faith*, 72.

> It was then and there that the net became greatly torn, when the two great whales had entered it, that is, the Supreme Priest wielding royal power with honour superior to the Emperor, and the second being the Emperor who, with his rule and offices, smuggled pagan power and violence beneath the skin of faith. And when these two monstrous whales began to turn about in the net, they rent it to such an extent that very little of it has remained intact.[29]

In Chelčický's imagination he could see these two monstrous whales spawning "scheming schools"

> first of all the hordes of monks in all manner of costumes and diversified colours; these were followed by hordes of university students and hordes of pastors; after them came the unlearned hordes with multi-form coats-of-arms."[30]

Chelčický lamented they all desired to rule and extend their rule:

---

29. Molnár, *Net of Faith*, 73.
30. Molnár, *Net of Faith*, 73.

Frontispiece Illustration of the 1521 Edition of The Net of Faith
Printed in the Monastery of Vilémov

(The net is held by four apostles and in the net are the righteous Christians. One sinner is falling overboard and another is escaping through a big hole in the torn net. Below, protruding from the open jaw of an infernal leviathan, the devil is roping in the pope, the emperor, the learned doctors, and other sinners.)

and in order to rule they divide; some are lords spiritual and some are lords temporal. The spiritual lords are the Pope, who is the lord over lords, the lord cardinal, the lord legate, the lord archbishop, the lord patriarch, the lord pastor, the lord abbot, the lord provost. . . . And the temporal lords are the lord Emperor, the lord king, the lord prince, the lord magnates, the lord burgrave, the lord knight, the lord page, the lord judge, the lord councillors, the lord mayor.[31]

31. Molnár, *Net of Faith*, 73.

Each appropriated to themselves various dominions and Christ is no longer lord at all. All this was an anathema to Chelčický who wrote:

> We find it clearly written in the Gospel that the apostolic man is bound to poverty, humility and work, in imitation of Christ and his apostles to whom he said, "Follow me, and I will make you fishers of men." They accepted the words of Christ and kept them until their death, not owning any business, estate or temporal fief. They kept his commandment. Sylvester [of Rome, who baptised Contantine] was duty bound to keep it, too. And he is guilty of transgression because he did not abide by his obligation.[32]

Chelčický followed this with chapters on the Pope's guilt and the Emperor's guilt. Chelčický further saw the Roman Church dividing society into three groups: (a) the lords, kings and princes, (b) the spiritual priesthoods, and (c) the workers in bondage. Again, these are the very categories and concerns which preoccupied Tolstoy. And like Tolstoy, Chelčický saw freedom from all this in a return to the law of Christ.[33]

6.2 Tolstoy and the Constantinian Heresy

Again, the two main post-conversion Second Tolstoy texts containing his Sermon on the Mount interpretations are *What I Believe* (1884) and *The Kingdom of God Is within You* (1893), or WB/KG as cited below. As was stated in subsection 2.2, similar to Luke/Acts, these two texts of Tolstoy relate each other as a continuation of something written earlier. As Luke began Acts with "in my former book," Tolstoy began KG with the sentence, "in 1884 I wrote a book entitled *What I Believe*." From that point he continued by setting up this second volume as a furtherance and development of the ideas in the first volume. There were nine intervening years where he was exposed to Chelčický and several other important people and groups who he had come to find out also were saying similar things; the Quakers, Abin Ballou, William Lloyd Garrison and others. Properly accessed the earlier volume (WB) has a textual and exegetical focus on the Sermon on the Mount whereas the second volume (KG) has more of a historical and doctrinal focus. Though there is an awareness in Tolstoy in the earlier volume, prior to any exposure to Chelčický of a Constantinian shift, it receives Tolstoy's greater attention in the second volume (KG). What he was

---

32. Molnár, *Net of Faith*, 77.
33. Molnár, *Net of Faith*, 75.

thinking, and aware of, in terms of a Constantinan shift at the time of the writing of the first volume is evident here:

> I examined the teachings of the early Fathers of the Church, and found them to agree in obliging no one to judge or condemn . . . the martyrs, by their acts, declared themselves to be of the same mind. I saw that Christianity before Constantine regarded tribunals only as an evil. . . . I turned to the Church commentaries. In all, from the fifth century onward.[34]

What he then described, though not using the term shift, was "contrary to the whole doctrine of Jesus."[35] Twenty pages later Tolstoy was back on the subject:

> Commentators of the Church, particularly those who have written since the fifth century, tell us that Jesus did not abolish the written law; that, on the contrary, he affirmed it. But in what way? How is it possible that the law of Jesus should harmonise with the Law of Moses? To these inquiries we get no response. The commentators all make use of a verbal juggle to the effect that Jesus fulfilled the law of Moses, and that the sayings of the prophets were fulfilled in his person . . . and the essential question for every believer how to harmonise two conflicting laws; each designed to regulate the lives of men, is left without the slightest attempt at explanation.[36]

He was referring to the Sermon on the Mount where again and again Jesus said, to paraphrase; you have heard that it was said but now I tell you something very different. Tolstoy wrote: "We must accept one commandment or the other; and Chrysostrom, like all the rest of the Church, accepted the commandment of Moses and denied that of the Christ, whose doctrine he nevertheless claims to believe. Jesus abolished the Mosaic law, and gave his own law in its place."[37] Tolstoy presented his awareness of a fourth and fifth century shift away from the Doctrines of Christ as coming to him solely though his own observations and study of the Gospels and early history of Christianity and Christendom. Still referencing at this point on from his earlier work he wrote of the New Life-Conception of the Sermon on the Mount as diametrically opposed to "the pseudo-Christian religion which

---

34. Tolstoy, *What I Believe*, 30–31.
35. Tolstoy, *What I Believe*, 30–31.
36. Tolstoy, *What I Believe*, 50.
37. Tolstoy, *What I Believe*, 52.

men had been teaching for fifteen hundred years."[38] Revealing much of his ill-regard for the rest of the New Testament, Tolstoy penned a version of the onset and progression of the Constantinian shift that neither Chelčický nor Luther would concur at least entirely with, nor would any modern adherents to the notion of a Constantinian heresy such as John Howard Yoder and Stanley Hauerwas:

> Therefore, the arbitrary separation of the metaphysical and ethical aspects of Christianity entirely disfigures the doctrine [of Jesus], and deprives it of every sort of meaning. The separation began with the preaching of Paul, who knew but imperfectly the ethical doctrine set forth in the Gospel of Matthew, and who preached a meta-physico-cabalistic theory entirely foreign to the doctrine of Jesus; and this theory was perfected under Constantine, when the existing pagan social organisation was proclaimed Christian simply by covering it with the mantle of Christianity. After Constantine, that arch pagan, whom the Church in spite of all his crimes and vices admits to the category of saints, after Constantine began the domination of the Councils, and the centre of gravity of Christianity was permanently displaced till only the metaphysical portion was left in view . . . until it has reached its present stage of development, as a doctrine which explains the mysteries of celestial life beyond the comprehension of human reason, and, with all its complicated formulas, gives no religious guidance whatever with regard to the regulation of this earthly life. . . . Psuedo-Christianity alone prescribes nothing . . . all that is necessary to the psuedo-Christian is the sacrament. . . . From the time of Constantine the Christian Church has prescribed no religious duties to its adherents. It has never required that they should abstain from anything. The Christian Church has recognised and sanctioned divorce, slavery, tribunals, all earthy powers, the death penalty and war.[39]

These brutal indictments against Christendom seen already in Tolstoy's earlier work (WB) are developed further in his second (KG).

The matters of hypocrisy and heresy take shape in the second volume (KG) as Tolstoy identified the hypocrisy of Christians and a Christian church that are in no way like Christ. Heresy becomes, for Tolstoy, the charge of any who side with Christ not the Church, who adhere to the teaching of Christ not the teachings of the Church. His questions are penetrating:

---

38. Tolstoy, *What I Believe*, 86.
39. Tolstoy, *What I Believe*, 150–51.

"May a Christian remain a Christian and still disobey the direct command of Christ; may he promise to conduct himself in a manner directly opposed to the doctrine of Christ by entering into military service and putting himself in training to be a murderer?"[40] Believing the answer is a categorical No, Tolstoy wrote; 'my book [WB] has been received just as all [heretical] denunciations have been, those denunciations of the clergy who have deviated from the law of Christ, with which history abounds since the time of Constantine the Great."[41]

This polarization of the Church's hypocrites and Christ's heretics is vivid for Tolstoy. The point of contention and divergence was the Credo, and for Tolstoy the Credo of the Church was, at best, a distraction from the Creed of Christ, and at worst the entire and diabolical displacement of it. Lost in the middle are the uninstructed masses for whom the Church Credo was unintelligible

> in the dogma of transubstantiation, the infallibility of the Pope, the bishops, and Scriptures, which is something utterly incomprehensible and nonsensical, requiring a blind faith, not in God or Christ, nor even in the doctrine, but a faith either in one person, as in Catholicism, or in many persons, as in Orthodoxy, or in a book, as in Protestantism. . . . Already, about the time of Constantine, the entire conception of the doctrine amounted to the resume formulated by the temporal power– the outcome of the discussions that took place in the council– to the Credo, in which it is said: I believe in this and that, etc., and at the end, "in the one holy, Apostolic Ecumenical Church," that is, in the infallibility of the persons who constitute it; so that it all amounted to this, that a man believed not in God, nor in Christ, as they revealed themselves to him, but in that which was believed by the Church.[42]

The contrast for Tolstoy was in the plain words of Jesus in the Sermon on the Mount. Jesus, he believed, brought from God words that were meant to be understood by the simple people of the world, and words that were to be lived. Yet, as Tolstoy saw them, heretics were merely those who believed differently than the Church and he pointed out that "each advance that has been made towards the comprehension and the practice of the doctrine [of Jesus] has been accomplished by heretics: Tertullian, Origen, Augustine,

---

40. Tolstoy, *Kingdom of God Is within You*, 36.
41. Tolstoy, *Kingdom of God Is within You*, 36.
42. Tolstoy, *Kingdom of God Is within You*, 56–57.

and Luther, Hus, Savonarola, Chelčický, and others were all heretics."[43] Tolstoy wrote:

> The Church as a Church, whether it be Catholic, Anglican, Lutheran, or Presbyterian, or any denomination whatsoever, inasmuch as it is the Church, cannot help striving after the same object as the Russian Church– namely to conceal the true meaning of the doctrine of Christ and to substitute a meaning of its own. . . . Do we not find Catholicism with its prohibition against reading the bible, and with its demand for implicit obedience to the clergy and the infallible Pope? Wherein does Catholicism differ in its preaching from the Russian Church? The same external worship, the same relics, miracles, and statues, miracle-performing Madonna and processions; the same vague and mystical utterances concerning Christianity in books and sermons, and all in support of the greatest idolatry. . . . The disparity between ecclesiastical creeds and the doctrine of Christ is so great that a special effort is required to keep mankind in ignorance . . . all these ideas evolved by the men of the fourth century."[44]

A full-length chapter in this project on the Constantinian heresy with these repeated and extensive citations is justified in the fact that in the history of Sermon on the Mount interpretation up to Tolstoy, the Constantinian shift framed, for Tolstoy, the broader historical-doctrinal context for rightly interpreting the Sermon and for returning to its message.

6.3 Embracing the Religion of the Sword, the Eusebian Myth, and the Unrealized Reformation

This is a major motif in Tolstoy's interpretation of the Sermon on the Mount, how, for eighteen-hundred years, these Doctrines of Jesus have been rejected and replaced. Counting his references to "eighteen hundred years" would extend into the multiple dozens of times in the main writings deemed here as Second Tolstoy. In an earlier identified Tolstoyan diatribe #7 (see subsection 2.3) his reiteration of this lapsed time period reaches a crescendo:

> The long experiment of Christian life by nation after nation, during eighteen centuries, has inevitably brought me to the necessity of deciding whether the doctrine of Christ is to be

---

43. Tolstoy, *Kingdom of God Is within You*, 64–65.
44. Tolstoy, *Kingdom of God Is within You*, 74–75.

accepted or refused.... Indeed, in the course of the eighteen centuries the best men in all of Christendom, through an inner spiritual medium, having recognised the truths of the doctrines, have borne witness of it, regardless of threats, privations, miseries and torture.... Eighteen centuries of the profession of Christianity have not passed in vain for those who have accepted it.... [T]hese eighteen centuries have made me realise all the miseries of the pagan state.[45]

Chelčický and Tolstoy both precisely pinpointed the time of departure, the fall of the Church, to the time of Constantine. In his biography of Chelčický, Murray Wagner wrote of the end of Chelčický's life when he met Réhor, who in later years would champion Chelčický's conceptions of a true and obedient church: "The old man [Chelčický] could only feel the tragedy of an unrealised reformation. In the imagery of his restitutionist metaphor, so few were willing to clear the thicket of underbrush, remove the debris and rotten timbers that had collected since Constantine, and begin to rebuild upon the church's one foundation on apostolic Christianity."[46] Regarding Constantine, Chelčický wrote: "He introduced the religion of the sword to the Christians.... Therefore, no Christian should deviate from the path of faith in order to follow the Emperor or his sword, for indeed, the way of Christ has not been repealed just because the Emperor is a 'Christian.'"[47] The emphasis casting doubt on *Christian* was his as "they have been seduced from faith by the Emperor; they no longer are of the faith of Christ but of the faith of the Emperor." (Tolstoy was equally unequivocal—"If the churchmen are Christians, then I am not a Christian, and visa versa.")[48] Chelčický saw the unholy alliance of spiritual and temporal powers behind the coercion of the sword to be a great evil:

> The Pope, having received temporal dominion from the Emperor, defends both by the sword, claiming by means of many texts and of sly and cunning reasonings that they are in the service of God. He covers Anti-Christ's footprints with Caesar's sword and has the Holy Spirit sitting on this new layer of sand.... Laban could not find the household gods because Rachel was sitting down on them (Genesis 31:34). Christ is the way and he who hides it with his sanctimoniousness commits a crime against the people who desire to take his way.... To his servants [Jesus]

---

45. Tolstoy, *The Kingdom of God Is within You*, 175–77.
46. Wagner, *Petr Chelčický*, 152.
47. Molnár, *Net of Faith*, 121.
48. Christian, *Tolstoy's Diaries: Volume II*, 246.

> gave a commandment to love their enemies and to do them good for evil deeds; to give them food and drink when they are hungry and thirsty, and to pray for them to God saying, "O Lord God, forgive them, for they know not what they are doing." This behaviour does not incite enemies to fighting, but it tames their anger and lust for war. They who want to live a Christian life must look for an example in Jesus Christ.[49]

Both Chelčický and Tolstoy believed the departure of the Church from the way of Christ, from the imitation of Christ, occurred during the reign of Constantine.

This negative narrative of a Constantinian heresy runs counter to the positive narrative most prominent in each of the major streams of Christendom today where the conversion of the pagan Constantine is considered (a) genuine, (b) a great triumph for God's Kingdom come on earth, (c) the end of the brutal early period of Christian persecution, and (d) "a model for Christian political practice today."[50] Certainly the early period of persecution was over. However, according to the negative narrative so central to the reformations of Chelčický and Tolstoy, the killing continued, and continues—in far larger numbers and on a global scale, only now with ecclesial complicity and justifications. Eusebius, the first proper historian of the Church, can be credited with starting the positive narrative. However, even articulate, modern defenders of Constantine's Christianity concede Eusebius was as much Caesar's cheerleader as he was any kind of observing objective historian.[51] Those who espouse the reality of a Constantinian heresy reject the Eusebian myth of a Great Church triumphant.[52] Chelčický was not reading Eusebius, rather he was directly influenced by the Waldensians and particularly their legend of the Donation of Constantine. The legend which came to Chelčický via the Austrian Waldensians of his day is as follows:

> The "manager" of the Church of God in the days of the rule of Emperor Constantine was "a certain Sylvester of Rome" who, being persecuted, led a miserable life "with his people on Mount Sirachyia." Moved by a dream that he had one night, the

---

49. Molnár, *Net of Faith*, 134.

50. Leithart, *Defending Constantine*, 11.

51. Leithart, *Defending Constantine*, 179. "[M]ainstream scholarship has long considered Eusebius nothing more than a 'political propagandist, a good courtier, the shrewd and worldly adviser of the Emperor Constantine, the great publicist of the first Christian emperor, the first in a long succession of ecclesiastical politicians, the herald of Byzantinism . . . and a caesaropapist." Leithart's citation is from Hollerich, "Religion and Politics in the Writings of Eusebius," 309.

52. Wagner, *Petr Chelčický*, 47.

Emperor asked to be baptised by Sylvester. Once baptised, the Emperor was miraculously cured from leprosy.

The Emperor, overjoyed by his recovery, stopped persecuting the Christians and their leader Sylvester; he even gave Sylvester "the imperial crown and dignity." Sylvester accepted the "donation" but his companions protested saying that "they have a commandment from the Lord, not to possess any land." On the night of the day in which the split occurred a voice from heaven was heard saying: "Today poison has been poured into the Church of God." The Christians departed from "Sylvester the arch-heretic upon hearing this voice" and continued to lead a life of poverty and renunciation. However, the greater part of the Church followed Sylvester and the hatred of these "pseudo-Christians" caused the persecution of the true "pauperes Christi" for many generations as if they were heathens of Jews.

These persecuted remnants finally gathered around the person of Peter Waldo who simply "corrected their order" (i.e. he did not found it!); he also studied the Scripture and inspired them to action "in accordance with the way of poverty." Hence, this was the origin of the Waldensians. By this legend the Waldensians wanted to justify their separation from the Church of Rome and their continuity as true descendants of the original "pure" church. Chelčický is much closer to this Waldensian interpretation of the Donation than to Wyclif's; on it be based his logic of separation of "Christ" and "Caesar."[53]

In just a couple short paragraphs of his *Net of Faith*, Chelčický used the term *poison* six times to describe what was poured into the Holy Church via the Donation of Constantine, AD 315.[54]

6.4 *Hic Sunt Leones*

Tolstoy deserves credit for being one of the only people in the last few hundred years to draw attention to the work of Petr Chelčický and the Constantinian shift.[55] He did so initially giving three pages to Chelčický and

53. Molnár, *Net of Faith*, 88n123. Cf. Holinka, *Traktáty Petra Chelcoikého*, 30ff.
54. Molnár, *Net of Faith*, 30ff.
55. Less noticeably, in 1923, the Dutch G. J. Heering published his *Fall of Christianity: A Study of Christianity, the State and War* calling attention to the Christus victor! "turning point" of Constantine's conversion, the Waldensians, and Tolstoy (Heering, *Fall of Christianity*, 54ff.). In 1981, Peter Brock devoted a few pages to the Constantinian shift, the Waldensians, and Chelčický in his *Roots of War Resistance: Pacifism from the Early Church to Tolstoy*.

Net of Faith in his *Kingdom of God Is within You*. In that space he briefly explained Chelčický's allegorical interpretation of Luke 5 by referring to what is written about *Net of Faith* in Pepin's *History of Czech Literature*. Tolstoy explained how from 1884–88 no copy of *Net of Faith* had been translated or was available for his review. He waited on a translation that was supposedly forthcoming but it never materialized in publication. Through a contact he had at the University of Prague he was able to get proof sheets of part of the translation that had been prepared. The veil over these writings and those like them struck Tolstoy as a validation of the revelation they contain:

> yet this book has remained out of print for centuries, and continues to be unknown except to a few specialists. One would think that works like these of the Quakers, of Garrison, of Ballou, and of Chelčický – which affirm and prove by the authority of the Bible, that the world misinterprets the teaching of Christ – would arouse an interest, would make a sensation, would give rise to discussions between clergy and their flocks. One might suppose that works which deal with the very essence of the Christian doctrine would be reviewed, and either acknowledged to be just, or else refuted and condemned. Not at all. Every one of these works suffers the same fate.[56]

In his dissertation on Chelčický, Enrico C. S. Molnár made an argument that "the whole ideological content of Czechoslovak Protestantism . . . for the great part [is] an uncharted map to Anglo-American Protestantism, which is still often compelled to inscribe the blank spaces with the legend *hic sunt leones*."[57] *Hic sunt leones* means "here be dragons" and is a old phrase for dangerous or unexplored territories which were marked on medieval maps by putting illustrations of sea monsters on the uncharted areas. Molnár's contention was the Czeck reformation of Chelčický, not even so much John Hus (who adopted the way of the sword), but Chelčický's Doctrine of Jesus is still to the Church a dangerous and unexplored way. Luther's doctrines of (Pauline) grace were difficult waters for the Church. Even more Chelčický's doctrines of Jesus, and Tolstoy's attempts to take them up, seem ill-fated to be marked *hic sunt leones*. In his preparatory comments to his transcription of Molnár's dissertation and translation of *Net of Faith*, Tom Lock sought to express the importance of bringing the work of *Chelčický* out in the mainstream of theological conversation:

---

56. Tolstoy, *Kingdom of God Is within You*, 27.
57. Molnár, *Net of Faith*, iii.

Why have I bothered to do this? The short answer is that the Holy Spirit told me it was important. Chelčický wrote the *Net of Faith* around 1443. 451 years later Tolstoy brought it to our attention in his *Kingdom of God Is within You*, lamenting its obscurity and exposing the "conspiracy of silence" that surrounds this part of the Gospel. It was another 53 years before Rev. Molnár made the first and only English translation, but his ultimate goal remained unfulfilled for 59 more years; his translation existed as a single copy – the original manuscript – in an academic library. Silence has reigned for 563 years.[58]

It is a similar sense of divine leading compelling this entire project as I concur with both Chelčický and Tolstoy's calls to return to a radical obedience to the Sermon on the Mount.

On my research trip to Yasnaya Polyana to the archives and personal library of Tolstoy, his personal copy of *Net of Faith* was located and discovered to have a four page, approximately 1800 word preface written by him some time late in the first decade of the new century. He began: "Written over 450 years ago by an unlearned man named Petr, from the town of Chelčice, exists a book, which is almost completely unknown."[59] Tolstoy dubbed Chelčický a "reviver . . . of Christian doctrine . . . despite him being a layman and uneducated in Latin, and although he was not a master in the seven arts, he was truthfully an implementer of the eight beatitudes and all of the Lord's commandments."[60] Tolstoy distinguished Chelčický from the other reformers in that he

> does not debate, like his predecessor Hus, and like Luther, Melanchthon, Calvin, that lived and acted after him, Papal ecclesial institutions and dogmas, he only shows that the lives of people considering themselves Christians, are not in themselves Christian, and that a Christian man cannot use power, cannot own land or slaves, live in splendour, or live a dissolute life, cannot execute, and most importantly, cannot kill or make war[61]

Tolstoy continued:

> The book is too far ahead of its time – the time of its fruitfulness has not yet come. The destruction of papal authority, the indulgences, and many other things created by Luther could be

---

58. Molnár, *Net of Faith*, vii.

59. Tolstoy, "Preface" (privately translated by Olga Sevastyanova for Steve Hickey, 2017), 1. Included in the appendices subsection 12.3.

60. Tolstoy, "Preface," 1–2.

61. Tolstoy, "Preface," 2.

handled by the modern men, however, the words of Chelčický could not be accepted, not because they were unclear or unjust, – on the contrary, all he said was too clear and too just – but because what he said was too far ahead of its time.[62]

It is quite evident Tolstoy felt Chelčický's work not only supported his own, but shared a similar fate:

> If the existing system were to be withheld, it means that Christianity must be renounced. And this is also frightening. What else was there left to do? One thing: forget what Christ, Chelčický and the conscience had said; and not think, not speak of it. This has also been the reason for the obscurity of Chelčický's book – the book was silenced, it had been forgotten. If a dozen scientists know about it, then they look at it only as a historical, literary record. Nonetheless, the spiritual wealth of mankind never perishes, but only ripens, like young fruit. And the longer they wait for their time, the more valuable they become. The same applies to Chelčický and his book. . . . Hundreds of thousands of copies of dozens of editions are printed of Nietzche, Zola and Verlaine. Everyone is familiar with the smallest details of these people's lives. However, the works of Chelčický have not yet to this day been printed, even in the Czech Republic and Germany, not to mention England and France.[63]

6.5 Chelčický, Tolstoy, and Jean Lasserre—Missing Voices in the Modern Dialogue

John Howard Yoder is typically credited with the conception of the terms Constantinian and the Constantinian Heresy to describe "the 'fourth-century shift' that created a gap between biblical Christians and us, a 'disavowal and apostasy.'"[64] Yoder offered his most complete articulation of the Constantinian heresy in a chapter of his 1984 book, *The Priestly Kingdom: Social Ethics as Gospel*.[65] Subsequently, Stanley Hauerwas remains known as the leading proponent of these concepts, himself being significantly influenced by Yoder. The most substantive challenge to Yoder and Hauerwas came in the 2010 publication of *Defending Constantine: The Twilight of an Empire*

62. Tolstoy, "Preface," 2.
63. Tolstoy, "Preface," 3.
64. Leithart, *Defending Constantine*, 1–2, 175.
65. Yoder, *Priestly Kingdom*. See chapter 7, "The Constantinian Sources of Western Ethics," 135–47.

and the Dawn of Christendom by Peter J. Leithart. Leithart expressly posited the main of his argument of his 350-page tome defending Constantine "is directed at Yoder" though "Hauerwas, and their increasing tribe" are very much in view.[66] Three years later Hauerwas and his increasing tribe responded with a book of essays edited by John Roth, *Constantine Revisited: Leithart, Yoder, and the Constantinian Debate*.[67] My intention here is not to properly review the important contributions of these books but only to acknowledge there is current and ongoing discussion of the notion of Constantinian Christendom, and that there are, in general, two divergent views represented by Leithart on the one end, and Hauerwas and his increasing tribe on the other. What is more important for the contribution of this project is not what has been said, but what is still missing from the conversation (forthcoming here in subsection 6.5 on Jean Lasserre), but especially a notable avoidance of Tolstoy and Chelčický particularly by Yoder.

Adding the page counts of these two modern, scholarly, and significant book-length treatments of the Constantinian Heresy, amounts to over six hundred pages. Quite noticeably in light of the work at hand on Tolstoy and Chelčický, there is no reference to either Tolstoy nor Chelčický by Leithart, Hauerwas, or any in their tribe. Yoder did refer to Chelčický six times in his book articulating his thoughts on a Constantinian shift, but not in reference to *Net of Faith* or to Chelčický's early articulations of the Constantinian Heresy.[68] Without reference to these earlier, major sources, Yoder is commonly considered the origin of this angle of critique. Additionally there is another important yet ignored person, still prior to Yoder and Hauerwas and known to both, who added significantly to the matter of a Constantinian Heresy. In 1965, twenty years before Yoder wrote his essay on Constantinianism, Bonhoeffer's influential French friend at Union Seminary Jean Lasserre wrote an entire chapter in his book *Christians and Violence* called *The Constantinian Heresy*.[69] Perhaps he was the first to ever use the precise term Constantinian heresy: "instead of speaking of the Constantinian

---

66. Leithart, *Defending Constantine*, 11.

67. Roth, *Constantine Revisited*. Perhaps the authors of the included essays could be considered members of the Yoder/Hauerwas tribe Leithart had in mind; John C. Nugent, Alan Krieder, Mark Thiessen Nation, William T. Cavanaugh, D. Stephen Long, Jonathan Tran, Branson Parler, Timothy J. Furry, Charles M. Collier, Caig Hovey, J. Alexander Sider, with the foreword written by Hauerwas and the afterword written by Leithart.

68. Yoder, *Priestly Kingdom*, 43, 88, 127, 146, 153, and 188.

69. Lasserre, *Les Chrétien et la Violence*. Chapter 3 is titled "The Constantinian Heresy," 81–94, and the related chapter 4 is called "The Paganism of War," 95–103. Citations from these chapters included in this chapter are translations from the French made for Steve Hickey by Rebecca Elder.

era we should rather refer to the Constantinian heresy."[70] It clearly was not Yoder. There is evidence Tolstoy, on the matter of the Constantinian heresy, was the influence for Jean Lasserre, and because these connections have not been made elsewhere, space was allotted in subsection 5.4 to deal with Bonhoeffer, Lasserre and Tolstoy. In brief review, it is enough to say Lasserre's father Henri was a Tolstoyan who wrote a book on Tolstoyan Communities, and he was a close friend of Tolstoy's personal secretary.[71] These connections and influences aside, Lasserre's contribution to the notion of a Constantinian heresy and a subsequent but directly related chapter on the *Paganism of War* merit the following analysis of Lasserre's chapter on the Constantinian heresy for what it contributes to the Constantinian shift so central to Chelčický's and Tolstoy's critique of the Church and Christian Dogma and reformation efforts.

On the subject of violence and war, Lasserre divided the history of the Church into two traditions; the first tradition was the tradition of the first three centuries:

> [T]here is not a single Christian text from this period which deals with the question of military service and of murder in general, without an outright condemnation and without proclaiming that the place of the Christian is not in the army. Nowhere do we find indulgence towards the Christian soldier. The testimony of the Fathers is unanimous: a Christian does not go to war. He will even refuse to be a judge, since a judge may be called upon to pronounce the death sentence.[72]

There are strong echoes of Tolstoy in these statements. Lasserre's daughter has written to me of how her father and grandfather discussed Tolstoyan pacifism, nonviolence and interpretations of the Sermon on the Mount.[73] Lasserre dedicated his earlier book, *Gospel and War*, to his Tolstoyan father. These material connections back to Tolstoy, and through Tolstoy back to Chelčický lend to the probability of Lasserre not coming to the Constantinian heresy on his own. What he wrote in his chapters on the topic should

---

70. Lasserre, *Les Chrétien et la Violence*, 90.

71. Lasserre, *Communities of Tolstoyans*.

72. Lasserre, *Les Chrétien et la Violence*. 81.

73. Christiane Lasserre (Jean's daughter) correspondence with Steve Hickey dated September 12, 2016. "I know that my grandfather Henri Lasserre met in Geneva a former secretar von Tolstoï. They became friends. Through that friend the influence of Tolstoï on my grandfather is sure and through Henri on my father. Probably my father spoke with Dietrich Bonhoeffer in New York about Tolstoï during their conversations."

be considered his subsequent developments of the Chelčickian/Tolstoyan historical/theological schema on the paganism of the Church.

The second tradition, Lasserre asserted, began in the fourth century:

> From the fourth century, we witness a complete reversal of the situation ... from then on, being a soldier will be accepted by the mass of the faithful and it is the conscientious objectors who will be excommunicated from the Church! Henceforth the bearing of arms will become normal for Christians, at least for those who are not priests, and the first pacifist tradition of the Church will be engulfed by a second tradition according to which homicide is completely compatible with the profession of the Christian faith, under certain conditions. These conditions are legitimate defence, just war, etc. Now we live under the influence of and within this second tradition. Everywhere in our 'Christian' countries, the Church and the army hold each other in mutual respect and cooperate willingly. It is normal and even glorious for a Christian to go to war and the first tradition has been forgotten to such an extent that conscientious objectors are seen as holding a scandalous position ... [a position] contrary to the sound teaching of the Church.[74]

In contrast to what was earlier called the Eusebian Myth of a glorious fourth century for the Church, Lasserre deemed "the fourth century was, in the history of the Church, a terribly dark and disappointing period... the about-turn was rapid and brutal!"[75] His reference there is to the consequences of a soldier seeking to obey the plain teaching of Jesus by refusing to take up arms being both executed and excommunicated.

Lasserre's most significant contribution to the arguments surrounding the Constantinian heresy were theological contributions, unlike anything made by Chelčický, Tolstoy, Liethart, Yoder or Hauerwas. Because the Constantinian period was marked by agreement with the Empire,[76] Lasserre's concern was in how the sovereignty of God and Lordship of Jesus Christ were compromised: "The decisive point about the Constantinian heresy is that it no longer believes in the unique sovereignty of Christ. From this time on this role must be shared with other lords."[77] Lasserre reminded his readers it was said in Acts 17:7 of the Christians during the first tradition period, "They say they have another king, Jesus."

74. Lasserre, *Les Chrétien et la Violence*, 84.
75. Lasserre, *Les Chrétien et la Violence*, 88.
76. Lasserre, *Les Chrétien et la Violence*, 89.
77. Lasserre, *Les Chrétien et la Violence*, 90.

> But there was a revision, and instead of the early creed 'Jesus Christ is Lord' was substituted a new restrictive creed, which marks a retreat: 'Jesus Christ is our Lord.' 'Our Lord' that is to say the Lord of the Church (and not of the state), of Christians (and not of pagans). . . . So the Constantinian heresy is characterised by the loss of the sense of the lordship of Jesus Christ over the whole world. From this time on the Church withdraws into the realm of personal piety, abandoning the empire to its own law and to its demons.[78]

These were points Tolstoy made but with little development. Lasserre can be considered a development of, or commentary on passages of Tolstoy such as this: "When a Christian promises to obey the commands or laws of men, he is like a craftsman who, having hired himself out to one master, promises at the same time to execute the orders of other persons. No man can serve two masters."[79] This shift of allegiance and lordship to another master resulted, in Lasserre's estimation, in five basic distortions of the Christian message:

> a) Christ lost his unique and preeminent place as 'only lord', a certain number of other lords began to scale the Christian heavenlies, in the exact course of this disgraceful fourth century: on the level of theology, the Church, the Tradition, the Papacy and the Virgin Mary became great lords who shared the prestige and authority of Christ; on the level of ethics it was Caesar and his empire. . . . [I]n the course of this disastrous century the mustard of nationalistic and paganism was added to the pure oil of the Gospel along with the vinegar of military paganism to made a rich and acid mayonnaise; and still today this mayonnaise is presented to us as Christianity.
>
> b) Henceforth, in Christian theology, the state is seen as being autonomous in relation to the authority of Christ. . . . Now once detached from Jesus Christ, these authorities have no other law than the law of the jungle. . . . Jesus Christ has been rejected, disqualified, expelled from the world of politics.
>
> c) There results a formidable split in Christian morality. Theology itself justified as bi-polar system, a real ethical dichotomy according to which a Christian would obey Jesus Christ in private life but would obey the state in civic life.
>
> d) At a stroke . . . Christian theology believed itself authorised to introduce into its ethics new moral criteria, such as the

---

78. Lasserre, *Les Chrétien et la Violence*, 91.
79. Tolstoy, *Kingdom of God Is Within You*, 190.

principle whereby the end justifies the means or the principle of efficiency. Now these principles are in direct contradiction to the Gospel . . . completely foreign to the Gospel. And one sees Christians who calmly and cooly justify torture, reprisals, the atom bomb, who knows what else? Jesus Christ has been well and truly eliminated from their thought processes.

e) The fifth . . . consists in the split in the human personality which has resulted for the vast majority of Christian; indeed they go as easily from Gospel morality to the law of the jungle, from the state of being a sheep led by the Good Shepherd to the state of a wolf pursuing its interests by force, as you go from long wave to short wave on the radio at the church of the knob.[80]

For Lasserre, the destruction of Christian discipleship, the following of Jesus, could not have been more complete: "Most Christians have made of the Gospel a kind of homeopathic remedy, which is taken in small dozes for little difficulties; but for serious issues, particularly in the realm of civic matters, they believe only in force and expediency."[81] Like the earlier reformers Chelčický and Tolstoy, Lasserre was asking: "Do our Churches not need Reformation by means of which they may rediscover the sense of the sovereignty of Christ?"[82] Confronting the critics of pacifism with the charge of compromising the sovereignty of Christ in the believer and in the world is this unique angle of argument used by Lasserre. It is unfortunate his writing on these points, until now, have been untranslated and off the radar of scholars and more importantly, of pastors and practitioners of the Gospel lifestyle and values of the Sermon on the Mount.

Lasserre's development of Chelčickian/Tolstoyan historical/theological schema on the paganism of the church continued into another chapter entitled "*The Paganism of War.*" Here again, it is all very Tolstoyan. *Pagan* was the term Tolstoy used to refer to the value system of Imperial Christianity. In the preface to his *Kingdom of God Is Within You* he wrote: "In this book I have endeavoured to show that our modern Christianity has been tried and found wanting, that the armed camp of Europe is not Christian, but Pagan, as is latter-day religion."[83] Tolstoy believed these values, so antithetical to Christianity, were of an altogether different spirit: "that a

---

80. Lasserre, *Les Chrétien et la Violence*, 91–93. As depicted above, Lasserre listed these five as—a, b, c, d, e. The paragraphs are direct quotations of sections of his argument under those points.

81. Lasserre, *Les Chrétien et la Violence*, 93.

82. Lasserre, *Les Chrétien et la Violence*, 93.

83. Tolstoy, *Kingdom of God Is Within You*, 7.

spirit inimical to true Christianity dwells in these authorities."[84] As Tolstoy drew from the Sermon on the Mount notions of not being able to serve two masters, God and the evil spirit Mammon, Lasserre developed this as it relates to violence and war. Under the section heading, "*Holding War as Sacred*," Lasserre expounded on ancient and modern war ceremonies and celebrations which still "trigger a reversal of all moral and social constraints: libations of alcohol abound, sexual inhibitions and moral constraints are cast aside; and it comes about that, as in the Roman Luercales, the slaves begin to command their masters."[85] These were points Tolstoy made again and again.[86] Lasserre referred to them as rites of "mass elation, where a sort of sacred passion or ecstatic drunkenness is manifested, resulting at times in acts of violence or abuse . . . and an altered state of mind."[87] Though both he and Tolstoy used the language of demon possession, Lasserre put a name on this god of war—Mars:

> The characteristic feature of all paganism is to enslave a human being to the deep tendencies of his carnal nature. We know that each deity in Antiquity exalted such instincts and glorified them; Diana, hunting; Bacchus, drunkenness; Eros and Venus, sex; Mammon, greed; Molech, violence; Mars, war. Despite the Christian gloss of our western civilisation, these gods are still universally regarded and revered. If you doubt this, just go to the cinema![88]

Lasserre noted: "all these pagan cults have a common dogma: when the god speaks, all must be sacrificed to him; all, even conscience, swiftly renounced and disqualified."[89] This sort of commentary on the rarely treated area of demonology offers an analysis and explanation that cuts across the pervasive deceptions and confusions about the spiritual realities and dynamics of the intersection of heavenly and earthly conflict. Lasserre pulled the veil off the face of Mars, the god of war:

> This god Mars certainly knows how to captivate and enthral his victims! With smoke and mirrors, by processions that are powerful and dazzling but religious, by his bewitching music, by his cunning exasperation of emotion and suffering, when he

---

84. Tolstoy, *Kingdom of God Is Within You*, 34.
85. Lasserre, *Les Chrétien et la Violence*, 96.
86. Tolstoy, *Kingdom of God Is Within You*, 65.
87. Lasserre, *Les Chrétien et la Violence*, 96.
88. Lasserre, *Les Chrétien et la Violence*, 97.
89. Lasserre, *Les Chrétien et la Violence*, 100.

reignites the flame of memory, he intoxicates humans, he makes them tremble with fear and mystical rapture, he exercises a real state of possession over them, overwhelming them with holy horror.... The pagan god has summarily transported them into another world, haunted by the heroes of old and the national gods, he has made them vibrate to a different life force, glorious and wild, for which they will always harbour a longing. Exactly like Eros, like Bacchus and Mammon, he succeeds perfectly in contriving for them this transcendence of the self which is characteristic of all forms of paganism and for which they will remain thirsty and in bondage. It is no doubt for this that men will enjoy recounting their memories of the barracks and adventures of war.[90]

The temptation is to continue with this captivating citation as Lasserre treated this with passion and vivid imagination. However, enough has been included here to demonstrate that Lasserre did not see the person Constantine as the problem though he was certainly a key part in the fall of the Church. Lasserre developed Tolstoy's sense that the spiritual realities more than the historical ones are what continue to displace Christ in the Church, and society. In other words, the problem is not with certain people past or present, it is with certain principalities which are as real and active today as they are ancient– namable, identifiable demonic spirits on specific unholy assignments, such as to glorify war and bloodshed. Tolstoy frequently used the language of possession and spiritual intoxication to describe warring society of his time and historically.[91] Tolstoy's (and even more Lasserre's) emphasis on the spiritual principalities more than the civil rulers is an emphasis not noted by Chelčický in the fourteenth century, or Yoder or Liethart in the present one. War, for Tolstoy and Lasserre, was a pagan god coming to enlist people to do evil work. When the Apostle Paul referred in 1 Timothy 4:1 to the "doctrines of demons" he perhaps was thinking along similar lines. Reformers fight hard over doctrines and the sad history of killing heretics illustrates how at times past reformers lost sight of the fact that their enemy was not flesh and blood. For Lasserre, for Tolstoy, the two masters had nothing in common and it was not possible to please them both, or obey both.

In part because it is not available anywhere else in English an extended section is included here on this point. The bullet points are Lasserre's:

---

90. Lasserre, *Les Chrétien et la Violence*, 98.
91. Tolstoy, *Kingdom of God Is within You*, 280–81.

Jesus, calmly, says no to Mars. He embraces a language which is the exact opposite of the pretentiousness of the pagan god.

- Mars persuades people that it is always what is strongest and cruellest that will prevail; but Jesus hopes that we will believe in the victory of his cross.
- Mars urges people to yield to their combative instinct, and to glory in it; but Jesus invites them to glory in their submission to the living God.
- Mars urges people to resign themselves to the worst, in a fatalism which grace cannot penetrate; but Jesus proclaims peacefully that he gives true life to those who will believe in him.
- Mars obtains for people an impressive exaltation in transcending themselves by following their animal instincts without any inhibition; but Jesus brings his disciples a transcendence of themselves in calm fellowship with the absolute Other, the personal God who speaks to sinners.
- Mars demands a total, unquestioning obedience, for the duration of the combat; but Jesus demands total, unquestioning obedience for the whole duration of our existence, even in times of crisis.
- Mars demands people who will sacrifice everything to him, because he has persuaded them that he alone can manage events from now on; but Jesus asks us to bring everything under a God who, far from destroying a human, safeguards and regenerates him.
- Mars promises, after the devastating infernos and slaughter that he provokes, an age of happiness and peace; but Jesus invites us to live peacefully in obedience and love while awaiting the coming of the Kingdom, which depends on God alone.
- Mars claims that good will emerge from the unleashing of evil; Jesus affirms on the contrary that evil must be overcome by good.
- Mars promises glory to the heroes who will have participated submissively in the great massacre of God's creatures; Jesus invites us to rejoice in his own glory, as manifested most notably in good samaritans' tiniest gestures of authentic love.

- Mars exalts the 'virile' courage of those who have given their lives in crushing their brothers; Jesus exalts the humble courage of those who give their lives in the service of their brothers.

- Mars hands out the 'cross' of war to his most valiant followers; but Jesus urges us simply to focus on his cross.

In truth, it is impossible to reconcile warlike paganism with the Gospel. But the pagan god, not at all put out, hides, deftly camouflages himself, and directly infiltrates the Church of Jesus Christ. And Christians, unaware, continue to sing the praises and the victory their Saviour, when their heart is already surrendered without resistance to the all-powerful domination of Mars, such is the extent to which he imposes himself on them.[92]

The work in this chapter has been to analyse Petr Chelčický and Jean Lasserre as related to Tolstoyan Sermon on the Mount interpretation and particularly the so-called Constantinian heresy. The reason for the selection of these two is in how these two significant and nearly lost reformers on each side of Tolstoy, reveal some amount of continuity between Chelčický and Lasserre, most probably through Tolstoy. Lasserre emerges as a modern voice for these long-buried contentions, and demonstrates a dependance on Tolstoy and Chelčický for his basis. These significant linkages and noted dependance, for reasons unknown, have been entirely ignored, or unnoticed, by Yoder and those after him, until here and now. It is hoped the work of this chapter will draw more attention to the unrealized Reformation in Bohemia and serve to draw the vital issues of embracing sword and empire into modern conversations of the shortcomings of Luther's Reform.

---

92. Lasserre, *Les Chrétien et la Violence*, 101–2.

~ 7.0 ~

Matual and Laurila
Plausible but Not Palpable, Loopholes and Tolstoy's Blindspot

WITHOUT QUESTION MUCH IS gained toward a better understanding of Tolstoy's interpretation of the Sermon on the Mount when careful consideration is given to what has been written by others engaging him critically on the Sermon. However, though there are those who have been critical of the religious Tolstoy, most only treat his doctrinal unorthodoxies, anti-clericalism and renunciations of the Church, mysticism and ritual. Those who actually engage his exegetical arguments on the Sermon on the Mount itself are very few in number, and even there, the criticisms are usually brief and not technical rebuttals of his extensive exegetical work and conclusions. This was even a point of lament for Tolstoy himself that people, especially Orthodox leaders, would reject him without responding to the main concerns he was raising from the Sermon on the Mount:

> All the criticisms of the statements contained in my own book [*What I Believe*] have given me a similar impression of a wish to ignore the subject.... The questions are put plainly and directly, and would seem to call for plain and direct answers. But no; my book has been received just as all previous denunciations have been, those denunciations of the clergy who have deviated from the law of Christ, with which history abounds since the time of Constantine the Great. Many words have been expended in noting the errors of my interpretation of this or that passage of the Scriptures, of how I am wrong in referring to the Trinity, the

Redemption and the Immortality of the soul, but never a word of that vital question: How are we to reconcile those lessons of forgiveness, humility, patience, and love toward all mankind, our neighbours a well as our enemies, taught us all by the Teacher, which dwell in the heart of each of us, with the necessities caused by military aggression against our own countrymen as well as against foreigners?[1]

While most of Tolstoy's adversaries avoided critically engaging his treatments of Matthew 5–7, there are two notable critical engagements of Tolstoy each contributing differently to our understanding of the religious Tolstoy. More recently was David Matual's book, *Tolstoy's Translation of the Gospels: A Critical Study*. Earlier was Kaarle S. Laurila's 1944 work, *Leo Tolstoy and Martin Luther as Interpreters of the Sermon on the Mount*.[2] Matual will be given attention here first, then Laurila will become the focus of the bulk of this chapter. In my review of the literature that constitutes criticism of Tolstoy's Sermon on the Mount interpretation, these two are the most significant and therefore become the focus of this chapter. There have been myriads of critics of the religious Tolstoy but apart from these two, there are no other (to my knowledge) significant treatments of Tolstoy's exegesis of these passages, particularly those on enemy love. This was a frustration for him as well, that people criticized him but did not rebut the arguments he was seeking to make. Especially he felt the Orthodox Church never answered the questions he was raising about obedience to the teaching of Jesus. We can await an English translation of recent book, *A Prophet Without Honor*, written by noted Tolstoy historian and scholar, Archpriest Father Georgy Orekhanov, now a Doctor of Church History at St. Tikhon Orthodox Humanitarian University in Moscow.[3] However it appears this new book is filling the important niche of the relationship between Tolstoy and the Orthodox Church, but perhaps there is engagement of Tolstoy's interpretation of the Sermon on the Mount as well.

---

1. Tolstoy, *Kingdom of God Is within You*, 36–37.

2. Laurila, *Leo Tolstoi und Martin Luther*. Laurila's work in its entirely was privately translated into English by Stuart Hay for use in this work. Citations of Laurila translated into English in this chapter are Hay's.

3. Father Georgy Orekhanov published two important dissertations: *Leo Tolstoy: The Russian Orthodox Church and Leo Tolstoy: the Reasons for the Conflict and Its Perception by Contemporaries* (2010) and *The Historical and Cultural Context of the Russian Orthodox Church—Leo Tolstoy Dichotomy* (2012). His recent book is *Leo Tolstoy: A Prophet without Honor*.

7.1 David Matual: Tolstoy as Translator

David Matual's main interests were in Tolstoy's "Gnostic Christ" and in Tolstoy's view of Logos, Church, and in Tolstoy as a self-taught exegete of the Greek New Testament. Even so, Matual provides those interested in Tolstoyan Christianity with a careful, book-length exegetical analysis of Tolstoy's treatment and translation of the Gospels and the Sermon on the Mount. Particularly frustrating though is Matual's repeated conflation and confusion of two separate Tolstoy works; his *Harmony of the Gospels* and his *Gospel in Brief*. Tolstoy is accused of taking a scissors to the Gospels, cutting out the miracles, the Resurrection, etc. That charge certainly is not true of Tolstoy's *Harmony of the Gospels* (see subsections 1.4–5), and it is only true of the *Gospel in Brief* if one dismisses entirely the purpose of the *Gospel in Brief* as a collection of the teachings of Jesus which Tolstoy believed were of great importance to following the way of Christ.

Of special interest for this project, Matual concluded with a chapter on Tolstoy's ethic and its basis in the Sermon on the Mount (154–71). Much in that chapter regarding Tolstoy and Matthew 5 is presented descriptively by Matual and covers no new ground than was already set forth in earlier sections of this project (particularly subsections 4.1.1–5). His analysis is mildly disparaging toward Tolstoy as translator, yet with evident ambivalence. Positively he is able to say:

> due to the fact that his translations of the pertinent gospel passages [referring to Matt 5–7] are, on the whole, more nearly accurate than any others. Linguistic manipulations and textual distortions still occur, of course, but on a far less ambitious scale. Moreover, the interpretations he gives to the verses he studies contain a certain measure of truth, or at least of plausibility. As a result, the radical ethical views derived from his gospel and disseminated throughout the world are both credible and intriguing, if not always palatable.[4]

What can be said is that any exegete of the Greek New Testament makes linguistic decisions that others who render a text differently might deem distortions or manipulations. Matual therefore voices what could be said of any Biblical interpreter with whom one disagrees. What remains are the high commendations Matual does give to Tolstoy's exegetical work and translation, especially regarding the Sermon on the Mount. He deems Tolstoy's translation as containing a measure of truth, plausible, credible and intriguing, even, as he notes, if they are not always plausible. The same could

---

4. Matual, *Tolstoy's Translation of the Gospels*, 53.

be said for the words of Jesus which is Tolstoy's main interest: What did Jesus mean? Matual falls into the trap of so many Tolstoy critics, the struggle to swallow Tolstoy's teaching becomes blurred with the struggle to swallow the sayings of Jesus, sayings which have never been that palpable.

Matual ends his project seeking to guard the Gospel (doctrinal orthodoxy) from Tolstoy who he believed disregards it.

> The *Union* and *Translation of the Four Gospels* is Tolstoy's attempt to liberate the ethical teachings of Christianity as he understood them from all those beliefs and institutions which undermine and pervert them. Among these is faith in the divinity of Christ and in the various miraculous events of his life that are meant to prove his divinity. The Tolstoyan religion is a creed without history, without heroes, without an incarnation of the Son of God – indeed without a personal God. The only deity is logos, and the only persons who are godlike are those who live by its decrees.[5]

It is true Tolstoy sought to liberate the ethical teachings of Jesus from the Church dogma and traditions which he believed perverted them, entirely. Also, it is true Tolstoy did not conceive of Christ as divine in any orthodox sense. However, it remains debatable that Tolstoy's deity was nothing more than an impersonal logos. What is not true in Matual's assessment is that Tolstoyan religion is creed without history. Tolstoy made a strong case for the teaching of Jesus in Christian history, with real heroes. *The Kingdom of God Within You* begins with a long rendition of the heroes of Sermon on the Mount Christianity. Matual misconstrues Tolstoyan religion to be about keeping decrees when it is more precisely about following a way, a path to life.

7.2 Kaarle Laurila: The Finnish Layman Who Offered the Lengthiest Critique to Date

The second substantial treatment of Tolstoyan Sermon on the Mount interpretations was much earlier than Matual's (1992) and was penned in 1944 by a Finnish professor at the University of Helsinki, Kaarle S. Laurila. Matual's analysis is mentioned first only because it is far more brief. Laurila's lengthy critique, written in German but translated for the first time for this project, will be evaluated in the central sections and remainder of this chapter. In the main he sought, unconvincingly in my view, to put forward

---

5. Matual, *Tolstoy's Translation of the Gospels*, 170–71.

Luther as the best retort to Tolstoyan Christianity. However, what Laurila does succeed at is to identify a significant weakness in Tolstoyan Sermon on the Mount interpretation related to the tension between loving neighbors and loving enemies.

Laurila's engagement spanned more than eighty pages and was published in 1944 as *Leo Tolstoi und Martin Luther als ausleger der bergpredigt* (translated; *Leo Tolstoy and Martin Luther as Interpreters of the Sermon on the Mount*) making it, up until this present work, the longest critical treatment of Tolstoy's Sermon on the Mount interpretation. A couple preliminary observations are in order related to Laurila's critique, the first being it is a lay critique. Laurila was not a churchman, per se, nor was he a Bible scholar or theologian. He was a professor of art philosophy and an aesthetics researcher. Laurila was vividly aware of his seeming lack of credentials to offer his assessment with any sort of academic authority. Even so, he believed the issues at stake warranted all people wrestle with these questions and settle the issues for themselves:

> These questions concern not only theologians and other specialists or specific groups; they affect us all, because the commandments in the Sermon on the Mount are not just purely religious but essential moral teachings that govern our conduct in all areas of life.[6]

He believed, and Tolstoy would agree, that the Sermon on the Mount was not for specialists only. It was given by Christ to unlearned people on a hillside and intended to be understood and obeyed. Laurila continued:

> The far-reaching nature of the questions raised by the Sermon on the Mount and the fact that they affect us all mean that clarifying them and solving them cannot be left to the theorists or any other group of specialists alone. We all must take a personal stance on these issues.

However, he added this caveat with which Tolstoy would surely not concur:

> Of course, that does not mean that all of us uneducated laymen should be in a position to give our own independent interpretation of the Sermon on the Mount, but we all need to decide for ourselves which interpretation we support and then take responsibility for this opinion.[7]

---

6. Laurila, *Leo Tolstoi und Martin Luther*, 3.
7. Laurila, *Leo Tolstoi und Martin Luther*, 3–4.

Laurila believed that Luther's interpretation of the Sermon on the Mount offers the best argumentation against Tolstoy's interpretation. Having Luther ready at hand to challenge Tolstoy's main theses gave Laurila (a layman) confidence to develop his critique. Tolstoy would have rejected any underlying insinuation that only a cleric-class can rightly discern the meaning of these passages, or that this is teaching the lay person can not apprehend alone.

7.3 An Intermittent Ethic: Laurila on Tolstoyan Reception in Finland

Related to the first observation, a second preliminary observation pertains to the geo-political context which gave Laurila reason to study Tolstoy's interpretations of the Sermon on the Mount for himself. Laurila writes of his country's warm embrace, "especially among the educated classes" around the turn of the century, of Tolstoy's "blistering, furious lectures condemning any kind of militarism."

> This [warm embrace of Tolstoy's anti-militarism] was largely due to the fact that we were entirely unable to think of applying Tolstoy's zeal for antimilitarism to ourselves, taking it as self-evident that Tolstoy was talking primarily about Russia and other great military countries. During its union with Russia, Finland did not have a national army which would have been tasked primarily with defending its own country. . . . Consequentially, personal experience had not granted us any insight into the necessity of a moral justification for national defence.[8]

Laurila surmised that it was only after Finland's independence in 1916 that she began to consider these matters in different light:

> Finland's independence had to be fought for through a hard war and at the cost of many victims. . . . The very first hour of independent Finland's life, then, showed that Tolstoy's nihilism, based on the Sermon on the Mount, was a dangerous heresy which, in reality, would have led to the Finnish people's inexorable downfall. In practice, this teaching would have led far more often to general peacelessness, uncertainty and anarchy . . . we had to learn the hard way, so to speak, that a minimum

---

8. Laurila, *Leo Tolstoi und Martin Luther*, 4.

of military power was absolutely essential to maintain internal calm and order in an independent Finland.⁹

Laurila was compelled to study Tolstoy himself and wrote because no one, to date, had "conclusively and exhaustively refuted" Tolstoy's interpretations of the Sermon on the Mount. In writing a critical analysis of Tolstoy himself, he was consciously filling a void left by others who only "studied in a brief and cursory way."¹⁰ He acknowledged and gave commendations for one such brief and cursory treatment by the Finnish theologian, Antti J. Pietilä, *Jeesuken siveysoppi ja nykyaika* (1935; trans. *The Ethics of Jesus in Modern Times*). During the first half of the twentieth century, Pietilä was one of the leading figures of the Christian Church in Finland. However, Laurila wrote because Finland, he believed, needed a timely, more developed and decisive refutation of Tolstoy than Pietilä had written. Laurila's work was an attempt to fill that void.

The reason the historical situation behind Laurila's critique bears preliminary mention is because it reveals a presupposition Tolstoy would reject when approaching the Sermon on the Mount. That presupposition is that it is an ethic for easy times, not hard times; for easy situations but not complex ones; for small scale personal problems, but certainly not conflicts on a national scale. To suggest the Sermon on the Mount is an ethic for one geographical place but not another, or for one time but not all time, for this situation but not that situation is an intermittent ethic; and intermittent ethics can only amount to an intermittent obedience. So many treatments of the Sermon on the Mount bear this intermittence, which serve as an escape clause from its demands, which for Tolstoy were absolute. A notable example drawn from related sections in this project is from the exchange between Dietrich Bonhoeffer and Reinhold Niebuhr. In an effort to persuade Bonhoeffer to forgo his fancies of traveling to India to see how Gandhi (applied Tolstoyanism) worked out Sermon on the Mount non-retaliation ethics there in India, Niebuhr advised those ideas might work in India under a more reasonable British rule but not back in Hitler's Germany.¹¹ In other words, at best, the Sermon on the Mount can only be applied situationally, intermittently.

Common in any critique of pacifism is the charge that anti-militarianism is an easy position to hold for ones-self as long as they have the luxury of living where others are out doing the dirty work for them. Tolstoy would reject the hypotheticals of those like Laurila who claim with a (false sense

9. Laurila, *Leo Tolstoi und Martin Luther*, 5.
10. Laurila, *Leo Tolstoi und Martin Luther*, 10.
11. Rasmussen, *Dietrich Bonhoeffer*, 213.

of) certainty what will or will not happen if deadly force is used or not used. Tolstoy's hermeneutic did not include these kinds of pragmatic filters. He did not read the teachings of Jesus through the lens of any what-ifs, what-abouts or what-thens. Tolstoy believed these matters of consequentialism were diversions from the plain doctrine of Jesus and entirely irrelevant to moral deliberation of one who follows the way of Christ. To use a nineteenth-century idiom (related to chopping wood with an axe without regard for where the chips land), not being a consequentialist, Tolstoy was happy to let the chips fall where they may. In his book on *Tolstoy's Pacifism*, Colm McKeogh stated:

> Tolstoy refuses to allow any consideration of consequences to dilute the wrongness of killing. The author, who had once described in great detail the unique and perplexing circumstances in which we can find ourselves, and the difficult moral choices which result, now saw life as starkly simple. The choice was always clear. One lived in accordance with the law of God, and paid no heed to what may come of it.[12]

> Tolstoy's pacifism is justified by reference to a divine revelation and not by claims of its supposed good consequences or just treatment of people. As Tolstoy does not argue for pacifism in terms of political consequences, he cannot be argued out of it by reference to its implications. Instead he asserts simply the 'moral impossibility' of killing [citing Tolstoy . . .].[13]

Not finding an adequate rebuttal of Tolstoyan Sermon on the Mount interpretation in any scholarship in Tolstoy's time up into the present day, Laurila looked prior to Tolstoy for a refutation and found what he was looking for in Martin Luther.

7.4 Pitting Luther against Tolstoy

As looming a force and figure as Tolstoy was in his day in both church and society, throughout all of vast Russia and far reaching internationally, still Luther dwarfs him. Laurila's decision to refute the strong Tolstoyan influence in early twentieth-century Finland using Luther served to bring one of Protestant Christendom's most respected expert witnesses against the case Tolstoy had been making for a simple and straightforward obedience to the demands of the Sermon on the Mount. As Laurila stated in his opening

---

12. McKeogh, *Tolstoy's Pacifism*, 104.
13. McKeogh, *Tolstoy's Pacifism*, 117.

salvo: "We will hand the judgment on these issues over to the most accomplished theologian of the Protestant world – Martin Luther himself."[14]

> What Luther achieved . . . provides such a detailed and precise answer to the misery and problems of our time and, more precisely still, to Tolstoy's thesis that it is almost as if Luther wrote his thoughts based on the crises of the contemporary era as a response to Tolstoy's teachings.[15]

One would get the impression Luther's case against Tolstoy is so watertight that it is settled for all time. Of course, it is not.

Laurila began by giving the context for Luther's commentary which is pertinent to these Sermon on the Mount themes so dear to Tolstoy. Laurila largely drew from Luther's 1523 essay, *Temporal Authority: To What Extent It Should Be Obeyed*.[16] There Luther himself explained the impetus for his treatment of the topic; many had written him with concerns over the relationship between Christians and the sword of the state and, how many were "perturbed over Christ's injunction in Matthew 5:39, 'Do not resist evil.'"[17] His intention was to "help people out of their moral dilemma and set them on the right track."[18] Luther's initial swipe was against the sophists (the Catholic theologians) who made artificial distinctions between commandments and counsels, counsels not being binding on all Christians but only on "über-Christians" of the priestly and monk classes. He rejected the notion of two classes of Christians common in Catholic theology; the perfect and the imperfect—"these words are meant for all Christians and were spoken as a categorical order."[19] Luther insisted the Sermon on the Mount was for all Christians, and here he would have had Tolstoy's strong agreement. However, Luther went on to insert his own artificial distinctions and classifications based on long-standing Augustinian frameworks of there being two cities, a city of God and a city of man. At this early point in Luther's theological thought, he was shaping this basic Augustinian framework into a more developed doctrine of the two kingdoms; the kingdom of God and the kingdom of this world. Luther insisted the Sermon on the Mount was for all Christians, but not for all situations and circumstances. Further, unlike Tolstoy, Luther gave no credence to the possibility that the Sermon on

---

14. Laurila, *Leo Tolstoi und Martin Luther*, 49–50.
15. Laurila, *Leo Tolstoi und Martin Luther*, 51.
16. Luther, "Temporal Authority," 75–129.
17. Laurila, *Leo Tolstoi und Martin Luther*, 52.
18. Laurila, *Leo Tolstoi und Martin Luther*, 52.
19. Laurila, *Leo Tolstoi und Martin Luther*, 53.

the Mount was intended for all of humanity, even though the crowd that gathered on the mountainside that day would seem to imply Jesus was bringing from heaven to earth a way of life that works wherever it is applied and by whomever.

Laurila celebrates Luther's view that "if the world were composed of real Christians, that is, true believers, there would be no need for benefits from prince, king, lord, sword, or law. . . . [I]t is impossible that the temporal sword and law should find any work to do among Christians, since they do of their own accord much more than all the laws and teachings can demand."[20] Laurila quotes Luther that "in this world (imagined of believers only), the rule of the Sermon on the Mount, i.e. the rule of love, would be quite sufficient."[21] It is at this point Luther found it necessary to make space for a second ethic, one that would work in a world that was dominated by non-Christians. As Laurila explained, "because the overwhelming majority of the world is made up of non-Christians, it is simply impossible for the evangelical rule of love to dominate. Another rule must be added."[22] Laurila found his retort to Tolstoy in Luther's dual ethic; one for Christians, and one for the world. Citing Luther: "God has ordained two governments: the spiritual, by which the Holy Spirit produces Christians and righteous people under Christ; and the temporal, which restrains the un-Christian and wicked so that – no thanks to them – they are obliged to keep still and to maintain an outward peace."[23] This became a relief to Laurila to see a "necessity of two rules for these very different classes of humans: the evangelical rule of the Sermon on the Mount for the Christians and the temporal rule of the sword for the non-Christians."[24]

Laurila ended his support for Luther's reading of the Sermon on the Mount by tagging on a perceptive arrangement, though it would seem it does the opposite of what he intended it to do. He posited there "lies an essential difference, even a contradiction, between the two men. . . . In general, Tolstoy typically represents a descending spiritual movement. . . . Luther, on the other hand, represents ascending movement, sunrise."[25] By a descending movement Laurila was referring to Tolstoy's move away from the aristocracy (power) wanting "to become countrified and 'plays' the peasant." Certainly this is accurate, there was for Tolstoy this descent. And significantly, but

20. Laurila, *Leo Tolstoi und Martin Luther*, 53.
21. Laurila, *Leo Tolstoi und Martin Luther*, 54.
22. Laurila, *Leo Tolstoi und Martin Luther*, 54.
23. Laurila, *Leo Tolstoi und Martin Luther*, 54.
24. Laurila, *Leo Tolstoi und Martin Luther*, 55.
25. Laurila, *Leo Tolstoi und Martin Luther*, 62.

seemingly undetected by Laurila, this was also the way of Christ, the way of the incarnation, the way of kenosis and humility, the way of the Beatitudes. By an ascending movement Laurila explained: "Luther, on the other hand . . . is a perfectly healthy offspring who rose from this broad, healthy basis to the highest culture. . . . [H]e has the highest social instincts." Laurila would seem to be saying Luther's movement was toward power in society whereas Tolstoy's was away from it. And this is perceptive as Luther gave theological permission for the state to crush the peasant class during their uprising, whereas Tolstoy pronounced the greatest of condemnations upon the state that runs rough over the least of these in society. Though Laurila's use of Luther, as shown here, does little more than make Tolstoy's point (that the theologians of the church add overtop the Sermon on the Mount a variety of dogmas that simply cancel out Christ's intended meaning), Laurila's own critique of Tolstoy's interpretation of the Sermon on the Mount, as will be detailed in the following two sections, contains more viable arguments than he had brought forth from Luther.

7.5 Laurila's Reading of Tolstoy's Sermon on the Mount Interpretation

Laurila's reading of Tolstoy's interpretation of the Sermon on the Mount begins with his observation that, for Tolstoy, everything is based on his exclusively religiocentric worldview (as if that is a bad thing); a consequence of Tolstoy having come to find no help in understanding the universe, or the purposes and problems within it, through philosophic and scientific conceptions of the world.[26] Tolstoy found Sermon on the Mount religion to be the sole satisfactory basis for both individual and human society. It is at this initial observation where Laurila first takes issue with Tolstoy, uncomfortable with the Sermon on the Mount being anything but an individual ethic. In short, for Laurila, a religiocentric worldview has value for believing individuals but conceiving the solutions for the greater problems of humanity and society from a mere religiocentric vantage point brought, for him, insurmountable complications, "an intrinsically impossible theory . . . if the removal of all means of coercion has the miraculous effect Tolstoy is hoping for – namely, that no one is inclined towards violence or other evil acts – why and for whom would we still need laws, courts, and police precautions? . . . [N]either sense nor humanity's thousand years of experience point to this optimistic conclusion on Tolstoy's part. It is no more than

---

26. Laurila, *Leo Tolstoi und Martin Luther*, 13.

a fanciful unfounded pipe dream."[27] For Laurila, religion-based non-violent sentiment was not sufficient to curtail the fallen human condition in greater society as he read Tolstoy to believe.

Central to Tolstoy's religiocentric worldview, according to Laurila's reading, are two related concepts: (1) Being a child of God and (2) reciprocal love:

> These two ideas mean that we, the people, are all children of God, his emissaries here on Earth and our purpose in life and our destiny can be found in carrying out the will of God, our holy Father. The will of God, in turn, is that his children should love one another. In this way, the doctrine of Christ is in essence a doctrine of mutual love, and universal brotherhood. . . .Tolstoy believes this general commandment of love (*Liebesgebot*) and peacefulness is at the heart of Christian teaching and he found it in abundance in the Sermon on the Mount.[28]

Tolstoy's five commandments derived from Matthew five codify these two basic concepts with the key being "love all people, including those from other nations."[29] From these two concepts, Laurila identified several principles which Tolstoy drew from the Sermon on the Mount. First, positively expressed as pacifism, negatively expressed as anti-militarism which, Laurila repeatedly asserted amounted to preaching absolute nihilism: "he believes that the best way to abolish war, and violence all together, is to kill the defensive spirit in people. Thus, he tackles the problem completely differently than how pacifists have generally done so, who wanted to curb violence at its source, i.e. the attacker."[30]

> Tolstoy advocates these views with full awareness of their meaning and implications. Indeed, he lays out the most extreme and appalling nihilistic consequences from his religious premise openly, honestly and without fear, as is his manner. These implications, so colossal and absurd for others, are for Tolstoy in no way unwanted or embarrassing. On the contrary, he confesses to feeling forced into these conclusions not only by logic but with joy and excitement. The nihilistic implications of his premise are for him the best proof of the validity of his argument.[31]

---

27. Laurila, *Leo Tolstoi und Martin Luther*, 36, 39–40.
28. Laurila, *Leo Tolstoi und Martin Luther*, 15.
29. Laurila, *Leo Tolstoi und Martin Luther*, 15.
30. Laurila, *Leo Tolstoi und Martin Luther*, 15.
31. Laurila, *Leo Tolstoi und Martin Luther*, 27–28.

The second principle identified by Laurila, negatively expressed, is anti-Patriotism (anti-militarism), or positively expressed, universal brotherhood. He read Tolstoy to be intolerant of any differentiation between a foreigner, even a hostile one, and the members of one's own family, community and nation. Patriotism, and national favoritism, Laurila identified as incompatible for Tolstoy's conception of universal brotherhood. Tolstoy believed "patriotism . . . perpetuates mutual distrust, suspicion and hatred in people and turns them against each other . . . [and] is the root cause of wars and the main obstacle to universal brotherhood."[32]

> Those in power . . . great scoundrels – use patriotism as a tool to mentally anaesthetise and wear down the docile and unsuspecting 'subjects' in order to pull the wool over their eyes to facilitate their own domineering and cunning plans . . . by fuelling their patriotic (i.e. separatist) instincts, leaders persuade their [docile and peaceful] subjects [they have to fight back if they don't want to sacrifice themselves and their country altogether] to be prepared to become soldiers, pay taxes, and generally help in any way with developing and preserving this giant rape machine, at whose centre stands the army and the entire military system. . . . But as soon as the government has this instrument for violence at hand, it uses it principally to suppress, exploit and enslave the very people who, out of patriotism, so willingly gave themselves us as a tool of the government and its instrument for violence.[33]

This is a fair summation of Tolstoy's view on the problem of patriotism and Laurila acknowledged it "[follows] fairly extensive exegetical discussion" in Tolstoy's presentation. Even so, Laurila was unable to agree with Tolstoy's rendering of Christ's word "enemy" as referring to "an enemy of the people" as opposed to "neighbour" referring to a compatriot. Offering no exegetical reasoning to support the traditional renderings of the text, Laurila was content to reject Tolstoy's rendering as "convenient" and putting a "distorted political meaning in to the words of the Sermon on the Mount which were clearly not there."[34] Calling for an "unbiased reading" which is apparently a reference to his own, Laurila added: "you get the distinct impression that Christianity's founder had no intention of acting as a political reformer or, indeed, of giving political and social instructions and rules of conduct. He is thinking only of the most important points, of salvation and the relationship

---

32. Laurila, *Leo Tolstoi und Martin Luther*, 19–20
33. Laurila, *Leo Tolstoi und Martin Luther*, 21.
34. Laurila, *Leo Tolstoi und Martin Luther*, 23.

of the individual with their God, their neighbours and their conscience."[35] Laurila reached for German theologian Ernst Troeltsch (1865–1923) to support his statement:

> The gospel contains no directly political and social instructions whatsoever – it is fundamentally apolitical. It concerns itself only with the highest goals of personal life and personal community and eager anticipates the realisation of these ideals which the approach of the end of the world and the coming kingdom of God will bring, next to which the world and its interests disappear altogether.[36]

Laurila accepted Troeltsch's generalisations as accurate, dubbing Tolstoy's "dubious (to put it mildly) exegesis" but not offering any of his own, or any to substantiate the comments from Troeltsch.[37] This would seem more of the same of which it was mentioned earlier that Tolstoy lamented—the renunciation of Tolstoy's ideas without properly engaging them, exegetically.

The third principle identified by Laurila central to Tolstoyan Sermon on the Mount interpretation is anarchism. In condemning and rejecting the political order of human societies as being based on violence, Laurila complained Tolstoy held that "all peacekeeping power, all laws, the entire judicial system – everything that the state has done to maintain peace and to protect lives of individuals and families, including the social order – is evil."[38] His weariness with Tolstoy and impatience with his ideas become more evident in this section. The abolition of all laws, and government in its entirety, through non-violence ("inaction and passive opposition"), individuals not defending themselves ("if some sort of barbarian breaks into and ransacks our peaceful home, strangles our innocent children or rapes our wife, sister or daughter, we may not, according to Tolstoy, lift a finger to stop him, because of the commandment 'do not resist evil!'"); to "substantiate these unusual conclusions, Tolstoy sometimes resorts to curious tricks of sophistry and acrobatic leaps of logic."[39]

> Tolstoy is of the optimistic belief that all evil people, criminals and hooligans would disappear or transform into good, peaceful

---

35. Laurila, *Leo Tolstoi und Martin Luther*, 23.

36. Laurila, *Leo Tolstoi und Martin Luther*, 23. Translator's note: "This is referenced by Laurila as having been given as part of a 1904 speech entitled *Politische Ethik und das Christentum* ('Political Ethics and Christianity'), cited in Otto Baumgarten's 1916 text *Politik und Moral*."

37. Laurila, *Leo Tolstoi und Martin Luther*, 23.

38. Laurila, *Leo Tolstoi und Martin Luther*, 26–27.

39. Laurila, *Leo Tolstoi und Martin Luther*, 34–35.

and honest people if there were no more violence to stop their evil desires running free. He never actually reveals why he believes and expects this. He probably did not know himself. He just believed it. Tolstoy, like all world changers and utopians ... believes, these people, thus far so criminal and evil, will suddenly turn into angels and will have evil desires no more. . . . However, several thousand years' experience has never provided even the slightest evidence to support such an optimistic expectation. Instead, experience has provided hard evidence time and again that law, order, peace and all the highest values of human life are irrevocably given up as long as they are not protected by real force against the destructive fury of the wrongdoer. But Tolstoy dismisses all of this.[40]

More accurately, Tolstoy would disagree with so much of it. Laurila afforded no appreciation for Tolstoy's view that the way of Christ would not always work for the better, or that it would even work at all for that matter, that this was indeed a pathway into persecution. As inconceivable as Tolstoy's ideas were to Laurila, even more inconceivable to Tolstoy would be the notion that Christ stood on that mountain and gave bad advice to people in the world, advice that would make society worse if applied in any significant way. Additionally, Laurila lacked the political imagination of Tolstoy, for example in Tolstoy's letter to the Tsar, that non-violent responses to evil did possess great power for positive change in the world. Tolstoy pleaded with the Tsar to not execute but forgive his father's assassins:

> if you were to do this, to summon these people, to give them money and to send them away somewhere to America, and were to write a manifesto headed by the words; 'but I say to you, love your enemies', – I don't know about others but I, a poor loyal subject, would be your dog and your slave. I would weep with emotion as I am weeping now, every time I heard your name. But what am I saying – 'I don't know about others?' I know that at these words goodness and love would flow across Russia like a torrent.[41]

As written in an earlier chapter here, Tolstoy's dream inspired him to put before the Tsar a dream, envisioning a Russia God could bless. Laurila had no such political imagination. Common in treatments of the Sermon on the Mount is a blindness to the possibility that God's thoughts are higher

40. Laurila, *Leo Tolstoi und Martin Luther*, 35–36.
41. Christian, *Tolstoy's Letters, Volume II*. "To the Emperor Alexander III, 8–15 March 1881, Letter #257," 340–47.

than ours, and his ways as well. Tolstoy's likely retort to Laurila's assertion that "several thousand years' experience has never provided even the slightest evidence to support such an optimistic expectation" would be that such is the case only because it has yet to be genuinely applied on such a large scale. Written in 1944, the present intensities of Hitler's attempts at world dominance and genocide would certainly be an overwhelming reality forefront in Laurila's thought-processes and the successes of Tolstoyan notions of non-violence in India, and in the civil rights advances in the southern United States would only later unfold. It is arguable that since the time of Laurila, and due in significant part to Tolstoy, the world does have examples in modern history, even besides Gandhi and Martin Luther King Jr.,[42] where central facets of Tolstoyan non-violence have been successfully applied. Tolstoyan anarchy is an area of political thought quite unexplored though that is changing as new work on Tolstoy's political theology is presently underway.[43]

7.6 Tolstoy's Blindspot; the Tension between Neighborly Love and Enemy Love

Despite being, until this project, the lengthiest critical treatment specific to Tolstoyan Sermon on the Mount interpretation, Laurila only set forth one thread of argumentation for which Tolstoy prepared no ready reply. Laurila rightly noted that Tolstoy seemed only able to construe enemy love from one side, that of the attacker, not the victim. Laurila asked: "what about the other part, the victim or victims? Should we also display non-Christian neighbourly love toward them, the victims?"[44]

> The only possible act of love toward someone threatened by violence lies in impeding, and protecting them from, the violence directed toward them. And if this is only possible by seizing the perpetrator by the scruff of the neck and treating them in such a rough manner. . . . If we do not do this, our neighbourly love is merely sounding brass or a tinkling cymbal. Thus it can be seen that Tolstoy's famous doctrine of non-resistance, which ought to be based on the instruction to love our neighbours, in fact, collapses in on itself as soon as this commandment of neighbourly

---

42. Wink, *Jesus and Nonviolence*, 2–3. "Non-violent general strikes have overthrown at least seven Latin American dictators."

43. Christoyannopoulos, "Tolstoy the Peculiar Christian Anarchist." Also, Christoyannopoulos, "Christian Anarchism"; Christoyannopoulos, *Tolstoy's Political Thought*.

44. Laurila, *Leo Tolstoi und Martin Luther*, 67.

love is complied with, i.e. when it is extended to the victims of the violence as well.[45]

Laurila rightly noted that Tolstoy overlooked that love can not possibly mean "let them do as they like and never act against their will and wishes.... [S]uch an interpretation of neighbourly love is clearly quite wrong, and above all deeply unChristian, even though Tolstoy declares his interpretation of love to be very Christian." Laurila offered helpful insights on Christian love as related to God's love:

> As an example of Christian love of one's neighbours, the love of God should serve the people. However, this love does not shy away from doing someone harm; rather, the idea is that God chastises those he loves, i.e. only if He loves them will He truly inflict pain on them.... True human love is very similar, or at least it is supposed to be, like God, it must not shy away from causing great pain to the object of love.... But it is not only children and minors who need this kind of physical force and opposition – true love often directly requires that we treat adults this way too... In the same way, love commands us to restrain a drunkard, a feverish person, a lunatic, or someone consumed by a sudden passion and therefore not of sound mind and clearly capable of doing something hasty and disastrous – again, with violence if need be.[46]

Laurila pointed to the thin spot on the ice in Tolstoy's interpretation of the Sermon on the Mount, raising the tensions that emerge when simultaneously seeking to both love neighbor and enemy. Tolstoy was clear; playing favorites with neighbors over enemies with love was not Christian. But the reverse is also unacceptable, to place the favoritism on the enemy against the neighbor.

Laurila was able to retreat to Troeltsch's doctrine of the two kingdoms and go easily along with violence against enemies. Yet neither Laurila, nor Tolstoy nor Luther wrestled with the unavoidable (Bonhoefferian) responsibility-guilt tensions common to any Christian caught in-between the challenge to simultaneously obey the commands to love enemies and neighbors. Luther, in fact, seemed to convey no guilt whatsoever in getting blood on his hands against evildoers. In Tolstoy, there is this blindspot toward what loving the victim might mean and his most famous disciple, Gandhi, is forced to build on (or deviate from) Tolstoyan non-resistance to evil (see subsection 5.3). In other words, resistance is allowable for the Christian,

---

45. Laurila, *Leo Tolstoi und Martin Luther*, 67.
46. Laurila, *Leo Tolstoi und Martin Luther*, 67–68.

as long as means are used that do not physically harm person/s. Perhaps Bonhoeffer then becomes a better choice than Luther to engage the Sermon on the Mount interpretations of Leo Tolstoy (see subsection 5.4).

The focus in this chapter on the lengthy critique of Tolstoyan Christianity by Kaarle S. Laurila provides a long overdue assessment of that neglected work. Its importance is both in its near geographical proximity to Tolstoy's Russia and its notability as a response to the substantial Tolstoyan influence in Finland in the first few decades of the century, particularly the easier pre-1916 period before Finland's independence. In Laurila's critique we are given an open window to the challenges Tolstoyan Christianity was to Christianity and State in a neighboring region. It is peculiar that, to date (at least to my knowledge), no one else has considered Laurila's essay on Tolstoy's interpretation of the Sermon on the Mount. Knowing a frequent lament and frustration for Tolstoy was that people quickly dismissed him without ever engaging his very arguments it is probable Tolstoy would have appreciated Laurila's rebuttal. Laurila, a layman, took it upon himself to offer a timely refutation to Tolstoy's views in the absence of anyone else rising to the occasion.

In this chapter an attempt has been made to host some interaction between Laurila's critique and Tolstoy's probable counterpoints. As this chapter has shown, Laurila comes at Tolstoy from Laurila's Lutheran standpoint and theological heritage. It has been demonstrated that Laurila found Luther's two kingdom framework to be, he believed, a direct and sufficient counter argument to Tolstoy. However, though making the traditional case for a doctrine of two kingdoms, Laurila neglected to offer any exegetical evidence to show Tolstoy's reading of enemy and neighbor as referencing compatriots and foreigners to be a erroneous reading. Tolstoy was led to his conclusion that the Sermon on the Mount applied to nation states also because of his exegesis. Laurila fought this point with Lutheran theology, and ignored Tolstoy's scriptural argument. For Tolstoy, Jesus' words trumped the dogmas of the church. Tolstoy's would have rejected the supposition that Jesus gave two ethics, one for the Christian and one for the world. One successful point in Laurila's critique was shown in this chapter to be in how he pointed out, what I'm calling, Tolstoy's blindspot. Laurila successfully made a case that there are times when the commands of enemy love and neighborly love come into conflict. To this line of argumentation, Tolstoy had no ready reply.

PART THREE

The Doctrine of the World

~ 8.0 ~

Sexual Self-Disarmament
Tolstoy's Eccentricity on Sex and Marriage

LEO TOLSTOY HAD SOME eccentric ideas about sex and marriage!

Such a remark might capture the consensus of the majority in his day and also our own. Yet any who lobby this complaint risk being shown a log in their own eye. Statistically, there is little integrity within the confines of Western Christendom to offer any constructive corrective to Tolstoy. Internet pornography use, affairs and various other sexual sins among clergy and pedophile priests are only part of the story. The statistics in the pews are no better and there is scant difference between the average pew-sitter in a Christian Church than there is in the hyper-sexualized culture in which they live.[1] Tolstoy presented a prophetic challenge that remains timely in calling followers of the way of Christ to take seriously, very seriously, Jesus' words on sex and marriage in the Sermon on the Mount.

This chapter and the next two chapters address only three of the five commandments Tolstoy gleaned from Matthew chapter five; the second, fourth and fifth commandments. Namely, *do not commit adultery* is the

---

1. Fifty-seven percent of pastors in the United States, and 64 percent of youth pastors have struggled in the past or present with pornography addictions. "Among born-again Christians, an extremely high 95 percent say that they have looked at pornography, with 54 percent indicating that they view it at least on a monthly basis and 44 percent admitting that they saw it at work within the past three months. Twenty-five percent of these firm believers confirm that they hide their Internet browsing history by erasing porn URLs on their computers and electronic devices . . . and 35 percent have cheated on their wives in an extramarital affair." Haverluck, "Survey"; see also, "Pastors and Porn."

focus of this chapter, and *resist not evil* and *do not make war* are the foci of the next and then the final chapter of this project. The reason space is not made for equal treatments of all five commandments is only because of the length requirements of this work. However, the first (*be not angry*) and the third (*take no oaths*) are given general introductions and overview in subsections 4.4.1 and 4.4.3. Additionally, though full-length chapter treatments of these remaining two commandments are not given, anger as a factor in violence and no oath-taking in tribunals are mentioned in these remaining chapters as they relate to the issues of non-violence. This chapter is concentrated on Tolstoy's second commandment, *do not commit adultery*, and his views on sex and marriage.

Tolstoy's most vulnerable point regarding his later views on sex, children, women, men and marriage lies in whether or not he was personally living up to the standard he espoused. As this chapter develops, his personal sexual integrity, word and deed, will be accessed. It will be shown that most of the calumny and confusion stem from placing his earlier sexual behavior and beliefs alongside the views he came to later in life, disregarding the actual chronology and evolution of his thinking about sexual matters, behavior. His most vulnerable point is not in his exegesis of the texts where Christ himself set a remarkably high bar for the sexual integrity of those who would follow his path to life. In six sections this chapter includes: (1) a brief critical appreciation for the psycho-biographical work by Daniel Rancour-Laferriere, *Tolstoy on the Couch: Misogyny, Masochism and the Absent Mother* followed by; (2) an analysis of Tolstoy's exegetical treatment of the relevant Gospel passages which speak to sex and marriage; (3) additional theological and pastoral contributions on overcoming sensual and sexual sin gleaned from Tolstoy's work, *The Christian Teaching*; (4) a biographical framework essential to properly understanding his views on sex and marriage; (5) extractions from and analysis of Tolstoy's prophetic novella *The Kreutzer Sonata* challenging the culture of his day toward Sermon on the Mount standards and practices for sex and marriage; and (6) some summarization of Tolstoy's views on sexual self-disarmament in the context of his broader interests of non-violence. The primary source material for consideration can be limited to three diverse works written by Tolstoy in the Second Tolstoy period each containing concentrated sections treating his views on sex and marriage; *The Christian Teaching* (1877); *What I Believe* (1884); and *The Kreutzer Sonata* (1889), and more so his *Postface* to this provocative and prophetic novel. Additionally and importantly, the diary of his wife Sophia contributes. And, important secondary source material will be drawn from Tolstoy friend Alymer Maude's chapter in the second volume of his biography of Tolstoy, a chapter titled, "*The Sex Question*."

Finally, helpful to the focus of this chapter are insights from Martin Green's trilogy comparing the two mahatmas, Tolstoy and Gandhi, as related to the sex question.

8.1 Tolstoy on the Secularist's Couch: Misogyny, Masochism, and the Absent Mother

Interdisciplinary scholarship on important subjects are welcome contributions toward better understanding and appreciation, especially of influential and important personalities in history. Certainly this is the case with the psychoanalysis of Leo Tolstoy by Daniel Rancour-Laferriere. It is hardly necessary to read past Rancour-Laferriere's title and subtitle to ascertain his diagnosis of the root causes of Tolstoy's behavior and beliefs about women and sexuality. Daniel Rancour-Laferriere thinly determined Tolstoy's misogyny, which is certainly present in his writings, goes beyond the norm of male and female relationship roles of late nineteenth century Russian culture. Regardless of whether his case is watertight, it remains that Tolstoy said shocking things to the modern ear. What is also true is that he said good things about women, and for women, that ran counter to the prejudice against women at his time. No one would disagree that Tolstoy was a complex figure in this regard.

The easy charge against Rancour-Laferriere and others who take on a psycho-analytical enterprise on a historical figure is that they do so without the person actually lying on the therapist's couch. Rancour-Laferriere's response is true:

> Quite frankly . . . no clinician ever had a patient about whom so much detailed and intimate information is available as we have about Leo Tolstoy. Not only did the introspective Tolstoy strive for maximal explicitness and honesty in his diaries, he had a wife, children, and other relatives, as well as many friends and colleagues who left behind detailed memoirs about their relationships with him . . . [forming] a rich psychological trove. Ordinarily a clinician merely works with a patient one-on-one, bringing family members and friends for consultation only occasionally, if ever. In Tolstoy's case the 'patient' has been described by so many witnesses, and from so many different perspectives, that it is possible to gain deep insight into his psyche – if one is actually willing, that is, to scrutinise the many volumes of available information.[2]

---

2. Rancour-Laferriere, *Tolstoy on the Couch*, 8.

Even so, tainting this careful work of Rancour-Laferriere is the secular bias behind it. Quickly, in fact on page one of a 270-page project, religion is dismissed as a source cause of Tolstoy's struggle sexually and his later views: "It was not a religious belief either, although Tolstoy did marshal quotations from the bible to support his thesis. Tolstoy's repudiation of sex was, rather, a fact of his particular biography, a strikingly personal declaration reflecting the state of his psyche at the time he made it."[3]

Tolstoy's famous dark night of the soul, known as the Arzamas Horror after the town in central Russian where he had his breakdown, is rendered by Rancour-Laferriere as separation anxiety and depressive anxiety (toska), a "crisis of vocation experienced upon the completion of a major work" made worse by being separated from his wife (woman/mother). Throughout Christian history, including the depression that Elijah experienced after the events at Mount Carmel, there are myriads of examples of people encountering demons, oppressions, and otherwise spiritual warfare in their weakened emotional states. Tolstoy's conversion took place over a number of years and the Arzamas Horror was a particularly defining moment in his spiritual journey. Rancour-Laferriere includes no consideration of spiritual realities affecting and at work in Tolstoy. From the vantage point of the discipline of theology, Tolstoy's struggle has significant context and explanation that are apparently beyond the purview of secular psychiatry. This can be demonstrated in modern readings of New Testament healings and deliverances which are downgraded to matters of mental illness and psychosis. It is true that past hurts and loss, as in the loss of Tolstoy's mother, are formative and stay with people throughout their lives. These are also the very touch points where people find salve in scripture and divine encounters. The contention throughout this project is that there is a more generous way to read Tolstoy as a follower of Christ. Especially in the area of sexuality, generally all men have long journeys toward self-control and sanity. In this chapter it will be shown that Tolstoy's journey led him toward agreement with both the teachings of Jesus and the Apostle Paul.

An additional point demonstrating the short-sightedness of a secular bias in psychoanalytical diagnosis, Rancour-Laferriere considers simple obedience to Jesus to be moral masochism:

> One way Tolstoy deals with his almost constant physical and psychical pain in 1889 is to actively welcome it. He is not satisfied merely to complain. He needs to gain some sort of mastery

---

3. Rancour-Laferriere, *Tolstoy on the Couch*, 1.

over (not necessarily pleasure in) his suffering, and for this he needs to actually seek out suffering.[4]

Rancour-Laferriere was referencing Tolstoy's statement that "You can only develop your spiritual essence by observing purity in your animal life, humbleness in your human (worldly) life, and love in your divine life."[5] Classic spiritual disciplines fostering self-control (the final fruit of the Spirit) such as chastity, abstinence and fasting, frugality, purity and holiness are inadvertently denigrated by Rancour-Laferriere as evidences of moral masochism. Fighting the urge to fornicate should rather be interpreted as striving to be faithful and loving to a spouse and as submission to the way of God which leads to life not destruction. It would seem evident from the therapist's couch that those who feed their animal desires reap a whirlwind of hurt and suffering as well. Additionally, this suffering (masochism) is not as miserable as Rancour-Laferriere makes it seem. Tolstoy found peace and happiness in such holiness on the path of Christ.

8.2 Tolstoy's Second Commandment: Abstinence in Singleness, Minimization in Marriage

Recall from chapter two, issues of sex and marriage take on commandment status for Tolstoy as he combined the lust/adultery and divorce sections of the Sermon on the Mount to comprise the second of five commandments he organized from his understanding of Matthew 5. In some sense each of the first four commandments are related to and support the fifth commandment against war; anger leads to murder, lust is at the root of aggression and dominance, oaths effectually surrender one's will to a warring commander in chief and, non-resistance to evil. Within the context of a broader call to disarmament, for Tolstoy, the ideals of abstinence in singleness and sexual constraint, its minimization and marginalization in marriage can be construed as sexual self-disarmament.

Speaking of this second commandment to guard against sensual desire and debauchery Tolstoy wrote: "The wisdom of this commandment impressed me profoundly. It would suppress all the evils in the world that result from the sexual relations."[6] Tolstoy argued that "license in sexual relations leads to contention" and to the "abandonment of the woman to whom

---

4. Rancour-Laferriere, *Tolstoy on the Couch*, 144.
5. Rancour-Laferriere, *Tolstoy on the Couch*, 144.
6. Tolstoy, *What I Believe*, 60.

I had first been united."[7] Within these statements run the threads of living at peace with all, aggression and dissension toward none, dominance of no one, and never turning against or away from anyone. Tolstoy believed "the law of humanity is to live in couples" and he viewed this text in Matthew 5:27–32 and also Matthew 19, Mark 10, Luke 16 and the first epistle of Paul to the Corinthians to be an "affirmation of the indissolubility of marriage."[8] He believed "monogamy is the natural law of humanity."[9] The exception clauses in Matthew 5 and 1 Corinthians he deemed to insert a "strange exception to the general rule . . . so entirely in contradiction with the fundamental idea."[10] As is more fully detailed in chapter two, Tolstoy resolved the contradictions by demonstrating how erroneous translations and scribal additions and errors obscured the original meaning of the commandment. He argued the exception permitting divorce, the fault of adultery, should not be interpreted as an act, but as a quality—namely libertinism, indulging sensual pleasures with no regard for moral principles. Traditional interpretation of these texts places the fault on the woman whereas Tolstoy's rendering relocated the fault with the man. Under no conditions should a man put his wife out and neither party should violate this union.[11] His re-rendering of the text for his *Gospel in Brief* shows clearly the decisions he made and conclusions he came to regarding its intended meaning:

> In the former law it was said: Do not commit adultery, and if you wish to put away your wife, give her a letter of divorcement. But I tell you that if you look lustfully at a woman's beauty you are already committing adultery. All sensuality destroys the soul, and so it is better for you to renounce the pleasures of the flesh than to destroy your life. And if you put away your wife, then besides being vicious yourself you drive her to wantonness too, as well as him with whom she may unite. So that is the second commandment: Do not think that love of a woman is good, do not desire women, but live with her with whom you have become united, and do not leave her.[12]

Prophetically against a culture where sexual debauchery and infidelity were pervasive and permissible, for the rest of his life, Tolstoy sought to

---

7. Tolstoy, *What I Believe*, 171.
8. Tolstoy, *What I Believe*, 60.
9. Tolstoy, *What I Believe*, 171.
10. Tolstoy, *What I Believe*, 60.
11. Tolstoy, *What I Believe*, 65.
12. Tolstoy, *Gospel in Brief*, 41–42.

live himself and persuade others to live this second commandment. In this regard he was a lone voice in the wilderness, and remains so today.

8.3 *The Christian Teaching* on Sensual and Sexual Sins

During the two year period 1875–77 Tolstoy wrote but did not finalise a manuscript entitled *The Christian Teaching* because other projects diverted his attention away. Two decades later, in 1897, it was published with his permission and the disclaimer that "this book was not intended by the author for publication in its present form." Tolstoy's statement was: "Certainly I regard this writing as unfinished and far from satisfying the demands which I myself should have put forward twenty years ago. But I now know that I shall not have time to finish it, to bring it to that degree of lucidity . . . and yet I think that even in its present form, there may be found in it something useful to men. . . . [T]herefore print and publish it as it and, God willing, if I become free from other works, and still have the strength, I will return to this writing and will endeavour to make it plainer, clearer and shorter."[13] Importantly, *The Christian Teaching*, contains substantial exposition from Tolstoy on the matters central to the concerns of this chapter. And more importantly it can be surmised from his disclaimer that his views expressed therein, though not polished to his satisfaction, by and large did remain fixed over the next two decades and beyond toward his life's end. He had the opportunity to note if there had been any development in his views, or change in them, and he only noted style and form corrections were in order, nothing substantive.

In *The Christian Teaching*, Tolstoy explained "the liberation of the spiritual being from the animal individuality" and referred to it as the birth of the spiritual being.[14] Prior to this new birth, "during infancy and childhood, and sometimes even later, man lives as an animal."[15] He did not view this born again experience to be instantaneous, it was "not accomplished at once, but like the physical birth by degrees . . . the pangs of birth alternate with pauses and reversions to the former position; manifestations of spiritual life alternate with manifestation of animal life."[16] Tolstoy expounded on sins that are obstacles to the manifestation of love. He defined sin as "obstacles to the manifestation of love" and listed six classifications of sins/obstacles: (1) sensual, (2) idleness, (3) avarice, (4) ambition, (5) sexual, and

13. Tolstoy, *Christian Teaching*, v–vi.
14. Tolstoy, *Christian Teaching*, 35.
15. Tolstoy, *Christian Teaching*, 36.
16. Tolstoy, *Christian Teaching*, 71.

(6) intoxication. The first and fifth, sensual and sexual sins (or obstacles to the manifestation of love) relate directly to our understanding of his views on lust, sex, adultery and marriage.[17] Sensual sin is committed when the needs of the body are placed first, particularly pleasures arising from a satisfaction of bodily needs. This is not exclusively a sexual sin (hedonism and debauchery) as it includes the variety of bodily needs including for food and drink (gluttony, intoxication), dress and lodging (vanity and luxury). Tolstoy parsed the sensual sin down more specifically in his fifth and sixth classifications of sexual sin and the sin of intoxication. Sex for the continuation of the race did not, for Tolstoy, constitute a sexual sin. He noted "complete abstinence from the sexual sin is possible" and that the line is crossed when sex is "to increase his personal welfare."[18]

> Man is, as it were, allowed the choice between two ways of serving God. Either by keeping free from married life and its consequences . . . or else, conscious of his own weakness, he may transmit to the posterity he has begotten, nourished and brought up the fulfilment, or at least the possibility of fulfilment, of that which he himself has neglected.[19]

For the Christian who has chosen the former way of serving God, and

> desires to keep chaste and to consecrate all his powers to the service of God, sexual sin will consist in any sexual intercourse whatever, even though it have for its object the birth and rearing of children. The purest married state will be such an innate sin for the man who has chosen the alternative of chastity.[20]

For the Christian who chooses the second alternative, either as a man or a woman, to marry, sexual relation is restricted to one person, and for the purpose of forming a family. Tolstoy believed sexual sin was committed in this case when sex is for pleasure while measures are taken to avoid the birth of children, "or becoming addicted to unnatural vices."[21] Tolstoy minced no words about the consequences of sexual sin:

> But for the sexual sin there would not exist the slavery and suffering of woman side by side with over-indulgence and depravity; there would be none of those quarrels, fights, murders, caused by jealousy, there would exist neither the degradation of

17. Tolstoy, *Christian Teaching*, 40.
18. Tolstoy, *Christian Teaching*, 55–56.
19. Tolstoy, *Christian Teaching*, 55.
20. Tolstoy, *Christian Teaching*, 56.
21. Tolstoy, *Christian Teaching*, 58.

> woman to the condition of an instrument of lust, prostitution or unnatural vice ... those dreadful diseases from which men now suffer, –nor forsaken children, nor infanticide.[22]

Indictments as such cut to the heart of life among the nineteenth-century Russian aristocracy as they do to twenty-first century society in the West.

In addition to the six sins, Tolstoy wrote of five snares,[23] five false justifications whereby people fall into the trap of convincing themselves the sin is excusable, and even necessary. The second is the family snare whereby a person justifies him or herself on the grounds of their children's welfare. Tolstoy believed it to be a lie and a deception that, in the name of love for our own families, people were released from the demands of justice toward others. The exploitation of the slave labour of others, depriving them of land and milk for their own children so there is milk for one's own children— these for Tolstoy were deceptions inherent to family life and contrary to the Kingdom of God on earth. It is at this point Tolstoy espoused ideas that frame what I suggested earlier constitutes white martyrdom (subsection 5.5, footnote 49); he sacrificed his family for Christ's sake:

> To avoid falling into this snare, many must refrain from intentionally developing himself this family love, from regarding this love as a virtue, and from yielding to it. . . . [K]nowing the snare, he must be always on his guard against it, so as not to sacrifice the divine for the family love . . . love for one's family is an animal instinct . . . many must endeavour to do for every stranger the same that he wishes to do for his family.[24]

Tolstoy did not believe animal lust in man was entirely extinguishable as the instinct is there for the continuation of the human race. He did believe "this lust may be reduced to very small dimensions, and by some even replaced by entire chastity."[25] He wrote of a "diminution and reduction" in the struggle against sexual sin. He wrote that

> reasonable consciousness, when awakened in many, demands the opposite [of animal sexual appetite], i.e. complete abstinence,

---

22. Tolstoy, *Christian Teaching*, 65–66.

23. Tolstoy, *Christian Teaching*, 73–74. (1) Personal snare, or snare of preparation— excusing ourselves with the justification that we are preparing for an activity useful in the future; (2) Family snare; (3) Snare of activity, or utility—excusing ourselves with the justification that something already begun needs to be completed; (4) Snare of fellowship, or fidelity—justifications that another with whom we are in close relationship will benefit; and (5) State snare, or the snare of the general good.

24. Tolstoy, *Christian Teaching*, 138–39.

25. Tolstoy, *Christian Teaching*, 183.

complete chastity . . . to overcome the habit of this sin, a man must first of all refrain from increasing it. If he be chaste, let him not infringe his chastity; if he be married, let him be true to his partner . . . when a man has succeeded in refraining from fresh sin, then let him labour to diminish that sexual sin to which he is still subject. . . . Although only in rare cases are men able to be altogether chaste, still everyone should understand and remember that he can always be more chaste than he formerly was, or can return to the chastity he has lost.[26]

Tolstoy friend and biographer Maude recalled an 1896 conversation he had with Tolstoy, then age seventy: "After saying that one should never be discouraged or cease to strive to attain what is good, he added, 'I was myself a husband last night, but that is no reason for abandoning the struggle; God may grant me not to be so again!'"[27] Maude remarked "the general verdict of Russian society was: 'Tolstoy is getting old. He has lost his vigour and the grapes are sour!'"[28] Such a sentiment and such an assumption are common to others who read Tolstoy's admonitions against sex and marriage. Rather than listen to the stinging indictment he brought to the widespread licentiousness in their own lives and societies, the messenger typically became the focus.

8.4 *Confession* and Diaries: A Whole Catalog of Active Sexual Life Going Back Twenty Years

Tolstoy the forthright diarist, the novelist of realism, the prolific thinker and philosopher can never be accused of having a secret sexual life. In his *Confession* he wrote the details of the loss of his virginity and of his road into sexual immorality. Five days before his wedding he shared painfully vivid diaries of his sexual past with his bride-to-be, scandalizing her for some time to come. Included in his long litany of sexual exploits and encounters he wrote of his very recent affair with one of his married peasants, the twenty-three year old Aksinia Bazykina (1836–1919), and of the child that came from that relationship, Timophey, who grew to become a coachman at Yasnaya Polyana and lived his entire life there. Such behavior was normal for estate owners of that time and place. Tolstoy's father also had a child with one of the serf girls at Yasnaya Polyana and the child also spent his life as a coachman at the estate. Biographer A.W. Wilson wrote that in 1859 Tolstoy

26. Tolstoy, *Christian Teaching*, 183–85.
27. Maude, *Life of Tolstoy, Vol. II*, 280.
28. Maude, *Life of Tolstoy, Vol. II*, 280.

was looking for a wife and that Tolstoy had "feelings which went beyond lust ... with whom he had a passionate and long-standing liaison since 1858" and quoted Tolstoy's diary which says: "I'm a fool. I'm a beast. I'm in love as never before in my life. She is pretty. ... Continue to see Aksinia exclusively. I looked for her. It is no longer the feelings of a stag but of a husband for a wife."[29] Even soon thereafter marrying Sophia, the mistress was never far away on the estate, a source of ongoing angst throughout the entirety of their marriage.[30] In her diary Sophia lamented Aksinya, and Tolstoy's bastard, and both are mentioned multiple times in the context of her early struggle to get beyond her husband's extensive and haunting sexual past:[31]

> I don't think I ever recovered from the shock of reading the diaries when I was engaged to him. ... I can still remember the agonising pangs of jealousy, the horror of that first appalling experience of male depravity. Here it all was, in one great dollop: the early whoring ... repeated doses of V.D. The gypsies, the Cossack girls– quasi-homoerotic devotion to his student friends, the flirtations in drawing rooms – a whole catalog of active sexual life going back twenty years. What was worst was the discovery that he had, until only a month or two before, been besottedly in love with his peasant mistress, Aksinya.[32]

Tolstoy hid nothing about his former relationship with Aksinya, he even wrote her as a character into his novels, *An Idyll*, and into *The Devil*. Three months before his death Tolstoy told his friend, follower and biographer Pavel Biriukov:

> You always write what is good about me. That is misleading and incomplete. The bad should also be told. When I was young I led a very bad life, and there are two occurrences in particular that torment me even now. I tell you this, and ask you to write it in my biography. Those occurrences were an affair with a peasant woman in our village before my marriage– which is referred to in my story The Devil. The other was the crime I committed

---

29. Wilson, *Tolstoy*, 184ff.
30. Tolstoy, *Diaries of Sofia Tolstoy*, 318, 529, 532.
31. "Now his actual wife met the earthly, common-law Aksinya and her little baby, Tolstoy's bastard. 'I think I shall kill myself with jealousy,' she told her diary. 'In love as never before' he writes. With that fat, pale peasant woman – how frightful! I looked at the dagger and the guns with joy. One blow, I thought, how easy it would be – if only it weren't for the baby. Yet to think that she is there, just a few steps away. I feel demented.'" Wilson, *Tolstoy*, 205.
32. Wilson, *Tolstoy*, 197.

> earlier with a maid servant, Masha, who lived at my aunt's. She was a virgin, I seduced her, and she was dismissed and perished.

What is also true is there is no indication that at any point after his wedding day to Sophia that he was anything but faithful to her and her alone. His prior sexual exploits were entirely pre-conversion and his later views on children and marriage were solidified after the last of his children was born. Maude defended Tolstoy from critics who had no regard for the chronology of his life conflating earlier behavior with later beliefs:

> I realise how inevitably he arrived at his views. From the first his progress was in one and the same direction, namely, towards greater and greater self-control. As a bachelor he struggled against his passion. As a married man he was faithful to his wife. And when at last he found his reaching checked by his wife's disagreement, and by the matrimonial bonds that help him to her, he wished to sacrifice his marital relations rather than his ideas. . . . Tolstoy's advice was the only advice he could give. . . . His outlook on life had begun to change seriously after fifteen years of marriage and had gone on changing for another twelve. . . . It was difficult to cling to his principles while held in the bonds of matrimony, and to aim at complete chastity was the only solution for a man of his character placed in such circumstances. . . Tolstoy is so interesting just because he honestly tells us what he thinks and feels, regardless of how it reflects on his own conduct. This is a rare and valuable practice which should be recognised and respected.[33]

In his biography chapter on *The Sex Question*, Maude mentioned how in 1888 Tolstoy read Alice B. Stockman's book *Tokology*. Stockman was an American gynecologist advocating sex only once a month within marriage and never during menstruation and pregnancy. It was significant to Tolstoy for any doctor at this time in history to espouse sexual practices near to his own views and those of the doctrine of Jesus.

8.5 *The Kreutzer Sonata* as a Prophetic Challenge to Immoral Society

Tolstoy's most developed expositions on the matters of sex and marriage come in his 1889 novella, *The Kreutzer Sonata*, and the *Postface* he wrote for it a year later to respond to the "large number of letters from people I

---

33. Maude, *Life of Tolstoy*, Vol. II, 276, 279.

do not know, asking me to explain in clear, simple terms what I think of the subject of the story." In the story, medical doctors of his day are portrayed in a very bad light; Tolstoy referred to them as "sharks" and "high priests of science" who "keep an eye on this problem, for a fee of course ... [T]hey assert that debauchery is good for the health, for it's they who have instituted this form of tidy, legalised debauchery. I even know mothers who take an active concern for this aspect of their son's health. And science directs them to the brothels."[34] Rather than tell patients the truth about what would surely eradicate the blight of syphilis entirely from society, abstinence, they were medicating the symptoms and perpetuating the deception that male sexuality could not and should not be bridled. Tolstoy considered this the first point intended in his book: "that in our society there has been formed the solid conviction, common to every class and receiving the support of a mendacious science, that sexual intercourse is an activity indispensable to health, and that since marriage is not always a practical possibility, extramarital sexual intercourse, committing a man to nothing except the payment of money, is something perfectly natural and therefore to be encouraged."[35] In line with his belief in the liveability of every aspect of the Sermon on the Mount, Tolstoy contended abstinence is possible and most beneficial, especially for any who desire to ascend from the plane of animality to the higher spirituality.

The Kreutzer Sonata is a story about a conversation on a long train ride with a man who had killed his wife and was acquitted by the jury because he was deemed a wronged husband who responded in an understandable rage defending his honour at finding his wife alone in the middle of the night with another man.[36] In literary circles Tolstoy's novels are known for the windows they open into the complex psychological world of his characters and this story is evidence of that skill; in regard to the man but also in regard to the psychology (of sexuality) of that society. Tolstoy began the story with citations of Matthew 5:28 and Matthew 19:10–12 on lust, marriage, and the higher calling of the eunuch for the Kingdom of Heaven's sake. The novella begins with passengers on the train talking about the ease of divorce, the European idea of marriage, love and the plight of women in the role of wife and mother. The ideal of love is discussed as "the exclusive preference for one man or one woman above all others."[37] Such a notion is rebuffed, as are things like spiritual affinity between and man and a woman and, shared

---

34. Tolstoy, *Kreutzer Sonata*, 136, 111.
35. Tolstoy, *Kreutzer Sonata*, "Postface," 299.
36. Tolstoy, *Kreutzer Sonata*, 152.
37. Tolstoy, *Kreutzer Sonata*, 104.

ideals. The reality in society is evident: "The husband and wife simply pretend to everyone that they're living in monogamy, when in actual fact they're living in polygamy and polyandry. It's not pretty, but it's feasible."[38] The cynicism of the story starts early and strong, "by the second month [of marriage, the couple comes to] loathe the sight of each other."[39] Debauchery is defined in the conversation as that which "takes place when you free yourself from any moral regard for the woman you enter into physical relations with."[40] As the conversation with the man progresses the language of snares is used repeatedly, the man and the woman become trapped by lust and the "licensed brothel [society] in which they live. . . . [M]arriages nowadays are set like traps. . . . [N]owadays a woman is like a slave in a market or a piece of bait for a trap."[41] And men, ironically, find themselves dominated by women as "the objects of your sensuality that will enslave you. . . . [H]e falls under her spell and loses his head."[42]

To those who would say sexual relations are necessary to the furtherance of the human race, the man in the novella retorts:

> Is the human race going to disappear from the face of the earth just because a dozen men don't want to go on living like pigs? . . . You ask how the human race would continue. . . . Why? We wouldn't exist otherwise. And why should we exist? . . . [W]hy should we live? If life has no purpose, if it's been given us for its own sake, we have no reason for living. If that is really the case, then the Schopenhauers . . . are perfectly right. . . . All the churches teach the end of the world, and all the sciences do the same. So what's so strange about morality pointing to the same conclusion?[43]

At this point in the novella Tolstoy inserted a positive comment about this being like what the Shakers preach and similar to the prohibitions against lust in Matthew 5. Matthew 5 makes several appearances in the book which lends to the probability the entire novella was Tolstoy's artistic, prophetic application of those truths to the society around him: "They asked me in court how I killed her, what I used to do it with. Imbeciles! They thought I killed her that day, the fifth of October, with a knife. It wasn't that day I killed her, it was much earlier. Exactly in the same way as they're killing

38. Tolstoy, *Kreutzer Sonata*, 106.
39. Tolstoy, *Kreutzer Sonata*, 106.
40. Tolstoy, *Kreutzer Sonata*, 109.
41. Tolstoy, *Kreutzer Sonata*, 117–19.
42. Tolstoy, *Kreutzer Sonata*, 120–21.
43. Tolstoy, *Kreutzer Sonata*, 125.

their wives, all of them." The point being murder starts with anger, and adultery with lust. Tolstoy was not treating symptoms as were the doctors of his day, he was cutting much deeper to expose and extract the root causes. The man in the novella became the prophetic voice of Tolstoy speaking of a necessary "radical shift in the opinion that many have of woman, and that woman has of herself. That shift will only occur when woman comes to consider virginity the most exalted condition a human being can aspire to."[44] The greater themes Tolstoy garnered from the Sermon on the Mount, those of non-violence, no murder and no war, are all connected to these matters of sex and sexuality. He did not shy away from condemnations of abortion, infanticide—"where they've murdered the child when it was still in its mothers womb. . . . No one even bothers to count these murders, just as no one ever counted the murders of the Inquisition, because they were supposed to be for the good of mankind."[45]

Tolstoy conveyed a deep cynicism about childrearing and marriage in a long dialogue that is the entire *The Kreutzer Sonata*. He painted a portrait of women living in constant fear of a child getting sick and dying, an occurrence commonplace to mothers of that time. He portrayed the busyness that is a full household to be detrimental to the soul as there "is never any time to study your conscience."[46] He portrayed children as unnecessary and marriage as a lesser calling, or as an allowable but compromised place for any who would aspire to moral perfection. Such a position was quickly rejected by the Orthodox Church, the Archbishop of Kherson denounced Tolstoy for undermining the Holy Sacrament of Marriage condemning his teaching "as undermining the whole edifice of society."[47] Tolstoy's views, though ghastly from the vantage point of modern Christian conceptions of marriage and child-rearing, do bear semblance to that of Paul in 1 Corinthians 7. In fact, in commenting on *The Kreutzer Sonata*, Maude noted Tolstoy gave "powerful presentments . . . of the Pauline morality" and in "*What Then Must Men Do?* of the pre-Mosaic morality. . . . It is all to the good that he gave us such forcible presentations of the two Biblical codes, but he carries us farther . . . [restating] in present-day language the case for aiming at the elimination or, as far as possible, the repression of sex feelings and activity . . . and the example of Jesus in this matter."[48] As much as any would try to make out Tolstoy's views to be eccentric he defended his positions: "these propositions

44. Tolstoy, *Kreutzer Sonata*, 136.
45. Tolstoy, *Kreutzer Sonata*, 138.
46. Tolstoy, *Kreutzer Sonata*, 147.
47. Maude, *Life of Tolstoy, Vol. II*, 280.
48. Maude, *Life of Tolstoy, Vol. II*, 274–75.

are merely the inevitable conclusions to be drawn from the Gospels, which we profess, or at least admit to be the basis of our conception of morality."[49] Maude continued: "[For his views on] repression of sex feelings and activity, he has been denounced and abused as though that ideal had never been heard before, and the example of Jesus in this matter had never been held in esteem. . . . [H]e simply represented the Biblical codes to us."[50]

In his *Postface* to *The Kreutzer Sonata,* Tolstoy took time to make abundantly clear what he was seeking to convey in the novella. First, that abstinence was possible. Second that marital infidelity had become, in all classes of society, commonplace. That such a "condition of animality is degrading to human beings" and thirdly, that procreation had entirely lost its meaning.[51] Fourthly, Tolstoy was calling out the fact that children had become "a hindrance to pleasure, as an unfortunate accident" and, he intended to portray contraception as bad, and abortion as murder.[52] He insisted: "we must stop raising the children of men as if they were the young of animals" which led to his fifth stated point: "we must give up thinking of carnal love as something particularly exalted, and must understand that a goal worthy of man, whether it be the service of mankind, of one's country, of science or of art (not to mention the service of God), as soon as we consider it as such, not attained by means of union with the object of our love either inside marriage or outside it. . . . [This is said] is the substance of what I was trying to say and of what I thought I had indeed said, in my story."[53]

More controversially he stated there "never has been and there never will be a Christian marriage." He dismissed it alongside notions of Christian property and a Christian army: "The Christian's ideal is the love of God and of one's neighbour; it is the renunciation of self for the service of God and of one's neighbour. Marriage and carnal love are, on the other hand, the service of oneself and therefore in all cases an obstacle to the service of God and men – from the Christian point of view they represent a fall, a sin."[54] He gave no consideration to marriage as a sacred covenant before a Covenant God, or as an image of the union of Christ and his Church, or of the importance of passing faith on to own's posterity. He did not appreciate the marriage union and family as the bedrock of human society. As these are each significant aspects to both the Pauline and Mosiac codes, their neglect

---

49. Tolstoy, *Kreutzer Sonata,* "Postface," 303.
50. Maude, *Life of Tolstoy, Vol. II,* 275.
51. Tolstoy, *Kreutzer Sonata,* "Postface," 300–1.
52. Tolstoy, *Kreutzer Sonata,* "Postface," 301.
53. Tolstoy, *Kreutzer Sonata,* "Postface," 302.
54. Tolstoy, *Kreutzer Sonata,* "Postface," 306–7.

in Tolstoy, contrary to Maude's assertion, show Tolstoy's view on sex and marriage was at best only partially-Pauline and partially-Mosaic. Tolstoy wrote: "For those who are able to enter upon it, this contraction of marriage, together with its consequences – the birth of children – specifies a new and more limited form of the service of God and men directly.... [T]he contraction of marriage reduces the scope of man's actions and obliges him to rear and educate his offspring, which is composed of future servants of God and men."[55] Regarding chastity as the ideal he wrote: "As soon as one makes of chastity an ideal and realises that every fall, no matter who the partners in it are, is a unique marriage that shall remain indissoluble for the whole of one's life, it becomes clear that the guidance given by Christ is not only sufficient, but it is the only guidance that is possible."[56]

8.6 Anke Pie and the Indian Tolstoy: Asceticism and Nonviolence

Tolstoy's most famous disciple—Gandhi, "read the story (*The Kreutzer Sonata*) literally, loved it, and recommended it widely"[57]—so stated Martin Green in the first of his three books comparing and contrasting these two mahatmas, Tolstoy and Gandhi. Green referred to Gandhi as the *Indian Tolstoy*, and to Tolstoy as *their master's great master*.[58] A couple of his comparisons as influencing factors in their (somewhat) similar views on sex are quite reaching—"both were notably unhandsome"—and even untrue; for example that they both had miserable sex lives in marriage.[59] That is perhaps true only in the case of Gandhi. Further, comparisons of Tolstoy and Gandhi fail if there is no mention that Gandhi was far more extreme, and hypocritical. Gandhi "refused to admit that there could be mutuality in sex, and asked his followers for sexual self-disarmament."[60] Tolstoy focused primarily on male sexual passions but not to the extent that women were not mutual participants. He even viewed women as more powerful in this regard, entrapping men in their own lusts. Unlike Tolstoy, there is a stain of hypocrisy in the aged Gandhi as Green recounted:

---

55. Tolstoy, *Kreutzer Sonata*, "Postface," 309.
56. Tolstoy, *Kreutzer Sonata*, "Postface," 310.
57. Green, *Challenge of the Mahatmas*, 135.
58. Green, *Challenge of the Mahatmas*, xi, 117.
59. Green, *Challenge of the Mahatmas*, 7.
60. Green, *Challenge of the Mahatmas*, 241.

Bose, who was Gandhi's secretary during his heroic pilgrimage to Noakhali in 1946–1947, resigned the post in protest against some things Gandhi did, including his sleeping in the same bed with women coworkers. Bose did not accuse Gandhi of lust, but of secrecy, and of allowing the women to involve themselves in a psychological situation beyond their capacity to handle, which fostered a possessiveness in them toward him, and a hysteria.[61]

Green complained Gandhi "encouraged Hindu sex-guilt. . . . [T]he young women who came under his spell were seduced into chastity." Importantly, Tolstoy was never the creepy old man. Interestingly, Green drew in a third generation notable adherent to Gandhian/Tolstoyan non-violence in Martin Luther King Jr.: "King was no Mahatma, and that was his strength; he was a guide in a movement with many leaders. He was a visionary but no Utopian, a man of God but no saintly eccentric. He felt no need to give up smart attire, good food, or sex, to be effectively non-violent."[62] In the area of sexual purity and integrity, comparing the three apostles of non-violence—King, Gandhi, and Tolstoy—perhaps surprisingly, Tolstoy was most saintly.

As the more recent example of a sexually-compromised champion of non-violence John Howard Yoder illustrates, the integrity of a person's adherence to true non-violence does hinge on their renunciation of animal passions, selfish exploitation, coercion and dominance of the weaker sex. In his article trying to make sense of the pacifist Yoder's sexual abuse, Stanley Hauerwas wrote:

> I also think we owe feminists a debt of gratitude for their critique of romantic love. For years in the core course in Christian Ethics, I assigned the work of Marie Fortune [*Sexual Violence: The Unmentionable Sin*, Pilgrim Press, 1983] because I thought her exposure of the violence present in romantic love to be a crucial insight. Fortune was not only important for exposing the violence occluded in romantic ideals of love, but she also helped make clear that nonviolence is not just about war.[63]

Tolstoy would have agreed with Fortune and Hauerwas that nonviolence is not just about war. And Green's comparisons are most equally helpful where he demonstrated the well-known asceticisms of both Gandhi and Tolstoy, from restricted diets (including vegetarianism) to sex all relate directly to the greater theme of non-violence.[64] As was mentioned earlier,

---

61. Green, *Challenge of the Mahatmas*, 241.
62. Green, *Challenge of the Mahatmas*, 240.
63. Hauerwas, "In Defence of 'Our Respectable Culture.'"
64. Green, *Challenge of the Mahatmas*, 19.

Gandhi did develop what he originally embraced from Tolstoy; narrowing Tolstoy's absolute non-retaliation to evil, to a non-violent retaliation to evil, significantly different conceptions. As regards to the relationship between sex and non-violence, Gandhi became more of a feminist than Tolstoy, "encouraging women to say no to their husbands sexual initiatives."[65] And, he concluded that "non-violence is the inherent quality of women." Green noted that some of the women admirers of Gandhi "have commented on Gandhi's literal womanliness and motherliness as elements in his attraction for them." Green quoted Gandhi as saying in 1944:

> I have repeated several times without number that nonviolence is the inherent quality of women. For ages men have had training in violence. In order to become nonviolent they have to cultivate the qualities of women. Ever since I have taken to nonviolence, I have become more and more of a woman.[66]

Reading Tolstoy's *Letter to Women* makes it seem possible he would have agreed with Gandhi on this point considering he ended his letter this way: "Therefore, in the hands of these women lies the highest power of saving men from the prevailing and threatening evils of our times. Yes, ye women and mothers, in your hands, more than in those of all others, lies the salvation of the world!"[67]

A metaphor in the Tolstoy home for things-that-which-one-should-give-up was Anke Pie. His wife Sophia was especially gifted in the kitchen and happily fed the many who visited Yasnaya Polyana, and fed them well, and with the best available to her. One particular cake was requested frequently in their family, Anke Pie, and it gets a mention in *War & Peace*. The recipe was from her own childhood and family of origin (and is available today in Sergei Beltyukov's publication *Leo Tolstoy's Family Recipe Book*).[68]

---

65. Green, *Challenge of the Mahatmas*, 41.
66. Green, *Challenge of the Mahatmas*, 42.
67. Tolstoy, "To Women."
68. Also here in an anonymous article ("Leo Tolstoj and Lemon Anke Pie"): "His wife, Sofya, named it after Dr Nikolai Anke, a friend of her mother's who had passed the recipe on to her family. "Ever since I can remember, on all festive occasions, big holidays and name days were always and invariably celebrated with Anke Pie. Without it, a meal wouldn't have been a meal, and a feast wouldn't have been a feast," wrote Tolstoy's son Ilya in his memoirs. . . . In an 1891 edition of *The Atlantic* magazine, the American writer Isabel P Hapgood recalled a visit to Yasnaya Polyana, Tolstoy's estate south of Moscow, during which the 63-year-old count gestured at the long dining table set by servants beneath the birch trees: 'You perceive the sinful luxury in which I live,' he told his guest, waving his hand towards the furniture, and saving what Hapgood saw as 'special bitterness for the silver forks and spoons.'" See also, Mosko et al., "Russian Oven."

In the summers (as fictionalized in *War & Peace*), the families would gather for feasts and the crescendo of the meal would be the delightful and delicious Anke Pie. Though it was a favorite treat he very much enjoyed, the dish became a point of personal angst for Tolstoy as it came to symbolise for him the greater tension between the life God wants people to live, and the Anke Pie life of self-indulgence. As this chapter has shown, sex for Tolstoy was Anke Pie. It was near the top of the list of things-that-one-should-give-up. If total abstinence was not one's calling, then at least the one committed to the doctrines of Jesus could practice diminution and reduction in their struggle against sexual sin. He knew such a narrow road would only be taken by a few but he also knew it was the only way to life, the other road leading to destruction. Against culture, prophetically, Tolstoy championed (his understanding of) the high standard Jesus gave for sex and marriage from the summit of the mount.

~ 9.0 ~

Matthew 5:38–39 as an Alternative Politic

REDUCED TO A SENTENCE or two, for Leo Tolstoy, the sum and substance of the Sermon on the Mount ethic is found in Matthew 5:38-39, "You have heard that it was said, 'Eye for eye, and tooth for tooth.' But I tell you, do not resist an evil person. If anyone slaps you on the right cheek, turn to them the other cheek also." Yet for Tolstoy this ethic was more than an ethic, it was an alternative politic, a politic that could hardly be obeyed in isolation. He believed the Sermon on the Mount was for the world, and that it undermined the present world order which had its foundation on a shifting cycle of violence. It was the way of the Kingdom of Heaven to be walked out by the peoples on the earth. Such a counter-cultural ideology could only be disruptive as it presented a direct challenge to the various prevailing ideologies of Tolstoy's time, and indeed of all time. In this chapter, Tolstoyan Sermon on the Mount interpretation, encapsulated in Matthew 5:38-39, will be set against the main political philosophies which were developing in his time, and ultimately successfully dominated his world and the world at large: Social Darwinism and Marxist-Leninism.

9.1 Tolstoy against Social Darwinism

Beginning a chapter on an alternative politic with a section on science requires some explanation. What significant, society-altering correlation could possibly exist between science and politics? One need look no further than climate science today to see how vastly global, political and societal implications emerge from scientific theory. And the climate science of our contemporary time was preceded by and related to an even more far reaching scientific theorem. Simply put, scientific Darwinian ideas and theory have had enormous consequences on society (in the form of Social Darwinism) and particularly on marginalized peoples, the sector of society most important to Tolstoy. It could not be said Tolstoy was anti-science. During his existential crisis and pre-conversation period, Tolstoy devoted long periods sincerely searching methodically through the various disciplines of human knowledge looking for any shred of meaning and purpose in life. For Tolstoy, science and philosophy were both a grand disappointment, a dry well, not a source of living water. In fact, Tolstoy did not just find an absence of life therein, he discerned the mechanisms of death in (scientific) Darwinism, and opposed those mechanisms as they presented themselves in Social Darwinism, writing against it in the very pages we find his expositions on the Sermon on the Mount. Though Tolstoy wrote against Darwinism, the more precise modern terminology of Social Darwinism is preferred here because it better captures the political aspects of the scientific theory, which he opposed. It was not biological matters about molecules and mammals which Tolstoy engaged and contested, it was what those Darwinian theories led to politically and socially, ala Social Darwinism—major things such as (1) the view of peoples as species to be categorised into favoured races, and that (2) society improves itself through violence against its weaker members. There is some conflation of Darwinism and Social Darwinism in Tolstoy's writings and the reader needs to be discerning to understand the distinctions as he saw a close connection between these two.

In investigating Tolstoy's angst toward Darwinian theory and its social and political ramifications, a good place to begin is with the very last letter he wrote, only a few days before his death. Terminal and beleaguered in bed at the Astapovo train station, Tolstoy wrote to his "dear children, Seryozha and Tanya." After explaining why it was best for them not to come to the station, he wrote that he wanted to add some advice to Seryozha:

> that you should think about your own life, who you are, what you are, what is the meaning of a man's life and how every reasonable man should live it. The views you have acquired about Darwinism, evolution and the struggle for existence won't explain to you the meaning of your life and won't give you guidance in your actions, and a life without an explanation of its meaning and importance, and without the unfailing guidance that steps from it is a pitiful existence. Think about it. I say it, probably on the eve of my death, because I love you. Goodbye;

try to calm your mother, for whom I have the most genuine feeling of compassion and love. Your loving father. L. Tolstoy[1]

In his parting words to his son, words about finding his way in life, Tolstoy could have cautioned against a variety of popular paths in life which he believed led to destruction, but he named Darwinism. And that he did call out Darwinism speaks as much to his own conviction that Darwinism, and more particularly Social Darwinism, was the antithesis of the Sermon on the Mount, as it tells us much about his son's interest in it. Set amidst the other admonitions given in the letter the former seems more probable. Reasonable weight can be placed on a dying man's last words of warning to loved ones, and the world. Such was the threat Tolstoy saw in Darwinian theory as it is applied politically and socially. However, this deathbed disdain was no recent conviction, it was a clear note he sounded across five decades of writing.

In his excellent chapter on *Tolstoy and Darwin*, Hugh McLean documents Tolstoy's exposure to Darwin and to many of the main articles and publications on Darwinism that Tolstoy for certain read, and those he likely did not read. Darwin's *On the Origin of Species by Means of Natural Selection, or the Preservation of Favoured Races in the Struggle for Life* was published in 1859, and 1864 in Russian. Tolstoy's first mention of Darwin comes in *War and Peace* (1867), three years later there is mention again in *Anna Karenina* (1870).[2] Without doubt, Darwin's ideas were well into the mainstream of Russian society within the short span of a decade, and "reached far beyond the frontiers of science."[3] In his *Confession* (1879–81), Tolstoy told of his

1. Christian, *Tolstoy's Diaries, Volume II*, 716–17.

2. Berman, "Darwin in the Novels," 331–51. "Although Tolstoy was deeply critical of Darwin in his notebooks, diaries, letters, and essays, his literary imagination was profoundly influenced by Darwinian theory.... *War and Peace* is set in a pre-Darwinian world where only the author, not the characters, has access to the new worldview opened up by ideas of evolution, natural selection and the struggle for existence. In this work, Darwinian ideas are manifest in the way Tolstoy conceived of the struggle of nations and individuals at the heart of the book and also in the 'Second Epilogue,' where he references Darwin directly to help explain and justify his theory of history. *Anna Karenina*, by contrast, unfolds in the new Darwinian age, where both the characters, as well as the author, engage with Darwin's theories. His influence can be felt in the structuring worldview of the author, which emphasizes chance over teleology and interweaves multiple plotlines. However, the characters' own engagements with Darwin are designed to undermine his ideas, vindicating faith over the new scientific worldview. Anna embraces the 'struggle for existence' as natural law and ends her life, while Levin turns away from Darwin and is saved from despair."

3. Vucinich, *Darwin in Russian Thought*, 3–4. "In theology [Darwinism] encouraged a novel and more comprehensive effort to assess the fundamental challenges of Darwinian heterodoxy.... [I]n the domain of ideology – the articulation of political

turn to science for the answers of life and the disappointment there: "If we turn to those branches of knowledge that attempt to provide solutions to the question of life . . . biology . . . we encounter a startling poverty of thought, extreme lack of clarity, and a completely unjustified pretension to resolve questions beyond their scope, together with continual contradiction between one thinker and another or even with their own selves."[4] Emerging from this extended season of searching out the question of life Tolstoy had found his answers in the teaching of Jesus which he came to believe spoke directly to the original condition of humankind: "The Christian doctrine [Sermon on the Mount] restores man to his original consciousness of self, not the animal self, but the Godlike self."[5]

9.1.1 Rudolf Steiner on Tolstoy and Darwin (1904)

One of the very few treatments of Tolstoy against Darwinian ideologies was by the Theosophist Rudolf Steiner in a series of lectures entitled *Origin and Destination of Humanity* in Berlin, November 3, 1904. Steiner took the side of Tolstoy pinpointing how the departure locus for Darwin and Tolstoy was in Darwin's superficial and shifting observations about outer forms:

> The origin and change of the forms of animals and plants in the struggle for existence [sic]. This confirms that the attention of science is directed to the outer form. And what did Darwin openly declare? He asserted that the plants and animals live out their lives in the most manifold forms but that originally, according to his conviction, there were forms into which life was breathed by a Creator of world. This is what Darwin himself says. His eyes are directed to the evolution of forms, of the outer form, and he himself feels that it is impossible to penetrate into what imbues these forms with life. He takes this life for granted and does not attempt to explain it. He pays no heed to it, the question for him being merely the shape and form which life assumes.[6]

---

beliefs and social goals – Darwinian debates echoed some of the most critical intellectual dilemmas of the day. . . . In literature Darwinism became a topic of direct concern or a target of endless allusions. References to the letter or spirit of Darwinian thought . . . [in] individual heroes of Dostoevsky's and Tolstoy's literary works provided graphic examples of the myriads of prisms refracting Darwinian science and showing the multiple strands of its impact on current thoughts and attitudes."

4. Tolstoy, *Confession*, 28–29.
5. Tolstoy, *Kingdom of God Is within You*, 97.
6. Steiner, *Origin and Destination of Humanity*.

This, Steiner argued, is the limitation of the materialistic view of the world. Steiner understood Tolstoy to rightly be rightly concerned with the deep matters of the soul to best answer the question of life:

> If you would truly understand form, you must look into its innermost essence . . . in Tolstoy the artist . . . he describes the soldier, the official, the human being belonging to some class of society, family or race – but everywhere he is looking for the soul. . . . Death is still the great stumbling block for the materialistic view of the world. . . . The riddle of life – in its scientific as well as in its religious aspect – lay at the very centre of the soul. . . . [Tolstoy] strove to understand this riddle. . . . Hence he has become the prophet of a new era. . . . That is why Tolstoy reaches out again for a higher kind of Christianity which he regards as the true Christianity – seek not the kingdom of God in outer manifestations – in the forms – but within you. . . . This is the inner morality, and inspiration. . . In his view, Christianity has been externalised. . . . The greatness of Leo Tolstoy lies in this: he has shown that the ideals are not to be found outside, in the material world, but can spring forth from the soul.[7]

Notwithstanding the flavours of Theosophism evident in Steiner's treatment of Tolstoy—his interest in the inner life of the Spirit—he has identified a most significant contrast between Darwin and Tolstoy.

9.1.2 Hugh McLean on Tolstoy and Darwin (2008)

Hugh McLean, mentioned earlier, is one of the other few who has given careful thought to research the ideological dynamics at play between Tolstoy and Darwin. His chapter, "Claws on the Behind" (which begins with some Tolstoyan humour regarding his own fingernails and the evolution of claws), is thorough in its inclusion and evaluation of Darwinian literature available to Tolstoy. Citing Tolstoy's October 28, 1900, diary entry, McLean recounts Tolstoy returning from a walk wondering why the fleshy end of his fingers were covered with nails. Darwin, he mused, argued the nails "originally grew everywhere, but except on the extremities the nails were useless and not retained."[8] With an obvious measure of sarcasm Tolstoy wrote briefly how it came about that we have a race without claws on our behinds. If there is any subtle insinuation equating claws to weapons we are left only to wonder. What was spelled out was that "[Social] Darwinism has all that is

---

7. Steiner, *Origin and Destination of Humanity*.
8. McLean, *In Quest of Tolstoy*, 159.

needed for a philosophy of the mob."⁹ McLean references Nikolai Strakhov, a close intellectual and personal friend of Tolstoy who wrote an important early response against Darwin's *Origin of Species*. Strakhov demonstrated Malthusian connections in Darwinian ideology and theory. From Strakhov's article: "When there are many children in a family and nothing to eat, [Thomas] Malthus simplemindedly takes this as a misfortune.... The weak will perish, and only the naturally selected, most privileged members will win the struggle, so that as a result progress will ensue, the betterment of the whole tribe." McLean notes that whether or not Tolstoy read the article itself, "the ideas it expressed, the horror aroused by the application of Darwinian principles to human life, became the dominant feature in Tolstoy's rejection of Darwinism and remained such the rest of his life." It can be said, for Tolstoy, the Sermon on the Mount does not just speak against soldiers, it speaks against [some] scientists too.

McLean raised another issue worthy of attention. Citing sources in Tolstoy's time (K. A. Timiriazev taking issue with Tolstoy's hero in *Anna Karenina*, Konstantin Levin), there is the charge against Tolstoy (the alter-ego of Levin) that he did not "read his Darwin very carefully, because in fact Darwin himself signifies not hatred and extermination, but on the contrary, love and protection."¹⁰ McLean noted Timiriazev made Darwin more "benign" but conceded "Darwin did indeed recognise the value of love, notably parental love, as a factor in survival.... Tolstoy, however, never recognised or made use of this potential support from Darwin for his doctrines of love."¹¹ McLean offered no reason for Tolstoy's disinterest in this point, but his reasons can be surmised. It remains speculation, but with solid basis, to say Tolstoy never acknowledged any supposed altruism and moral capacity to love in Darwin's theory because, for Tolstoy, any Darwinian parental love toward survival could only be a love of the lower sort, loving only those who love in return, as the pagans do. In Tolstoy's three conceptions of life, the pagans were of the animal sort. The highest conception, the New Life-Conception of the Sermon on the Mount, reflected our God-like capacity, a capacity Darwin never noticed. Tolstoy would not have seen any evidence in species self-survival that demonstrated Sermon on the Mount-style Godly love, love toward even those who are hostile toward us. For Tolstoy, the Darwinian love was entirely self-concerned. McLean used the term "scientific despotism" to refer to how Tolstoy viewed the real mechanics in Darwin's

---

9. McLean, *In Quest of Tolstoy*, 159.
10. McLean, *In Quest of Tolstoy*, 171.
11. McLean, *In Quest of Tolstoy*, 171.

theory, "which [do] not hesitate to sacrifice one or more individuals if common interest required it."

A chapter in Tolstoy's 1893 *The Kingdom of God Is within You* (KG) is entitled "Misconception of Christianity by Scientists." The significance is in how the Sermon on the Mount, for Tolstoy, was not just about individual piety, and the challenge it presented was not just a challenge to the Church (as was the case with other reformers in Christendom). He presented the values of the Sermon on the Mount as a challenge to all the social and political structures in society, culture and government. Looking back now, in terms of a Sermon on the Mount revolution against evolution, Darwinian social ideologies, not Tolstoyan Christianity, prevailed. Extensive work on the bitter fruit of Social Darwinism since Tolstoy's time has been done by Richard Weikert.[12] Weikert writes about Adam Sedgwick, Darwin's mentor in natural science at Cambridge, who wrote Darwin in 1859:

> There is a moral or metaphysical part of nature as well as a physical. A man who denies this is deep in the mire of folly. Tis the crown and glory of organic science that it does, thro' final cause, link material to moral; . . . You have ignored this link; and, if I do not mistake your meaning, you have done your best in one or two pregnant places to break it. Were it possible (which, thank God, it is not) to break it, humanity, in my mind, would suffer a damage that might brutalise it, and sink the human race into a lower grade of degradation than any into which it has fallen since its written records tell us of its history.[13]

As Weikert chronicles in his three extensively documented books on Social Darwinism, Sedgwick's prophetic worry, as I think of it, sadly came true. It is with hope that it is not too late to reconsider Tolstoy's use of the Sermon on the Mount as a dismantling of the tenants of Social Darwinism. Since references are frequent in the corpus of Second Tolstoy, the following is intentionally cursory.

9.1.3 The Sermon on the Mount as the Antithesis of Survival of the Fittest

Having now, in brief, engaged notable points in Steiner and McLean as related to their treatments of Tolstoy and Darwin, the remainder of this

---

12. See Weikart, *From Darwin to Hitler*. Also Weikart, *Hitler's Ethic*; Weikart, *Socialist Darwinism*.
13. Weikart, *From Darwin to Hitler*, 1.

section will feature the voice of Tolstoy cast only through his main Sermon on the Mount exposition, *What I Believe* (WB). During this time of popularity for Social Darwinism, Tolstoy held up Jesus' admonition to judge not: "Discrimination of persons is forbidden, as well as any judgment that shall classify persons as good or bad" (WB, 29). Contrasting Darwin's struggle for life and disregard for weaker human beings with the commandment of Jesus: "I found in Matthew 5:21–26 the first commandment of Jesus: . . . Never look upon a human as being worthless" (WB, 59). "God makes no distinction among peoples, and lavishes gifts upon all men; men ought to act exactly in the same way toward one another, without distinction of nationality, and not like the heathen, who divide themselves into distinct nationalities" (WB, 73). In his exposition on Jesus' teaching for sexual restraint Tolstoy rejected base animal desires and instincts, advocating a very different path for those who would follow Christ (WB, 63). Regarding the struggle for existence Tolstoy wrote: "The doctrine of Jesus, which teaches us that we cannot possibly make life secure, but that we must be ready to die at any moment, is unquestionably preferable to the doctrine of the world, which obliges us to struggle for the security of existence" (WB, 137). Notions that human beings must compete with each other in the struggle for life are foreign to anything Tolstoy found in the doctrine of Jesus, in fact it was the antithesis of it. As prophetic as Tolstoy was in various regards, one of his predictions remains entirely unfulfilled: "I firmly believe that, a few centuries hence, the history of what we call the scientific activity of this age will be a prolific subject for the hilarity and pity of future generations. For a number of centuries, they will say, the scholars of the western portion of a great continent were the victims of epidemic insanity" (WB, 90–91).

9.2 Tolstoy against Marxist-Leninism

In the last decade of his life, indeed the last few years of that last decade (1908–11), around the time of his eightieth birthday, the social and political ideas of Tolstoy's were countered by notable Marxist-Leninist revolutionaries, namely Vladimir Lenin, and Leon Trotsky (1879–1940).[14] Between the years 1908 and 1911, Lenin wrote seven articles on Tolstoy, in the first calling him the "mirror of the Russian revolution."[15] In September, 1908, Leon Trotsky wrote an article on the occasion of Tolstoy's eightieth birthday, initially entitled "*Tolstoy, Poet and Rebel.*"[16] These concise but high caliber

---

14. Wolfe, *Three Who Made a Revolution*.
15. Lenin, *Articles on Tolstoi*.
16. Trotsky, "Tolstoy, Poet and Rebel."

charges from Lenin and Trotsky toward Tolstoy will both be considered shortly, and briefly.

Within this same time frame, at the Garrick Theatre in London on Sunday morning February 6, 1910, American attorney and self-confessed Tolstoy disciple Clarence Darrow (later of Scopes Trial fame) debated Arthur Morrow Lewis. Lewis was a scholar from England who originally trained for the ministry before becoming a Socialist Party educator in the United States lecturing not only in favour of socialism but against Christianity. The transcript of the debate originally published in 1910 was titled the *Darrow-Lewis Debate on the Theory of Non-Resistance*, however, subsequent printings assumed the title, *Marx Versus Tolstoy: A Debate*. Additional comments and insights from the Darrow-Lewis debate fall victim to space constricts herein.

Such prominent personalities responding so publicly to Tolstoy is a testament to the weightiness of his ideas and their popularity as an alternative politic to that of Marxist-Leninist ideologies. In his December 27, 1867, review of Marx's *Das Kapital*, Friedrich Engels wrote that Marx "was simply striving to establish the same gradual process of transformation demonstrated by Darwin's natural history as a law in the social field . . . [and that] science was for Marx a historically dynamic revolutionary force."[17] The one addresses the natural and organic field and the other the social order. In his book *The Students Marx* (1892), Marx's son-in-law Edward Aveling made the same observation: "That which Darwin did for Biology, Marx has done for economics."[18] Though there are important differences, an exposition on the ideological origins and overlap of the two would take us beyond the scope of concern here, except in how they both conflict with Tolstoy at similar points. Those points are the focus of this section and Tolstoy will be given a hearing first, followed by a brief treatment of the aforementioned articles by Lenin and Trotsky.

9.2.1 Tolstoy on the Superstition of Progress, Human Brotherhood, and Non-violent Means

The basic point of conflict between Tolstoy and Marxism is in Tolstoy's rejection of any and all violent means as progress toward any moral good. Tolstoy, even prior to his spiritual crisis, was never a revolutionary socialist. He claimed his view during his early to mid-adult years was that of "a nihilist . . . a man who believed in nothing" (WB, 10). Yet he was deeply troubled

17. Cohen, *Revolution in Science*, 347.
18. Cohen, *Revolution in Science*, 347.

from very early on by the "miseries of humanity . . . and the wars and massacres" (WB, 14). He considered these emerging progressive ideologies in biology and economics to be prevailing "superstition[s] of progress" and likened the people of the world to be as "a person in a boat being carried along by wind and waves and who when asked the most important vital question, 'Where should I steer?' avoids answering by saying, 'We are being carried somewhere'" (CF, 12). He was awakened to the precariousness of this superstition of progress on his first trip to Paris (1857) where he saw executions—"the heads being separated from the bodies and heard them thump, one after the next into the box I understood, and not just with my intellect but with my whole being, that no theories of the rationality of existence and progress could justify this crime" (CF, 12–13). Tuberculosis resulting in the death of his beloved older brother Nikolay (d. 1860) deeply pained him, further underscoring for him the inadequacy of this superstition of progress. Tolstoy decidedly rejected the prevailing notions that "everything is evolving and I am evolving" and that brutal society "acting in the name of progress" was evolving toward any sort of moral good or better life and living. His existential and spiritual crisis, and long conversion[19] were well underway during this period. In due time, as if emerging into the light at the end of a long tunnel, Tolstoy decidedly embraced the way of Christ in the Sermon on the Mount, the Kingdom of God within, and decidedly embarked on that path for the remainder of his life. Revolutionary Marxist justifications for violent means were the anti-thesis of the Doctrine of Jesus as understood by Tolstoy:

> Revolutions are attempts to shatter the power of evil by violence. Men think that by hammering upon the mass they will be able to break it in fragments, but they only make it more dense and impermeable than it was before. External violence is of no avail. The disruptive movement must come from within when the molecule releases its hold upon molecule and the whole mass falls into disintegration. (WB, 179)

Those are among the closing lines in his exposition of the Sermon on the Mount. The disruptive movement within was developed even further in his follow-up book, *The Kingdom of God Is within You*. Tolstoy saw the Kingdom of God expressed in the Doctrines of Jesus as *the* disruptive movement which alone had the power to change the world for the better. The Doctrines of the World as he called them—Darwinism and Marxism—hardly progressive at all, amount to the wide road leading many to destruction.

---

19. Medzhibovskaya, *Tolstoy and the Religious Culture*.

Tolstoy became deeply concerned for those being run over by the wheels of social progress, and this too became a notable point of conflict with Marxism. He came to love the *muzhik*, the peasant of the working population:

> What happened was that the life of our class, the rich and learned, became not only distasteful to me, but lost all meaning. All our activities, our discussion, our science and our art struck me as sheer indulgence. I realised that there was no meaning to be found here. It was the activities of the labouring people, those who produce life, that presented itself to me as the only true way. (CF, 66)

His new fascination with, and affinity for, the lower classes went beyond romanticized notions of a simpler existence. He was awakened to the humanity of all people, the divine in all people, and classism and caste quickly became a stench to him. Tolstoy noticed Jesus revealed the way of life to the ordinary and unlearned people on that mountainside and came to believe.

> God makes no distinctions between people. (WB, 73)

> I know now that my fellowship with others cannot be shut off by a frontier, or by a government decree which decides I belong to some particular political organisation. I know that all men everywhere are brothers and equal. . . . I understand now that true welfare is possible for me only on the condition that I recognise my fellowship with the whole world. (WB, 175)

Tolstoy discerned a hatred-toward-the-other at work in the politics of his day that served to divide men, all of which ran counter to what he had come to affirm about universal love (WB, 78). Marxism was devoid of any love for the least. Tolstoy contended:

> the fourth condition of happiness[20] is sympathetic and unrestricted intercourse with all classes of men. And the higher a man is placed in the social scale, the more certainly is he deprived of this essential condition of happiness. The higher he goes, the narrower becomes his circle of associates; the lower sinks the moral and intellectual level of those to whose companionship he is restrained. . . . Is not the whole system like a great prison where each inmate is restricted to association with a few fellow convicts? (WB, 130–31)

20. Tolstoy's conditions of happiness mentioned in the citation above were (1) the link between man and nature should not be severed; (2) work; (3) family; (4) sympathetic and unrestricted intercourse with all classes of men; and (5) bodily health.

In a precise summation of the import of his reading of the Sermon on the Mount as related to social order Tolstoy wrote: "Jesus says, 'Your social system is absurd and wrong. I propose to you another.' And then he utters the teachings reported by Matthew v. 38–42" (WB, 69). For Tolstoy, the Sermon on the Mount was an alternative politic incompatible with political ideologies that separated classes of men, fuelled animosities, and deemed violence as a means to any desired end. And since Revolutionary Marxism was merely a violence begat by violence, for Tolstoy, there could be no common ground with Marxism. He could not participate in the violence of the State, nor in violent counter-measures against it. "My very existence, entangled with that of the State and the social existence organised by the State, exacts from me an anti-Christian activity directly contrary to the commandments of Jesus" (WB, 24).

Shortly it will be shown these were for Tolstoy the driving factors behind his pioneering ideas later dubbed Christian anarchy. Though popular and superficial understandings of anarchy result in false assumptions that anarchy means violent means, for Tolstoy it was only about non-participation in the state and not violence against it. He believed Jesus only approved of non-violent means, and he believed in a total disengagement with the "entire social fabric founded upon principles that Jesus reproved" (WB, 35). His reproach of the Church was far greater than his reproach of the state: "If the progress [of non-violence] is slow, it is because the doctrine of Jesus . . . has been cunningly concealed from the majority of mankind under an entirely different doctrine falsely called by his name" (WB, 41). Tolstoy argued the Doctrines of the Church and the Doctrines of the World, both Darwinism and Marxism, all were the antithesis of the Doctrine of Jesus.

9.2.2 Lenin: The Weakness and Subtle Poison of Tolstoy's Sermon on the Mount

Hindsight and hypotheticals as related to historical events make for bestselling books in the genre of alternative histories. There is the seed of a good hypothetical account in the early connections, not made until this writing, between the boy Lenin and the aging prophet Tolstoy. Referring to Tolstoy's virtually unknown 1881 letter to Tsar Alexander III (the subject of subsection 5.2), had the Tsar heeded Tolstoy's plea for mercy for those who assassinated Alexander II, it is quite conceivable the Russia of Lenin's youth and formative years would have been changed for the good, perhaps tempering the myriads of insurrectionists who continued to surface in the terrorist phase of nineteenth century Russia. Instead, political hostilities against

Russian Absolutism were only emboldened as Tolstoy has prophesied in his 1881 letter to the Tsar. Lenin's beloved elder brother Sasha (Aleksandr Ilyich Ulyanov) was executed six years later by Alexander III for his leading role in a foiled regicide plot. The execution of his brother "shook [Lenin] to the very core. Everything changed. He was radicalised politically by the event and its aftermath."[21] Lenin began "working for a revolution 25 years before 1917"—without a radicalized Vladimir Lenin, "there would have been no socialist revolution in 1917."[22]

Lenin lived the rest of his life never mentioning his brother's name in his writings or speeches, which total fifty-five volumes today. Yet, this deep personal loss solidified into a cold revolutionary and calculated retaliation. After Lenin's death Winston Churchill wrote of Lenin, "The execution of the elder brother deflected this broad white light through a prism: and the prism was red."[23] Lenin's elder brother was identified to the authorities by a couple of young men of weak constitution in his inner circle when they were being interrogated and pressured to name the leader of the assassination plot. Lenin would not expose himself in the future to such weakness and did not hesitate to purify the ranks of his resistance as well as in Russian society after the 1917 revolution.[24] To provoke additional dialogue I will assert this bold claim: The death penalty gave the world Vladimir Lenin.

---

21. Ali, *Dilemmas of Lenin*, 69. The following is important to set the contrast with Lenin before and after his brother's execution. He was not the product of a revolutionary household. Tariq Ali writes: "When *The People's Will* decapitated the head of state in March 1881, the three oldest children of the Ulynovs (Lenin's family name) in Simbrisk . . . were aged fifteen, thirteen and eleven respectively. . . . [Their liberal-conservative] father, who denounced the terrorists as criminals, donned his uniform and rushed off to attend Mass for the dead tsar at the local cathedral. . . . Denunciations of the regicides became a ritual in schools and at church assemblies on Sunday. . . [Lenin at age 16 was] a conformist as far as politics and religion were concerned. Sasha was much more political and disdained religion, calmly refusing to attend Mass and up-setting his fervently Orthodox father" (Ali, *Dilemmas of Lenin*, 58, 63). After his brother's execution in 1887, Lenin immediately began reading his brother's radical books, especially that of Chernyshevsky, *What Is to Be Done?*

22. Ali, *Dilemmas of Lenin*, 2, 12.

23. Ali, *Dilemmas of Lenin*, 70.

24. Ali, *Dilemmas of Lenin*, 74. "But then, after the execution of my brother, knowing that Chernyshevsky's novel was one of his favourite works, I began what was a real reading and pored over the book not several days, but several weeks. Only then did I understand its full depth. It is a work which gives one a charge for a whole life . . . what a revolutionary should look like, what rules he should follow, how he should approach his goal and what means and methods he should use to achieve it. . . . Before I came to know Marx, Engels, Plekhanov, only Chernyshevsky wielded a dominant influence over me, and it all began with What Is To Be Done." (Ali reprints this Lenin quote taken from Valentinov, *Encounters with Lenin*)

Lenin read enthusiastically in his youth all the literature of the noteworthy Russian novelists including Leo Tolstoy. Lenin biographer Tariq Ali captured the shaping role literature played in the political culture during Lenin's formative years and throughout his life.

> Lenin knew better than most that classical Russian literature had always been infused with politics. . . . In his polemics, Lenin often attacked his opponents by comparing them to almost always unpleasant and sometimes minor characters drawn from Russian fiction. Where the country's writers differed . . . was on the means necessary to topple the regime. Pushkin supported the 1825 Decembrist uprising that challenged the succession of Nicholas I. Gogol satirised the oppressions of serfdom before rapidly retreating. Dostoevsky's flirtation with anarcho-terrorism was transformed into its stunted opposite after a terrible murder in St. Petersburg. Tolstoy's assault on Russian absolutism delighted Lenin, but the count's mystical Christianity and pacifism left him cold.[25]

A little known fact is that it was not Marx's *Das Kapital* that first changed and guided Lenin. It was a radical Russian novel by Nikolay Chernyshevsky (son of a priest, turned atheist) called *What Is To Be Done?* published in 1863. The novel was a response to Ivan Turgenev's (Tolstoy friend and fellow novelist) book *Fathers and Sons* (1862). Tolstoy wrote his own book using Chernyshevsky's title *What Is To Be Done?* (Tolstoy, 1886, also translated *What Then Must We Do?*) and Lenin followed with his own *What Is To Be Done?* (Lenin, 1902).[26] The political theory and evolution of thought ongoing in Lenin during these years is detailed elsewhere, however as Bertram Wolfe noted: "*What's to Be Done?* contained, some in germ, some fully developed, virtually all of the ideas on politics and party organisation which would later be known as 'Leninist.'"[27] For here, the point is to establish the fact that Tolstoy's prophetic letter to the Tsar had the potential to change the political and social hostilities in Russia after 1881 which could only have

---

25. Ali, "Lenin's Love of Literature."

26. Each title intentionally echoing Luke 3:10–14: "'What should we do then?' the crowd asked. John answered, 'Anyone who has two shirts should share with the one who has none, and anyone who has food should do the same.' Even tax collectors came to be baptized. 'Teacher,' they asked, 'what should we do?' 'Don't collect any more than you are required to,' he told them. Then some soldiers asked him, 'And what should we do?' He replied, 'Don't extort money and don't accuse people falsely—be content with your pay.'"

27. See Harding, *Lenin's Political Thought*; Wolfe, *Three Who Made a Revolution*, 156.

produced a very different Lenin, and that Tolstoy's prophetic literature was part of the political conversation underway in and around the radicalizing and retaliating Vladimir Lenin. It is regrettable neither Tolstoy's letter to the Tsar, nor his subsequent writings were enough to realize the hypothetical proposed here.

The inundation of Russian State press articles and stories in liberal papers on the occasion of Tolstoy's eightieth birthday, and even more on the occasion of his death two years later, provoked Vladimir Lenin to put forth his own assessments of Tolstoy and Tolstoyan Christianity and nonviolence as an alternative politic. Lenin wrote one article on the occasion of the birthday and six more notably briefer articles after Tolstoy's death. The first article published September 11, 1908, in the *Proletary No. 35*, bore a peculiar title considering Lenin's disdain for Tolstoyan political theory; *Lev Tolstoi as the Mirror of the Russian Revolution*. The title is peculiar because Lenin's charge was that Tolstoy failed to understand the Revolution and remained aloof from it. But he deemed Tolstoy as a mirror of the revolution in the sense that he mirrored what was presently wrong with it, a mirror in the sense of revealing the weaknesses of it. Lenin's assessment came only a couple years after the failed 1905-6 uprising, a failure he laid at the feet of Tolstoy: "Tolstoi-an non-resistance to evil, which was the most serious cause of the defeat of the first revolutionary campaign" (Lenin, 8).[28] Lenin wrote that "the mortal blow [of this defeat] struck at the . . . softness and flabbiness of the masses" (Lenin, 8). His hope was that from the defeated masses of the revolutionary Social-Democrat, socialist proletariats and the peasantry there would "inevitably advance from their midst more and more steeled fighters who will be less capable of falling into our historical sin of Tolstoi-ism!" (Lenin, 8).

Lenin viewed the sin of Tolstoy-ism, the weakness of Tolstoy-ism, to be twofold. First, Lenin famously had no regard for any religious basis for society and politics. A fierce Marxist, Lenin likewise saw religious sentimentality as the opiate of the masses. This well-known remark of Marx is not often quoted in its entirety: "Religion is the sigh of the oppressed creature, the heart of a heartless world, and the soul of soulless conditions. It is the opium of the people (Die Religion . . . ist das Opium des Volkes)."[29] Lenin took an even harsher view than Marx. Whereas this statement of Marx equates religion with a drug that helps soothe someone in pain, Lenin saw religion, particularly the Sermon on the Mount religion as a deadly

---

28. Citations within the text of this section are from Lenin, *Articles on Tolstoi*.

29. From the introduction of Marx, *A Contribution to the Critique of Hegel's Philosophy of Right*.

poison: "[Tolstoy's] preaching of a new purified religion, that is to say, of a new, refined, subtle poison for the oppressed masses" (Lenin, 12). Lenin considered this to be "the preaching of one of the most odious things on earth, namely religion . . . the crackpot preaching of submission, 'resist not evil' with violence'" (Lenin, 6). This softness and flabbyness which Tolstoyan religion produced in the masses is the second of the sins of Tolstoy, in Lenin's view. The first again being its basis in religion, and the second being the resulting flabbiness.

Lenin's interest in writing on Tolstoy appears to be motivated by a desire to leverage moments of nation-wide interest in him and harness additional support for additional waves of violent revolution. In writing that Tolstoy was a mirror of the Russian Revolution, Lenin was saying Tolstoy reflected its weaknesses but also embodied its passions and complaints. Lenin wrote how Tolstoy was "absurd as a prophet" but that Tolstoy

> is great as the spokesman of the ideas and sentiments that emerged among the millions of Russian peasants at the time the bourgeois revolution was approaching in Russia. . . . Tolstoi's ideas are a mirror of the weakness, the shortcomings of our peasant revolt, a reflection of the flabbiness of the patriarchal countryside and of the hidebound cowardice of the 'enterprising muzhik.' . . . Tolstoi reflected the pent-up hatred, the ripened striving for a better lot, the desire to get rid of the past – and also the immature dreaming, the political inexperience, the revolutionary flabbiness." (Lenin, 7–9)

Lenin's limited compliments of Tolstoy, and even gratitude, are in how he viewed him as successful in "raising so many problems" via his artistic genius which Lenin considered vital to the "epoch of preparation for revolution. . . . [H]e succeeded in conveying with remarkable force the moods of the large masses that are oppressed by the present system, in depicting their condition and expressing their spontaneous feelings of protest and anger" (Lenin, 10–11). During this period where articles on Tolstoy were in every paper, Lenin used Tolstoy to rebuke both the State and liberal press. At the death of Tolstoy, the State newspapers, Lenin asserted, "shed crocodile tears, professing their respect for 'the great writer' while at the same time defending the 'Holy' Synod" in their excommunication of Tolstoy (Lenin, 13). Lenin chided the liberal press for holding up the late Tolstoy as "the great conscience" while at the same time rejecting his religious fanaticism. The substance of three of the articles of Lenin on Tolstoy are specific to the proletarian struggle. In them Lenin continued to convey Tolstoy's success in his "indictment of the ruling classes" and in his articulation of the pain of the proletarian class, but insisted "Tolstoi did not understand" that "which alone is capable of destroying the old world which Tolstoi hated" (Lenin, 22). He was referring to bloodied struggle as the "win[ning]" path to "a better life."

Lenin's assessment was that "Tolstoi-ism, in its real historical content, is an ideology of an Oriental, and Asiatic order. Hence the asceticism, the non-resistance to evil" (Lenin, 30). These oriental origins of the ideas of the Sermon on the Mount were raised also by Arthur Lewis in his aforementioned debate with Clarence Darrow on Tolstoy versus Marx. These attempts to disparage Sermon on the Mount lifestyles as somehow antiquated and of an era gone-by fit the progressive ideologies of Lenin's and Lewis' time. Using Tolstoy against himself, Lenin wrote "'There is no general law of human progress,' says Tolstoi, 'and this is proved by the quiescence of the Oriental peoples'" (Lenin, 30). Lenin continued by writing what reads like a eulogy of any sort of Tolstoyan Sermon on the Mount as a viable alternative politic:

> The period of 1862–1904 was just such a period of upheaval in Russia, a period in which, before everyone's eyes, the old order collapsed, never to be restored, in which the new system was only just taking shape. . . . The year 1905 marked the beginning of the end of 'Oriental' quiescence. Precisely for this reason that year marked the historical end of Tolstoi-ism, the end of an epoch that could give rise to Tolstoi's teachings and in which they were inevitable. . . . A quarter of a century ago, the critical elements in Tolstoi's doctrine might at times have been of practical value. . . . In our days . . . the series of events mentioned above has put an end to "Oriental" quiescence. . . . [I]n our days, the most direct and most profound harm is caused by every attempt to idealise Tolstoi's doctrine, to justify or to mitigate his "non-resistance," his appeals to the "Spirit," his exhortations for "moral self-perfection," his doctrine of "conscience" and universal "love," his preaching of asceticism and quietism, and so forth. (Lenin, 32)

With historical hindsight, comparing the legacy of Leninism with the legacy of Tolstoyanism is to lay the death of tens of millions in Lenin's revolutionary wake alongside the liberation of hundreds of millions of Indians who, through Gandhian non-violence, practiced Tolstoyan Sermon on the Mount lifestyles as an alternative and truly transformatory politic. Ironically, during the very time frame Lenin was writing this eulogy of sorts for Tolstoyan ideas, Mahatma Gandhi was voraciously reading Tolstoy's *Kingdom of God Is within You* envisioning a heretofore unseen non-violent mass resistance against tyrannical powers. In light of Jesus' death of the seed metaphor of John 12:24, Lenin clearly was premature in eulogizing Tolstoyan ideas. Time and subsequent events have shown what the seed of the dying Tolstoy would grow into as applied to oppressions in South Africa, India, and ultimately civil rights in America and numerous other nations.

9.2.3 Leon Trotsky's 1908 Tribute to Leo Tolstoy

Because of events that drew into question his loyalties, Leon Trotsky was considered by Lenin to be a Judas.[30] However as an ideological ally, after the Revolution of 1917, Trotsky became a formidable leader in the early Bolshevik government being appointed head of the Red Army. Trotsky was the mastermind behind and practitioner of the Red Terror—a three year period of political cleansing, paranoia and payback, brutal repressions and retributions, concentration and labour camps, and summary executions of 200,000 people. After Lenin's death, Trotsky was exiled ultimately to Mexico where he was assassinated with an ice ax to the head by order of Joseph Stalin. Such a violent history of living and dying by the sword demonstrates the trajectory of the man who wrote quite unflatteringly in 1908 of the peaceful Tolstoy on the occasion of his eightieth birthday. Trotsky's piece now known as his 1908 Tribute to Tolstoy was originally titled Tolstoy, Poet and Rebel. The latter title is more fitting as traditionally a tribute is a statement of respect and admiration and there is little of either in Trotsky's piece. As with Lenin's 1908 article on the occasion of Tolstoy's birthday, Trotsky appears to be using the occasion of the myriad of Tolstoy tributes in the press to make his own statements about the future of the Russian Revolution.

Also like Lenin, Trotsky viewed Tolstoy and Tolstoyan-ism as something soon to be in the past. He wrote of him as "this last apostle of Christian forgiveness."[31] In mocking terms, Trotsky discounted the genuineness of Tolstoy's conversion and his hypocritical simple home life: "in the wrath of repentance" Tolstoy renounced vain and worldly lifestyles and

> returns to God, accepts the teachings of Christ, and rejects the divisions of labor, and along with it culture and state, he becomes the preacher of agricultural labor, of the simple life and of non-resistance to evil by force. . . .

---

30. Lenin, "Judas Trotsky's Blush of Shame," 45.
31. Page numbers are not identified in the document. All quotations in section 9.2.3 are from Trotsky, "Tolstoy, Poet and Rebel."

> [A] famous poet, a millionaire, one of "our own milieu," and an aristocrat to boot, wears out of moral conviction a peasant shirt, walks in bast-shoes, chops wood. It is as if here was a certain redemption of the sins of a whole class, of a whole culture.... [O]ne would have to say that for the last thirty years of his life, Tolstoy, the moralist, has stood completely alone. Truly his was the tragic position of a prophet crying in the wilderness.

> He divests himself of all material cares connected with business and enrichment and dons peasant clothing as if performing a symbolic rite, renouncing culture. But what lurks behind this symbolic act?

With notable contempt, Trotsky pushed back on how Tolstoy "cast aside 'the superstition of progress universally prevalent in our times.'"

> "It's all very well," he cries, "to have electricity, telephones, exhibitions and all the gardens of Arcadia with their concerts and performances, along with all the cigars and match boxes, suspenders and motors; but I wish them all at the bottom of the sea. And not only them but also the railroads and all the manufactured cotton and wool cloth in the world. Because to produce them 99 out of every 100 people must be in slavery and perish by the thousands in factories where these items are manufactured."

Trotsky balked at any insinuation that Tolstoy ever really was "an apologist for serfdom." He reminded readers Tolstoy "was 33 years old when serfdom was abolished in Russia" and that he was "the descendant of 'ten generations untouched by labor.'" His argument was Tolstoy only gave thought to those situated at the opposing poles of the ancient order—landlord and peasant—and "never feels a need to understand . . . to peer into [the] souls [of] . . . the German superintendent, the merchant, the French tutor, the physician, the 'intellectual', and finally, the factory worker with his watch and chain." Tolstoy's preaching of the humanity of all was deemed hollow by Trotsky and his loving concern limited.

Having shown what he clearly saw as the disingenuousness of Tolstoy's spirituality and moralisms, Trotsky turned to a brief assessment of "Tolstoy's social philosophy . . . in the form of the following 'programmatic' theses." These summary points of Trotsky demonstrate his understanding of Tolstoy's alternative politic:

1. It is not some kind of iron sociological laws that produce the enslavement of people, but legal codes.
2. Modern slavery rests on three statues: those on land, taxes and property.
3. Not only the Russian state but every state is an institution for committing, by violence and with impunity the most horrible crimes.
4. *True social progress is attained only through the religious and moral self-perfection of individuals.*
5. "To get right of states it is not necessary to fight against them with external means. All that is needed is not to take part in them and not to support them." That is to say:
    a. not to assume the calling of either soldier or field marshall, minister or village elder, juryman or member of parliament;
    b. not to pay taxes, direct or indirect, to the state voluntarily;
    c. not to utilise state institutions or governmental funds whether for salary or pensions; and
    d. not to safeguard one's property by measures of state violence.

Trotsky intentionally used italics for the fourth point suggesting that by simply removing religious aspects entirely, Tolstoy's program became "a rather rounded anarchist program." In "removing the religious-moral thesis, we actually remove the single nerve which connects this whole rationalistic structure with its architect: the soul of Lev Tolstoy. . . . Tolstoy seeks to revive – by dint of a religious-moral idea – life under a purely natural economy." Trotsky's reading of Tolstoy's "social philosophy" as workable without the inner religious impetus does indeed take the soul out of Tolstoy's Kingdom-of-God-is-Within-You program.

Admittedly there is more historical recounting and political theorizing in these sections than there is exegetical exposition and nuancing, however, that is the nature of Tolstoyan Sermon on the Mount interpretation. Prevailing Social Darwinian and Marxist-Leninist thinkers did not only have to deal with Tolstoyan ideas in theory, but in practice. His interpretations were applied conceptions during periods of great national unrest and not just notions bantered about by musing philosophers and political and social scientists. Lenin and Trotsky decisively dismissed any modern relevance for ancient and oriental ways whereas Tolstoy held firmly on his conviction that the Sermon on the Mount was for all people, in all times and ages. There is no progressing passed it, and history shows what Lenin and Trotsky viewed as the best way forward became just another blood-wrought path to destruction. The historical backdropping in these sections is therefore essential to the bigger picture accessing the workability of these competing sets of social programs.

In this chapter, the two major social movements and political philosophies of Social Darwinism and Marxist-Leninism developing in Tolstoy's Russia and in the larger world of that time were set against Tolstoyan Sermon on the Mount interpretation. Tolstoy was shown to be against biological Darwinism and moreso against the social and political ramifications of Darwinian theory. For Tolstoy, presumptions of favoured races and survival of the fittest were antinomic to all Jesus taught on the mountainside. Tolstoy rejected base animal desires insisting human progress and flourishing only come through the doctrine of Jesus and not through lower life conceptions. Ideological links between Social Darwinism and Marxist-Leninism were given as the chapter proceeded to discuss Vladimir Lenin's and Leon Trotsky's written challenges to Tolstoyan Christianity. These political leaders of the radical left rejected the softness of Tolstoyan love and considered it a poison in the populace, even the very cause of the failure of the 1905 Russian Resolution. Tolstoyan non-violence was presented as the distinct difference between his teaching and the main doctrines of the world of his time.

~ 10.0 ~

Tolstoy against State Violence
Theo-tactical Altruism (TtA)

Though widely known as, and considered both a pacifist and an anarchist, both of these designations inadequately capture important nuances and substantive differences in Tolstoy's religio-political thought and practice. Both terms, anarchism and pacifism, are tired, burdened and heavy-laden, and most concerning is in how each are conversation stoppers with people who are otherwise predisposed to be sympathetic to, and supportive of the radical teachings of Jesus. Both terms, *Christian anarchy* and *Christian pacifism*, will be jettisoned in the paragraphs that follow and arguments will be made to replace them both with one new, more modern, and more precise designation—*theo-tactical altruism*, or simply *theo-tactics*. This new term will be carefully defined in this chapter. The important matter of what *theo* meant to Leo Tolstoy was treated earlier in subsection 4.5.1.

The stimulus behind suggesting this long-overdue change is the hope that Tolstoyan Sermon on the Mount-style alternative politics will take on a whole new life, interest and following in the world today. Tolstoy's most famous disciple, Mahatma[1] Gandhi, took Jesus/Tolstoyan-style non-vio-

---

1. In this chapter there will not be consistency in the spelling of Gandhi's name as either Mahatma or Mohandas are acceptable as related to the person Gandhi. My preference is Mahatma, but I have kept the spelling of others who refer to him otherwise in the pages that follow. Mohandas is a name, whereas Mahatma is a title. "He employed peaceful means to accomplish this end, and so came to be revered among the people. The reverence is reflected in the title Mahatma, which is defined as a revered person or sage who, some suggest possesses supernatural powers. The use of titles as if they were names should not be surprising. Some illustrative examples are Jesus *Christ*, Julius

lence (his theo-tactics) as a political strategy and recaptured it and repackaged it in a vernacular his culture could better understand; he coined the now-famous term satyagraha, a Sanskrit spiritual word that translates into holding onto truth, a spiritual love and truth force marked by non-violent resistance. In his book on Jesus and non-violence, Walter Wink wrote of the Brazilians in their non-violent struggle adopting the term, "firmeza permanente or relentless firmness" (which is a careful "translation of the New Testament virtue of hupomonē" from Luke 21:12–19 where Jesus told his followers they would go to jail and stand before kings and governors but "by standing firm (ὑπομονή) you will win true life for yourselves."[2] Wink lamented "many people have not aspired to Jesus' Third Way because it has been presented to them as absolute pacifism."[3] Wink's own new designation, Third Way, and Gandhi's satyagraha will be discussed later in this chapter. For now it is enough to see there is both precedence and justification, and even urgency for new language.

In an important book on Tolstoyan political thought and Christian anarchy, Christian Anarchism: A Political Commentary on the Gospel, Alexandre Christoyannopoulos explained how anarchy was not a term Tolstoy liked:

> Tolstoy himself avoided the word "anarchism" to describe his thought, because he associated the word with the violent revolutionaries which he strongly disagreed with. His understanding of anarchism as an intellectual position improved over time, however, and he eventually accepted this term to describe his position as long as it was understood that his anarchism was strictly non-violent and based on the Sermon on the Mount.[4]

Even though Tolstoy settled into a measure of tolerance with the term, others who are far less invested and informed have trouble getting passed it. All that considered, it is probable that Tolstoy would object to future generations continuing to use it since the verbiage remains so burdened with off-putting and imprecise baggage that it quickly and unnecessarily distances

---

Caesar, Genghis *Khan*." See "Difference between Mohandas and Mahatma Gandhi."

2. Wink, *Jesus and Nonviolence*, 105–6. Wink was making reference to the peasants in Alagamar, Brazil who struggled non-violently to keep their lands from being illegally expropriated by multi-national corporations colluding with local politicians and military forces. On one particular day, a number of peasants were arrested and jailed and hundreds of their friends marched to the house of the judge to demand they be arrested as well. The judge decided to send them all home and release those jailed that day. This was firmeza permanente, the virtue of hupomonē, taken from Luke 21:12–19.

3. Wink, *Jesus and Nonviolence*, 102.

4. Christoyannopoulos, *Christian Anarchy*, 15.

many serious followers of Christ around the world from any sort of solidarity with his views, and especially so if a better term was proposed. If these ideas are going to gain greater traction today among those in the world who do have regard for a radical and radicalized adherence to the teachings of Jesus, again this new terminology is needed.

10.1 The Sermon on the Mount Is Not State-Crafting, Nor Is It Theocracy

The CIA World Fact Book lists well over thirty types of government with indication of variance and overlap creating an even longer listing.[5] The point being, nation by nation, simple and fixed labels can only serve generally not precisely as descriptions. Though anarchy is loosely fitting, and even probably the closest fitting of the options of possible traditional labels for Tolstoy's political thought, it remains an unworkable and inadequate designation. For three reasons the term falls short and should be avoided.

First, the term today is impossibly linked with the very opposite of much of what Tolstoy stood for. The term today is popularly regarded, and definitionally regarded, as lawlessness. At best, lawlessness and rebellion only generally and superficially fit the philosophy of Tolstoy. More precisely he aspired to follow eternal laws, greater laws, the law of love and to submit to a greater Kingdom coming on earth. His rebellion was against a rebellion against God's laws. Occasionally tired eyes and mild dyslexia have tricked at least one into seeing antichrist when reading anarchist. A doltish personal anecdote as such is probably not worthy of mention in a serious treatment of this subject however it is not too far reaching to say more than a few good people do see the word anarchist and immediately associate it with rebellion against God and against good orderly and civil society. Even so, there are greater reasons yet which make the word not worth salvaging as related to Tolstoyan political thought. The designation fails to convey important nuances and substantive differences between Tolstoyan Sermon on the Mount interpretation and classic, political anarchy categories and subcategories.

---

5. Absolute monarchy, anarchy, authoritarian, commonwealth, communist, confederacy, constitutional, constitutional democracy, constitutional monarchy, democracy, democratic republic, dictatorship, ecclesiastical, emirate, federation, federal republic, Islamic republic, Maoism, Marxism, Marxism-Leninism, monarchy, oligarchy, parliamentary democracy, parliamentary government, parliamentary monarchy, presidential, republic, socialism, sultanate, theocracy, and totalitarian. See https://web.archive.org/web/20160304061219/https://www.cia.gov/library/publications/the-world-factbook/fields/2128.html.

The second reason to seek other designations to replace anarchy (and pacifism) is to better articulate central distinctives unique, and particular to Tolstoy's views. In this project, in putting forth the word altruism, and the conceptual conjunction theo-tactical altruism, it is hoped more dialogue will be forthcoming. Perhaps there are fine-tuned variations that need to be suggested, or other phraseology entirely; what is important is that those who are sympathetic to the importance of presenting Tolstoyan Sermon on the Mount interpretation as an alternative politic in our time move past the associations with anarchy, and pacifism. Others have made suggestions toward this end, namely Eller, Cavanaugh, and Christoyannopoulos; Theonomy (the rule of God), Acraticism or the redundant Acratic-Theonomy, Christianarchy, and even Eucharistic-Anarchy.[6] At present, Christian Anarchy is most widely used.

Anarchy in the classic sense stresses the absolute freedom of the individual. Yet, Tolstoy was an advocate for a universal brotherhood, the rights and dignity of others over one's own, and for taking a path of self-renunciation for the betterment of others which is better deemed altruism (altruism comes from the Latin root altrui/alteri which means other people, somebody else). Though there are camps underneath the general umbrella designation of anarchy for which this is not the case, generally anarchy is not driven by altruism, it is not about others, it is against others and more self-concerned. Increasingly today and despite the classic technical definitional work of political theorists, anarchy is understand to be violent and the destructive, toward people and property. Even adding the modifier Christian to anarchy fails to overcome the problems with the term as related to Tolstoy. Words were the lifework of Leo Tolstoy and over many years via many articles and books he worked to carefully articulate himself.

Though a century of Sermon on the Mount commentators have made lofty claims like the Sermon on the Mount is the Constitution of the Kingdom, or the Magna Carta of the Kingdom of God, in Tolstoy's view it was nothing of the sort; and this is the third reason to not consider the Sermon on the Mount to be Christian anarchy, or a Christian anarchist's manifesto. For Tolstoy, the Sermon on the Mount was not state-craft; he did not view it as a portrait of a perfect society, or a charter or blueprint for making one.[7] For Tolstoy, the Sermon on the Mount did not contain instructions on establishing an alternative kingdom in the world, rather, it was God's strategy for how to live in the midst of the kingdoms that already exist on earth.

---

6. Christoyannopoulos, *Christian Anarchy*, 216, 236. Referencing Eller, *Christian Anarchy*, 3; also, Cavanaugh, "City," 194.

7. Christoyannopoulos, *Christian Anarchy*, 31.

Tolstoy was not one to give much consideration or credence to outcomes, or to the consequences of Christ-like living. His concern was simple obedience regardless. He dismissed accusations that his ideals were utopian mainly because he was not trying to create a utopia, or advocate for one. For Tolstoy, the Sermon on the Mount, as will be argued here, was theo-tactical, not theocratical.[8] In other words, he did not see the doctrines of Jesus to be descriptive of life under God's rule. For him the commands of Jesus in Matthew five were prescriptive, how God wants his followers to live in the present and in the midst of earthly rulers, under violence-based governments. For this reason, Tolstoy's political thought does not fit traditional political categories for types of ordering in society.

10.1.1 Tolstoy Was a Radicalized, Radical, Theo-tactical Altruist

Tolstoy was less a revolutionary Christian anarchist than he was a radicalized, radical, theo-tactical altruist.[9] To coin a much-needed new term, Tolstoy was a theo-tactician, a proponent of God's ways—he was a radicalized, radical, theo-tactical altruist. Theo-tactical altrusim will be parsed and defined shortly, but first some comments on the seeming redundancy in initial modifiers which are intentional to underscore important aspects of Tolstoy's theo-tactical altruism. The latter adjective radical is there to distance Tolstoyan theo-tactical altruism from a general humanitarian altruism (an anthro-tactical altruism, if you will). Tolstoy's theo-tactical altruism was Christian not humanitarian, it was other-worldly in a Sermon on the Mount, second-mile sense. In the Sermon on the Mount Jesus differentiated between a general human regard for others (as mile one), and a far surpassing regard expected of the follows of Christ (as mile two). In taking his followers out into the second mile of the Sermon on the Mount Jesus repeatedly said, "you have heard that it was said . . . but I say to you"—he advocated a "righteousness that surpasses" that of the religious people of his day. Tolstoy's theo-tactical altruism was of this radical sort. The term radical is preferred even over the term religious as Tolstoyan Sermon on the Mount interpretation calls the follower of Christ beyond religion. The former adjective radicalized was chosen because Tolstoy's ideas were also

---

8. In this chapter theo-tactics are considered as distinct and different from theocracy; theocracy is one of the classic forms of government (i.e. monarchy, democracy, theocracy, autocracy, etc.), theocracy being where God's representatives on earth order society according to God's laws—examples include the ancient Kingdom of Israel and the modern efforts in the world to establish Shari'ah as the rule of law under an Islamic caliphate.

9. Theo-taktischer Altruismus in German, and l'altruism théo-tactique, in French.

his actions. His political theory quickly became more than theory. He had been radicalized by the Doctrines of Jesus and this radicalization quickly put him at odds with State. This radical, radicalized theo-tactical altruism, he believed, had the power and potential to change the world for the better. Before defending the term theo-tactical altruism to describe Tolstoyan political theory, additional reasons are needed to justify the discontinuation of well over a century of simplistic, superficial associations of Tolstoy with political anarchy, even Christian anarchy.

10.1.2 The Juxtaposition of Anthro-tactics with Theo-tactics

There are several advantages to using the term theo-tactical altruism to describe Tolstoyan political and social ideas. Definitionally, tactical is a term of, or relating to combat—small scale actions with a larger purpose, and strategic manoeuvring. Tolstoy's theo-tacticism, and Gandhi's later developments upon it were small scale actions with a greater purpose. Pacifism and passivity, despite the best efforts of those who correctly espouse the important differences between them, are popularly considered synonyms. Theo-tacticism as a suggested new term for Tolstoyan Sermon on the Mount interpretation, is not passive, it is very much tactical combat and engagement using divine weaponry as ways. To better understand it, theo-tactics can be juxtaposed with another newly conceived antonym; anthro-tactics—human ways, notably in-kind retaliation which comes so natural to human nature—as in Proverbs 14:12: "there is a way that seems right to a man but in the end it leads to death." Theo-tactics, unlike anthro-tactics, have the effect of defeating the enemy of our enemy, the one who is not flesh and blood presently opposing us. Loving (engaging with divine weaponry) the opposing one, whom God also loves (or as Tolstoy would say, also a child of God), causes both sides to win.[10] Love and altruism are theo-tactical in a win-win way, ideally, but always ultimately, according to Tolstoy. Theo-tactical altruism breaks the cycle of violence which Tolstoy argued is the basis of the State.[11] Tolstoy used the word expedient, as in an accelerant to

---

10. Wink, *Jesus and Nonviolence*, 46.
11. First Samuel 8:10–18 on the violence-based State: "Samuel told all the words of the Lord to the people who were asking him for a king. He said, 'This is what the king who will reign over you will claim as his rights: He will take your sons and make them serve with his chariots and horses, and they will run in front of his chariots. Some he will assign to be commanders of thousands and commanders of fifties, and others to plow his ground and reap his harvest, and still others to make weapons of war and equipment for his chariots. He will take your daughters to be perfumers and cooks and bakers. He will take the best of your fields and vineyards and olive groves and give them

intensify, in writing of the four expedients to the cycle of State violence: (1) Intimidation, (2) Bribery, (3) Hypnotism and, (4) Conscription (KG, 171–74). Theo-tactical altruism, for Tolstoy, in later Bonhoefferian terms, was the cog in the wheel of the violence-based State. Tolstoy had come to see God's way of warfare as theo-tactical altruism, and that theo-tactical altruism is the path toward Christlikeness. Theo-tactical altruism is bigger than a political theory or sub-stream within classic categories of the same. Theo-tactical altruism, for Tolstoy, is how heaven comes to earth—obeying the Sermon on the Mount, particularly the enemy love of Matthew 5:43–48. Heaven coming to earth, theo-tactically, does not easily fit classic political and social categories, at best it transforms them.

Inherent to the concept of altruism is an intrinsic motivation which was essential for Tolstoy as the location of this Kingdom of Heaven is within. He rendered Matthew 5:48 "be good as your heavenly father is always good." His view of the Kingdom was that the King was good, always good, and this good starts within a person and proceeds outward into the world around them. Tolstoy was not so much striving for State collapse, but for societal transformation, possible only through the transformation of State by the rule/reign of Christ, the Kingdom of God on earth. In his letter to Tsar Alexander III after the occasion of the assassination of his father Alexander II, Tolstoy enthusiastically said he'd be the first to follow the Tsar if the Tsar would follow the non-retaliation path of Christ.

> If you do not forgive, but execute the criminals, you will only have uprooted 3 or 4 individuals from among hundreds and, and evil begetting evil, 30 or 40 will grow up in place of these 3 or 4, and you will have lost for ever the moment which alone is worth more than a whole lifetime – the moment when you could have fulfilled God's will but did not do so. . . .
>
> Forgive; return good for evil, and from among hundreds of evil-doers, dozens will come over – not to you and not to them (that is not important) but will come over from the devil to God, and thousands, even millions of hearts will tremble with joy and emotion at the sight of this example of goodness from the throne at such a terrible moment for the son of a murdered father.

---

to his attendants. He will take a tenth of your grain and of your vintage and give it to his officials and attendants. Your male and female servants and the best of your cattle and donkeys he will take for his own use. He will take a tenth of your flocks, and you yourselves will become his slaves. When that day comes, you will cry out for relief from the king you have chosen, but the Lord will not answer you in that day.'"

> Sire! If you were to do this, to summon these people, to give them money and to send them away somewhere to America, and were to write a manifesto headed by the words: "but I say to you, love your enemies", – I don't know about others but I a poor loyal subject, would be your dog and your slave. I would weep with emotion as I am weeping now, every time I heard your name. But what am I saying – "I don't know about others?"
>
> I know that at these words goodness and love would flow across Russia in a torrent. . . . As wax before fire, every revolutionary struggle will melt away before the Tsar-man who fulfils the law of Christ.[12]

The State was less the issue for Tolstoy than the cycle of violence it was enmeshed in. In this important citation is it possible to see (a) that Tolstoy viewed violent revolutionary tactics (arguably the popular conceptions of anarchy) as evil; (b) that Tolstoy left the door quite open to the possibility of a Tsar and a State that could fulfil the law of Christ on earth; and (c) that Tolstoy would happily submit, like a dog and slave, to the Tsar who fulfilled the law of Christ. The issue for Tolstoy was the fulfilment of the law of Christ and not any sort of statelessness, and this should separate him more than it does from anarchist theory. Tolstoy's letter to the tsar needs to carry more weight than it previously has in discussions about Tolstoy and the state, and his various writings about state. This was a letter he anguished over, writing five or six drafts, carefully articulating his view of state to the leader of the state. It is hardly the case that this is one throw-away citation that stands against others. The suggestion here is that this letter be used as a key to rightly interpreting other Tolstoyan passages. This can only result is distancing Tolstoy even further from traditional anarchy ideology.

In her primer on anarchy, Ruth Kinna characterizes anarchy as a movement "from below."[13] By contrast, Tolstoyan theo-tactics are strategies from above, having their source and mandate in the revelation of the will of God for followers of Jesus. Practically, Tolstoyan theo-tactics work wherever applied, even from the top, as in the case of his letter to the Tsar. Kinna begins her primer with a definition for anarchy: "Anarchism is a doctrine that aims at the liberation of peoples from political domination and economic exploitation by the encouragement of direct or non-governmental action."[14] Though he was concerned for these very things, they were not the primary goals of Leo Tolstoy. His foremost concern was discerning and following

---

12. Christian, *Tolstoy's Letters, Volume II*, 345–47.
13. Kinna, *Anarchism*, 4.
14. Kinna, *Anarchism*, 3.

the will of God. Kinna develops a concise sketch of the history of anarchy: "its roots in a critique of revolutionary government advanced in the course of the French Revolution" where "'the children of Marx' . . . were presenting 'basically Marxist ideas as anarchism.'"[15] It is not the case that anarchy equals Marxism but there are common origins that continue to stereotype anarchy negatively in public opinion today. Kinna posits modern anarchy has its earliest expression in 1968 when American "student rebellion put anarchism back on the political agenda." Her choice of the word rebellion further distinguishes conceptional anarchy from Tolstoyan Christianity. Anarchy is associated with rebellion and Tolstoy was concerned with obedience and submission to God's rule. Kinna makes the very points driving my case for new vocabulary and for disassociation with anarchy as related to Tolstoy.

> [A]narchists have not been able to communicate their ideas very effectively and, instead of being accepted as a term that describes a possible set of futures, anarchy is usually taken to denote a condition of chaos, disorder and disruption . . . anarchism is the ideology of anarchy – a term that has been understood in both the history of ideas and in popular culture to imply the breakdown of order, if not violent disorder. As many anarchists have pointed out, the problem . . . is not only the confusion . . . but its broadness: disorder can imply anything from disorganisation to barbarism and violence . . . anarchy remains a problematic concept.[16]

Kinna cites a noted anarchy scholar (John Moore) who finds the existing "57 varieties" of anarchism to be "unedifying."[17]

> Anarchists have appended a dizzying array of prefixes and suffixes to 'anarchism' to describe their particular beliefs. Anarchism has been packed in anarcho-syndicalist, anarcha-feminist, eco-anarchist and anarcho-communist, Christian, social, anarcho-capitalist, reformist and primitivist varieties.[18]

Even using simplifying charts for categories of anarchy in her book, Kinna writes that "what emerges from this matrix is a picture of confusion . . . the boundaries between schools increasingly diffuse. . . . 'New' anarchists are

---

15. Kinna, *Anarchism*, 30–31, citing The Anarchist International, *Bulletin of the Anarchist International,* http://www.wassamattayou.com/anarchy/ai.html.

16. Kinna, *Anarchism*, 6, 10, 11.

17. Kinna, *Anarchism*, 19.

18. Kinna, *Anarchism*, 18.

no more homogeneous ... than their predecessors. Indeed, new anarchists have little regard for each other and often profess a deep antipathy for each other's work."[19]

Despite areas of common concern and overlap, anarchy as an ideology can only be weakly attributed to Tolstoy and the baggage that comes with the designation does not lend itself to any clarification of Tolstoy's views. Though Tolstoy read and resonated with what he was able to read of the writings of the Russian revolutionary anarchist, Peter Kropotkin, he had a very different set of core beliefs than Kropotkin.[20] As much as Kropotkin and Tolstoy are understood to be anti-government, again, Tolstoy was pro-God's government on earth, though not in any theocratical sense comparable to forced Shari'ah law and Islamic caliphate. For Tolstoy, God's reign comes on earth through the lived values of people who seek to live like Christ. It is through theo-tactics (Sermon on the Mount lifestyles) that the Kingdom of God comes on earth. God's goodness becomes seen in the goodwill, charity, compassion, selflessness and love of the followers of Christ—in theo-tactical altruism.

The best treatments of Tolstoy as anarchist (Hopton, Christoyannopoulos—both given more attention later in the chapter) each direct the reader to

> return to the quotation that expresses Tolstoy's views. "The Anarchists are right in everything; in the negation of the existing order, and in the assertion that, without Authority, there could not be worse violence than that of Authority under existing conditions. They are mistaken only in thinking that Anarchism can be instituted by a [violent] revolution."[21]

A superficial reading leaves the impression that Tolstoy was basically an anarchist, just not of the violent sort. However, a careful reading takes note that Tolstoy was expressing that anarchists were entirely missing the active ingredient of the Sermon on the Mount program for social and political change—the Kingdom of God within and the greater spirituality and philosophy of the Doctrine of Jesus, which became his primary message (the Gospel of Second Tolstoy). As Michael Elliot explained, the "starting point is not a social, economic or political theory. It springs instead from what we might call the religious impulse."[22] This colossal difference between the

19. Kinna, *Anarchism*, 24, 27
20. Christian, *Tolstoy's Letters, Volume II*, 576–77.
21. Hopton, "Tolstoy, God and Anarchism." Citation from Tolstoy, "On Anarchy," in *Government Is Violence*, 67.
22. Elliot, *Freedom, Justice, & Christian Counter-Culture*, 152.

anarchists and Tolstoy is more easily seen in reference to his most famous disciple, Gandhi.

10.1.3 Theo-tactics as a Pressurised Faucet or Well-Spring, Not a Deep Bucket

The famous Salt March of Gandhi was termed by Gandhians as Dandi Satyagraha. Satyagraha is a very dynamic word coined to precisely capture the spiritual life, the love and truth (satya) force (agraha) of the Gandhian movement, which was very much a Tolstoyan movement. To call the Salt March a march is to minimise the tactic by eliminating the grand spirituality that energized, engineered, and embodied it. Indeed Gandhi did use the term march, and Martin Luther King Jr. did use the term bus boycott, just as Tolstoy used terms like non-violence and anti-conscription. But Tolstoy's phrase of choice was to speak of the New Life-Conception of the Sermon on the Mount. Gandhi re-captured that by coining a new word for his context, Satyagraha. To regard Tolstoyan Christianity as anti-this or non-that is to etymologically bind it negatively to minimalizing expressions incapable of conveying the positive and far greater spiritual force—the truth, love and life force that Tolstoyan Christianity was, and as he deemed it.[23] The anti's and non's miss entirely the redemptive intention behind Tolstoy's theo-tactical altruism, concerned and purposed to win the enemy, not defeat and destroy them. Limited terms like Christian anarchy and pacifism also fail to capture the greater inner and outer workings of the New Life-Conception. The suggestion here is that theo-tactics is a more precise and more workable, big picture word that better articulates the entirety of Tolstoyan Sermon on the Mount interpretation. The spiritual truth and force that Satyagraha was a couple generations ago in the East can possibly be re-rendered theo-tactics for present and future generations here in the West. Speaking as one, those who resist labels like anarchist and pacifist (because such labelling is so limiting, misconstrued and stigmatised) are more inclined to a designation like theo-tactics, or theo-tactical altruism.

Perhaps a few word pictures will serve well to summarize and clarify even more the need for a new vocabulary. Returning again briefly to the brilliance of Gandhi's Satyagraha, this was not a deep-bucket term which

---

23. Michael C. Elliot did offer a positive spin on Christian Anarchy subsequent to his analysis of Tolstoy: "A Positive Programme of Christian Anarchy: 1. Devolution of authority; 2. Decentralization of power; 3. Distribution of Wealth; 4. Demythologizing of work; 5. Deschooling of Society; 6. Degree of technology; 7. Development of land." See Elliot, *Freedom, Justice, & Christian Counter-Culture*, 151.

was so generalized it encompassed many diverse facets of his spiritual and political theory and practice. It is more a term that can be seen as a pressurised faucet, a well-spring word from which many tributaries ultimately flow. Here again is the dissatisfaction with present terms which seek to place Tolstoyan ideas in various existing and traditionally-labeled buckets. To call him an anarchist or a pacifist or even non-violent is to slap a tag on a tributary and not draw attention to the creative catalyst pressurizing it. Precisely conceived, and properly understood, a well-spring word like theo-tactics better describes what people see when they see a demonstration, a march, or a young man refusing to enlist. Such a well-spring word may indeed help people over the impasse presented by reductionary discussions limited to the pros and cons of downstream outflows.

10.1.4 Tolstoy Did Not Envision a Stateless, Lawless Utopia[24]

Tolstoyan political theory scholar Alexandre Christoyannopoulos provided a helpful and succinct recap of what Tolstoyan political expositions are and what they are not: "Tolstoy's political musings do not amount to a full or systematic political theory. Rather, his writings are those of a political critic – a prophet, as it were. He plays a role analogous to the Socratic gadfly about violence and about the suffering inflicted by structures which we constitute and legitimise."[25] And just as it is not possible to find in Tolstoy a systematic political theory, it is not precise to label him as fully an adherent to one, or another—namely anarchy and pacifism.[26] Granted, across the corpus of

---

24. Though he did not give a definition, Tolstoy's use of the term State is probably best understood along the lines of German sociologist and political economist Max Weber who later described the State as "human community that (successfully) claims the monopoly of the legitimate use of violence within a given territory." That definition captures the pieces which were so distasteful to Tolstoy; the monopoly over society by a central government based on force, coercion and compliance. See Weber, "Politics as a Vocation, 1919."

25. Christoyannopoulos, "Eccentric Yet Still Prophetic," 23.

26. On the subject of Tolstoy and Gandhi against coercion, Kenneth Rivett noted: "Gandhi may have been wrong in thinking Tolstoy was not an anarchist, but he certainly was not one himself" (Rivett, "Gandhi, Tolstoy, and Coercion," 42nn67, 69 [The Collected Works of Mahatma Gandhi (CWMG) Delhi, Government of India Ministry of Information and Broadcasting, 1958–1984, 10:249 (21 May 1910) and CWMG 86:424 (16 Feb 1947)]). "I cannot pretend to speak for Tolstoy, but my reading of his works has never led me to consider that, in spite of his merciless analysis of institutions organised and based upon force, that is governments, he in any way anticipates or contemplates that the whole world will be able to live in a state of philosophical anarchy.... I do not conceive of such a golden age. But I do believe in the possibility of a predominately non-violent society. And I am working for it."

Second Tolstoy there are myriad of texts and articles that, together, have earned him association, rightly and wrongly, with anarchists and pacifists. Christoyannopoulos' book *Tolstoy's Political Thought* draws from all the pertinent Tolstoy texts. For our purposes here, that wider corpus survey is not needed. In fact, a few concentrated passages will suffice to draw out the arguments this chapter seeks to make. The following concentrated passage is from a primary source collection of Tolstoy writings published today as *Writings on Civil Disobedience and Nonviolence*:[27]

> "Carthago delenda est."[28] Government is violence. Christianity is meekness, non-resistance, love. And, therefore, government cannot be Christian, and a man who wishes to be Christian must not serve government. Government cannot be Christian. A Christian cannot serve government.

From sentiments of that sort, which in various forms are frequent throughout Second Tolstoy, arise all the different facets of Tolstoyan theo-tactical altruism: anti-government, anti-authority, anti-conscription, anti-war, anti-tribunals (courts), conscientious objection, labor strikes, marches, imprisonments and martyrdom; also including more modern activist measures like sit-ins, solidarity boycotts and divestitures.[29] All of the above is a direct outcome of Tolstoyan theo-tactical altruism which entails not serving the present State, but following the way of Jesus which is meekness, non-resistance and love.[30]

In another concentrated article, "Church and State," written in 1882, published in 1904, Tolstoy wrote:

---

27. Tolstoy, *Writings on Civil Disobedience and Nonviolence*, 172.

28. Tolstoy begin the final paragraph in a letter to Dr. Eugen Heinrich Schmitt with a short quote from second century BC Roman Senator Cato the Elder, who, speaking in the Forum at the onset of the Third Punic War against Carthage said, "Carthage must be destroyed."

29. With great political imagination, Gene Sharp has listed 198 methods of nonviolent protest in volume two of his three-book work, *The Politics of Nonviolent Action, Part Two: The Methods of Nonviolent Action*. Within Sharp's superb listing, there are a number that would be anthro-tactical, not theo-tactical. An anthro-tactic, as I conceive them, is any tactic God is not wanting employed at any given time, place and situation. Additionally, a theo-tactic for one situation might be an anthro-tactic in another situation. Theo-tactics are not a box of tools, but rather a discernment of ways, God's ways.

30. Matthew 10:16, being shrewd as snakes and as innocent as doves is a helpful delineator between theo-tactics and anthro-tactics. Not included in this listing are some of the modern anarchical tactics of a malicious and deceptive nature which Tolstoy would likely have rejected: doxxing, infiltration, intimidation, and de-platforming.

> The sanctification of political power by Christianity is blasphemy; it is the negation of Christianity. After fifteen hundred years of this blasphemous alliance of pseudo-Christianity with the State it needs a strong effort to free oneself from all the complex sophistries by which always and everywhere (to please the authorities) the sanctity and righteousness of State-power, and the possibility of its being Christian, has been pleaded. In reality the term "Christian State" resembles "hot ice". The thing is either not a State using violence, or it is not Christian.[31]

The last sentence in particular can be read to imply the possibility exists that a State could exist without violence, though history has yet to produce such an example. Tolstoy's issue was with violence, not the existence or nonexistence of a State per se.

As mentioned earlier in his letter to Tsar Alexander III, it can be said that Tolstoy would have tolerated, and even supported and submitted to a State that took seriously the non-violence mandates of Jesus.[32] However, in all his wide reading of human history such a State was unknown to him. Had Tolstoy had more eschatological interest, or belief in a future messianic reign of God on earth (of the big-government-sort spoken of in Isaiah 9:7—"of the increase of his government and peace there will be no end") more could be said about his theo-tactical goals not necessarily being statelessness. Tolstoy was drawn to previous agricultural eras, simpler living in agricultural communities, and therefore his concerns were more immediate in disengaging from State-using-violence and less long-term to clarify what he envisioned as a governing replacement. It cannot be said Tolstoy embraced an anarchical form of government, lawlessness or statelessness. He had no answer for those who wondered what form of society should replace the present one.

> To the question, how to be without a State, without courts, armies, and so on, an answer cannot be given, because the

---

31. Tolstoy, "Church and State," in *The Works of Leo Tolstoy*, 12:338.

32. This claim places a greater weight on the letter to the Tsar than on Tolstoy's numerous other statements that are typically read to be total rejections of state. The assertion here is the care of thought behind this letter to the Tsar and its various drafts is evidence of this being his most held belief, that being his willingness to submit to a state that reflects the values of Christ. Once his other "anti-state" passages are seen through the interpretive key of that important text, they can be better understood. This further distances Tolstoy from classic anarchist theory. Most of his other statements against state are against the state that does not follow the way of Christ, coercion-based states, not of the state in any form. He was very much an advocate for the kingdom of heaven on earth which he believed to come as the values of Jesus were lived by people on earth, including people in government.

> question is badly formulated. The problem is not how to arrange a State after the pattern of today, or after a new pattern. Neither, I, nor any of us, is appointed to settle that question.
>
> But, though voluntarily, yet inevitably must we answer the question, how shall I act faced with the problem which ever arises before me? Am I to submit my conscience to the acts taking place around me, am I to proclaim myself in agreement with the Government, which hangs erring men, sends soldiers to murder, demoralizes nations with opium and spirits, and so on, or am I to submit my actions to conscience, i.e., not participate in Government, the actions of which are contrary to my reason?
>
> What will be the outcome of this, what kind of a Government here will be – all of this I know nothing of that I don't wish to know; but that I cannot. I only can know that nothing evil can result from my following the higher guidance of wisdom and love, or wise love, which is implanted in me.[33]

Wise love amounts to theo-tactics. Tolstoy's main concern and contribution was how to live theo-tactically in the present violence-based society. He was not envisioning statelessness; nor was he asking what kind of state or lack thereof we should live in. He was asking how shall we live in the present state? His answer was to not participate in it.

Experiments with small-scale alternative societies in Tolstoyan communities throughout Russia during Tolstoy's lifetime can, at best, only be interpreted as attempts to embody what he envisioned for a society living according to the Doctrines of Jesus here in the meanwhile.

> In order that men may live in a common life without oppressing each other, there is necessary, not an organisation supported by force, but a moral condition in accordance with which people act from their inner conviction and not coercion. Such a condition does not exist [except] in religious communities in America, in Russia, in Canada. Here people do indeed, without laws enforced by violence, live in the communal life without oppressing each other. Thus the rational activity proper to our time for men of our Christian Society is only one: the profession and preaching by words and deed of the last and highest religious teaching known to us, of the [vital and true] Christian teaching [Doctrine of Jesus].[34]

---

33. Tolstoy, "On Anarchy," in *Government Is Violence*, 68–69.
34. Tolstoy, "An Appeal to Social Reformers," in *Government Is Violence*, 63.

Certainly Gandhi interpreted a Tolstoyan society to be similarly situated in small scale communities based on Christian virtues and values, as did later expressly Tolstoyan expressions of it by Dorothy Day and the Catholic Worker Movement in the United States. This disengagement with violence-based States, if indeed it is properly a form of anarchy, still falls short of what can more precisely be called Tolstoyan theo-tactics. To classify Tolstoy as an anarchist, unfortunately because of popular perceptions (and ignorance of the actual varieties of anarchy), is to insinuate he had a rebellious and ungovernable spirit which, is not compatible with what we do know about his interest in present rule and reign of God on earth, and submission to God's ways and his eternal laws. An ungovernable spirit is the inverse of meekness. If anything, flavours of anarchy in Tolstoy were at best transitional, for the meanwhile, a means to a better life together under divine rule, and peace. Even as Christoyannopoulos clarifies that "Christian anarchists do not envision a chaotic society, but an organized one based on real consent, love and mutual help rather than on the fictional granting of the legitimacy of violence to some monstrous Leviathan," there remains far too much chaos associated with anarchy proper to recover that term in any helpful way.[35]

10.2 Walter Wink and the Third Way

At the very top of a stack of the best books and commentaries on enemy love and Matthew 5:38–41 should sit Walter Wink's little volume, *Jesus and Non-violence: A Third Way*.[36] It is remarkably Tolstoyan, though Tolstoy is not mentioned once. Rather, as is so unfortunately commonplace, Gandhi is given all the glory. Wink marvelously captures the grander spirituality and dynamics of Satyagraha which is to say in doing so he makes great progress in better articulating the spiritual, social and political theories Tolstoy drew from his reading of the Sermon on the Mount. Though he skips right over Tolstoy in tracing Satyagraha back to the Sermon on the Mount, his insights bear directly on what Tolstoy had passed off to Gandhi.[37]

---

35. Christoyannopoulos, *Christian Anarchism*, 46.
36. Wink, *Jesus and Nonviolence*.
37. Gandhain scholars would be right to challenge the generalization in this sentence which may seem to disregard the fact that for Gandhi, and for Tolstoy too, theo-tactical altruism emanated also from Hinduism, Buddhism and other religious traditions. What is true however is that it was the Sermon on the Mount not other religious traditions that brought theo-tacticalism to Tolstoy's attention and it was Tolstoy's reading of the Sermon on the Mount that captured Gandhi's interest and secured his following. Other religious tradition was used by both men to support the Doctrines of Jesus in the Sermon on the Mount.

That a stalemate has been reached between followers of Christ on the matters of resistance and non-resistance, submission to government and anarchic-revolution, just-war and pacifism, and that conversations about non-violence are presently stymied by the use of these failed terms are concerns echoed in the work of Walter Wink on nonviolence:

> There are good reasons for reluctance to champion nonviolence. The term itself is negative. It sounds like no-doing, the putting all of ones energy into avoiding something bad rather than throwing one's total being into doing something good. . . . "Turn the other cheek" became a divine ultimatum to slaves and servants to accept flogging and blows obsequiously. "Love of enemies" was twisted to render the oppressed compliant from the very heart, forgiving every injustice with no thought of changing the system. Non-violence meant, in the context of this perverse inversion of the gospel, passivity. And the fact that "pacifism" and "passivism" sound so alike only made the confusion worse. . . . When the court translators working in the hire of King James chose to translate *antistenai* as "resist not evil" they were doing something more than rendering Greek into English. There were translating nonviolent resistance into docility. . . . [T]he King would not want people concluding they had recourse against his or any other sovereigns unjust policies. Therefore the populace must be made to believe that there are two alternatives and only two: flight or fight. Either we resist not or we resist. And Jesus commands us, according to these king's men, to resist not. Jesus appears to authorize monarchical absolutism. Submission is the will of God. And most modern translations have meekly followed in that path. Neither of these alternatives has anything to do with what Jesus is proposing. . . . Jesus abhors both passivity and violence as responses to evil. His is a third alternative not even touched by these options.[38]

Wink carefully expounds Tolstoy's famously favorite texts in a way that further solidify the foundation of the interpretations Tolstoy had come to embrace, and espouse. The three examples given by Jesus in Matthew 5:38–41, turning the other cheek, giving the remaining garment to one's debtor, and going the second mile, are each shown by Wink to be "aikido-like. . . Jesus' teaching is a kind of moral jujitsu, a martial art for using the momentum of evil to overthrow it."[39] Wink grasps hold of words that are rich with eastern

---

38. Wink, *Jesus and Nonviolence*, 3, 10, 12–14.
39. Wink, *Jesus and Nonviolence*, 21, 43.

spiritual and religious philosophical flavouring to give greater definition to this Third Way of Jesus.

10.2.1 The Theo-tactics of the Turned Cheek, Extra Cloak and Second Mile

Wink expressed simply the two alternatives, both of which can be deemed anthro-tactical, alongside this Third Way, deemed in this chapter to be the way of theo-tactical altruism:[40]

Flight	Fight
• Submission	• Armed Revolt
• Passivity	• Violent Rebellion
• Withdrawal	• Direct Retaliation
• Surrender	• Revenge

The Third Way
• Seize the moral initiative
• Find a creative alternative to violence
• Assert your own humanity and dignity as a person
• Meet force with ridicule and humor
• Break the cycle of humiliation
• Refuse to submit to or accept the inferior position
• Expose the injustice of the system
• Take control of the power dynamic
• Shame the oppressor into repentance
• Stand your ground
• Force the Powers to make decisions for which they are not prepared
• Recognize your own power
• Be willing to suffer rather than retaliate
• Cause the oppressor to see you in a new light
• Deprive the oppressor of a situation where a show of force is effective
• Be willing to undergo the penalty for breaking unjust laws
• Die to fear of the old order and its rules

Wink draws each of these Third Way tactics from his multi-page exegesis and exposition of what exactly Jesus was directing followers to do in his

---

40. Wink, *Jesus and Nonviolence*, 27–28.

three examples with the turned cheek, extra cloak and second mile. He showed Jesus to have a divinely-inspired and therefore creative, innovative, transformative, and redemptive political imagination not limited by the failed anthro-tactics which come so natural, those being either flight or fight.

10.2.2 The Cross as Theo-tactical

In subsequent chapters Wink gave mention to how these theo-tactics were successfully employed by Gandhi, and many others.[41] In one example from the American South during the civil rights movement, Wink recalls the time Martin Luther King Jr.'s theo-tactical altruists (to use this chapters suggested term), in front of Alabama State Troopers and bigoted Sheriff Jim Clark sang out responsively, "Do you love Martin King?" "Certainly, Certainly, Certainly, Lord!" "Do you love Jim Clark?" "Certainly, Certainly, Certainly, Lord!" The minister at the microphone then said, "It's not enough to defeat Jim Clark – Do you hear me Jim? – we want you converted. We cannot win by hating our oppressors. We have to love them into changing."[42] Fast forward now to the end of the story, Jim Clark eventually did have a change of heart. Echoing the limitations of reason, also a Tolstoyan conclusion, Wink emphasised the spirituality and the grace permeation and supernatural basis of theo-tactical altruism:

> I don't believe that non-violence is something you can arrive at rationally. We can develop it as a spirituality and can obtain the grace necessary to practice it, but not as a result of reason. Not that it is anti-reason, but that it is not natural. The natural thing to do when somebody hits you is to hit them back. We are called upon to be supernatural. We reach that way of being, not as a result of nature, but of prayer.[43]

---

41. Wink, *Jesus and Nonviolence*, 2–3: "Non-violent general strikes have overthrown at least seven Latin American dictators. . . . In 1989–90 alone, four nations underwent nonviolent revolutions, all of them successful except Romania. These revolutions involved 1.7 billion people. If we total all the nonviolent movements of the twentieth century, the figure comes to 3.4 billion people, and again, most were successful. And yet there are people who still insist that nonviolence doesn't work! Gene Sharp has itemized 198 different types of nonviolent actions that are a part of the historical record, yet our history books seldom mention any of them, so preoccupied are they with power politics and wars." Drawing from Sharp, *Politics of Nonviolent Action*, 117–434.

42. Wink, *Jesus and Nonviolence*, 64–65.

43. Wink, *Jesus and Nonviolence*, 86.

This pressurised faucet, this Third Way, to use his term, Wink contends, "it is not a last minute strategy that can be donned at will like an asbestos suit. The cross also means not necessarily winning." Though Wink insisted this Third Way is a win/win in an ultimate sense for each party in a conflict, he was forthright to align this Third Way with martyrdom and the way of the Cross: "I cannot really be open to the call of God in a situation of oppression if the one thing I have excluded as an option is my own suffering and death."[44] Also, like Tolstoy who called out Church-sanctioned violence and war as the greatest obstacle to the Great Commission, Wink wrote "I have come to believe that creative non-violence has to be a constitutive element of evangelisation and the proclamation of the gospel."[45] How could it be any other when theo-tactic altruism was the constitutive element Christ embodied on the Cross; meekness and love, non-retaliation and forgiveness? These constitute theo-tactical altruism; they came from within Jesus, as a wellspring with the intention being to win the (human) enemy not defeat and destroy them. "Father forgive them for they know not what they are doing" comes from theo-tactical altruism, not anarchy. Though Wink, skipping right over Tolstoy, held up King and Gandhi locating the source of these theo-tactics in the Sermon on the Mount, Wink succeeds in giving what can been construed as a precise articulation and conceptual development of Tolstoyan Sermon on the Mount interpretation.

10.2.3 Theo-tactics for the Most Intense Times in the Most Brutal of Places

A final significant piece can be drawn from Wink which bears heavily on Tolstoy's interpretation of the Sermon on the Mount. The persistent concern continues to be whether or not the Sermon on the Mount works for every situation and location, especially in the most intense times and in the most brutal of places. As has been previously mentioned, Niebuhr advised Bonhoeffer to not go to visit Gandhi because those tactics may work under British oppression but not in Nazi Germany. Wink calls attention to these tactics working in the Philippines and Poland where non-violent "solidarity irreversibly mobilised popular sentiment against the puppet communist regime. . . . [Wink concluding] this undercuts the oft-repeated claim that what Mohandas Gandhi did in India or Martin Luther King Jr. did in

---

44. Wink, *Jesus and Nonviolence*, 88.
45. Wink, *Jesus and Nonviolence*, 85.

the American South would never work under a brutal, Soviet-sponsored government."[46]

> An argument once heard in Latin America and South Africa is that while nonviolence is certainly the biblical norm, it can only be used against governments that have achieved a minimum moral level. It can work with genial British in India, but not with the violent defenders of apartheid or the brutal communists. This argument has been exploded by events, however, since the entire eastern bloc has collapsed under non-violent pressure. As for the British in India, they were no more genial than the Romans in Palestine. Had Jesus waited for the Romans to achieve a minimum moral level, he never would have been able to articulate the message of non-violence to begin with. On the contrary, his teaching does not presuppose a threshold of decency, but something of God in everyone. There is no one, and surely no entire people, in whom the image of God has been utterly extinguished.[47]

Theo-tactics are transforming wherever applied. No matter the intensity of the temptation to vengeance and violent retaliation, theo-tactics amount to the divine way not just of escape, but of entrance into divine life and living.[48]

10.3 John Howard Yoder on Tolstoy as a Pacifist

John Howard Yoder put forth a significant contribution in a little book naming the varieties of pacifism seen throughout history; his listing included seventeen types of pacifism. Gandhi's pacifism he labeled "The Pacifism of Nonviolent Social Change." Importantly, the "pacifism" of Tolstoy was not listed, and neither was the "pacifism" of Jesus. Yoder did mention "The Pacifism of Absolute Principle" would be the closest of the seventeen categories to Tolstoy's non-violence:

> There is the ancient ethical tradition of the imitation of Jesus. It makes the same moral claims as the pacifism of moral law (III above) but its content is not abstract commands but the life and word of Jesus. His command and example are to be followed

---

46. Wink, *Jesus and Nonviolence*, 1–2.
47. Wink, *Jesus and Nonviolence*, 66–67.
48. In the sense of 1 Corinthians 10:13: "No temptation has overtaken you except what is common to mankind. And God is faithful; he will not let you be tempted beyond what you can bear. But when you are tempted, he will also provide a way out so that you can endure it."

without calculation of social possibilities. Its major spokesman have been Peter Waldo, Peter of Chelčice and Leo Tolstoy. It does not expect widespread acceptance, but neither does it acquiesce in the world's noncompliance with Jesus' norm, as do the other minority approaches.[49]

That the pacifisms of Tolstoy, and Jesus, are of the sort that they defy traditional labelling and designation is significant and additional basis for jettisoning the term pacifism altogether in reference to Tolstoy. As Yoder insisted, Tolstoy, Chelčický and Waldo were seeking to live out the life and word of Jesus. They were theo-tacticians in this sense, and not pacifists. They were following the way of Christ. Gandhi was also a theo-tactician in the Tolstoyan sense but as was seen in subsection 5.3, he followed this path only in part.

10.4 Hopton and Christoyannopoulos on Tolstoy and Anarchism

Three scholarly treatments of Tolstoy and anarchy appeared in the Anarchist Studies publication in the years 2000, 2008 and 2010; the first by Terry Hopton of the University of Central Lancashire, and the latter two by Alexandre Christoyannopoulos of Loughborough University.[50] Hopton began his article by expressing one of the initial observations also mentioned earlier in this project; that "these later writings [of Tolstoy] have never received the attention that they deserve, apart, that is from the light they shed on Tolstoy's biography."[51] Prior to Hopton, the treatments of Tolstoy and anarchy were scant and critically superficial, the main ones being identified ahead in subsection 10.4.2. Post-Hopton, Alexandre Christoyannopoulos has substantially built upon the earlier works and continues to produce a good amount of critical study on Tolstoy's political thought.[52] It would be quite a challenge to find primary or secondary Tolstoy material on, or related to anarchy that has escaped his purview. Time is better spent engaging his analysis; some

---

49. Yoder, *Nevertheless*, 20.

50. Hopton, "Tolstoy, God and Anarchism"; Christoyannopoulos, "Leo Tolstoy on the State"; Christoyannopoulos, "'Bethink Yourselves or You Will Perish,'" 11–18.

51. Hopton, "Tolstoy, God and Anarchism," 27.

52. Including: Christoyannopoulos, "Eccentric Yet Still Prophetic"; Christoyannopoulos, *Christian Anarchy*; Christoyannopoulos, "Turning the Other Cheek"; Christoyannopoulos, "Tolstoy the Peculiar Christian Anarchist"; Christoyannopoulos, "Christian Anarchism."

of which has already been done in this chapter in proposing altogether new designations. Since Christoyannopoulos intended his initial essay to build on Hopton's work, that will be the starting place here as well, and the utmost of brevity will hopefully not do it a disservice.

10.4.1 Tolstoy an Adherent of the Christianity *of Christ*

Hopton traced out the framework upon which Tolstoyan anarchy rests; the heavy burden of moral responsibility that should rest on the individual, the self-deception at play in negations and evasions of that responsibility, and the fundamental problem of the meaning of life and the corruption of Christianity since Constantine. Hopton then asserted "Tolstoy's simple and categorical objection to the State is that it is the dominant institutional form of violence," and that "man cannot serve two masters. . . . Government is violence and Christianity is meekness, non-resistance and love."[53]

> For Tolstoy, the state represents the systemic evasion of our moral responsibility. Thus, oaths are only one of many ways in which we can abdicate our responsibility for the consequences of our actions and transfer it to others. . . . Each individual member of the state can believe that he or she is not to blame for the wrong that is done. . . . They should first ask if such a system ought to continue. . . . Only the most profound transformation in the moral life of the people who currently populate the system can change things. If this were to occur, then there would be no system any more. . . . For Tolstoy, to demand the end to war is to demand the end to state.[54]

Additionally, state violence, as Tolstoy saw it, must be seen in a far wider sense including economic exploitation which is "as bad as physical violence."[55] The entire economic system of the State creates a master–slave disparity. Tolstoy's solution, in Hopton's reading, begins with thinking for oneself as individuals and then admitting the fallacy and deception of the whole social order. Quoting Tolstoy on this revolution within:

> There can only be one permanent revolution – a moral one: the regeneration of the inner man. How is this revolution to take place? Nobody knows how it will take place in humanity, but every man feels it clearly himself. And yet in our world everybody

---

53. Hopton, "Tolstoy, God and Anarchism," 36.
54. Hopton, "Tolstoy, God and Anarchism," 37–38.
55. Hopton, "Tolstoy, God and Anarchism," 39.

thinks of changing humanity, and nobody thinks of changing themselves.⁵⁶

What form of society replaces the State was not much of a concern for Tolstoy. Hopton wrote: "For Tolstoy the important thing is simply that we do God's will, and accept that what follows from this is his will."⁵⁷ Hopton ultimately concluded "Kropotkin was not wrong to include Tolstoy's 'Christian Anarchism' in the tradition of anarchist thought."⁵⁸

Before moving on to Christoyannopoulos, a couple of quick comments on Hopton's reading. How love, enemy love, which for Tolstoy is God's will, can be so compatible with an inherently-aggressive-and-angry anarchy is a central point that ought to be more of a unsettling matter than it seems to be for those, like Hopton and Kropotkin, who place Tolstoy comfortably among the anarchists. And, regarding a point that will become important in the following paragraphs, Hopton is right to assert "the belief in nonviolence is inseparable from Tolstoy's religious worldview. . . . In Tolstoy's case the principle on which the new life must be based is Christianity. . . . Tolstoy makes a sharp distinction between the Church and its Christianity on the one hand, and the Christianity of Christ on the other."⁵⁹

10.4.2 The Twentieth-Century Struggle to Hear Tolstoy's Voice

Christoyannopoulos begins by identifying what has been written in the last century; which is "still very little thorough discussion on Tolstoy in anarchist circles."⁶⁰ Among just a few others he specifically referenced Hopton, Woodcock and Stephens stating: "What all this suggests, therefore, is that the substance of Tolstoy's anarchism has largely been left aside (albeit usually respectfully acknowledged) by academic analyses of anarchism, and this also largely as a whole."⁶¹ In his 2010 article in Anarchist Studies, at the centenary of Tolstoy's death, Christoyannopoulos shared similar zeal with what lies behind this project, that Tolstoy's later writings are "just as urgent

---

56. Hopton, "Tolstoy, God and Anarchism," 43.

57. Hopton, "Tolstoy, God and Anarchism," 45.

58. Hopton, "Tolstoy, God and Anarchism," 28. Referencing the originally published 1905 essays on the history of anarchism by Peter Kropotkin, now published under the title "Anarchism and Anarchist Communism."

59. Hopton, "Tolstoy, God and Anarchism," 46–47.

60. Christoyannopoulos, "Leo Tolstoy on the State," 23.

61. Christoyannopoulos, "Leo Tolstoy on the State," 23. See Hopton, "Tolstoy, God and Anarchism"; Stephens, "Non-Violent Anarchism of Leo Tolstoy"; and Woodcock, *Anarchism*.

today as [they were] at the time of [their] writing" (citations to follow in the remainder of section 10.4.2 are all noted here).[62] He sought to restate some of what caused Tolstoy "to spend the last thirty years of his life tirelessly articulating his view and trying to convince the wider public of its rationale." Christoyannopoulos wrote: "Tolstoy has a lot to say about today's world, and what he says about it, he says well. . . . [I]t is probably even more important than a century ago that Tolstoy's prophetic critique is heard and seriously considered."

Perceptive is Christoyannopoulos' analysis of what happened to drown out Tolstoy's voice since his death in 1910. Several factors emerge: "The world and especially Russia became engulfed in such turmoil that his voice was drowned by the louder and more numerous ones calling for violence, war and revolution." There were "deliberate efforts to mute Tolstoy's voice and followers. . . . [H]e was depicted as a brilliant illustrator of the Russian peasantry and aristocracy but one whose late political writings could be swept aside was the made ramblings of a foolish eccentric."

> [T]he rest of Europe was busy with a huge economic crisis, clashing ideologies, and mounting nationalist passions and military tension that reached their climax in 1939. The ensuing Cold War framed post-war ideological options in a Manichean binary [black/white] that neatly kept views like Tolstoy's safely at bay. In other words, Tolstoy's voice would always struggle to be heard in the twentieth century.

Christoyannopoulos offered Gandhi as the only significant example of any continuation of Tolstoyan ideas in the twentieth century, at least what is generally agreed to be the most significant part of his political thought; non-violence and resistance to the State. It is at this point, Christoyannopoulos' reading took a turn worthy of further conversation. Christoyannopoulos asserted:

> Tolstoy's Christian anarchism was nominally 'Christian' because it was from Jesus that it drew its rejection of violence and (hence) the state, Jesus for Tolstoy was not a divine but simply a rational teacher. Tolstoy believed that what he preached was not particularly Christian but reasonable, and this intelligible to all. In short, he took Jesus' teaching on love and violence out of its Christian case and couched it in the 'universal' language of reason, where non-Christians (like Gandhi) could also hear it. . . .

---

62. Christoyannopoulos, "'Bethink Yourselves or You Will Perish,'" 11–18. Subsequent citations in this section are from this source.

One could argue that Tolstoy was not really a Christian. He did not go to church, did not believe in key church dogmas, and did not see Jesus as anything more than a rational but normal human being.

The argument of this project (considering passages like Matt 5:19, "whoever practices and teaches these commands will be called great in the kingdom of heaven"), was that Tolstoy was a Christian of the greatest sort for he spent thirty years of his life seeking to practice himself, and teach others the injunctions of the Sermon on the Mount. It is not the case that Tolstoy separated Christ from his teaching, or removed love and non-violence from its Christian case. When Christoyannopoulos states Tolstoy "took Jesus' teaching on love and violence out of its Christian case" it can only be true if by *Christian case* he means the Christianity of orthodox Christendom. Tolstoy viewed the Christianity of orthodox Christendom as an unrecognizable deviation from Christ Jesus. It is true Tolstoy was a nominal Christian, if even one at all, according to the standards of what constituted Christianity at his time. It is not true Tolstoy distanced himself from Jesus the teacher on the mount. Certainly Tolstoy separated Christ from the teaching of the Church, from Orthodox rituals, superstitions, dogmas and doctrines, even major matters like the doctrine of the Trinity, miracles and the Resurrection. However, it cannot be said he separated the teachings of Jesus from the Teacher, Jesus. In fact, to read him correctly is to notice he was ever a proponent of the Doctrines of Jesus. Tolstoy's was not a Christ-less Christianity. It was the very opposite. Furthermore, it was not a mere reason and Enlightenment rationality. For him, it was divine revelation and faith in God's ways. Tolstoy pointed the world to the way of Christ, and drew from other religious and philosophies only where they supported the teachings of Christ.

With our shared interest and desire to draw greater attention to these later writings of Tolstoy and to gain a wider hearing and acceptance for them, there is the feeling of walking a loose tightrope as long as we continue trying to describe Tolstoyan theo-tactics as *Christian Anarchy*. As was argued earlier in this chapter, there are those who are very inclined to the teachings of Jesus who quickly lose interest when they hear the term *anarchy*. And, as Christoyannopoulos noted, secular anarchists are similarly turned away because of their "unease at the 'Christian' epithet to Tolstoy's anarchism." If indeed Christ is a stumbling block for secularists, perhaps the more generic *theo*-tactics is a step toward placation and conciliation. However, it would be more than unfortunate, in fact, a disservice and gross misreading of Tolstoy if the trend in Tolstoyan contributions in future discussions of resistance theory come at expense of the secularization of Tolstoy.

The trajectory of Tolstoy's life was from secular to spiritual, from the Church to Christ, and then embracing Christ's way for the world. While acknowledging the evident continuity between Tolstoy's earlier and later writing, this project holds fast on a reading of Tolstoy that his conversion was genuine and substantive. Tolstoy came to the end of human reason and he turned with a measure of faith to the counter-intuitive and otherworldly teachings of Christ. It is true and very much the case that he rejected *Church*-ianity; that is the ecclesial institutions, dogmatic traditions and formulations of it, and that he was both anti-clerical and anti-supernatural (yet only regarding Biblical miracles and Orthodox mysticisms). However, the divinity of the teachings of Christ was his conviction, even if the divinity of Christ was not. And, even there, hard and fast judgments about whether or not he was truly a Christian can only be conjecture. We are left to say that for Tolstoy, Jesus and this Kingdom of God within was a matter of the heart, not just the head. We are left to trust the statements of those who knew him best, like his family. After his death his beloved cousin Countess A. A. Tolstoy said that at the very mention of Christ's name (Jesus), Tolstoy's "voice quivered and his eyes gleamed moistly. This memory consoles me to this day; without admitting it to himself he loved the Redeemer with the deepest love and felt him to be more than an ordinary man."[63] The secularization of Tolstoy is not to merely fillet off a thin layer, it effectually disembowels his theo-tactics of the divine. The spirituality of adherence to the doctrine of Jesus was primary, and secondary were any manifestations of the Spirit of Jesus in Tolstoy that bore resemblance to political categories of anarchy. Important for a new generation to hear Tolstoy's voice clearly will be a resistance to any present-day trends towards a secularizing distortion of it. With Tolstoy's insistence on the importance of the Kingdom of God within, a theo-centric reading of the political implications of his thought is important to maintain.[64]

---

63. Nigg, "Heretic in the Eastern Church," 389, citing Countess A. A. Tolstoy, *Erinnerungen an Leo N. Tolstoj*, 38.

64. Tolstoy believed, like the later Russian novelist and Soviet-critic Aleksandr Solzhenitsyn, who wrote in *The Gulag Archipelago*: "Gradually it was disclosed to me that the line separating good and evil passes not through states, nor between classes, nor between political parties either — but right through every human heart — and through all human hearts" (Solzhenitsyn, *Gulag Archipelago*, 615).

10.5 A Modern Appropriation: Antifa, the Righteous Wind, and Theo-tacs

This final chapter points toward modern appropriations of Tolstoyan theo-tactical altruism based on the conviction that, now more than ever, the Sermon on the Mount is needed in the world, and that "the Sermon on the Mount is perhaps the main conversation the Holy Spirit wants to have with the Church today."[65] What follows are some comments about the alignment of clergy and churches with violence-inclined, anarchical activism, particularly in the United States. A couple of decades of personal involvement and leadership in both politically left-leaning and politically right-leaning activism has taught me the religious left (Red Letter Christians[66] for example) is aligned now with the political left in such a way they are losing their prophetic stance against it.[67] And worse, their alignment with it gives its violent practitioners and society at large a false assurance of God's approval of their tactics. Of particular concern is the alignment of the religious left with violent counter-movements, namely Antifa. Tolstoy would prophetically stand a distance away from these movements denouncing their justifications of their violent tactics.[68] He kept his distance from the violent anarchists of his day and would certainly not march alongside them, and with them, as we see Christians justify doing today in their zeal for matters of social righteousness. At least in America at the present time,

---

65. Hickey, *Obtainable Expectations*, in the Foreword by Mike Bickle, 15.

66. See Guthrie, "When Red Is Blue."

67. In religious political activism in American there is an unfortunate bifurcation of the Psalm 89:14 depiction of the earthly reign of God: "righteousness and justice are the foundation of your throne." The religious left now aligns with social justice and not so much with moral righteousness. Perhaps a similar assessment can be made of the religious right in activism for moral righteousness but not so much for social justice.

68. Bray, *Antifa*, 169. Three justifications are given for "punching Nazis" and the various physical confrontations and violent methods employed: (1) debate has failed, (2) militancy works, and (3) fascist violence necessitates self-defence. Bray decries all the people today who watch films in the cinema and cheer on the violent demise of the Nazis in 1940s Germany, but seem to not be able to justify the use of violence against nazis now, before things ever get that bad. Perhaps there is his fourth justification for violence: to avoid greater uses of violence later. Bray quotes an Antifa-Baltimore member named Murray who wrote: "You fight them by writing letters and making phone calls so you don't have to fight them with fists. You fight them with fists so you don't have to use knives. You fight them with knives so you don't have to use guns. You fight them with guns so you don't have to fight them with tanks." In that is evident a tactic of intensification of violence, which is entirely anthro-tactical, that the tactics start with small arms. The theo-tactical way of Jesus starts by laying down small arms, not raising the fist, but turning the cheek. In theo-tactics there is the de-escalation of violence. In anthro-tactics, violence escalates.

there are more than a few sightings in street protests of collared-clerics arm and arm with black-hooded Antifa foot soldiers (who shortly prove to be armed in some fashion; and who, as they press toward escalation, proceed to carry out violence against police, persons and property).[69]

Antifa is an abbreviated conjunction for a global and growing movement of anti-fascists in the world today. In an irony its adherents and militant activists rigorously deny, fascist tactics are justified and employed to fight what they deem fascist in the world; these tactics include fascism in the flavours of intolerance and censorship, denials of free speech and free assembly enforced through coercion and violence.[70] A best-selling modern handbook for these resistance groups is Saul Alinski's *Rules for Radicals*.[71] Such is a thoroughly anthro-tactical manual and those who employ them can hardly be said to have the righteous wind at their backs.[72] The argument

---

69. A notable example of clergy participation in intentionally-violent civil unrest was in Charlottesville, Virginia in August, 2017 (see Jenkins, "Clergy Who Stared Down White Supremacists"). Rev. Lisa Sharon Harper, the founder and organizer of FreedomRoad.us, (a cleric ordained by the same denominational body which ordained and oversees me) said it "felt like Selma after Bloody Sunday." The grand difference is the violence at Selma was one-directional, whereas the violence at Charlottesville was not. Both sides that day came prepared to bloody the other. Gandhi did not stand beside the violently inclined, or just behind them praying for their success. The military chaplain Father George Zabelka, who prayed for and blessed the planes and crews as they left the airfield to drop atomic bombs on Hiroshima and Nagasaki, has since repented and written passionately about his errors: "Look, I am a Catholic priest. In August of 1945, I did not say to the boys on Tinian, 'You cannot follow Christ and drop those bombs.' But this same failure on the part of priests, pastors and bishops over the past 1700 years is, I believe, what is significantly responsible for Hiroshima and Nagasaki and for the seemingly unceasing 'Christian' blood-letting around the globe. It seems to me that Christians have been slaughtering each other, as well as non-Christians, for the past 1700 years, in large part because their priests, pastors and bishops have simply not told them that violence and homicide are incompatible with the teachings of Jesus" (Magliano, "Conversion of the Catholic Priest"). Notably converted, Father Zabelka later wrote the foreword for Tolstoy's *Writings on Civil Disobedience and Nonviolence*.

70. "The legitimation of violence against a demonized internal enemy brings us close to the heart of fascism." Quotation from Robert Paxton's *The Anatomy of Fascism* cited in D'Souza, *Big Lie: Exposing the Nazi Roots*, 195.

71. Alinsky, *Rules for Radicals*.

72. A phrase commonly heard in social justice circles today notably used by Barack Obama in his 2004 speech at the Democrat National Convention: "I feel like we got a righteous wind at our backs here, but we're going to have to work. We're going to have to struggle. We're going to have to fight." The phrase is possibly based on Jeremiah 18:17: "Like a wind from the east, I will scatter them before their enemies; I will show them my back and not my face in the day of their disaster." However, some believe it is attributed to the writings of Chairman Mao: "The ill wind of opportunism is falling, the righteous wind of socialism is on the rise" (Zedong, *Writings of Mao Zedong*, 680). In any case, this is a good example of religious political rhetoric being used to justify tactics.

in this chapter has been for theo-tactics, and to even abbreviate this even more—or a new generation of young theo-tacs to emerge in the spirit of Jesus, not in the spirit of Mars or in the spirit of Chairman Mao; in the spirit of Tolstoy, not in the spirit of Marx; in the spirit of Gandhi and of Martin Luther King Jr., not the spirit of Malcolm X, Che Guevara, or the spirit of the Black Panthers, or of Saul Alinski, or today's Antifa.

10.5.1 The Wind of Righteous Rhetoric

A final word about words; certainly an apropos section in a project on the greatest sermon and, as some believe of Tolstoy, the greatest storyteller. It is too much to say the Sermon on the Mount was a street rally speech to a discomforted mob, but it is not too much to say it was intended to speak strategically and theo-tactically into those very settings in societies throughout all ages. In part, the belaboring throughout this chapter on conceiving and using better terminology is motivated by a concern that rhetoric and messaging (weaponized wording), become the strategic, creative and innovative but mostly the inspired dimension of the political imagination needed to win an enemy without violence. In terms of academic disciplines, this project emerges within the constructs of Christian Ethics. More specifically, it is concerned with the ways Jesus wants his followers to live, at least how Tolstoy viewed such Christlike lifestyles and living. Theo-tactics are therefore the concern of Christian ethicists; discerning and articulating God's ways which are higher than ours, and his thoughts which are higher than ours, and also, his way of word-smithing which has the righteous wind behind it.

The sound-bytes of the Sermon on the Mount have reverberated verbatim throughout the centuries. They have lost none of their piquant properties. Jesus, the greatest moral voice the world has ever seen, spoke and left people on that hillside in awe and taken aback by the authority in which he spoke. There was a connection between his moral authority and his messaging, an incarnation of Word into word. What Jesus said was tight and sometimes terse. As a double-edged sword his words cut both to the heart and through the deception and the spin. His words were sometimes ironic and hyperbolic, deep yet simple, heartening and humorous, clever riddles and ridiculing, and even earthy and parabolic. He did not bother to be polite, sanitized, politically-correct, or to tip-toe around the proverbial elephant in the room. There was love, yet righteous indignation, and both passion and urgency. Tolstoy too, as a master wordsmith, used words and short-stories theo-tactically. Christian ethicists need to (prayerfully) work hard(er) at bridging the gap between academic research and anointed rhetoric. Rhetoric is a both a grace and a proficiency (a competency) for theo-tacticians of the Christ-like sort, and of the Tolstoyan sort.

~ 11.0 ~

Conclusion

THERE ARE SEVERAL FIRSTS within these pages. This is the first book-length treatment of the Sermon on the Mount in Second Tolstoy. Within, there is the first parallel, technical comparison of Matthew 5–7 in Tolstoy's *Gospel in Brief* with a contemporary English translation (NIV-UK). There are several first time appearances of material that has, heretofore, not been considered critically and heretofore not translated into English; newly found and newly translated material on Tolstoy and Chelčický, on Tolstoy and Lassarre, on Tolstoy and Laurila, and especially there are new historical connections uncovered between Tolstoy and Bonhoeffer. There are new assertions that have never been made before on Tolstoy's conversion, Tolstoy's marriage, Tolstoy's political thought, his letter to the Tsar as related to Lenin, and on Tolstoy as prophet and reformer. Tolstoy remains a formidable challenge to Constantinian Christianity. Quite importantly, there is new verbiage and vernacular given in these pages to better describe Tolstoyan Christianity to a new generation. That verbiage being theo-tactics. And there is a delightful new find, included in the appendices (subsection 12.5) which I am calling the *Tolstoy Anathema Iron*, making its first appearance in Tolstoyan studies.

If there is one missing piece in this project, it is that there was not space to treat Tolstoy's Diaries. Major and minor commentary has been given on all of the main pieces of Second Tolstoy in some way, except his Diaries. Early on his Diaries were acknowledged but reasons were given for narrowing the focus to the six main works of Second Tolstoy, two in particular. Even so, some space in chapter five was given to his Letters, but not to his Diaries. It is this history of the unfolding of his actual life that makes Tolstoy as a Sermon on the Mount interpreter come alive. Sometimes it can be hard to tell what theology professors actually believe—their subjects are separated from themselves—they write eloquently about what others think but it is not who they are, and they escape from the mandates of the material themselves. Tolstoy is the antithesis of that making him all the more interesting and important as an interpreter of the Sermon on the Mount. He is a good example of being both a hearer and a doer; of combining the double-charge given twice in the Sermon on the Mount (like a parentheses at the beginning and the end): "whoever *practices* and *teaches* these commands will be called great in the kingdom of heaven" (Matt 5:19) and "everyone who *hears* these words of mine and *puts them into practice* is like a wise man who built his house on the rock" (Matt 7:24).

11.1 Three Misreadings: What We Get Wrong

Significant arguments have been made in the preceding pages and chapters justifying this long overdue, generous reading of Leo Tolstoy's interpretation of the Sermon on the Mount. There have been a couple guiding presuppositions throughout the project. First, that (1) little concern be given to his theological (Christian) unorthodoxies. They exist. However, they do not cancel what he did get right in his reading of, obedience to, and reverence for the Sermon on the Mount. Once this dense fog of doctrinal consternation regarding 'Tolstoy the Heretic' lifts off, what remains is a pretty clear pathway. In fact, it is the pathway Christ called his followers down in Matthew 5–7.

The second guiding presupposition throughout this project, one of the marks of this entire work, is the (2) credence given to Tolstoy's conversion to the Christian way, the way of Christ. The controversial title itself, *Second Tolstoy*, points toward the legitimacy of his Christian conversion: "Therefore if anyone is in Christ, he is a new creature; the old things passed away; behold, new things have come" (2 Cor 5:17). It has been meticulously shown in part one of this project (chapters one through five) how there is a vast amount of Second Tolstoy material, and it is this Second Tolstoy corpus which awaits further academic, and more importantly, popular engagement. Also, in treating Tolstoy's conversion seriously, there is the hope that Tolstoy will be welcomed back to the fold and given some measure of standing within Christendom, for he is indeed one of our troubled and troubling prophetic voices.

In drawing this project to its close, there are three common misreadings of Tolstoy to mention by way of precaution. Following a brief mention of those, the pervasive question of this project will be summarily addressed;

What did Tolstoy get right? By way of findings and conclusions, this project has come upon four that set Tolstoy apart. However first, the three common misreadings.

11.1.1 The Marginalization of Tolstoy

There remains, ongoing, *the marginalization of Tolstoy*. Due mostly to his unorthodoxies, but also to his radicalization of discipleship, it has been shown in the preceding chapters that Tolstoy has been marginalized as any sort of important Christian thinker or theologian, or practitioner of the ways of Christ. By and large, unfortunately, he is not read alongside other Christian thinkers; pastors and seminarians are not encouraged or required to read Tolstoy, and sadly his significant influence and contribution are largely lost to modern followers of Christ. The average Christian has heard of Luther, but only know of Tolstoy as a writer of great fiction. In these pages a case has been made that Tolstoy should be treated as a major Christian contributor, a prophetic voice. Granted his Christianity was not the dogma-laden Christianity of the Church, but it was Christianity in the sense of the Christianity of Christ, the doctrine of Jesus. The marginalization of Tolstoy is perhaps also due to a misreading of his life and weak attempts to live the doctrines of Jesus. It is wrongly assumed he failed at living it, that he failed at his marriage and his life ended in tragedy, therefore he should be set to the side as not being anyone worthy of admiration. Arguments have been set forth in these chapters proposing a very different reading; that according to Christ's criteria (Matt 5:19), Tolstoy could be called "great in the Kingdom" and that his adherence to the ways of Christ put him at odds with the world, even at odds with his wife. Instead of marginalizing Tolstoy, this project argued he is an good example of faithfulness resulting in green, white and grey martyrdoms.

11.1.2 The Secularization of Tolstoy

The second precaution is against *the secularization of Tolstoy*. Though understandable, this too is an unfortunate misreading. Particularly in the area of Tolstoy's contribution to political thought and theory there is a temptation to brush aside *his* Christianity to gain a wider support for his supposed anarchy or pacifism. Tolstoy's departure from (Christian) doctrinal orthodoxy, combined with his keen interest in Eastern religious traditions and teachings have led many to incorrectly assume he merely took moral principles from Christ, and left Christ behind. Arguments have been made in preceding pages that this was not the case. To be true to Tolstoy is to not veer far from Christ on the Mount. Tolstoy's was not a Christ-less Christianity (this would actually be an outright inversion of his view). Tolstoy viewed the Christianity of his time to be Christ-less and that the doctrines of Jesus were entirely eclipsed by subsequent centuries of dogma and ritual. Earlier in this project there was a measure of lament in how, too often, Gandhi gets the glory for what was really Tolstoyan. The danger of the secularization of Tolstoy bares a similar grievance if indeed Tolstoy is given the glory for what he received from Jesus.

11.1.3 The Pluralization of Tolstoy

The third caution is against *the pluralization of Tolstoy*. Related to the second danger, attempts to claim Tolstoy as a universalist, or a convert to Buddhism, Hinduism, or that he was an early adherent to Baháʼísm are all significant misreadings. Dragan Milivojevic was right: "Tolstoy sought to discover in Oriental religions an affirmation of his own spiritual values derived from Christianity."[1] Acknowledging universal moral principles and ascribing to universalism are two different things and the admonition here is that they be properly distinguished. Arguments have been made in these chapters showing Tolstoy drew from other faiths to support the teachings of Christ, yet he sternly rejected the aspects of other faiths that were distinctly not compliant with the doctrine of Jesus. Tolstoy as pluralist assertions are problematic because they perpetuate a false endorsement of pluralism by Tolstoy. Tolstoy's message was not that all roads lead to the same desired place. His message was that the way of Christ leads to life and all other ways do not. Temptations to make Tolstoy more palpable to modern ears by construing him as a universalist should be resisted.

11.2 Four Main Findings: What Tolstoy Got Right

Tolstoy's driving concern in his reading of the Sermon on the Mount was that it be obeyed, not reasoned against or watered down. Tolstoy can be viewed as a forerunner in a (hopefully) forthcoming obedience movement the Church has really yet to see. There have been dozens of significant and positive movements throughout the history of Christianity, each calling the

---

1. Balasubramanian, *Influence of India on Leo Tolstoy*, 13, citing Milivojevic, "Tolstoy's Concept of Reason," 105–13.

Church back to an area of neglect, or in Tolstoy's words . . . to a new truth;[2] holiness movements; monastic movements; ecumenical and social gospel movements; Zionist and restoration movements; faith, charismatic, health/wealth and signs and wonders movements; missions movements; and the Church globally is enjoying a prayer movement presently taking shape in a variety of ways including a New Monasticism movement. However, in two thousand years, has the Church ever seen a significant obedience movement to the doctrine of Jesus?

11.2.1 Simple Obedience

In subsequent research to that presented here, I have a particular interest to give more attention to how Bonhoeffer can be seen as a ideological descendant of Tolstoy, at least as related to Sermon on the Mount obedience. Bonhoeffer is widely considered a major Sermon on the Mount interpreter; the middle section of his famous *(Cost of) Discipleship* being his commentary on Matthew 5-7. Bonhoeffer gave great definition to the matters of simple obedience to the Sermon on the Mount, and his very life became a struggle with a sense of responsibility under the demands of the Sermon on the Mount in the brutal and unforgiving context of Adolf Hitler in Nazi Germany. One of the new contributions of this project to these areas of academic inquiry has been in uncovering important connections between Tolstoy and Bonhoeffer through Bonhoeffer's friend Jean Lasserre, and between Gandhi and Bonhoeffer on Tolstoyan Sermon on the Mount interpretations (see subsection 5.4).

Life together in Sermon on the Mount-based communities, religionless Christianity, costly grace, discipleship, responsibility, and simple obedience are popular and much written about Bonhoefferian notions. Until now, the suggestion that each bear a distinct Tolstoyan flavour has gone unnoticed and unmade; and each are deserving of further critical analysis and comparison. Whether any further real dependance of Bonhoeffer on Tolstoy can be more firmly established (than in subsection 5.4) is less important than appreciating Tolstoy's earlier (and unfortunately largely hidden) influence advocating these very ideas. The basis of this likeness between Tolstoy and Bonhoeffer is a return to simple obedience, and to the Sermon on the

---

2. In speaking of his discovery of the New Life-Conception, found in the Sermon on the Mount, as a "new truth" Tolstoy was referring to truth that was new to him. In the context of the various movements in Christian history it might help to speak of present truth, or truth that God is underscoring at the present time. Tolstoy did not believe truth was situational or relative.

Mount. Bonhoeffer minced no words, the Christian has only two choices—obedience or disobedience: "When Jesus demanded voluntary poverty of the rich man, the young man knew that his only choices were obedience or disobedience" (DBW-D, 77).[3]

> Only one thing was demanded . . . entrusting themselves to the word of Jesus Christ, believing it to be a stronger foundation that all the securities of the world. The forces that wanted to get between the word of Jesus and obedience were just as great back then as they are today. (DBW-D, 77)

Bonhoeffer listed some of those ever-present forces; reason objected, conscience, responsibility, piety and even the old Reformation accusation made again by Lutherans of Bonhoeffer's time against this sort of "lawless 'enthusiasm'" and "irrational opinions" (DBW-D, 77). In vintage Bonhoeffer vernacular he wrote: "Whenever simple obedience is fundamentally eliminated, there again the costly grace of Jesus' call has become the cheap grace of self-justification" (DBW-D, 77).

Tolstoy wrote of a feeling he first had as a child, what he called "the feeling of the Cross."[4] The commands of Christ and the call of Christ, for both Tolstoy and Bonhoeffer, came with this feeling of the Cross. When Christ's commands are interpreted by his followers in ways that remove any such sense of Cross it is apparent they have talked themselves out of simple obedience. Whether or not Bonhoeffer ever heard of Tolstoy's 'feeling of the Cross' he certainly would have concurred: "Whenever Christ calls us, his call leads us to death" (DBW-D, 87). Bonhoeffer remarked in his chapter on *Simple Obedience* in *Discipleship* how a reversal so often takes place; instead of putting one's full dependance on the word of God, dependance is placed elsewhere:

> Anywhere else in the world where commands are given, the situation is clear. A father says to his child: go to bed! The child knows exactly what to do. But a child drilled in pseudotheology would have to argue thus: Father says go to bed. He means you are tired; he does not want me to be tired. But I can also overcome my tiredness by going to play. So, although father says go to bed, what he really means is go play. . . . The situation is supposed to be different only with respect to Jesus' command. In that case simple obedience is supposed to be wrong, or even to constitute disobedience. (DBW-D, 79–80)

---

3. Bonhoeffer, "Simple Obedience," in *Dietrich Bonhoeffer Works Volume 4: Discipleship*, 77–83.

4. Biriukov, *Leo Tolstoy*, 54.

Such a reversal, regardless of the pious reasoning behind it, is open rebellion and disobedience. It is to not trust the word of God, and to not trust the word of God not only makes one disobedient, it produces for the Christian and for the Church a false sense of communion with Christ. Bonhoeffer wrote, "the promise of community with Jesus is given to this obedience" (DBW-D, 79). Tolstoy would agree and add that community with Jesus and community within Christendom are not the same.

11.2.2 Living Martyrdoms

Both Tolstoy and Bonhoeffer became what I earlier termed, grey martyrs (see subsection 5.5, Note 50). A grey martyr is one whose obedience to and 'enthusiasm' for the word of God results in being disfellowshipped and excommunicated. Such is the irony that communion with Christ can, at times, sever one from their ecclesiastical community; and communion ecclesiastically can, at times, separate us from Christ and full dependance on his word. For both Tolstoy and Bonhoeffer, communion with Christ was not based on Creed but on obedience. Bonhoeffer wrote of.

> the road to faith passing through the obedience to God's call. . .
> . Only the obedient believe, and only the believer obeys. . . . The call goes out, and without any further ado the obedient deed of the one called follows. The disciple's answer is not a spoken confession of faith in Jesus. Instead it is the obedient deed. (DBW-D, 63, 68)

Tolstoy said very similar things against the Creed; actually, he was far more intense. Regardless, the point was the same. The contention here is that Tolstoy may never have been a red martyr, but he was a green, white and grey martyr. Bonhoeffer was both a red martyr and a grey one. The call to come and die means more than mere red martyrdom. Each of the four martyrdoms can be equally gruelling and all demanding. Each are living martyrdoms.

Bonhoeffer ended his lengthy treatment on the Sermon on the Mount in his *Discipleship* in the same place Tolstoy left off, and in the same place Jesus ended his famous Sermon with obedience to the word being the difference between the wise and foolish builder:

> This word, which I accept as valid for myself; this word . . . immediately draws me into acting, into obedience, is the rock on which I can build my house. This word of Jesus coming from eternity can only be answered by simply doing it. Jesus has

spoken; the word is his; our part is to obey . . . the only thing that exists besides action is inaction. There is no such thing as intending to act and not doing it. Those who treat the word of Jesus any other way except by acting on it assert that Jesus is wrong; they say no to the Sermon on the Mount; they do not do his word. All our questions, complications, and interpretations are inaction. (DBW-D, 182)

As was shown earlier in subsection 5.4, at Finkenwalde, Bonhoeffer envisioned followers of Christ gathering in community, into new forms of monasticism—a new monasticism that has nothing in common with the old except an uncompromising allegiance to the Sermon on the Mount. His desire to go visit Gandhi's ashram demonstrated his interest in seeing at least one expression of a [Tolstoyan] Sermon on the Mount community in action. Much more work needs to be done to flesh out what both he, and Tolstoy, envisioned.

11.2.3 Enemy Love

The third significant finding in this project is the matter of *love* and more specifically, *enemy love*. For Tolstoy, the point was not mere nonviolence, or anti-war; it was that love can never be violent, and love is fully incompatible with war of any sort. The command was to love and therefore Tolstoy could not be loving and also support executions, or the killing of animals. Yet, it is not enough, or precise, to simply categorise him, for example, as a vegetarian. Properly viewed, he was loving and therefore a vegetarian. Love is the basis for subsequent behavior and to read Tolstoy properly is to look beyond the behavior to that from which it flows; love. Particularly Tolstoyan, is in how he stressed the Sermon on the Mount calls the follower of Christ beyond love of neighbor out into the place of enemy love.

Søren Kierkegaard wrote of love in a way that can be construed as blind love or one-sided love. His exposition on blind love provides a helpful commentary for better understanding enemy love as conceived by Tolstoy. Like Kierkegaard, Tolstoy collapsed neighborly love into enemy love; and any distinction of *friend* or *enemy* in the object of love is eliminated entirely. Kierkegaard explained:

> Men think that it is impossible for a human being to love his enemies, for enemies are hardly able to endure the sight of one another. Well, then, shut your eyes– and your enemy looks just like your neighbour. Shut your eyes and remember the command that you shall love. . . . When you shut your eyes, you do

> not see the distinctions of earthly existence. And when you shut your eyes, your mind is not diverted and confused just when you are to listen to the words of the command. And when your mind is not disturbed and confused by looking at the object of your love and the distinction of your object, then you become all ears for the words of the command, which speak one thing and one thing only to you, that you ought to love your neighbour.... [W]hen your eyes are closed and you have become all ears for the command, you are on the way of perfection in loving your neighbour.[5]

This can be helpful in understanding the movements within Tolstoy's conception of Christian love. The only thing that matters is obedience to the command of Christ. It does not matter what was done to us, or by whom. Retaliation is never a factor, or ever an option, because the driver is our love, not anything of the other. For Tolstoy, love can not be retaliatory. The collapsing of the friend and enemy distinction in Tolstoy (and Kierkegaard) separates the Christian (one who is like Christ) from the non-Christian (one who is not like Christ). Christ was loving and therefore forgiving, and the Christian is one who is like Christ in these Christlike manners. Tolstoy viewed Christian love as blind and one-sided. It is of no relevance at all whether or not love is reciprocated.

11.2.4 Theo-tactics

The world would be far better off if more were concerned with theo-tactics, if more lived theo-tactically, and taught others to do the same.[6] This is the fourth significant finding of this project, the discernment of *theo-tactics*. The arguments and proposals in chapter ten putting forth the new term

---

5. Kierkegaard, *Works of Love*, 79.

6. Time to pioneer some Theo-tactical Seminaries! Here's how I would define that: A Theo-tactical Seminary is a short-term, residential community that teaches how God wants people to live today. It is a development on Tolstoyan communities, and even more a development of what Bonhoeffer might have envisioned at Finkenwalde. The basis being that God sent his Son, the Way, to show the way to life eternal, and also the way to live now. As such, a Theo-tactical Seminary is focused on the emulation of Christ and the Sermon on the Mount, which is Christlikeness. It is a specialty seminary focused on putting Christ of the Mount and Christlikeness back in to the centre of what it means to be a Christian. Once down off that "mountainside" it would be said of graduates that it is evident they have been with Jesus. As noted in the dedication of the book, envisioned herein is a future generation of Siders, that is mountainsiders – those who gather together desiring to radically adhere to the way of Jesus given on that mountainside.

and notion of theo-tactics (to best capture Tolstoyan Sermon on the Mount interpretation) perhaps constitute the major contribution of this project—but that may be better left for others to decide. This new vocabulary offers better definition of Tolstoy's conceptions. He was not a passivist, nor was he merely a pacifist. He was heeding God's ways for winning enemies; he was a theo-tactician. Tolstoy was not an early anarchist only of a non-violent sort. He did not believe the Sermon on the Mount to be state-crafting. Theo-tactically he understood the Sermon to be about how God wanted his people to live in the midst of the kingdoms that already exist in the world. Theo-tactics are about discerning, apprehending, and obeying how God wants his people to live now, in present situations, in present confrontations; in whatever country one happens to live in, at whatever time in history. Theo-tactics are about sorting out God's will here on earth [now] as it is in heaven. Theo-tactics are what Jesus spoke of on the mountainside. Tolstoy called it the New Life-Conception; today it is best defined as theo-tactics.

~ 12.0 ~

Appendices

APPENDICES ARE TYPICALLY THE place to bury supporting material that would otherwise burden down the reader if such were included in the main sections of the book. The appendices chosen for this project go beyond this traditional purpose.

Appendices subsection 12.1 is my NIV-UK/TGB Parallel Comparison of Matthew 5–7 which is a vital accompaniment to the comments in subsection 1.6, in fact it is the basis for them. The hope is the reader will be able to study the comparison and see for themselves Tolstoy's renderings, additions and changes. Also, this is the first complete and careful comparison to be done, or at least to be published as such, and its inclusion in these appendices serve to ensure its ease of availability for use and consideration by additional scholars and scholarship.

Second, in subsection 12.2, the inclusion of Tolstoy's Letter to Tsar Alexander III is motivated by a desire to bring this important document out of the forgotten archives of history, dust it off and set it in the midst of a new generation for consideration. As explained in subsection 5.2, I contend this letter is of even higher caliber than Dr. King's famous *Letter from the Birmingham Jail*. A sample of Tolstoy's handwriting is included to give the reader a feel for the original document, written out several times in several drafts, to state what Tolstoy felt led to communicate following the dream that prompted the letter. Also, the reader will be able to get a sense of the scribbles Sofia Tolstoy worked with as she rewrote seven times (at least) by hand his succession of revised manuscripts of *War and Peace*. The collected works of Tolstoy fill over ninety volumes and with the exception of later and mainly formal correspondence it was all handwritten. Later in his life

Tolstoy was given a Remington understroke typewriter but his spirituality did not incline him to use labor-saving machines. His daughter Alexandra sat at this typewriter for hours each day doing her father's correspondence and typing out his handwritten manuscript drafts. In the deathcast of his writing hand, deep grooves are present from a long life with a pen in hand. Thoughts of that hand writing this letter to the tsar leave an impression—though the intended impression on the world was never made. Including the letter here is done with prayerful hope the letter will make its way to another leader somewhere who has the power to heed and respond to its prophetic message.[1]

Third, in subsection 12.3, is the first English translation of Tolstoy's foreword to Chelčický's *Net of Faith*, which was done exclusively for my research by Olga Sevastyanova. Subsection 6.5 spells out the importance of Chelčický's *Net of Faith* to Tolstoy's understanding of the Constantinian shift, and also the difficulty he had obtaining a copy of this work. That he wrote a preface to it in 1907 is virtually unknown, far moreso than even this largely unknown work of Chelčický itself. Tolstoy's preface was a discovery on my June 2017 research trip to Yasnaya Polyana and the Tolstoy archives there. It is with an awareness that others would be well-served to have easier access to this preface the English translation is made available here. There is more in the preface than was highlighted in my use of it in subsection 6.5 and readers will surely benefit from all of Tolstoy's comments on this important Chelčický work.

In subsection 12.4, there are several works of art that either were important to Tolstoy or tell their own story about the reception of Tolstoyan Sermon on the Mount interpretation. The medium of art, for Tolstoy, was certainly part of his prophetic mode of communication and these images are included here to give another window into his Sermon on the Mount views, and the reaction of others for, or against them.

Lastly, in subsection 12.5, are a couple of pictures of what I have named the *Tolstoy Anathema Iron*. This was a delightful find during the course of my research. It is certainly relevant to the matter of persecution (grey martyrdom) for adherence to the doctrines of Jesus expressed in the Sermon on the Mount.

---

1. A PDF is available here https://stevehickey.files.wordpress.com/2018/08/ltr-to-tsar.pdf.

12.1 NIV-UK/TGB Parallel Comparison of Matthew 5–7

KEY: Double underline in the NIV-UK text are <u>omissions</u> not found in the TGB text.
Single underline in the TGB text are <u>additions</u> not found in the NIV-UK text.

NIV-UK (New International Version - UK)
Matthew 5-7

Introduction to the Sermon on the Mount

> *Note 1. Tolstoy began with a paraphrase of Matthew 4:23 and crafted it into a summary introduction of his view that Jesus went about in all the towns and villages teaching all men the happiness of doing the Father's will. Tolstoy then relocated here Matthew 9:35 the text about Jesus having compassion on the crowds as they were like sheep without a shepherd. Again, his emphasis is doing the will of God and having knowledge of what true life consists of.*

5:1 Now when Jesus saw the crowds, he went up on a mountainside and sat down. His disciples came to him, 2 and he began to teach them.

The Beatitudes

He said:
3 'Blessed are the poor in spirit,
   for theirs is the kingdom of heaven.

4 Blessed are those who mourn,
   for they will be comforted.
5 <u>Blessed are the meek,
   for they will inherit the earth.</u>
6 Blessed are those who hunger and thirst <u>for righteousness</u>, for they will be filled.
7 <u>Blessed are the merciful,
   for they will be shown mercy.</u>
8 <u>Blessed are the pure in heart,
   for they will see God.</u>
9 <u>Blessed are the peacemakers,
   for they will be called children of God.</u>

10 Blessed are those who are persecuted <u>because of righteousness</u>,
   for theirs is the kingdom of heaven.
11 'Blessed are you when people insult you, persecute you and falsely say all kinds of evil against you <u>because of me</u>. 12 Rejoice and be glad, because

TGB (Tolstoy's Gospel Brief)
Translated from the original Russian manuscript by Alymer Maude, 1893

THE KINGDOM OF GOD (Chapter Four of TGB)

Therefore the will of the Father is that all men should have life and happiness.

"THY KINGDOM COME"

JESUS went about in the towns and villages and taught all men <u>the happiness of doing the Father's will</u>. And he was sorry for people because they perish without <u>knowing what true life consists of</u>, and trouble and torment themselves without knowing why, like scattered sheep that have no shepherd.

Once many people came to Jesus to hear his teaching and he went up on a hill and sat down. His pupils surrounded him. And he began to teach the people

<u>what the Father's will is</u>.

He said:
Blessed are the poor <u>and the homeless</u>,
for they live in <u>the will</u> of the Father.

If they are hungry they shall be satisfied, and if they sorrow and weep they shall be comforted.

> *Note 2. Tolstoy's rendering of the blessings are reordered following closely the parallel woes in Luke's Sermon on the Plain. Tolstoy's emphasis is God's concern for those in physical poverty as against those who have earthly wealth. Note thought he did insert "poor in spirit" at very end of this section*

If people despise them, thrust them aside, and drive them away,
let them be glad of it,

great is your reward in heaven, for in the same way they persecuted the prophets who were before you.

> *Note 3. Again, Tolstoy's Beatitudes are reordered from the blessings in Matthew and follow closely the woes in Luke 6:20-26.*

Salt and light

13 'You are the salt of the earth. But if the salt loses its saltiness, how can it be made salty again?

It is no longer good for anything, except to be thrown out and trampled underfoot.

14 'You are the light of the world. A town built on a hill cannot be hidden. **15** Neither do people light a lamp and put it under a bowl. Instead they put it on its stand, and it gives light to everyone in the house. **16** In the same way, let your light shine before others,

that they may see your good deeds and glorify your Father in heaven.

The fulfilment of the law

17 'Do not think that I have come to abolish the Law or the Prophets; I have not come to abolish them but to fulfil them. **18** For truly I tell you, until heaven and earth disappear, not the smallest letter, not the least stroke of a pen, will by any means disappear from the Law until everything is accomplished. **19** Therefore anyone who sets aside one of the least of these commands and teaches others accordingly will be called least in the kingdom of heaven,
but whoever practises and teaches these commands will be called great in the kingdom of heaven.

for so God's people have always been treated and they receive a heavenly reward.

But woe to the rich, for they have already got what they wanted, and will get nothing more. Now they are satisfied, but they too will be hungry. Now they rejoice, but they too will be sad. Woe to those whom everyone praises, for only deceivers are praised by everybody.

Blessed are the poor and homeless; but blessed only if they are poor not merely outwardly but also in spirit-

just as salt is good only when it has saltness in it and is not salt merely in appearance.

So you also, the poor and homeless, are the teachers of the world; you are blessed if you know that true happiness is in being homeless and poor. But if you are poor only outwardly then, like salt that has no savor, you are good for nothing.

> *Note 4. Tolstoy's own conversion and testimony shine through in these references to the poor and homeless being the teachers of true happiness for in his search for happiness and the meaning of life he learned more of the way of life from the peasant class than from any philosopher or theologian. (A Confession, Chapters 10, 15.)*

You are the light of the world, therefore do not hide your light but let men see it. When a man lights a candle he does not put it under the bench but on the table that it should give light to everyone in the room. So you, too, should not hide your light but show it by your actions, that men may see that you have the truth,
and seeing your good deeds may understand your heavenly Father.

And do not think that I free you from the law. I teach not release from the law but fulfillment of the eternal law. As long as there are men under heaven the eternal law remains. There will be no release from law till men of themselves fulfill the eternal law completely. And now, I give you the commandments of that eternal law. If anyone releases himself from any of these short commandments and teaches others that they may do so, he shall be least in the kingdom of heaven, but he who fulfills them and thereby teaches others to fulfill them shall be great in the kingdom of heaven.

APPENDICES

20 For I tell you that unless your righteousness surpasses that of the <u>Pharisees and the teachers of the law</u>, you will certainly not enter the kingdom of heaven.

Murder

21 'You have heard that it was said to the people long ago, "You shall not murder, and anyone who murders will be subject to judgment." **22** But I tell you that anyone who is angry with a brother or sister will be subject to judgment. Again, anyone who says to a brother or sister, "<u>Raca</u>," is <u>answerable to the court</u>. And anyone who says, "You fool!" <u>will be in danger of the fire of hell</u>.

23 'Therefore, if you are <u>offering your gift</u> at the altar and there remember that your brother or sister has something against you, **24** leave your gift there in front of the altar. First go and be reconciled to them; then come and offer your <u>gift</u>.

25 '<u>Settle matters quickly with your adversary who is taking you to court. Do it while you are still together on the way, or your adversary may hand you over to the judge, and the judge may hand you over to the officer, and you may be thrown into prison. 26 Truly I tell you, you will not get out until you have paid the last penny.</u>

> *Note 8. The additional sentences Tolstoy inserted here infer 1 Samuel 15:22 – "Does the LORD delight in burnt offerings and sacrifices as much as in obeying the LORD?"*
> *Note 9. He also took the liberty at the end of each section of these five New Commandments to provide summary sentences to expound his interpretation of these New Commandments of Jesus.*

Adultery

27 'You have heard that it was said, "You shall not commit adultery."

28 But I tell you that anyone who looks at a woman lustfully has already committed adultery with her in his heart. **29** <u>If your right eye causes you to stumble, gouge it out and throw it away. It is better for you to lose one part of your body than for your whole body to be thrown into hell. 30 And if your right hand causes you to stumble, cut it off and throw it away.</u> It is better for you to lose one part of your body than for your whole body to go into hell.

For if your virtue is no more than the virtue of the <u>Orthodox legalists</u> you will never reach the kingdom of heaven.

<u>These are the commandments:</u>

In the former law it was said: Do not kill, and if anyone kills another
he must be judged. But I tell you
that everyone who grows angry with his brother-man deserves judgment, and <u>still more to blame</u> is he who <u>speaks abusively</u> to his brother-man.

> *Note 5. Saying only "more to blame" Tolstoy omitted specific mention of the consequences; i.e. answerable to the court and danger of the fire of hell.*

So if you wish to <u>pray</u> to God, first think whether there is anyone who has something against you. If you remember even one man who considers that you have offended him, leave your <u>prayers</u> and go first to make peace with your brotherman, and then you may <u>pray</u>.

> *Note 6. Again, Tolstoy omitted the specific consequences; court, judge, officer, prison until the debt is settled.*
> *Note 7. He then added a summation of the commandment against anger in the following:*

<u>Know that God requires neither sacrifice nor prayer, but only peace, concord, and love among men; and that you can neither pray nor think of God if there is a single man towards whom you do not feel love.</u>

<u>So this is the first commandment: Do not be angry, and do not rail; and if you have spoken harshly to anyone make peace with him and do it so that no one should have a grudge against you.</u>

In the former law it was said: Do not commit adultery, and if you wish to put away your wife, give her a letter of divorcement. But I tell you that if you look lustfully at a woman's beauty you are already committing adultery.

<u>All sensuality destroys the soul</u>, and so it is better for you to <u>renounce the pleasures of the flesh</u> than to destroy your life.

Divorce

31 'It has been said, "Anyone who divorces his wife must give her a certificate of divorce." **32** <u>But I tell you that anyone who divorces his wife, except for sexual immorality, makes her the victim of adultery, and anyone who marries a divorced woman commits adultery</u>.

> *Note 10. Tolstoy added a summation of his second commandment which combined into one New Commandment, Jesus' teaching against adultery and divorce.*

And if you put away your wife, then besides being <u>vicious</u> yourself you <u>drive her to wantonness too</u>, as well as him with whom she may unite.

<u>So that is the second commandment: Do not think that love of a woman is good, do not desire women, but live with her with whom you have become united, and do not leave her.</u>

Oaths

33 'Again, you have heard that it was said to the people long ago, "Do not break your oath, but fulfil to the Lord the oaths you have made."

34 But I tell you, do not swear an oath at all: <u>either by heaven, for it is God's throne; **35** or by the earth, for it is his footstool; or by Jerusalem, for it is the city of the Great King</u>. **36** And do not swear by your head, for you cannot make even one hair white or black.

> *Note 11. Tolstoy added commentary explaining how swearing to anything is evil and he inserts a second time how nothing more should be said except a simple yes to following the will of God.*

37 All you need to say is simply "Yes," or "No"; anything beyond this comes from the evil one.

> *Note 12. Tolstoy added a summation of his third New Commandment against oath-swearing.*

In the former law it was said: <u>Do not utter the name of the Lord God in vain</u>, do not call upon God when lying, and do not dishonor the name of your God. Do not swear to any untruth and so profane your God. But I tell you that <u>every oath is a profanation of God.</u> Therefore do not swear at all.

Man cannot promise anything, for he is wholly in the power of the Father. He cannot make one gray hair black.
<u>How then can he swear beforehand that he will do this or that, and swear to it by God? Every oath is a profanation of God</u>, for if a man is compelled to fulfill under an oath that which is against <u>the will of God</u> it shows that he had promised to act contrary to <u>God's will</u>, and so <u>every oath is an evil</u>. But when men ask you about anything, say Yes if it is yes, or no if it is no; anything added to that is evil.

<u>So the third commandment is: Never swear anything for anyone. Say Yes when it is yes, No when it is no, and understand that every oath is evil.</u>

Eye for eye

38 'You have heard that it was said, "Eye for eye, and tooth for tooth."

39 But I tell you, do not resist an evil person.

If anyone slaps you on the right cheek, turn to them the other cheek also. **40** And if anyone wants to sue you and take your shirt, hand over your coat as well. **41** If anyone forces you to go one mile, go with them two miles. **42** Give to the one who asks

In the former law it was said that if a man killed another he must give a life for a life, an eye for an eye, <u>a tooth for a tooth, an arm for an arm, an ox for an ox, a slave for a slave, and much else</u>. But I say to you: Do not fight evil by evil, and <u>not only do not exact at law an ox for an ox, a slave for a slave, a life for a life</u>, but do not resist evil at all. If anyone wishes to take an ox from you, give him another; if he wants to take your coat by law, give him your shirt as well;

if anyone <u>knocks out a tooth on one side</u>, turn the other side to him. If he would make you <u>do one piece of work for him, do two</u>. If men wish to take your property, let them have it.

you, and do not turn away from the one who wants to borrow from you.

Note 13. Tolstoy relocated the entirety of the Sermon on the Mount's prohibition against judging (Matthew 7:1-6) to this location after Matthew 5:42. Such a reordering follows his understanding of the fourth New Commandment – "do not return evil, do not judge or go to law, do not sue, and do not punish." A parallel comparison on 7:1-6 is forthcoming in the traditional place within the Sermon on the Mount.

Love for enemies

43 'You have heard that it was said, "Love your neighbor and hate your enemy." **44** But I tell you, love your enemies and pray for those who persecute you, **45** that you may be children of your Father in heaven. He causes his sun to rise on the evil and the good, and sends rain on the righteous and the unrighteous. **46** If you love those who love you, what reward will you get? Are not even the tax collectors doing that? **47** And if you greet only your own people, what are you doing more than others? Do not even pagans do that? **48** Be perfect, therefore, as your heavenly Father is perfect.

Note 14. The most notable variance in Tolstoy's paraphrase of Matthew 5:43-47 are his repeated precise mentions of the primarily applications of these commands to nation-states and relations between ones own countrymen and foreigners from other nations. Tolstoy exegesis of this text led him to conclude Jesus was not referring merely to interpersonal relationships but rather that enemy love was the command of Jesus for a nation as well.

Note 15. At this point comes the longest addition of Tolstoy to the text of the Sermon on the Mount. He included a review and summary of the five New Commandments in this and previous sections.

If they owe you money and do not return it, do not demand it.

And therefore: Do not judge or go to law, do not punish, and you yourself will not be judged or punished. Forgive everyone and you will be forgiven; but if you judge others they will judge you also. You cannot judge, for men are all blind and do not see the truth. How can you see a speck in your brother's eye when there is dust in your own? You must first get your own eye clear-but whose eyes are perfectly clear? Can a blind man lead the blind? They will both fall into the pit. And those who judge and punish are like blind men leading the blind. Those who judge, and condemn others to violent treatment, wounds, mutilation, or death, wish to correct them, but what can come of their teaching except that the pupils will learn to become just like their teacher? What then will they do when they have learnt the lesson? Only what their teacher does: violence and murder. And do not expect to find justice in the courts. To entrust one's love of justice to men's courts is like throwing precious pearls to swine: they will trample on them and will tear you to pieces.

And therefore the fourth commandment is: However men may wrong you, do not return evil, do not judge or go to law, do not sue, and do not punish.

In the former law it was said: Do good to men of your own nation and do harm to foreigners.
But I tell you: Love not only your own countrymen, but people of other nations also. Let others hate you, attack you, and wrong you, but speak well of them and do good to them. If you are attached only to your own countrymen, remember that all men are attached to their own countrymen, and wars result from that. But behave equally well to men of all nations, and you will be sons of the Father. All men are His children, so they are all brothers to you.

And so this is the fifth commandment: Treat foreigners as I have told you to treat one another. To the Father of all men there are no separate nations or separate kingdoms: all are brothers, all sons of one Father. Make no distinctions among people as to nations and kingdoms.

And so:

1. Do not be angry, but live at peace with all men.
2. Do not indulge yourself in sexual gratification.
3. Do not promise anything on oath to anyone.
4. Do not resist evil, do not judge and do not go to law.
5. Make no distinction of nationality, but love foreigners as your own people.

All these commandments are contained in one:
All that you wish men to do to you, do you to them.

> *Note 16. Here Tolstoy inserted a transitional passage to conclude his review of the five New Commandments and tie them to an important aspect in the coming section; that being rewards. However, it is noteworthy his conception of rewards is not of eternal rewards.*

<u>Do not fulfill these commandments for praise from men. If you do it for men, then from men you have your reward. But if you do it not for men, your reward is from your heavenly Father.</u>

Giving to the needy

6 'Be careful not to practise your righteousness in front of others to be seen by them. <u>If you do, you will have no reward from your Father in heaven.</u> 2 'So when you give to the needy, do not announce it with trumpets, as the hypocrites do in the synagogues and on the streets, to be honoured by others. <u>Truly I tell you, they have received their reward in full.</u> 3 But when you give to the needy, do not let your left hand know what your right hand is doing, 4 so that your giving may be in secret. Then your Father, who sees what is done in secret, <u>will reward you.</u>

So if you do good to others do not boast about it before men.

That is what the hypocrites do, to obtain praise. And they get what they seek.

But if you do good to men, do it so that no one sees it, and that your left hand should not know what your right hand does.
And your Father will see it and will <u>give you what you need.</u>

Prayer

5 'And when you pray, do not be like the hypocrites, for they love to pray standing in the <u>synagogues</u> and on the street corners to be seen by others. Truly I tell you, they have received their reward in full. 6 But when you pray, go into your room, close the door and pray to your Father, who is unseen. Then your Father, who sees what is done in secret<u>, will reward you.</u>
7 And when you pray, do not keep on babbling like pagans, <u>for they think they will be heard because of their many words</u>. 8 Do not be like them, for your Father knows what you need before you ask him.

And if you wish to pray, do not do it as the hypocrites do. They love to pray in the <u>churches</u> and in the sight of men. They do it for men's praise, and from men receive what they aim at.
But if you wish to pray, go where no one will see you, and pray to the Father <u>of your spirit</u>, and He will see <u>what is in your soul and will give you what your soul desires.</u> When you pray, do not wag your tongue as the hypocrites do.

Your Father knows what you need before you open your lips.

9 'This, then, is how you should pray:

'"Our Father in heaven,

hallowed be your <u>name</u>,
10 your kingdom come, your will be done,
on earth as it is in heaven.
11 Give us today our daily bread.
12 And forgive us our debts,
as we also have forgiven our debtors.
13 And lead us not into temptation,
but deliver us from the evil one."

Pray only thus:

Our Father, without beginning and without end, like the heavens!
May Thy <u>being</u> alone be holy.
May power be Thine alone, so that Thy will may be done, <u>without beginning and without end</u>, on earth.
Give me the food of life this present day.
Efface my former <u>mistakes</u> and wipe them out, as I efface and wipe out all the <u>mistakes</u> my brothers have made; that I may not fall into temptation, but be saved from evil.
<u>For the power and strength are Thine, and the decision is Thine.</u>

14 For if you forgive other people when they sin against you, your heavenly Father will also forgive you. 15 But if you do not forgive others their sins, your Father will not forgive your sins.

If you pray, free yourself above all from <u>malice</u> against anyone.
For if you do not forgive others their faults, your Father will not forgive you yours.

33 But seek first his kingdom and his righteousness, and all these things will be given to you as well.

Take care to be in the Father's will. Desire that which alone is important, and the rest will come of itself. Seek only to be in the will of the Father,

34 Therefore do not worry about tomorrow, for tomorrow will worry about itself. Each day has enough trouble of its own.

and do not trouble about the future, for when it comes its trouble will come too. There is enough evil in the present.

> Note 17. Tolstoy reordered this next section (7:1-6) and placed it following Matthew 5:42. It is re-inserted here for the sake of this parallel comparison.

Judging others

7 'Do not judge, or you too will be judged. 2 For in the same way as you judge others, you will be judged, and with the measure you use, it will be measured to you. 3 'Why do you look at the speck of sawdust in your brother's eye and pay no attention to the plank in your own eye? 4 How can you say to your brother, "Let me take the speck out of your eye," when all the time there is a plank in your own eye? 5 You hypocrite, first take the plank out of your own eye, and then you will see clearly to remove the speck from your brother's eye.

You cannot judge, for men are all blind and do not see the truth.

How can you see a speck in your brother's eye when there is dust in your own?

You must first get your own eye clear-but whose eyes are perfectly clear?

> Note 18. Here Tolstoy borrowed from Matthew 15:14 about the blind leading the blind and both falling into a pit.

Can a blind man lead the blind? They will both fall into the pit. And those who judge and punish are like blind men leading the blind.

> Note 19. In keeping with the discoveries made in his word studies on κρίνω, Tolstoy inserts commentary here that Jesus was expressly referring to juries and court tribunals and not to interpersonal relationships.

Those who judge, and condemn others to violent treatment, wounds, mutilation, or death, wish to correct them, but what can come of their teaching except that the pupils will learn to become just like their teacher? What then will they do when they have learnt the lesson? Only what their teacher does: violence and murder. And do not expect to find justice in the courts. To entrust one's love of justice to men's courts is like throwing precious pearls to swine: they will trample on them and will tear you to pieces.

6 'Do not give dogs what is sacred; do not throw your pearls to pigs. If you do, they may trample them under their feet, and turn and tear you to pieces.

Ask, seek, knock

7 'Ask and it will be given to you; seek and you will find; knock and the door will be opened to you. 8 For everyone who asks receives; the one who seeks finds; and to the one who knocks, the door will be opened. 9 'Which of you, if your son asks for bread, will give him a stone? 10 Or if he asks for a fish, will give him a snake? 11 If you, then, though you are evil, know how to give good gifts to your children, how much more

will your Father in heaven give good gifts to those who ask him!
12 So in everything, do to others what you would have them do to you, for this sums up the Law and the Prophets.

Ask and it shall be given you; seek and ye shall find; knock and it will be opened to you.

Where is there a father who would give his son a stone instead of bread, or a snake instead of a fish? Then why do you think if we wicked men can give our children what they need, that your Father in heaven will not give you what you truly need, if you ask Him? Ask, and the heavenly Father will give the spirit of life to them that ask Him.

> Note 20. The Golden Rule is omitted here but is relocated in vague form – "Treat foreigners as I have told you to treat one another" – in his summary of the fifth New Commandment above.

The narrow and wide gates

13 'Enter through the narrow gate. For wide is the gate and broad is the road that leads to destruction,

Narrow is the path to life, but enter by that narrow way. There is only one entry to life-a strait and

and many enter through it. **14** But small is the gate and narrow the road that leads to life, and only a few find it.

True and false prophets

15 'Watch out for false prophets. They come to you in sheep's clothing, but inwardly they are ferocious wolves. **16** By their fruit you will recognise them. Do people pick grapes from thorn-bushes, or figs from thistles? **17** Likewise, every good tree bears good fruit, but a bad tree bears bad fruit. **18** A good tree cannot bear bad fruit, and a bad tree cannot bear good fruit. **19** Every tree that does not bear good fruit is cut down and thrown into the fire. **20** Thus, by their fruit you will recognise them.

> *Note 21. Tolstoy gleaned verbiage from the related material in Luke's Sermon on the Plain (6:44-45) and inserted it here after this Sermon on the Mount section on how to recognize false teachers.*

True and false disciples

21 'Not everyone who says to me, "Lord, Lord," will enter the kingdom of heaven, but only the one who does the will of my Father who is in heaven. **22** Many will say to me on that day, "Lord, Lord, did we not prophesy in your name and in your name drive out demons and in your name perform many miracles?" **23** Then I will tell them plainly, "I never knew you. Away from me, you evildoers!"

The wise and foolish builders

24 'Therefore everyone who hears these words of mine and puts them into practice is like a <u>wise</u> man who built his house on the rock. **25** The rain came down, the streams rose, and the winds blew and beat against that house; yet it did not fall, because it had its foundation on the rock. **26** But everyone who hears these words of mine and does not put them into practice is like a foolish man who built his house on sand. **27** The rain came down, the streams rose, and the winds blew and beat against that house, and it fell with a great crash.'

28 When Jesus had finished saying these things, the crowds were amazed at his teaching, **29** because he taught as one who had authority, and not as their teachers of the law.

narrow one. Great and wide is the field around, but it leads to destruction. The narrow way alone leads to life, and few find it. <u>But do not be afraid, little flock! The Father has prepared the Kingdom for you.</u>

Only, beware of false prophets and teachers; they come to you in sheep's clothing, but inwardly are ravening wolves. By their fruits-by what comes from them-you will know them. From the burdock you do not gather grapes, nor apples from an aspen. A good tree bears good fruit and a bad tree bad fruit.

So you will know these men by the fruits of their teaching.
<u>A good man out of his good heart brings forth all that is good. But an evil man out of his evil heart brings forth all that is evil. For from the overflow of the heart the lips speak. And therefore if teachers tell you to do to others what would be bad for yourselves, if they teach violence, executions, and wars-then you may know that they are false teachers.</u>

For it is not those who say: 'Lord, Lord!' who will enter the kingdom of heaven, but those who fulfill the will of the heavenly Father. The false teachers will say: 'Lord, Lord! We taught <u>your doctrine</u>, and by your teaching drove out evil.

But I will disown them and say: 'No, I never recognized you and do not recognize you now, Go away from me; you do what is unlawful.'

He who hears these words of mine and acts on them is like a <u>reasonable</u> man who builds his house on a rock.

And his house will stand against all storms.
But he who hears these words of mine and does not act on them is like a foolish man who builds his house on the sand. When a storm comes his house will fall

and all in it will perish.

And the people were all astonished at this teaching, for <u>the teaching of Jesus was quite different</u> from that of the <u>Orthodox professors of the law</u>.

Fasting

16 'When you fast, do not look sombre as the hypocrites do, for they disfigure their faces to show others they are fasting. Truly I tell you, they have received their <u>reward</u> in full. **17** But when you fast, put oil on your head and wash your face, **18** so that it will not be obvious to others that you are fasting, but only to your Father, who is unseen; and your Father, who sees what is done in secret, will <u>reward</u> you.

If you fast, do so without any parade of it before others. The hypocrites fast that people should see it and praise them-and people do praise them, so they get what they wanted. But you should not do so; if you suffer want, go about with a cheerful face that men may not see,

but that your Father may see and give you <u>what you need</u>.

Treasures in heaven

19 'Do not store up for yourselves treasures on earth, where moths and vermin destroy, and where thieves break in and steal. **20** But store up for yourselves treasures in heaven, where moths and vermin do not destroy, and where thieves do not break in and steal. **21** For where your treasure is, there your heart will be also.
22 'The eye is the lamp of the body. If your eyes are healthy, your whole body will be full of light. **23** But if your eyes are unhealthy, your whole body will be full of darkness. If then the light within you is darkness, how great is that darkness!
24 'No one can serve two masters. Either you will hate the one and love the other, or you will be devoted to the one and despise the other. You cannot serve both God and Money.

Do not lay up store for yourself on earth. On earth maggots consume, and rust eats, and thieves steal: but lay up for yourselves heavenly riches. Heavenly riches are not consumed by maggots, nor eaten away by rust, nor do thieves steal them.
Where your riches are, there will your heart be also.

The light of the body is the eye, and the light of the soul is the heart. If
your eye is dim
your whole body will be in darkness. And if the light of your heart is dim your whole soul will be in darkness.
You cannot serve two masters at the same time. If you please the one you will offend the other. You cannot serve both God <u>and the flesh</u>. Either you will <u>work for the earthly life</u> or for God.

Do not worry

25 'Therefore I tell you, do not worry about your life, what you will eat or drink; or about your body, what you will wear. Is not life more than food, and the body more than clothes?
26 Look at the birds of the air; they do not sow or reap or store away in barns, and yet your heavenly Father feeds them. <u>Are you not much more valuable than they</u>?

Therefore do not be anxious about what you will eat or drink, or how you will be dressed. For the life is more wonderful than food and clothing and God has given you this.
Look on God's creatures, the birds. They do not sow or reap or gather in the harvest, yet God feeds them.<u> In God's sight man is not less than a bird. If God gave man life, He will be able to feed him too. And you yourselves know that you can do nothing of yourselves, however you may strive.</u>

27 Can any one of you by worrying add a single hour to your life? **28** 'And why do you worry about clothes? See how the flowers of the field grow. They do not labour or spin. **29** Yet I tell you that not even Solomon in all his splendour was dressed like one of these. **30** If that is how God clothes the grass of the field, which is here today and tomorrow is thrown into the fire, will he not much more clothe you – you of little faith?

You cannot lengthen your life by an hour. And why do you trouble about clothing?
The flowers of the field do no work and do not spin, but they are adorned as Solomon in all his luxury never was. And if
God has so adorned the grass which grows to-day, and to-morrow is cut down,
will He not clothe you?

31 So do not worry, saying, "What shall we eat?" or "What shall we drink?" or "What shall we wear?" **32** For the <u>pagans</u> run after all these things, and your heavenly Father knows that you need them.

Do not be afraid and do not worry; do not say that you must think of what you will eat and how you will be clothed. <u>All men</u> need these things and God knows that you need them. So do not trouble about the future. Live in the present day.

> *Note 22. The Sermon on the Mount traditionally ends with the parable of the wise and foolish builders. Tolstoy added to the traditional conclusion with references to how in Jesus Christ the prophecies of Isaiah 9 were fulfilled. Functionally he used Isaiah 9 in a similar way to how Luke in chapter four used Isaiah 61 to communicate the same about Christ.*

They taught a law that had to be obeyed, but Jesus taught that all men are free. And in Jesus Christ were fulfilled the prophecies of Isaiah: that a people living in darkness, in the shadow of death, saw the light of life. That he who brought this light of truth did no violence or harm to men, but was meek and gentle. To bring truth into the world he neither disputes nor shouts, nor is his voice raised, and he will not break a straw or put out the smallest light, and all the hope of men is in his teaching.

ENGLISH WORD COUNT: 2,586   **ENGLISH WORD COUNT: 3,012 (16.5% longer)**

Copyrights

NIV-UK
Holy Bible, New International Version® Anglicized, NIV® Copyright © 1979, 1984, 2011 by Biblica, Inc.® Used by permission. All rights reserved worldwide.

TGB
Tolstoy, Leo. *The Gospel in Brief* (1883). Translated by Aylmer Maude. Guildford, UK: Free Age Press (White Crow Books & White Crow Productions Ltd.), 2010.

Tolstoy, Leo. *The Complete Works of Count Tolstoy – Volume 15: The Four Gospels Harmonized and Translated, Vol II.*, Edited and Translated by Leo Wiener. Boston: Dana Estes & Company Publishers, 1904.

On pages 386-387 of the second volume of his *The Four Gospels Harmonized and Translated*, cited above, Tolstoy listed the *"Contents of Gospel in Brief"* to identify where the passages were taken from and reordered in his *Gospel in Brief*. The Sermon on the Mount is found in Chapter four of the TGB and his citations are as follows: "Chapter IV.: Matt. ix. 35-36; v. 1-2. Luke vi. 20-25, 20. Matt. v. 13-24; xix. 7, 9; v. 33-34, 37-41. Luke vi. 30, 37. Matt. vii. 1, 3. Luke vi. 39-40. Matt. vii. 6; v. 39, 43-44, 46; vii. 12; vi. 1-12. Mark xi. 25-26. Matt. vi. 16-34. Luke xi. 9. Matt. vii. 9-11, 13-14. Luke xii. 32. Matt. vii. 15-17. Luke vi. 45. Matt. vii. 21-27. Luke iv. 32. Matt. iv. 14, 16; xii. 19-21." This listing is generally accurate but not exhaustive. The few additional inferences from other Biblical passages are noted in the blue notation texts of this NIV-UK/TGB comparison.

12.2 Letter to Tsar Alexander III, 8–15 March 1881

Your Imperial Majesty,

I, an insignificant, unqualified, poor, weak man, am writing a letter to the Russian Emperor and advising him what he should do in the most complex, difficult circumstances which have ever existed. I feel how strange, improper and impudent this is, and yet I am writing. I think to myself: if you write this letter, it will be of no use, and it will either not be read or it will be read and found to be harmful, and you will be punished for it. This is all that can happen. And there will be nothing for you to regret about it. But if you don't write this letter and learn afterwards that no one had told the Tsar what you meant to say, and that the Tsar thought and said to himself afterwards when it was too late to change anything: if only someone had told me then! If this happens, you will for ever regret not having written what you thought. And therefore I am writing to Your Majesty to say what I think.

I am writing from the depths of the country and I know nothing for certain. What I know, I know from newspapers and from rumours, and I may therefore be writing unnecessary nonsense about something which may not be so at all; if so, pray forgive my presumption, and believe me when I say that I am not writing because I think highly of myself, but only because I am already so much to blame towards everybody that I am afraid of being even more to blame through not doing what I can and ought to do.

(I am not going to write in the tone in which people usually write letters to emperors – with flourishes of false and servile eloquence which only obscure both feeling and thought. I shall write simply as man to man. My genuine feeling of respect for you, as a man and as a Tsar, will be more evident without these adornments.)

Your father, the Russian Tsar, a kind old man who had accomplished much good and had always wished people well, was inhumanly mutilated and killed – not by personal enemies, but by enemies of the existing order of things. He was killed in the name of the supposed greater good of mankind. You have taken his place, and have before you those enemies who poisoned your father's life and caused his death. They are your enemies because you occupy your father's place, and for the sake of the illusory general good which they seek, they are bound to wish to kill you too.

In your soul there must be a feeling of vengeance towards these people as the murderers of your father, and a feeling of terror at the obligation which you have had to take upon yourself. It is impossible to imagine a more terrifying situation – more terrifying because it is impossible to imagine a stronger temptation to do evil. Enemies of the fatherland and of the people, despicable rascals, godless creatures who have ruined the tranquillity and the lives of millions of people who are your subjects – they are also your father's murderers. What else is there to do but to cleanse the Russian soil of this infection, and to crush them like vile serpents? This is not required of me by my personal feelings, nor even by a desire to avenge my father's death; it is required of me by my duty, it is expected of me by the whole of Russia.

The whole terrifying nature of your situation lies in this temptation. Whoever we may be – Tsars or shepherds – we are all men, enlightened by Christ's teaching.

I am not speaking of your obligations as a Tsar. Before the obligations of a Tsar there are the obligations of a man, and they must form the basis of the obligations of a Tsar and coincide with them.

God will not ask you to fulfil the obligations of a Tsar; he will not ask you to fulfil a Tsar's obligations, but he will ask you to fulfil human obligations. Your situation is terrifying and for that reason alone Christ's teaching is necessary in order to guide us in those fearful moments of temptation which fall to the lot of men. To your lot has fallen the most terrifying of temptations. But however terrible it is, Christ's teaching overcomes it, and all the snares of temptation which encompass you will vanish like dust for a man who fulfils the will of God. Matt. 5, 43: Ye have heard that it hath been said, Thou shalt love thy neighbour, and hate thine enemy. But I say unto you, Love your enemies . . . do good to them that hate you – That ye may be the children of your Father which is in heaven. Matt 5, 38: Ye have heard that it hath been said, An eye for an eye, and a tooth for a tooth: But I say unto you, That ye shall resist not evil. Matt. 18, 20: I say not unto thee, Until 7 times: but, Until 70 times 7. Do not hate your enemy, but do good to him, do not resist evil, do not cease to forgive. This is said to man and any man can fulfil it. And no considerations, whether the Tsar's or the state's, may break these commandments. Matt. 5, 19: Whosoever therefore shall break one of these least commandments, and shall teach men so, he shall be called the least in the kingdom of heaven; but whosoever shall do and teach *them*, the same shall be called great in the kingdom of heaven. Matt. 7, 24: Therefore, whosoever heareth these sayings of mine, and doeth them, I will liken him unto a wise man, which built his house upon a rock: And the rain descended, and the floods came, and the winds blew and beat upon that house; and it fell not: for it was founded upon a rock. And everyone hearing . . . [there is a gap in the text here].

I know how far the world in which we live is from those divine truths which are expressed in the teachings of Christ, and which live in our hearts – but the truth is the truth, and it lives in our hearts and calls forth our admiration and the desire to draw near to it. I know that I, an insignificant, worthless man whose temptations are 1,000 times weaker and those which have fallen on you, have given in not to truth and goodness, but to temptation, and that it is impertinent and mad of me, having done evil to man, to require of you a spiritual strength which has no precedent; to require that you, the Russian Tsar, under pressure from all who surround you, and being a loving son, should after a murder forgive the murderers and return them good for evil; but I cannot help wishing this, nor can I help seeing that your every step in the direction of forgiveness is a step towards good; or that every step in the direction of punishment is a step towards evil. And so, just as in quiet moments when I experience no temptation, I hope and wish with all my heart and soul to choose the path of love and goodness for myself, so I now wish it for you, and cannot help hoping that you will strive to be as perfect as your father is in heaven and to do the greatest thing in the world and overcome temptation; that you, the Tsar, will set the world the greatest example of the fulfilment of Christ's teaching – that you will return good for evil.

Return good for evil, resist not evil, forgive everyone.

This and this alone needs to be done; this is the will of God. Whether one has or does not have the strength to do this is another question. But we must wish for this alone, we must strive towards this alone, we must consider this alone to be good and must know that all considerations to the contrary are temptations and seductions – *all considerations to the contrary, all* are groundless, unsound and unenlightened.

But, apart from the fact that every man can and must be guided in his life by nothing other than these expressions of God's will the fulfilment of these divine commandments is at the same time the most sensible course of action for your own life and for the lives of your people. Truth and goodness are always truth and goodness on earth as well as in heaven. To forgive these terribly transgressors of human and divine laws and to return them to good for evil will seem to many people, at best, idealism or madness, and to many others an ill-intentioned act. These latter will say: 'What is needed is not to forgive, but to purge the corruption, to put out the fire.' But if one challenges those who say this to prove their opinions, both madness and ill-intent will be found to be on their side.

About 20 years ago a nest of people was formed – mostly young people – who hated the existing order of things and the government. These people imaged a different order of things, or even no order at all, and by every godless, inhuman means – by fires, robberies, murders – tried to destroy the existing system of society. For 20 years people have been fighting against this nest. Like a beehive, it constantly brings forth new workers and to this day this nest has not only not been destroyed, but has been growing bigger, and these people have gone so far as to commit the most terrible acts of cruelty and audacity which upset the course of the life of the state. People who tried to fight this plague with superficial, external remedies, employed two types of remedy: the one, that of directly cutting away what was diseased and rotten by harsh punishments; the other, that of allowing the disease to run its course without regulating it. The latter were the liberal measures intend to satisfy the discontented forces and to diminish pressure from the harmful ones. For people who look at the matter from a material point of view, there are no other ways – either firm measures of excision or liberal weakness. Wherever any people gathered to discuss what needed to be done in the present circumstances, and whoever they were – friends in a drawing room, members of a committee, meetings of representatives – if they talked about what should be done in order to excise the evil, they would never go beyond these two views on the subject: either excision – harshness, executions, exiles, the police, tightening of the censorship etc., or liberal indulgence – freedom, a moderate relaxation of penal measures, even representative government, a constitution, an assembly. People can say a great deal more that is new with regard to the details of the one or the other manner of action: many people from one and the same camp will be in disagreement over many things and will argue, but neither the one nor the other will abandon their positions – some will look to the remedy of the forcible excision of evil, others will look to the remedy of giving an outlet to, and not curbing the growing unrest. Some people will treat the illness by firm remedies against the illness itself; other people will not treat the illness, but will attempt to place the organism in the most advantageous and most hygienic conditions, in the hope that the illness will go of its own accord. It is very possible that both will say much that is new in detail, but they will not say anything new, because both systems have been tried and both have not only failed to cure the sick man, but have had no effect at all. The illness continues to the present day, gradually growing worse. And therefore I think that one should not without more ado call the application of God's will to political affairs a daydream or madness. If we regard the fulfilment of God's will, that holiest of holies, as a remedy against everyday, worldly evil, then we must not look on it disdainfully once it has become evident that all worldly wisdom has not helped and cannot help. They treated the sick man with strong remedies and then they stopped giving him strong remedies and allowed his organism to function freely, but neither system has helped: the sick man is getting sicker. There remains yet another remedy – a remedy about which the doctors are completely ignorant, a strange remedy. Why not try it? This remedy has one primary and inalienable advantage over the others and that is that the others have been used with no success while this one has never been used.

People have tried in the name of the state's need to secure the good of the masses, to restrict freedom, to exile and execute; they have tried in the name of the same need to secure the good of the masses, to give freedom, and the result was just the same. Why not try in the name of God only to fulfil His law, without thinking about either the state or the good of the masses. There can be no evil in the name of God and the fulfilling of His law.

The second advantage of a new remedy – also an indubitable one – is that the other two remedies were bad in themselves: the first consisted in force and executions (no matter how justified they may have appeared, everyone knew that they were evil) and the second consisted in a not entirely honest connivance at freedom. The government gave this freedom with one hand and held it back with the other. The application of both these remedies, however useful they may have seemed to the state, was not a good thing for those who applied them. But the new remedy is such that it is not only natural to man's soul, but it also brings supreme joy and happiness to man's soul. Forgiveness and the returning of good for evil are good in themselves. Therefore the application of the two old remedies must be repugnant to the Christian soul and must leave behind a feeling of regret, while forgiveness brings supreme joy to the one who practices it.

The third advantage which Christian forgiveness has over repression or the artificial direction of harmful elements relates to the present moment and has special importance. Your own condition and that of Russia now is like the condition of a sick man going through a crisis. One false step, or the application of an unnecessary or harmful remedy can destroy the sick man for ever. In the same way, a single action now in one sense or the other: whether avenging evil by cruel executions or convening representatives – may seal our future. Now in these 2 weeks when the criminals are being tried and sentenced, a step will be taken which will select one of 3 paths at the crossroads before us: the path of suppressing evil by evil, the path of liberal indulgence (both paths already tried and leading nowhere), or a new path – the path of Christian fulfilment of God's will by the Tsar, as a man.

Sire! As a result of some fatal, terrible misunderstandings a terrible hatred against your father flared up in the souls of the revolutionaries – a hatred which led them to commit a terrible murder. This hatred can be buried with him. The revolutionaries could – although unjustly – have blamed him for the death of dozens of their comrades. But you are pure in the eyes of all Russia and in their eyes. There is no blood on your hands. You are the innocent victim of your position. You are pure and innocent in your own eyes and in the eyes of God. But you stand at the crossroads. A few days more, and if those people triumph who say and think that Christian truths are only for conversation, and that in the life of the state blood must flow and death must reign, then you will pass for ever from that blessed state of purity and life in God, and will enter on the dark path of the needs of the state which justify everything, even the transgression of God's law for man.

If you do not forgive, but execute the criminals, you will only have uprooted 3 or 4 individuals from among hundreds and, evil begetting evil, 30 or 40 will grow up in place of these 3 or 4, and you will have lost for ever the moment which alone is worth more than a whole lifetime – the moment when you could have fulfilled God's will but did not do so; you will leave for ever the crossroads where you could have chosen good instead of evil, and will be forever entangled in evil deeds called the interests of the state. Matt. 5, 25.

Forgive; return good for evil, and from among hundreds of evil-doers, dozens will come over – not to you and not to them (that is not important) but will come over from the devil to God, and thousands, even millions of hearts will tremble with joy and emotion at the sight of this example of goodness from the throne at such a terrible moment for the son of a murdered father.

Sire! If you were to do this, to summon the people, to give them money and to send them away somewhere to America, and were to write a manifesto headed by the words: 'but I say unto you, love your enemies', – I don't know about others but I, a poor loyal subject, would be your dog and your slave. I would weep with emotion as I am weeping now, every time I heard your name. But what am I saying – 'I don't know about others?' I know that at these words goodness and love would flow across Russia in a torrent. The truths of Christ are alive in the hearts of man, and they only are alive, and we love others only in the name of these truths.

And you, the Tsar, would proclaim this truth, not in word but in deed. But perhaps this is only a dream and nothing can be done about it. Perhaps, even though it is true that (1) there is more probability of success with actions not yet tried than with actions which have been tried and proved useless, and (2) that such an action is undoubtedly good for the one who performs it, and (3) that you now stand at the crossroads and that this is the only moment when you can act according to God's law, and that if you allow this moment to escape you can never bring it back – perhaps all this is true, but it will be said that it is impossible. If you did this you would ruin the state.

But let us suppose that people are used to thinking that divine truths are truths only for the spiritual world and are not applicable to the earthly one; let us suppose that doctors say: we do not accept your remedy because, although it has not been tried and it is not harmful in itself and it is true that there is a crisis now, we know that it is no use and can do nothing except harm. They will say: Christian forgiveness and returning good for evil are all right for each man, but not for the state. The application of these truths to the government of the state will ruin the state.

Sire! This is a lie, a most evil, most perfidious lie, to say that the fulfilment of God's law will ruin people. If this is the law of God for man, then it is always and everywhere the law of God, and there can be no other law to express His will. And there are no more blasphemous words than to say: God's law is no good. In that case it is not God's law. But let us suppose that we forget that God's law is above all other laws and we forget that it is always applicable. Very well: God's law is not applicable and if we fulfil it, the evil will become even worse. If the criminals are forgiven, if they are all released from prison and from exile, the result will be an even worse evil. But why should this be? Who said so? How do you prove it? By your own cowardice. You have no other proof. Moreover, you have no right to reject anybody else's remedy because everyone knows that yours are no good.

People will say: if you release all the criminals, there will be a massacre, because when a few are released, there are minor disorders, so when a great many are released, there will be major disorders. They reason in this way and speak of revolutionaries as if they were bandits or a gang which had joined together and would be finished once they were caught. But it is not like that at all: it is not their number which is important, nor is it important to destroy or exile a few more of them, but it is important to destroy this ferment, and replace it by a different ferment. What are revolutionaries? They are people who hate the existing order of things, find it evil, and envisage the foundations of a future, better order of things. One cannot fight them by killing and destroying them. It is not their number which is important but their ideas. To fight against them one must fight spiritually. Their ideal is a general sufficiency, equality, and freedom. To fight against them, one must oppose their ideal with another ideal which will be superior to, and will include their ideal. The French, the English, and the Germans are fighting them now, and also without success.

There is only one ideal which can be opposed to them. It is the one from which they have themselves proceeded, without understanding it and blaspheming it, one which includes their ideal – the ideal of love, forgiveness and the returning of good for evil. Only one word of forgiveness and Christian love, spoken and fulfilled from the height of the throne, and the path of Christian rule which is there for you to tread, can destroy the evil gnawing away at Russia.

As wax before fire, every revolutionary struggle will melt away before the Tsar-man who fulfils the law of Christ.

12.2.1 Tolstoy's handwriting: Draft of 1881 Letter to Tsar Alexander III[2]

[2]. Polnoe sobranie sochineniia (Gosudarstvennoe izdatel'stvo khudozhestvennoi literatury, 1934) T. 63.

12.3 First English Translation of Tolstoy's Foreword to Chelčický's *Net of Faith*

Preface by Leo Tolstoy, Translated for Steve Hickey by Olga Sevastyanova

Written over 450 years ago by an unlearned man named Petr, from the town Chelčice, exists a book, which is almost completely unknown. In the book, titled "The Net of Faith" we not only find a simple, clear, powerful and truthful exposure of the terrible lies in which people lived, and still continue to live, maintaining beliefs most distant from that of true/unfeigned Christianity, and imagining that they confess true Christian teachings; in this book we also find clear guidance towards the one and only good way of life, that was revealed to Man by Christ.

Although any life truth that must serve as regulation for Man's actions/behaviour is uncovered swiftly in the minds of saints, in that of the majority is uncovered slowly, hesitantly, unnoticeably, in bursts, sometimes as if almost fully concealed, sometimes reappearing triggered by the new forces similar to the labours of birth. This is still happening in Christianity now, as it did then. Christian doctrine became initially adopted by a relatively small number of simple, lower class, unwealthy people in its full significance. However, as it spread throughout larger groups of people, including people of great status and wealth, the truth became more and more distorted, and by the establishment of the church (stated by Chelčický to be from the time of Constantine), was distorted to such a great extent, that its main, true meaning/significance in life was entirely concealed from the people, and replaced by extraneous forms that had become estranged to the essence of Christianity.

Truth, however, that comes into the minds of men, cannot be silenced. Outwith the church, still remained loyal people who understood and upheld true Christian teachings, what the churchmen called heresies. And so occurred again and again newer pulls towards its rebirth. And every time greater and greater numbers of people became participants in the Christian truth in its true sense.

This was the type of loyal believer and reviver that Chelčický was to the Christian doctrine. His main publishing, "The Net of Faith" serves as an indication to what the Christian community should be in regard to its original founders' teachings, and what it had become through its distortion.

This is what is said to the preface of the book:

> This book, bearing the title "The Net of Faith," written by Petr from Chelčice, who lived in the times of Master Rokizana, who was well known to him and with whom he often talked. He wrote many useful books on the Lord's Laws for the church, in the battle with the antichrist and his delusions/influences, and if the world has still not seen this book, then the reason for this must be the church clergy, which has not ceased to present Petr Chelčický's books as misguided and blasphemous to the world, and all because it condemns his way of life. Considering this, many people from all social classes (estates) readily read not only this publication, but also many of Chelčický's others, despite him being a layman and uneducated in Latin, as although he was not a master in the seven arts, he was truthfully an implementer of the eight beatitudes and all of the Lord's commandments, and was in this sense a real Czech doctor. In this book, Chelčický touches on all classes (estates): beginning with the emperors, then kings, princes, pans, knights, townsfolk, labourers, and ending in rural dwellers; but, Chelčický especially draws attention to the clergy: the popes, cardinals, bishops and archbishops, abbots, and all institutional monks, deacons, rectors and vicars. The first half of the book outlines how and by what means the terrible falsehoods (promiscuity) had found their way into the holy church, and proves that only by the removal of all human fabrications, can it ascend to its truthful origin – Jesus Christ; the second half of the book discusses the

emergence and popularisation of various classes (estates) within the church, that only hinder the true knowledge of Christ, for they are full of a prideful spirit, and forcefully conflict with Christ's meekness and humility."

And indeed, Chelčický, as in this book as well as in his other works, does not debate, like his predecessor Hus, and like Luther, Melanchthon, Calvin, that lived and acted after him, Papal ecclesial institutions and dogmas, he only shows that the lives of people considering themselves Christians, are not in themselves Christian, that a Christian man cannot use power, cannot own land or slaves, live in splendour, or live a dissolute life, cannot execute, and most importantly, cannot kill or make war.

Chelčický does not argue whether or not salvation can be achieved through actions or faith, he does not defend predetermination or argue about dogmas; he requires only for the decrees of the church to be accessible to the understanding of the people. He does not reject those decrees, but speaks about the lives of Christians, showing that the lives of world rulers, armies, courts and the nobility are incompatible with that of a Christian (he even believed that the lives of city dwellers were incompatible with Christianity). Most importantly, he shows that executions and wars are inconceivable to a Christian. He shows that the interconnection between Christianity and the state, which has since occurred, has led to the demise and destruction of Christianity. On the contrary, what should happen is the opposite: Christianity combining with the state, must destroy the state. And so he proves that it is possible for the absence of state power to not only maintain order in people's lives, but also destroy the chaos and evil from which people suffer.

This has been the reason for the obscurity of the book and the actions of Chelčický: in the field of Christianity they occupy the same position that Christianity occupies in all of mankind. The book is too far ahead of its time – the time of its fruitfulness has not yet come. The destruction of the papal authority, the indulgences, and many other things created by Luther could be handled by the modern men, however, the words of Chelčický could not be accepted, not because they were unclear or unjust, – on the contrary, all he said was too clear and too just – but because what he said was too far ahead of its time.

Chelčický's demands could not even be accepted today, and thus even less so in his time. To refute Chelčický's statements was impossible; at least then people were honest enough to consider it impossible to deny that Christ taught the things he taught i.e. that people love not only those who love them, but also their enemies, that they tolerated grievances, repaid evil with kindness, and considered all men brothers; and that such teachings were incompatible with the pre-existing structure of life. And so the question inevitably arose: what to withhold - Christianity or the established societal structure? If Christianity was to be withheld, then it is clear that the powerful must renounce their power, the wealthy renounce their wealth, the middle class to renounce to secure themselves by violence, the poor and powerless to renounce their obeisance to what contradicts Christian law – and in a state all societal actions contradict Christian law – thus exposing themselves to persecution. And this is frightening.

If the existing system were to be withheld, it means that Christianity must be renounced. And this is also frightening. What else was there left to do? One thing: forget what Christ, Chelčický and the conscience had said; and not think, not speak of it.

This has also been the reason for the obscurity of Chelčický's book – the book was silenced, it had been forgotten. If a dozen scientists know about it, then they look at it only as a historical, literary record.

Nonetheless, the spiritual wealth of mankind never perishes, but only ripen, like young fruit. And the longer they wait for their time, the more valuable they become. The same applies to Chelčický and his book.

His book was only recently printed for the first time by the Russian Academy of Sciences, and nobody – naturally – not only did not read, but did not hear of it, like with all else that is costly and is with great importance printed in the Academy's publications. Hundreds of thousands of copies of dozens of editions are printed of Nietzsche, Zola and Verlaine. Everyone is familiar with the smallest of details of these people's lives. However, the works of Chelčický have not yet to this day been printed, even in the Czech Republic and Germany, not to mention England and France.

And almost nothing is known about Chelčický himself. It is believed that he was born around 1390 and died around 1450. Some think he was a nobleman, others - that he was a peasant, a shoemaker or a farmer. I believe he was a farmer.

I come to conclude that he was a farmer, a peasant (muzhik), firstly from his strong, simple and clear writing style; secondly from the book's wisdom, as the author always knows what is important and what is less important, always putting what is important first; thirdly from the naivety and heart he sometimes talks simply, coarsely, forcefully, and with bitter ridicule about things that are clearly heavy on his heart.

"The net of faith" is an old book in time, but in meaning and content it is the newest book – so new that the people of our time are still far from prepared for the true enlightenment allowing its comprehension. But its time will come, and is drawing nearer.

After all, Christianity is not a human invention, and so it is not one of the temporary forms in which human societies are formed, but is truth, if not appearing on the stone tablets on Mount Sinai, is written even harder than in stone – in the hearts of all men, and once it is uttered, it cannot be scratched from their minds. This truth has waited and will still wait, but this will only make it more evident and only more urgently require its fulfilment.

One cannot remove the idea from Christianity that Christians, as Chelčický says, should "not be participants in world wisdom," not be officials, judges, or soldiers, but bear all injustice humbly, patiently, without repaying evil for evil, and without complaining or seeking revenge. No matter how they tried, and continue to try and dispel these truths, truths they remain, and even through the sophisms invented over the centuries in an attempt to conceal them, they continue to directly and uninhibitedly capture people's hearts.

But how can it be? Until now, the dilemma had been solved by silencing Christianity, or rudely lying about it to uphold the state. But it is time for the people to try the different, alternative decision, by giving up the state and giving themselves to Christianity. This decision would be considerably more wise, as the states' corrupt systems have not only withheld their promised benefits, but continue to increase the corruption people must bear more and more, which causes the people to lose faith in them.

It is to this new and wise solution Chelčický's wise, heartfelt and necessary book contributes.

A few of the passages from this book are placed in the weekly readings "The Circle of Reading."

—Leo Tolstoy

12.4 Depictions of Tolstoyan Christianity in Art

12.4.1 *What Is Truth*, Nikolay Ge

Ge's *What Is Truth* is a piece that was censored in Russia because it depicted Christ's confrontation with Government. Tolstoy's favourite artist and friend Nikolay Ge captured the facedown of the Doctrine of Jesus with the Doctrine of State. Tolstoy loved Ge's work and viewed it as a "new epoch in Christian art" and a long overdue shift away from depictions of "saints, the Madonna, and Christ as God."

> Then Ge took the most simple motif . . . Christ and his teaching in conflict with the teaching of the world. . . . Christ, after being led, tormented, beaten and dragged from one jail to the other and from one official to another, is brought before the governor, a very kindly fellow who is not concerned for Christ or the Jews, still less with any truth explained to him, an acquaintance of all the scholars and philosophers of Rome, by this ragamuffin; his only concern is not to be at fault in the eyes of a superior official. Christ sees before him a deluded man bloated with fat, but he decided not to spurn him just because of his appearance, and so begins to express to him the essence of his teaching. But the governor is not concerned with this. He says, What is truth? and goes away. And Christ looks sorrowfully at this impenetrable man.[3]

---

3. Christian, *Tolstoy's Letters: Volume II*. From Letter #352, June 30, 1890, "To P.M. Tretyakov," 460, 462, 467, 508.

12.4.2 *Tolstoy in Hell*, Fresco, 1883

In the lower tier at the far right of this fresco (originally in the church at the village of Tazovo in the Kursk Province), Tolstoy is shown embraced by Satan who received him in hell while the holy prelates and apostles of Orthodoxy gave blessing to the act. The Fresco was removed at Lenin's special order during the Bolshevik crusade against religion in the early years of the Soviet regime. The fresco was later transferred to the Museum for the History of Religion and Atheism of the Soviet Union in Moscow.

12.4.3 *Christ Embracing Tolstoy*, by Jan Styka

This painting, also known as the "Excommunicated" portrays Tolstoy not as a heretic and false teacher who renounced Jesus as Lord and Christ, but as a Christian who bowed his head before the Lord as a sign of humility.

> That I have renounced the Church which calls itself Orthodox is quite correct. But I have renounced it not because I have revolted against the Lord; but on the contrary, only because I desire to serve him with all the powers of my soul. . . . I began by loving my Orthodox faith more than my peace; then I loved Christianity more than my Church; and now I love truth more than anything in the world. And until now the truth coincides for me with Christianity was I understand it and I profess this Christianity, and in that measure in which I do profess it I peacefully and joyously live and peacefully and joyously am approaching death.[4]

4. Leo Tolstoy, April 4, 1901 (From the "Response to the definition of the Synod of February 20-22 and the letters I received on this occasion").

12.4.4 Ilya Glazunov's *Eternal Russia*

On my June 2017 research excursion to the land of Tolstoy, friends at Yasnaya Polyana took me to see a painting on a wall (measuring 3 x 6 meters!) called *Eternal Russia* by the artist Ilya Glazunov. Glazunov painted it in 1988 for the millennial celebrations of Russia to visually show in one panorama the entire thousand year history of Russia. Note their most celebrated literary giant but then excommunicated prophet Tolstoy in the lower right with the words "non-resistance" on his chest pointing the nation toward the divine way (Sermon on the Mount, the Doctrine of Jesus) which leads beyond the abode of the dead.[5]

---

5. Also on the placard situated on Tolstoy's chest is the unfortunate inclusion of a masonic symbol which only perpetuates the myth in Russia that Tolstoy was any sort of Freemason. The myth likely stems from his famous leading character in War and Peace who, for a time, tried to take Freemasonry seriously. Tolstoy was not a Freemason.

12.4.5 *Do Not Repay Evil with Evil*: Petr Chelčický at Vodňany by Alfons Mucha (1918)[6]

Depicting a scene from the Hussite Wars in 1420, artist Alfons Muche sought to capture the aftermath of the invasion of the Tabor army having plundered and set fire to the town of Vodňany. Residents fled to the nearby village of Chelčice, home to Petr Chelčický, or Petr of Chelčice. Amidst the wounded and dead, Petr Chelčický grabbed hold of a man's hand raised to vow a bloody revenge. The painting shows Chelčický trying to dissuade him from taking vengeance into their own hands and responding to violence with more violence. Chelčický also renounced Tabor aggressions, likened Jan Žižka to the devil, but wrote decisively against retaliation.

6. Source: http://www.kalab.nl/en/p/mucha/12.html

12.5 Matthew 5:11 and the Tolstoy Anathema Iron

> Blessed are you when they revile and persecute you,
> and say all kinds of evil against you falsely for My sake.
>
> —MATTHEW 5:11

After Tolstoy's excommunication he was, of course, considered an anathema and household irons bearing his depiction were produced in great numbers.[7] The story behind its production is not clear or certain, though it is claimed a priest name Iliodor complained to Tsar Nicolas II of Tolstoy's heresies and Rasputin obtained the correspondence and replied instead:

> "[F]orget about this Iliodor, if anything happens to us people will never remember us, but they will remember him." But Iliodor did not want to listen. He took a portrait of Leo Tolstoy and put it on altar and made believers spit on it. When Rasputin heard about this, he sent another letter and condemned the priest and soon he died. Tolstoy was critical of everything. After his death the royalty punished him. Knowing the story with Iliodor, they started the production of irons.[8]

The Tolstoy Anathema Iron, as I have named it, is a large iron with a top pipe inlet for burning coal. On the foot of the iron is a closable clean out vent which bears the face of Tolstoy. The purpose of the design was twofold, to symbolically place the heretic in the fire (of hell) against the hot coals, and so each day the women of Russia could spit on his face when they check if the iron was hot enough to use.

---

7. Today only a few remain as private possessions and in museums such as the Vereysky Local History Museum and the Museum Etnomir. See https://ethnomir.ru/posetitelyam/muzei/muzey-utyugov/. Last accessed March 15, 2018.

8. Email to Steve Hickey from Маргарита Бабакина, July 27, 2017.

~ 13.0 ~

Bibliography

UNIVERSITIES THAT TEACH RUSSIAN literature and the literature of Tolstoy abound and continue to raise up Tolstoyan scholars and much scholarship. Consequently, bibliographies relating to the literary Tolstoy are extensive and available with ease. Dozens and dozens of articles and books have been written in each decade since his death, and even before. Anthony Briggs, the preeminent Russian scholar, Tolstoy translator, and now Professor Emeritus Professor of Russian Language and Literature at Birmingham University, remarked that the field by now is so saturated in commentary that any new work today in Tolstoy studies can only amount to small nuances.[1] Yet he is referring only to First Tolstoy literature, he himself having not even read *The Kingdom of God Is within You*.[2] Admittedly feeling ill-qualified and out of his areas of expertise to comment, he and other experts in the Tolstoyan literary community have left Tolstoy's departure into religious fanaticism well enough alone deeming it the task of theological scholars to take notice if any of it were indeed important.

Part of this project has been to draw together, draw in, and draw from the relatively scant sources that relate to and treat what I have come to see as the neglected and under-appreciated religious Tolstoy of the Second Tolstoy

---

1. Jones, *New Essays on Tolstoy*, 109, "Most of Tolstoy's better known works have by now settled down to enjoy an acknowledged reputation. Their merits and demerits have been established so that new studies tend to add detail to what has gone before, or make slight changes in emphasis, rather than produce bold revelations. Any casual assessment of Tolstoyan scholarship would conclude that the pioneering work was out of the way, at least as far as his major works are concerned."

2. "I do not know much about The K of G is W Y, never having read it." Personal correspondence of Steve Hickey with Dr. Briggs, February 16, 2016.

period. Therefore what is captured in this bibliography does go beyond a reciting of the sources already cited in the previous chapters for their direct contribution to this project. Whether cited or not, it has been this wider reading which incalculably contributed to the view of the religious Tolstoy expressed and argued in this project.

In this bibliography, I purposely break from expected norms of style and form by occasionally indenting and listing some chapter titles in Tolstoy books, compilations and secondary sources. His moral teachings permeated a variety of his short stories and other literature and the hope is to provide a basic indexing here of where that material can be found. What follows is what would have been most helpful to me in the early days of my study of Tolstoy. Second Tolstoy related articles and spread widely over many publications and many years they can be hard to locate, especially since sets of his collected works are increasingly hard to come by. It is hoped that by calling attention to them in this way it will make them easier for interested persons to locate and obtain. It is hoped this bibliography will serve well to aid the work of others toward a greater treatment of the Second Tolstoy which again, the First Tolstoy has already long been afforded in both academic and popular settings.

13.1 Primary Source Material[3]

13.1.1 Tolstoy Non-fiction Work

Chelcicky, Petr. *Siet Viery* (Siet Viery is Czeck for *Net of Faith*); s českago izložil J. S. Annenkov, s predisloviem L. N. Tolstogo i s vvedeniem I. V. Jagič (Translated

---

3. Notes on the choice and availability of translations and editions. Tolstoy's decision to release all copyrights on his later and mainly religious writings perhaps contributed to the variety of editions that are still readily available today and also to the version uncertainty, confusion, and oft-poor quality and layout of publications as well. The original *Collected Works of Count Tolstoy* were half in Russian, edited and with translations by Leo Wiener (Boston: Dana Estes & Company, 1904). Though credit is formally given to Weiner for his early work on the *Collected Works (1904)*, Anthony Briggs in his *Brief Life: Leo Tolstoy* clarifies: "One of the greatest achievements in the publishing world was accomplished in the twentieth century by a team of Soviet scholars working for three decades on the *Complete Works* of Leo Nikolaevich Tolstoy (1928–58), which ran to ninety large volumes" (p. 7). Wiener also translated *The Kingdom of God is With You* (CW 1905, 1932), as did Aline P. Delano (the authorised translation, 1894) and Constance Garnett (1894). There is also a twenty-one volume *Collected Works of Count Tolstoy* all in English. Neither of these collected works are easily found today; however, in December 2014 the ninety-volume collection was made available for sale online, readable through Kindle; and, it is all available in Russian for free: http://tolstoy.ru—a "mammoth digital corpus—which includes novels, diaries, letters, religious tracts, philosophical treatises, travelogues, and the original *Complete Collected Works*," (the

from the Czeck by J. S. Annenkov, with an introduction by L. N. Tolstoy and a foreword by I. V. Jagič. Moscow: Posrednik, 1907.

Christian, R. F., ed. and trans. *Tolstoy's Diaries: Volume I, 1847–1894*. New York: Scribner, 1985.

———. *Tolstoy's Diaries: Volume II, 1895–1910*. New York: Scribner, 1985.

———. *Tolstoy's Letters: Volume I, 1828–1879*. Selected, edited, and translated by R. F. Christian. London: University of London Press, 1978.

———. *Tolstoy's Letters: Volume II, 1880–1910*. Selected, edited, and translated by R. F. Christian. London: University of London Press, 1978.

Tolstoy, Leo. *A Calendar of Readings: Daily Thoughts to Nourish the Soul—Written and Selected from the World's Sacred Texts by Leo Tolstoy* (1904). Introduction, translation, and compilation by Peter Sekirin. New York: Scribner, 1997.

———. *The Christian Teaching*. Translated by V. Tchertkoff. New York: Stokes, 1897.

———. *A Confession* (1882) [includes: *What Is Religion, and What Does Its Essence Consist Of?* (1902)]. Translated by Anthony Briggs. London: Hesperus, 2010.

———. *A Confession and Other Religious Writings* [*What Is Religion and of What Does Its Essence Consist?* (1902); *Religion and Morality* (1893); *The Law of Love and the Law of Violence* (1908)]. Translated by Jane Kentish. London: Penguin, 1987.

———. *Christianity and Patriotism*. Translated by Leo Wiener. Cabin John, MD: Wildside, 2013.

English version of that site is still under construction as of July 7, 2016). A new one-hundred-plus volume of collected works is being prepared in Russia at this time. The editions of Tolstoy's religious writings used for this monograph are those published by *Free Age Press, the Centenary Editions*. *Free Age Press* is the original Tolstoy publishing house in Britain founded by his disciple and friend Vladimir Chertkov. Two recent articles have been written about the still-ongoing Tolstoy translation wars. David Redneck of *The New Yorker* wrote "The Translation Wars." Also, notable Tolstoyan translator Rosamund Bartlett wrote "Tolstoy Translated." Opinions are strong when it comes to these translation issues and anonymous chat-room comments of Tolstoy enthusiasts such as the following are interesting; "Garnett is the old standard. The usual line is stay away from Constance Garnett — she bowdlerized, made mistakes, etc. Joseph Brodsky sniped that the 'reason English-speaking readers can barely tell the difference between Tolstoy and Dostoevsky is that they aren't reading the prose of either one. They're reading Constance Garnett.' She worked so fast that when she came across an awkward passage she would leave it out. She made mistakes. But her stylish prose, which made the Russian writers so accessible, and seemingly so close to the English sensibility, ensured that her translations would remain for many years the authoritative standard of how these writers ought to sound and feel. Louise and Aylmer Maude are the best." In personal correspondence during the research for this monograph, Anthony Briggs, pre-eminent Russian scholar and acclaimed Tolstoy translator wrote: "First, don't believe those people who denigrate Constance Garnett, a valiant pioneer in translating Russ Lit who got better as she went along. I do not believe you will be seriously misled by her translation of this work. If she made any mistakes they would be of a detailed character that would not affect T's overall message. . . . Do not worry about getting the very best version. T wrote at such length that any version of the minor works is likely to be nearly as good as any of its successors. And I am not aware that [*The Kingdom of God Is within You*] has been retranslated at all during the last century." (Dr. Briggs personal note to Steve Hickey, February 16, 2016). See also "Appendix I - English Translations of Tolstoy" in Maude, *The Life of Tolstoy*, 1:456–67.

———. *Essays from Tula*. With an Introduction by Nicolas Berdyaev. London: Sheppard, 1948.
  Bethink Yourselves (May, 1914)
  The Slavery of Our Times (July, 1900)
  An Appeal to Social Reformers (July, 1900)
  True Criticism (Tolstoy's Preface to the Russian edition of the German Novel *Der Butnerbauer* by Von Polenz; July, 1901)
  I Cannot Be Silent: An Indictment of the Russian Government (May, 1908)
  Thou Shalt Kill No One (August, 1907)
  A Letter on the Peace Conference (1899)
  The End of the Age: An Essay on the Approaching Revolution
  Love One Another

———. "The First Step." Introduction written by Tolstoy for Howard Williams's 1892 book, *The Ethics of Diet: A Catena of Authorities Deprecatory of the Practice of Flesh-Eating*. Nordestedt: Hansebooks, 2018.

———. *The Gospel in Brief*. 1883. Translated by Aylmer Maude. Guildford, UK: Free Age, 2010.

———. *The Gospel in Tolstoy: Selections from His Short Stories, Spiritual Writings, and Novels*. Edited by Miriam LeBlanc. New York: Plough, 2015.
  Finding God
    The Three Hermits
    Levin Looks for Miracles (from *Anna Karenina*)
    The Death of Ivan Ilyich (a selection)
    My Way to Faith (from *Confession*)
  Love of Neighbour
    Three Questions
    Where Love Is, God Is
    Master and Man (a selection)
    What Men Live By
  Peace and NonViolence
    The Empty Drum
    Nikolai Meets the Enemy (from *War and Peace*)
    How to Resist Evil (from *The Kingdom of God Is within You*)
    What Pierre Learned from Platon the Peasant (from *War and Peace*)
  Forgiveness
    God Sees the Truth, But Waits
    A Spark Neglected Burns the House
    Nekhlyudov Seeks Redemption (from *Resurrection*)
    The Healing of Prince Andrei (from *War and Peace*)
    The Repentant Sinner
  Living Simply
    A Grain as Big as a Hen's Egg
    Ivan the Fool
    What Is the Meaning of Life (from *The Kingdom of God Is within You*)
  The Way of the Kingdom
    A Talk among Leisured People
    Walk in the Light While There Is Light

———. *Government Is Violence: Essays on Anarchism and Pacifism*. Edited and introduced by David Stephens. London: Phoenix, 1990.
  The Non-Violent Anarchism of Leo Tolstoy by David Stephens
  The End of the Age
  An Appeal to Social Reformers
  On Anarchy
  Thou Shalt Not Kill
  Patriotism and Government
  The Kingdom of God Is within You (selections)
  The Slavery of Our Time
  On Socialism: State and Christian
———. *Great Short Works of Leo Tolstoy*. Introduction by John Bayley. New York: Harper & Row, 1967.
———. *The Kingdom of God Is within You*. 1893. Authorised Translation from the original Russian manuscript by Aline P. Delano. Guildford, UK: Free Age, 2010.
———. *The Law of Love and The Law of Violence*. 1908. Translated by Mary Koutouzow Tolstoy, with a Foreword by Baroness Budberg. New York: Holt, Rinehart and Winston, 1970.
———. "Letter to a Hindu: The Subjection of India—Its Cause and Cure." In *The Works of Leo Tolstoy, Volume 21*, translated by Aylmer Maude, 427–28. Tolstoy Centenary Edition. Oxford: Oxford University Press, 1934.
———. *My Religion—What I Believe*. 1884. Translated by Huntington Smith. Guildford, UK: Free Age, 2009.
———. *On Life*. Translated by Mabel and Agnes Cook, based on the French version of the Countess Tolstoy and M. M. Tastevin, edited by A. C. Fifield. London: Free Age, 1883.
———. *The Physiology of War; Napoleon and the Russian Campaign*. Translated from the 3rd French edition by Huntington Smith. New York: Crowell & Co., 1888.
———. "Preface." In *Net of Faith*, privately translated by Olga Sevastyanova for Steve Hickey. 2017. (Included in the appendices subsection 12.3.)
———. "Thoughts and Aphorisms." In *The Complete Works of Count Tolstoy*, edited and translated by Leo Wiener, 19:196–97. London: Howell, 1905.
———. *Tolstoy as Teacher: Leo Tolstoy's Writings on Education*. Edited by Bob Blaisdell, translated by Christopher Edgar. New York: Teachers & Writers Collaborative, 2000.
———. *Tolstoy on Education*. Introduction by Reginald D. Archambault. Chicago: Chicago University Press, 1967.
———. "To Women." http://www.online-literature.com/tolstoy/2740/.
———. *What I Owe to Garrison*. (A letter to V. Tchertkoff later became the preface of *A Short Biography of William Lloyd Garrison*, by V. Tchertkoff and F. Holah.) London: Free Age, 1906.
———. *What Is Religion? And Other Writings*. 1902. Translated by V. Tchertkoff and A. C. Fifield. Guildford, UK: Free Age, 2010.
———. *The Works of Leo Tolstoy, Volumes 1–21*. Tolstoy Centenary Edition. Translated by Aylmer Maude. Oxford: Oxford University Press, 1934.[4]

4. *Polnoe sobrnie sochineny* (PSS) is the name of the ninety-volume *Tolstoy Works* published in Moscow under the editorship of V. G. Chertkov (Gosizdat) 1928–1958. Additionally, a twenty-one-volume *Tolstoy Centenary Edition* (London, 1928–1937)

———. *Writings on Civil Disobedience and Nonviolence.* Introduction by David H. Albert, foreword by George Zabelka. Philadelphia: New Society, 1987.
The Beginning of the End
Two Wars
"*Notes for Officers*"
"*Notes for Soldiers*"
On Patriotism
Carthago Delenda Est
Patriotism or Peace?
Letter on the Peace Conference
Letter to a Non-Commissioned Officer
The Beginning of the End
Letter to Dr. Eugen Heinrich Schmitt
A Reply to Criticisms
Another Reply to Critics
"*Thou Shall Not Kill*"
Help!
The Emigration of the Dukhobors (1899)
Nobel's Request
Letter to Ernest Howard Crosby
Nikolai Palkin
Church and State
Postscripts to the "Life and Death of Drozhin"
On the Negro-Question
The Inevitable Revolution

was translated by Louise and Aylmer Maude and published by Oxford University Press. This, along with *The Life of Tolstoy*, and in the *World's Classics* series (London, 1906–1940) became available in a sixteen-volume set. Also in English is the twenty-four-volume *Complete Works of Count Tolstoy* translated and edited by Leo Wiener, London (Dent), 1904–1905. This edition includes a bibliography of Tolstoy works and articles in French, German and English. The twenty-four volumes are designated as such: Vol 1: *Childhood, Boyhood, Youth; The Incursion*; Vol 2: *A Landed Proprietor; The Cossacks; Sevastopol*; Vol 3: *A Moscow Acquaintance; The Snow-storm; Domestic Happiness; Miscellanies*; Vol 4: *Pedagogical Articles; Linen-measurer*; Vol 5–8: *War and Peace*; Vol 9–11: *Anna Karénin*; Vol 12: *Fables for Children; Stories for Children; Natural Science Stories; Popular Education; Decembrist; Moral Tales*; Vol 13: *My Confession; Critique of Dogmatic Theology*; Vol 14–15: *The Four Gospels Harmonized and Translated*; Vol 16: *My Religion; On Life; Thoughts on God; On the Meaning of Life*; Vol 17: *What Shall We Do Then? On the Moscow Census; Collected Articles*; Vol 19: *Walk in the Light while Ye Have Light; Thoughts and Aphorisims; Letters; Miscellanies*; Vol 20: *The Kingdom of God Is within You; Christianity and Patriotism; Miscellanies*; Vol 21: *Resurrection*, Vol 1; Vol 22: *Resurrection*, Vol 2; *What is Art? The Christian Teaching*; Vol 23: *Miscellaneous Letters and Essays*; Vol 24: *Latest Works; Life; General index; Bibliography*.

13.1.2 Related Tolstoy Fiction

Tolstoy, Leo. *Anna Karenina* (1874–76). Translated by Rosemary Edmonds. Middlesex: Penguin, 1954.
———. *Childhood, Boyhood, Youth*. (Trilogy originally published separately: 1852–57.) Translated by Rosemary Edmonds. Middlesex: Penguin, 1964.
———. *The Death of Ivan Ilyich and Other Stories*. 1882. Translated by Anthony Briggs. London: Penguin, 2008.
———. "Father Sergius." In *The Kreutzer Sonata and Other Stories* (1899–1900), translated by David McDuff and Paul Foote. London: Penguin, 2008.
———. *How Much Land Should a Man Own?* 1836. Translated by Ronald Wilks. Penguin Little Black Classics 57. Middlesex: Penguin Random House, 2015.
———. *The Kreutzer Sonata and Other Stories*. 1899–1900. Translated by David McDuff and Paul Foote. London: Penguin, 2008.
———. *Resurrection*. 1899–1900. Translated by Anthony Briggs. London: Penguin, 2009.
———. *War & Peace*. 1865–68. Translated by Anthony Briggs. London: Penguin, 2005.
———. *War & Peace*. 1865–68. Translated by Louise and Aylmer Maude, includes the 1868 *Appendix—Some Words about War & Peace*. Oxford: Oxford University Press, 1991.

13.1.3 Tolstoy Family

Tolstoy, Count Ilya. *Reminiscences of Tolstoy*. Translated by G. Calderson. London: Chapman and Hall, 1914.
Tolstoy, Countess A. A. *Erinnerungen an Leo N. Tolstoi*. https://www.gutenberg.org/files/41371/41371-h/41371-h.htm.
Tolstoy, Countess Alexandra. *Tolstoy: A Life of My Father*. Translated by E. R. Haploid. New York: Harper, 1953.
———. "Tolstoy and the Russian Peasant." *Russian Review* 19.2 (1960) 150–56.
Tolstoy, Count Sergei. *Tolstoy Remembered by His Son*. Translated by Moura Budberg. London: Weidenfeld and Nicolson, 1961.
Tolstoy, Nikolai. *The Tolstoys: Twenty-Four Generations of Russian History 1353–1983*. London: Hamilton, 1983.
Tolstoy, Sofia. *The Diaries of Sofia Tolstoy*. Translated by Cathy Porter, foreword by Doris Lessing. Surrey, UK: Alma, 2009.
Tolstoy, Tatyana. *Tolstoy Remembered*. Translated from the French by Derek Coltman. London: Joseph, 1977.

13.2 Secondary Source Material
13.2.1 Books, Journal Articles, Essays and Papers

Abraham, J. H. "The Religious Ideas and Social Philosophy of Tolstoy." *International Journal of Ethics* 40 (1929) 105–10.

Adams, Maurice. "The Ethics of Tolstoy and Nietzsche." *International Journal of Ethics* 11.1 (1900) 82–105.

Ali, Tariq. *The Dilemmas of Lenin: Terrorism, War, Empire, Love, Revolution.* London: Verso, 2017.

———. "How Lenin's Love of Literature Shaped the Russian Revolution." *The Guardian*, March 27, 2017. https://www.theguardian.com/books/2017/mar/25/lenin-love-literature-russian-revolution-soviet-union-goethe.

Alinsky, Saul David. *Rules for Radicals: A Practical Primer for Realistic Radicals.* New York: Vintage, 1972.

Alston, Charlotte. *Tolstoy and His Disciples: The History of a Radical International Movement.* London: Taurus & Co., 2014.

Armytage, W. H. G. "J. C. Kenworthy and the Tolstoyan Communities in England." *American Journal of Economics and Sociology* 16.4 (1957) 391–404.

Augustine. *The Lord's Sermon on the Mount (DE SERMONE DOMINI IN MONTE).* Translated by John J. Jepson. Ancient Christians Writers Series 5. New York: Newman, 1948.

Balasubramanian, Radha. *The Influence of India on Leo Tolstoy and Leo Tolstoy's Influence on India: A Study of Reciprocal Receptions.* Foreword by Galina Alekseeva. Lewiston, NY: Mellen, 2013.

———. "Leo Tolstoy from 1901–2010 in Two Leading English-Language Newspapers in India." *Tolstoy's Studies Journal* 23 (2011) 61–68.

Ballou, Adin. *Christian Non-Resistance: In All Its Important Bearings, Illustrated and Defended.* Philadelphia: M'Kim, 1846.

Basinsky, Pavel. *Leo Tolstoy: Flight From Paradise.* Translated from Russian by Huw Davies and Scott Moss. London: Glagoslav, 2015.

Bartlett, Rosamund. *Tolstoy: A Russian Life.* London: Profile, 2010.

———. "Tolstoy Translated: Rosamund Bartlett Describes How the Works of Russia's Greatest Writer Were Introduced to the English-Speaking World." *Financial Times*, August 8, 2014. http://www.ft.com/cms/s/2/9cb5c9e0-1e40-11e4-ab52-00144feabdc0.html.

Bartolf, Christian. "Tolstoy's Legacy for Mankind: A Manifesto for Nonviolence." Paper presented at Second International Conference on Tolstoy and World Literature, Yasnaya Polyana and Tula, RU, August 2000. http://fredsakademiet.dk/library/tolstoj/tolstoy.htm.

Bauman, Clarence. *The Sermon on the Mount: The Modern Quest for Its Meaning.* Macon, GA: Mercer University Press, 1985.

Berlin, Sir Isaiah. *The Hedgehog and the Fox: An Essay on Tolstoy's View of History.* New York: Mentor, 1957.

Berman, Anna A. "Darwin in the Novels: Tolstoy's Evolving Literary Response." *The Russian Review* 76.2 (2017) 331–51.

Bethge, Eberhard. *Dietrich Bonhoeffer: A Biography.* London: Collins, 1970.

Biriukov, Pavel. *Leo Tolstoy: His Life and Works, Autobiographical Memoirs, Letters, and Biographical Material.* New York: Scribner, 1906.

Birukoff, Paul. *Paroles de Tolstoï.* French pamphlet, [1918]. No longer extant.

Blavatsky, H. P. "Leo Tolstoi and His Unecclesiastical Christianity." *Lucifer* 7 (1890) 9–15.

Bonhoeffer, Dietrich. *Dietrich Bonhoeffer Works, Volume 4: Discipleship.* Minneapolis: Fortress, 2003.

———. *Dietrich Bonhoeffer Works, Volume 9: The Young Bonhoeffer, 1918–1927*. Minneapolis: Fortress, 2003.
———. *Dietrich Bonhoeffer Works, Volume 13: London 1933–1935*, Minneapolis: Fortress, 2007.
———. *Letters and Papers from Prison*. New York: Simon & Schuster, 1971.
Boot, Alexander. *God and Man according to Tolstoy*. New York: Palgrave Macmillan, 2009.
Bowman, Archibald A. "The Elements and Character of Tolstoy's Weltanschauung." *International Journal of Ethics* 23.1 (1912) 59–76.
Bray, Mark. *Antifa: The Anti-Fascist Handbook*. London: Melville, 2017.
Briggs, Anthony. *Brief Lives: Leo Tolstoy*. London: Hesperus, 2010.
Brock, Peter. *The Roots of War Resistance: Pacifism from the Early Church to Tolstoy*. Nyack, NY: Fellowship of Reconciliation, 1981.
———. "Tolstoyism and the Hungarian Peasant." *Slavonic and Eastern European Review* 58.3 (1980) 345–69.
Bryan, William Jennings. *In His Image*. Freeport, NY: Books for Libraries, 1971.
Bulgakov, S.N. editor., *On the Religion of Lev Tolstoy*, Moscow: Put', 1912.
Bullitt, Margaret M. "Rousseau and Tolstoy: Childhood and Confession." *Comparative Literature Studies* 16.1 (1979) 12–20.
Bunin, Ivan. *The Liberation of Tolstoy: A Tale of Two Writers*. Edited, translated from the Russian, and with an introduction and notes by Thomas Gaiton Marullo and Vladimir T. Khmelkov. Evanston, IL: Northwestern University Press, 2001. (Originally published in Russian in 1937 under the title: *Osvobozhdenie Tolstogo*.)
Butkevich, Timofei Ivanovich. нагорная проповедь [Sermon on the Mount]. Kharkov: Tip. Gub Provleniia, 1892–93. (By the "Khar'kov heresiologist"—professor of Apologetics and Theology at Kharkov' University, Orthodox Archpriest—a polemic against Tolstoyan Sermon on the Mount interpretation.)
Carmody-Wynne, Diane. "Martin Green, Gandhian Critic." *Cross Currents* 36.2 (1986) 140–46.
Cavanaugh, William T. "The City: Beyond Secular Parodies." In *Radical Orthodoxy: A New Theology*, edited by John Milbank et al., 182–200. London: Routledge, 1999.
Charfield, Charles, and Ruzanna Mikhailovna, eds. *Peace/mir: An Anthology of Historic Alternatives to War*. New York: Syracuse University Press, 1994.
Chelčický, Petr. *The Net of Faith: The Corruption of the Church Caused by Its Fusion and Confusion with Temporal Power*. N.p., 1521.
Christoyannopoulos, Alexandre. "Alexandre on Tolstoy and Anarchism." Interview with C. S. Soong. Blog Talk Radio's *Against the Grain*, September 8, 2008. http://www.blogtalkradio.com/draaibaarheidsfactor/2009/11/16/alexandre-on-tolstoy-and-anarchism.
———. "'Bethink Yourselves or You Will Perish': Leo Tolstoy's Voice a Centenary after His Death." *Anarchist Studies* 18.2 (2010) 11–18.
———. "Christian Anarchism: The Forgotten Politics of Jesus' Rule of Love." Paper presented at the World International Studies Conference, Ljubljana, SI, July 2008.
———. *Christian Anarchy: A Political Commentary on the Gospel*. Abridged ed. Exeter, UK: Imprint Academic, 2011.
———. "Eccentric Yet Still Prophetic: Leo Tolstoy's Christian Anarchist Thought." Paper prepared for 7th ECPT General Conference, Bordeaux, FR, September 2013.

———. "Leo Tolstoy on the State: A Detailed Picture of Tolstoy's Denunciation of State Violence and Deception." *Anarchist Studies* 16.1 (2008) 20–47.

———. "Leo Tolstoy's Anticlericalism in Its Context and Beyond: A Case against Churches and Clerics, Religious and Secular." *Religions* 7.5 (2016) 1–20.

———. "Tolstoy the Peculiar Christian Anarchist." Paper presented at *God Save the Queen: Anarchism and Christianity Today*, All Hallows Church, Leeds, June 2006.

———. *Tolstoy's Political Thought: Christian Anarcho-Pacifist Iconoclasm Then and Now*. New York: Routledge, 2019.

———. "Turning the Other Cheek to Terrorism: Reflections on the Contemporary Significance of Leo Tolstoy's Exegesis of the Sermon on the Mount." *Politics and Religions* 1 (2008) 27–54.

Chute, Patricia. *Tolstoy at Yasnaya Polyana: His Life and Work in the Charmed World of His Estate*. New York: HarperCollins, 1991.

Coetzee, J. M. "Confession and Double Thoughts: Tolstoy, Rousseau, Dostoevsky." *Comparative Literature* 37.3 (1985) 193–32.

Cohen, I. Bernard. *Revolution in Science*. Cambridge, MA: Belknap, 1985.

Crosby, Ernest Howard. *Tolstoy and His Message*. New York: Funk & Wagnalls, 1903.

Craufurd, Alexander H. *The Religion and Ethics of Tolstoy*. London: Unwin, 1912.

Darrow, Clarence, and Arthur M. Lewis. *Marx Versus Tolstoy: A Debate*. Chicago: Kerr and Company, 1911.

Davis, Dena S. "Bonhoeffer and Gandhi." Paper for the International Bonhoeffer Society English Language Section, Dallas, TX, November 1980. Available at the Burke Library Bonhoeffer Archives at Union Theological Seminary; Bonhoeffer Secondary Sources; Series 1A, Box 2, folder 23; Conferences & Lectures: AAR Conferences.

"The Difference between Mohandas and Mahatma Gandhi." *Quirky Science*, August 28, 2015. http://www.quirkyscience.com/difference-between-mohandas-and-mahatma-gandhi/.

D'Souza, Dinesh. *The Big Lie: Exposing the Nazi Roots of the American Left*. Washington, DC: Regnery, 2017.

Edgerton, W. B. "The Artist Turned Prophet: Leo Tolstoj after 1880." In *American Contributions to the Sixth International Congress of Slavists*, edited by William H. Harkins, 2:61–85. The Hague, NL: Mouton, 1968.

———, trans. and ed. *Memoirs of Peasant Tolstoyans in Soviet Russia*. Bloomington: Indiana University Press, 1993.

Edwards, Anne. *Sonya: The Life of Countess Tolstoy*. New York: Simon and Schuster, 1981.

Eikhenbaum, B. M. "On Tolstoy's Crises." In *Tolstoy: A Collection of Critical Essays*, edited and translated by Ralph E. Matlaw, 52–55. Englewood Cliffs, NJ: Prentice-Hall, 1967.

Eller, Vernard. *Christian Anarchy: Jesus' Primacy over the Powers*. Eugene: Wipf & Stock, 1987.

Elliott, Michael C. *Freedom, Justice, & Christian Counter-Culture*. London: SCM, 1990.

Ellul, Jacques. *Violence: Reflections from a Christian Perspective*. New York: Seabury, 1969. https://web.archive.org/web/20150910074958/http://www.religion-online.org/showchapter.asp?title=573&C=712.

Eltzbacher, Paul. "Tolstoi's Teaching." In *Anarchy*, 126–52. Radford, VA: SMK, 2011.

Flew, A. "Tolstoi and the Meaning of Life." *Ethics: An International Journal of Social, Political, and Legal Philosophy* 73 (1963) 110–18.

Follett, Westley. *Céli Dé in Ireland: Monastic Writing and Identity in the Early Middle Ages*. Suffolk, UK: Boydell, 2006.
Fueloep-Miller, Rene. "Tolstoy the Apostolic Crusader." *The Russian Review* 19.2 (1960) 99–121.
Gallie, W. B. *Philosophers of Peace and War: Kant, Clausewitz, Marx, Engels and Tolstoy*. Cambridge: Cambridge University Press, 1978.
———. "Tolstoy: From 'War and Peace' to 'The Kingdom of God Is within You.'" In *Philosophers of Peace and War: Kant, Clausewitz, Marx, Engels and Tolstoy*, 100–132. Cambridge: Cambridge University Press, 1978.
Gandhi, M. K. *An Autobiography or the Story of My Experiments with Truth*. Translated from the Gujarati by Mahadev Desai. Ahmedabad: Navajivan, 1927.
———. *The Collected Works of Mahatma Gandhi*. 100 vols. 6th rev. ed. New Delhi: Ministry of Information and Broadcasting, Govt. of India, 2000-1.
———. "Letter to Adolf Hitler." https://www.mkgandhi.org/letters/hitler_ltr1.htm.
———. *My Non-Violence*. Compiled and Edited by Sailesh Kumar Bandopadhyay. Ahmedabad: Navajivan, 1955.
———. *My Religion*. Compiled and Edited by Bharatan Kumarappa. Ahmedabad: Navajivan, 1960.
Garrison, William Lloyd. *Non-Resistance*. New York: Nation, 1924.
Grayling, A. C. *Wittgenstein: A Very Short Introduction*. Oxford: Oxford University Press, 1996.
Green, Martin. *The Challenge of the Mahatmas*. New York: Basic, 1978.
———. *The Origins of Nonviolence: Tolstoy and Gandhi in the Historical Settings*. University Park: Pennsylvania State University Press, 1986.
———. *Tolstoy and Gandhi, Men of Peace: A Biography*. New York: Basic, 1983.
Greenwood, E. B. *Tolstoy: The Comprehensive Vision*. London: Dent & Sons, 1975.
Guseinov, A. A. "Faith, God, and Nonviolence in the Teachings of Lev Tolstoy." *Russian Studies in Philosophy* 38.2 (1999) 89–103.
Gustafson, Richard F. *Leo Tolstoy Resident and Stranger: A Study in Fiction and Theology*. Princeton: Princeton University Press, 1986.
Guthrie, Stan. "When Red Is Blue: Why I Am Not a Red-Letter Christian." *Christianity Today*, October 11, 2007. http://www.christianitytoday.com/ct/2007/october/33.100.html.
Harding, Neil. *Lenin's Political Thought*. London: Macmillan, 1977.
Harnack, Adolf. *Militia Christi: The Christian Religion and the Military in the First Three Centuries*. Translated by David McI. Gracie. Philadelphia: Fortress, 1981.
Hauerwas, Stanley. "In Defence of 'Our Respectable Culture': Trying to Make Sense of John Howard Yoder's Sexual Abuse." *ABC Religion and Ethics*, October 18, 2017. http://www.abc.net.au/religion/articles/2017/10/18/4751367.htm.
Haverluck, Michael F. "Survey: Alarming Rate of Christian Men Look at Porn, Commit Adultery." *OneNewsNow*, October 9, 2014. https://web.archive.org/web/20170902221655/https://www.onenewsnow.com/culture/2014/10/09/survey-alarming-rate-of-christian-men-look-at-porn-commit-adultery.
Heering, G. J. *The Fall of Christianity: A Study of Christianity, the State and War*. Translated from the Dutch by J. W. Thompson. London: Allan & Unwin, 1930.
Hickey, Steve. "Jean Lasserre and the Tolstoy Bonhoeffer Never Knew." Paper given at *Reading Bonhoeffer for the Life of the Church Conference*, St. John's College, Durham, September 2016.

———. *Obtainable Expectations: A Timely Exposition of the Sermon on the Mount.* Alachua, FL: Bridge Logos Foundation, 2012.

———. *Tolstoy's Novel Idea: Obey the Sermon on the Mount.* Soldotna, Alaska: Mountainside, 2021.

Holinka, Rudulf. *Traktáty Petra Chelcoikého; O trojim lidu – O cirkci svaté.* Prague: Melatrich, 1940.

Hollerich, Michael J. "Religion and Politics in the Writings of Eusebius: Reassessing the First 'Court theologian.'" *Church History* 59 (1990) 309.

Holman, Michael J. De K. "Translating Tolstoy for the Free Age Press: Vladimir Chertkov and His English Manager Arthur Fifield." *The Slavonic and East European Review* 66.2 (1988) 184–97.

Hopton, Terry. "Tolstoy, God and Anarchism." *Anarchist Studies* 8 (2000) 27–52.

Hunt, James D. "Gandhi, Tolstoy, and the Tolstoyans." In *An American Looks at Gandhi: Essays in Satyagraha, Civil Rights and Peace,* 37–55. New Delhi: Promilla & Co., 2005.

Jacoby, Susan. "The Wife of the Genius." *New York Times,* April 19, 1981. http://www.nytimes.com/1981/04/19/books/the-wife-of-the-genius.html?mcubz=1.

Janaway, Christopher. *Schopenhauer: A Very Short Introduction.* Oxford: Oxford University Press, 2002.

Jenkins, Jack. "Meet the Clergy Who Stared Down White Supremacists in Charlottesville." *Think Progress,* August 16, 2017. https://thinkprogress.org/clergy-in-charlottesville-e95752415c3e/.

Jones, E. Stanley. *The Christ of the Mount: A Working Philosophy of Life.* New York: Abingdon, 1931.

———. *Mahatma Gandhi. An Interpretation.* Nashville: Abingdon-Cokesbury, 1948.

Jones, Malcolm, ed. *New Essays on Tolstoy.* Cambridge: Cambridge University Press, 1978. Nine essays, including:
"Tolstoy and Religion," by E. B. Greenwood
"The Purleigh Colony: Tolstoyan Togetherness in the Late 1890s," by Michael J. De K. Holman

Kant, Immanuel. *Critique of Pure Reason.* Translated by F. Max Müller. New York: MacMillan, 1922.

Kaufmann, Walter A. *Religion from Tolstoy to Camus.* New York: Harper & Brothers, 1961.

Kelly, Geoffrey B. *An Interview with Jean Lasserre. Union Seminary Quarterly Review Jahrgang* 27 (1972) 149–60.

Kennan, George. "A Visit to Count Tolstoy." *The Century* 34 (1887) 252–65.

Kierkegaard, Søren. *Works of Love.* Translated by Howard Hong and Edna Hong. New York: Harper Perennial Modern Classics, 2009.

Kinna, Ruth. *Anarchism: A Beginners Guide.* London: Oneworld, 2005.

Kis-Lev, Jonathan. *Dear Tolstoy, Yours Gandhi: A Novel Based on True Correspondence.* London: Goldsmith, 2016.

Kissinger, Warren S. *The Sermon on the Mount: A History of Interpretation and Bibliography.* ATLA Bibliography Series 3. Metuchen, NJ: Scarecrow and American Theological Library Association, 1975.

Kokobobo, Ani: "Authoring Jesus: Novelistic Echoes in Tolstoy's Harmonisation and Translation of the Four Gospels." *Tolstoy Studies Journal* 20 (2008) 1–13.

Kubalkin, S. *Petr Chelčický, český Tolstoj XV. století* [Peter Chelčický the Czech Tolstoy of the Fifteenth Century]. Prague: Vestnik Evropy, 1909.

Kuzminskaya, Tatyana A. *Tolstoy as I Knew Him: My Life at Home and at Yasnaya Polyana.* New York: Macmillan, 1948.
Laurila, Kaarle S. *Leo Tolstoi und Martin Luther als ausleger der bergpredigt.* Translated by Stuart Hay. Helsinki: Suomalainen Tiedeakatemie, 1944.
Lasserre, Henri. *The Communities of Tolstoyans and Their Significance for the Cooperative Community Movement of Today.* Translated from the French by Purcell Weaver. Toronto: Rural Cooperative Community Council and Canadian Fellowship for Cooperative Community, 1944.
Lasserre, Jean. *Les Chrétien et la Violence.* 2nd ed. Preface by Frédéric Rognon. Lyon, Fr: Olivetan, 2008.
———. *War & the Gospel.* Translated by Oliver Coburn. Foreword by the Very Rev. George F. Macleod. London: Clarke & Co., 1962.
Lavrin, Janko. "Tolstoy and Gandhi." *Russian Review* 19.2 (1960) 132–39.
Leithart, Peter J. *Defending Constantine: The Twilight of an Empire and the Dawn of Christendom.* Downers Grove: IVP Academic, 2010.
"Leo Tolstoj and Lemon Anke Pie." https://web.archive.org/web/20190709131743/ https://itinerariesoftaste.sanpellegrino.com/how-we-were/leo-tolstoj-and-lemon-anke-pie.
Lenin, Vladimir Ilyich (Ulyanov). *Articles on Tolstoi.* Moscow: Progress, 1951.
———. "Judas Trotsky's Blush of Shame." In *Lenin Collected Works,* edited by George Hanna, translated by Dora Cox, 17:45. Moscow: Progress Publishers, 1974. https://www.marxists.org/archive/lenin/works/1911/jan/02.htm.
Levitysky, Ihor. "The Tolstoy Gospel in the Light of the Jefferson Bible." *Canadian Slavonic Papers / Revue Canadienne des Slavistes* 21.3 (1979) 347–55.
Love, Jeff. *Tolstoy: A Guide for the Perplexed.* London: Continuum, 2008.
Luther, Martin. "Temporal Authority: To What Extent It Should Be Obeyed—1523." In *Luther's Works,* edited by Jaroslav Pelikan and Helmut T. Lehman, 45:75–129. 55 vols. St. Louis: Concordia, 1955–86.
———. "The Sermon on the Mount (Sermons)." In *Luther's Works,* edited by Jaroslav Pelikan and Helmut T. Lehman, 21:1–294. 55 vols. St. Louis: Concordia, 1955–86.
———. "Whether Soldiers, Too, Can Be Saved 1526." In *Luther's Works,* edited by Jaroslav Pelikan and Helmut T. Lehman, 46:88–137. 55 vols. St. Louis: Concordia, 1955–86.
Magliano, Tony. "The Conversion of the Catholic Priest Who Blessed the Atomic Bomb Crews." *National Catholic Reporter,* August 3, 2015. https://www.ncronline.org/blogs/making-difference/conversion-catholic-priest-who-blessed-atomic-bomb-crews.
Markovitch, Milan I. *Jean-Jacques Rousseau et Tolstoï.* Paris: Librairie Ancienne Honoré Champion, 1928.
Marshall, Peter. "Leo Tolstoy: The Count of Peace." In *Demanding the Impossible: A History of Anarchism,* 362–83. London: Fontana, 1992.
Marx, Karl. *A Contribution to the Critique of Hegel's Philosophy of Right.* Deutsch-Französische Jahrbücher: Paris, 1844.
Matlaw, Ralph E., ed. *Tolstoy: A Collection of Critical Essays.* Englewood Cliffs, NJ: Prentice-Hall, 1967.
Matual, David. "The Gospel according to Tolstoy and the Gospel according to Proudhon." *The Harvard Theological Review* 75.1 (1982) 117–28.
———. *Tolstoy's Translation of the Gospels: A Critical Study.* Lewiston, NY: Mellen, 1992.

Maude, Aylmer. *The Life of Tolstoy, Vol. I: First Fifty Years*. Oxford: Oxford University Press, 1987.
———. *The Life of Tolstoy, Vol. II: Later Years*. Oxford: Oxford University Press, 1987.
———. *Tolstoy and His Problems: Essays by Aylmer Maude*. London: Grant Richards, 1902.
McArthur, Harvey K. *Understanding the Sermon on the Mount*. London: Epworth, 1961.
McDowell, Andrea Rossing. "Lev Tolstoy and the Freedom to Choose One's Own Path." *Journal for Critical Animal Studies* 5.2 (2007) 1–18.
McLean, Hugh. *In Quest of Tolstoy*. Boston: Academic Studies, 2008.
McKeogh, Colm. *Tolstoy's Pacifism*. Amherst, NY: Cambria, 2009.
Medzhibovskaya, Inessa. "Terror Unsublimated: Militant Monks, Revolution and Tolstoy's Last Master Plots." *Tolstoy Studies Journal* 22 (2010) 17–38.
———. *Tolstoy and the Religious Culture of His Time: A Biography of a Long Conversion, 1845–1887*. Latham, MD: Lexington, 2008.
———. "Tolstoy's Hieromonk." *Tolstoy Studies Journal* 11 (2009) 55–63.
———. "Tolstoy's Response to Terror and Revolutionary Violence." *Kritika: Explorations in Russian and Eurasian History* 9.3 (2008) 505–31.
Meyer, Dietrich. *Dietrich Bonhoeffer Nachlass*. Munich: Chr. Kaiser, 1987.
Mikhaylovsky, Nikolay Konstantinovich. "The Left and Right Hand of Count Leo Tolstoy." Essay, 1873.
Milivojevic, Dragan. "Tolstoy's Concept of Reason Applied to Buddhism." In *Literary History and Culture*, edited by Wimal Dissanayake and Steven Bradbury, 105–13. Honolulu: University of Hawaii Press, 1989.
Molnár, Enrico C. S. *A Study of Peter Chelčický's Life and a Translation from Czech of Part One of His Net of Faith*. BDiv thesis, Pacific School of Religion, 1947.
Morris, Brian. *Tolstoy and Anarchism*. http://www.spunk.org/library/pubs/freedom/raven/sp001746.html.
Mosko, Alexey, et al. "Russian Oven: Anke Pie, the Feast That Stole Leo Tolstoy's Heart." *Russia Beyond*, July 22, 2016. https://www.rbth.com/multimedia/video/2016/07/22/anke-pie-the-feast-that-stole-leo-tolstoys-heart_611671.
Müller, Reich Bishop Ludwig. *The Word of God—A Germanization from the Sermon on the Mount*. Translated by Stuart Hay for Steve Hickey. 4th ed. Weimar: German Christian Publishing Group, 1936.
Murphy, Daniel. *Tolstoy on Education*. Newbridge, IE: Irish Academic, 1992.
Nag, Kalidas. *Tolstoy and Gandhi*. In Gandhi's Foot-steps 4. Foreword by M. S. Aney, introduction by K. N. Katju. Patna: Pustak Bhandar, 1950.
Neck, Serge van. "Tolstoy's Views on the Baháʼí and Mormon Faiths." *Commonalities: A Bahai-Mormon Dialogue*, March 23, 2015. https://commonalities.wordpress.com/2015/03/23/tolstoys-views-on-the-bahai-and-mormon-faiths/.
Nickell, William. *The Death of Tolstoy: Russia on the Eve, Astapovo Station, 1910*. New York: Cornell University Press, 2010.
Niebuhr, H. Richard. *Christ and Culture*. New York: Harper & Brothers, 1951.
Nigg, Walter. "The Heretic in the Eastern Church: Leo Tolstoy." In *The Heretics: Heresy Through the Ages*, edited and translated by Richard Winston and Clara Winston, 377–99. New York: Dorset, 1962.
———. *The Heretics: Heresy Through the Ages*. Edited and translated by Richard Winston and Clara Winston. New York: Dorset, 1962.
Nikitina, Nina. *A Tour of the Estate with Lev Tolstoy*. Yasnaya Polyana: Yasnaya Polyana Publishing, 2004.

Orekhanov, Archpriest Georgy. *Leo Tolstoy: A Prophet without Honor.* Moscow: Izdatel'stvo Eksmo, 2016.[5]

Orwin, Donna Tussing, ed. *The Cambridge Companion to Tolstoy.* Cambridge: Cambridge University Press, 2002.

Palmer, Brian. "What Do Anarchists Want from Us?" *Slate*, December 29, 2010. http://www.slate.com/articles/news_and_politics/explainer/2010/12/what_do_anarchists_want.html.

Paperno, Irina. *"Who, What Am I?": Tolstoy Struggles to Narrate the Self.* Ithaca: Cornell University Press, 2014.

Pevear, Richard. "Introduction." In War and Peace, by Leo Tolstoy, translated by Richard Pevear and Larissa Volokhonsky, vii–xvi. New York: Knopf, 2007.

Popoff, Alexandra. *Sophia Tolstoy.* New York: Free, 2010.

———. *Tolstoy's False Disciple: The Untold Story of Leo Tolstoy and Vladimir Chertkov.* New York: Pegasus, 2014.

"Pastors and Porn: The Struggle Is Real." *CBN News*, January 29, 2016. https://www1.cbn.com/cbnnews/us/2016/January/Pastors-and-Porn-The-Struggle-is-Real.

Plekhanov, Georgi. *Selected Philosophical Works.* 5 vols. Moscow: Progress, 1974–81.

Puzin, Nikolai. *The Leo Tolstoy House-Museum in Yasnaya Polyana.* Yasnaya Polyana: Yasnaya Polyana Publishing, 2010.

Rancour-Laferriere, Daniel. *Tolstoy on the Couch: Misogyny, Masochism and the Absent Mother.* New York: New York University Press, 1998.

———. *Tolstoy's Quest for God.* New Brunswick, NJ: Transaction, 2007.

Rasmussen, Larry L. *Dietrich Bonhoeffer: Reality and Resistance.* Nashville: Abingdon, 1972.

Redfearn, David. *Tolstoy: Principles for a New World Order.* Exeter: Shepheard-Walwyn, 1992.

Redneck, David. "The Translation Wars: How the Race to Translate Tolstoy and Dostoyevsky Continues to Spark Feuds, End Friendships and Create Small Fortunes." *The New Yorker Magazine*, 7 November 2005. http://www.newyorker.com/magazine/2005/11/07/the-translation-wars.

Redpath, Theodore. *Tolstoy.* London: Bowes & Bowes, 1960.

Reuss, Eduard. *Die Geschichte der Heiligen Schriften Neuen Testaments.* Halle: Schwetschke und Sohn, 1842.

———. *History of the Sacred Scriptures of the New Testament.* Translated by E. L. Houghton. 2 vols. Boston: Houghton Mifflin, 1884.

Rivett, Kenneth. "Gandhi, Tolstoy, and Coercion." *South Asia (Australia)* 11.2 (1988) 29–56.

Root, Martha L. "Count Leo Tolstoy and the Baha'i Movement." *Baha'i Talks*, May 10, 2011. http://bahaitalks.blogspot.co.uk/2011/05/count-leo-tolstoy-and-bahai-movement-by.html.

Roth, John D., ed. *Constantine Revisited: Leithart, Yoder, and the Constantinian Debate.* Eugene, OR: Pickwick, 2013.

Rousseau, Jean-Jacques. *Confessions.* Translated by Angela Scholar. Oxford: Oxford University Press, 2008.

5. Also by Orekhanov are two dissertations: *Leo Tolstoy: The Russian Orthodox Church and Leo Tolstoy: The Reasons for the Conflict and Its Perception by Contemporaries* (2010) and *The Historical and Cultural Context of the Russian Orthodox Church—Leo Tolstoy Dichotomy* (2012).

Scanlan, James P. "Tolstoy among the Philosophers: His Book on Life and Its Critical Reception." *Tolstoy Studies Journal* 18 (2006) 52–69.
Schardt, Bill, and David Large. "Wittgenstein, Tolstoy and the Gospel in Brief." *The Philosopher* 89.2 (2001).
Schmitt, Carl. *The Concept of the Political*. Chicago: University of Chicago Press, 1996.
Schopenhauer, Arthur. *The World as Will and Representation*. Translated from the German by E. F. J. Payne. 2 vols. New York: Dover, 1969.
Sekirin, Peter, ed. *Americans in Conversation with Tolstoy: Selected Accounts, 1887–1923*. London: McFarland & Company, 2006.
Sharma, Satish. *Gandhi's Teachers: Leo Tolstoy*. Ahmedabad: Gujarat Vidyapeeth, 2009.
Sharp, Gene. *The Politics of Nonviolent Action, Part Two: The Methods of Nonviolent Action*. Boston: Porter Sargent, 1973.
Shreiner, Susan E. "Martin Luther." In *The Sermon on the Mount through the Centuries: From the Early Church to John Paul II*, edited by Jeffrey P. Greenman et al. Grand Rapids: Brazos, 2007.
Simmons, Ernest J. *Leo Tolstoy*. London: Lehmann, 1949.
Solzhenitsyn, Aleksandr. *The Gulag Archipelago Volume 2: A Experiment in Literary Investigation*. London: Collins and Harvill, 1975.
Spence, Gordon William. "Suicide and Sacrifice in Tolstoy's Ethics." *Russian Review* 22.1 (1963) 157–67.
———. *Tolstoy the Ascetic*. Edinburgh: Oliver & Boyd, 1967.
———. "Tolstoy's Dualism." *Russian Review* 20.3 (1961) 217–31.
Stanoyevich, Milivoy S. "Tolstoy's Theory of Social Reform." *The American Journal of Sociology* 31.6 (1926) 744–62.
Stanton, Leonard J. *The Optina Pustyn Monastery in the Russian Literary Imagination: Iconic Vision in Works by Dostoevsky, Gogol, Tolstoy, and Others*. New York: Lang, 1995.
Stassen, Glen H. "Peacemaking." In *Bonhoeffer and King: Their Legacies and Import for Christian Social Thought*, 191–206. Minneapolis: Fortress, 2010.
Steiner, Edward A. *Tolstoy the Man*. Lincoln: University of Nebraska Press, 2005.
Steiner, George. *Tolstoy or Dostoevsky: An Essay in Contrast*. London: Faber and Faber, 1959.
Steiner, Rudolf. *Theosophy and Tolstoy*. Fifth lecture in the series entitled: "Origin and Destination of Humanity," given November 3, 1904 in Berlin. German text in available in *Nachrichtenblatt* 23.20–22 (1946); also in *Gegenwart* 18.2 (1956). English translation by Dorothy S. Osmund retrieved online at Rudolf Steiner Archives. http://wn.rsarchive.org/Lectures/19041103p01.html.
Stendardo, Luigi. *Leo Tolstoy and the Bahá'í Faith*. Welwyn, UK: Ronald, 1985.
Stephens, David. "The Non-Violent Anarchism of Leo Tolstoy." In *Government Is Violence: Essays on Anarchism and Pacifism*, by Leo Tolstoy, edited by David Stephens, 7–19. London: Phoenix, 1990.
Stepun, F. "The Religious Tragedy of Tolstoy." *Russian Review* 19 (1960) 157–70.
Struve, Gleb. "Tolstoy in Soviet Criticism." *Russian Review* 19.2 (1960) 171–86.
Tchertkoff, V., and F. Holah. *A Short Biography of William Lloyd Garrison*. London: Free Age, 1904.
Thompson, Caleb. "Wittgenstein, Tolstoy and the Meaning of Life." *Philosophical Investigations* 20.2 (1997) 96–116.

TNN. "Gandhi to Hitler / Dear Friend Hitler." *Times of India*, July 4, 2011. https://timesofindia.indiatimes.com/entertainment/movie-previews/bollywood/Gandhi-to-Hitler-/-Dear-Friend-Hitler/articleshow/9100479.cms?referral=PM.

Trotsky, Leon. "Tolstoy, Poet and Rebel." *World Socialist Web Site*, December 2, 2010. https://www.wsws.org/en/articles/2010/12/tols-d02.html.

Troyat, Henri. *Tolstoy*. Translated from the French by Nancy Amphoux. New York: Doubleday, 1967.

Urban, Wilbur B. "Tolstoy and the Russian Sphinx." *International Journal of Ethics* 28.2 (1918) 220–39.

Valentinov, Nikolay. *Encounters with Lenin*. Oxford: Oxford University Press, 1968.

Venturi, Franco. *Roots of Revolution: A History of the Populist and Socialist Movements in Nineteenth Century Russia*. Translated from the Italian by Francis Haskell, introduction by Isaiah Berlin. London: Weidenfeld & Nicolson, 1960.

Verney, Victor. *Petr Chelčický and Pacifism: Unity of the Brethren and Lost Hussite Roots*. Self-published, Amazon Digital Services, 2013. Kindle.

Viesel, Mikhail. "War and Peace: 7 Little-known Facts about Russia's Greatest Epic." https://www.rbth.com/arts/literature/2015/11/11/war-and-peace-7-little-known-facts-about-rusias-greatest-epic_539471

Vucinich, Alexander. *Darwin in Russian Thought*. Berkeley: University of California Press, 1988.

Wagner, Murray L. *Peter Chelčický: A Radical Separatist in Hussite Bohemia*. Studies in Anabaptist and Mennonite History 25. Scottdale, PA: Herald, 1983.

Walsh, Charles. *Strange Glory: A Life of Dietrich Bonhoeffer*. New York: Knopf, 2014.

Weber, Max. "Politics as a Vocation, 1919." https://www2.southeastern.edu/Academics/Faculty/jbell/weber.pdf.

Weikart, Richard. *From Darwin to Hitler: Evolutionary Ethics, Eugenics, and Racism in Germany*. New York: Palgrave Macmillan, 2004.

———. *Hitler's Ethic: The Nazi Pursuit of Evolutionary Progress*. New York: Palgrave Macmillan, 2004.

———. *Socialist Darwinism: Evolution in German Socialist thought from Marx to Bernstein*. San Francisco: International Scholars, 1998.

Wenzer, Kenneth C. *An Anthology of Tolstoy's Spiritual Economics: Volume II of the Henry George Centennial Trilogy*. New York: University of Rochester Press, 1997.

Wilson, A. N. *Tolstoy*. London: Atlantic, 2012.

———. "Tolstoy's Georgist Spiritual Political Economy (1897–1910): Anarchism and Land Reform." *American Journal of Economics and Sociology* 56.4 (1997) 639–67.

Windisch, Hans. *The Meaning of the Sermon on the Mount*. Philadelphia: Westminster, 1951.

Wink, Walter. *Jesus and Nonviolence: A Third Way*. Minneapolis: Fortress, 2003.

Wolfe, Bertram D. *Three Who Made a Revolution: A Biographical History of Lenin, Trotsky, and Stalin*. New York: Cooper Square, 2001.

Woodcock, George. *Anarchism: A History of Libertarian Ideas and Movements*. Harmondsworth, UK: Penguin, 1975.

Yoder, John Howard. *The Christian Witness to the State*. Scottdale, PA: Herald, 1964.

———. *Nevertheless: Varieties and Shortcomings of Religious Pacifism*. Scottdale, PA: Herald, 1971.

———. *The Politics of Jesus: Vicit Agnus Noster*. 2nd ed. Grand Rapids: Eerdmans, 1994.

———. *The Priestly Kingdom: Social Ethics as Gospel*. Notre Dame: University of Notre Dame Press, 1984.

Zedong, Mao. *The Writings of Mao Zedong 1949–1976. Volume II: September 1945– December 1955*. Edited by Michael Y. M. Kau and John K. Leung. Armonk, NY: Sharpe, 1992.

13.2.2 Video and Documentary

Tolstaya, Alexandra. *BBC's Yesterday's Witness: Tolstoy, Narrated by Tolstoy's Daughter.* 30 Minutes of interview footage taken from the *National Archives*, 1970. https://www.youtube.com/watch?v=SGQu6lu41dI. (Comment: Excellent and interesting portrait of Tolstoy as a loving Father and of his wife Sophia's bitter resentment of his adherence to the teachings of Jesus. Alexandra Tolstaya also wrote a book called *The Father and the Daughter.*)

Yentob, Alan. *The Trouble with Tolstoy*. BBC, 2001. Digital Classics DVD, 2011.

13.2.3 Annotated Bibliographies and Online Searchable Archives

Egan, David R., and Melinda A. Egan. *Leo Tolstoy: An Annotated Bibliography of English-Language Sources to 1978*. Metuchen, NJ: Scarecrow, 1979.

———. *Leo Tolstoy: An Annotated Bibliography of English Language Sources from 1978 to 2003*. Metuchen, NJ: Scarecrow, 2005.

http://tolstoy.ru is the Tolstoy archive and searchable collection of all Tolstoy's works. However, the English version of this website continues to remain "under construction." Leo Tolstoy's entire body of work is "free – all 46,000 pages of it – in PDF, FB2 and EPUB formats for Kindle, iPad or almost any other ebook reader." The ninety-volume edition of Tolstoy's Collected Works was "scanned and proofread three times by more than 3,000 volunteers from 49 countries." Truly an incredible crowdsourcing feat.[6]

---

6. http://www.openculture.com/2013/09/the-complete-works-of-leo-tolstoy-online.html.

www.ingramcontent.com/pod-product-compliance
Lightning Source LLC
Chambersburg PA
CBHW061425300426
44114CB00014B/1543